Tartaria
A S I A
EVROPA
Carthaio
Turchestan
Mar de Bachu
China
Iapan
Natolia
Persia
Corasan
Barbaria
Aegyptus
Guzarate
India orientalis
Arabia
AFRICA
Nubia
Abissini
Manicongo
Melinde
Zeilan
Lantchidol mare
MAR DI INDIA
Duo Compagne
Los Romeros
Tristan de Acuña
Gonsalo Aluares
Plitacorum regio, sic à Lusitanis appellata ob incredibilem earum auium ibidem magnitudinem.
Vastissimas hic esse regiones ex M. Pauli Veneti et Lud: Vartomanni scriptis peregrinationibus constat.
S NONDVM COGNITA.

Pennsylvania

ADVENTURES IN TIME AND PLACE

ADOPTED IN 1907, OUR STATE'S FLAG SHOWS THE STATE COAT OF ARMS ON A BLUE BACKGROUND. TWO BLACK HORSES HOLD A SHIELD WITH A SHIP, A PLOW, AND THREE BUNDLES OF WHEAT. THE SHIP STANDS FOR BUSINESS AND THE PLOW AND WHEAT STAND FOR AGRICULTURE. LEFT OF THE SHIELD IS A STALK OF CORN, A SYMBOL OF PLENTY. TO THE RIGHT IS AN OLIVE BRANCH, A SYMBOL OF PEACE. THE BALD EAGLE AT THE TOP STANDS FOR BRAVERY, SPEED, STRENGTH, AND WISDOM. BELOW THE SHIELD IS THE MOTTO "VIRTUE, LIBERTY, AND INDEPENDENCE."

James A. Banks

Barry K. Beyer

Gloria Contreras

Jean Craven

Gloria Ladson-Billings

Mary A. McFarland

Walter C. Parker

PROGRAM AUTHORS

Dr. James A. Banks
Professor of Education and Director of the Center for Multicultural Education
University of Washington
Seattle, Washington

Dr. Barry K. Beyer
Professor Emeritus, Graduate School of Education
George Mason University
Fairfax, Virginia

Dr. Gloria Contreras
Professor of Education
University of North Texas
Denton, Texas

Jean Craven
District Coordinator of Curriculum Development
Albuquerque Public Schools
Albuquerque, New Mexico

Dr. Gloria Ladson-Billings
Professor of Education
University of Wisconsin
Madison, Wisconsin

Dr. Mary A. McFarland
Instructional Coordinator of Social Studies, K-12, and Director of Staff Development
Parkway School District
Chesterfield, Missouri

Dr. Walter C. Parker
Professor and Program Chair for Social Studies Education
University of Washington
Seattle, Washington

NATIONAL GEOGRAPHIC SOCIETY
Washington, D.C.

SENIOR CONSULTANTS

Dr. Ruth Shirey
Professor of Geography and Regional Planning
Indiana University of Pennsylvania
Indiana, Pennsylvania

Robert Heinly
Special Studies Supervisor
Rose Tree Media School District
Media, Pennsylvania

Stephen Bullick
Social Studies Supervisor
Mt. Lebanon School District
Pittsburgh, Pennsylvania

GRADE-LEVEL CONSULTANTS

Melvin Garrison
Philadelphia City Schools
Philadelphia, Pennsylvania

Carole Briggs
Support Teacher
Brookville Area School District
Brookville, Pennsylvania

Sharon Laverdue
Teacher
J.M. Hill Elementary School
East Stroudsburg, Pennsylvania

Bill Cornell
President, Retired
Pennsylvania Historical Association
Wormleysburg, Pennsylvania

CONSULTANTS FOR TEST PREPARATION

The Princeton Review is not affiliated with Princeton University or ETS.

ACKNOWLEDGMENTS
The publisher gratefully acknowledges permission to reprint the following copyrighted material:
From *Leaves of Grass*, edited by Harold W. Blodgett and Sculley Bradley. Copyright © 1965 by New York University. From *Life on the Mississippi* by Mark Twain (Samuel L. Clemens). Copyright © 1950 by Harper & Brothers. From *An American Childhood* by Annie Dillard. Copyright © 1987 by Annie Dillard. HarperCollins Publishers, Inc. From *Amish Women: Lives and Stories* by Louise Stoltzfus. Copyright © 1994 by Good Books. Good Books, Intercourse, PA. From *Scientists Who Study Ancient Temples and Tombs* by Mel Higginson. Copyright © 1994 by The Rourke Corporation. From *Pennsylvania: A History of the Keystone State*, courtesy of Historical Society of Pennsylvania. From *Shh! We're Writing the Constitution*, text copyright © 1987 by Jean Fritz. Reprinted by permission of G. P. Putnam's Sons. From *The American Heritage History of Railroads in America* by Oliver Jensen, American Heritage, Bonanza Books, NY, Copyright © 1975. From "A Pennsylvania Boyhood" by John Culbertson, in *American Heritage*, Copyright © December 1966. Verse from "25th Anniversary of Freedom" by Frances E. W. Harper, Leon Gardiner Collection, Historical Society of Pennsylvania. From "Down in a Coal Mine," from the Archive of American Folk Songs, Library of Congress. From "Susquehanna: America's Small-Town River" by Peter Miller in *National Geographic*, Vol. 167, No. 3, Copyright © March 1985. Adapted from "A Memorial to Save Others" by Jon Rutter in the Lancaster Sunday News, March 17, 1996. From *Voices from Marshall Street: Jewish Life in a Philadelphia Neighborhood 1920-1960* by Elaine Krasnow Ellison and Elaine Mark Jaffe. Copyright © 1994 by Ellison & Jaffe, Camino Books, Inc., Philadelphia.

McGraw-Hill School Division
A Division of The McGraw-Hill Companies

McGraw-Hill School Division
Two Penn Plaza
New York, New York 10121

Printed in the United States of America

ISBN 0-02-149116-X / 4

7 8 9 VHJ 06 05 04

Teacher's Multimedia Edition

ISBN 0-02-149113-5

2 3 4 5 6 7 8 9 VHJ 02 01 00 99

CONTENTS

UNIT ONE The Geography of Pennsylvania

UNIT TWO Early Pennsylvania

UNIT THREE Forming a New Country

UNIT FOUR Challenge and Growth

UNIT FIVE

Pennsylvania Today

200

REFERENCE SECTION

STANDARDIZED TEST SUPPORT

FEATURES

SKILLS LESSONS

CITIZENSHIP

LEGACIES

Primary Sources

Literature

Music

Art

INFOGRAPHICS

LINKS

DID YOU KNOW?

CHARTS, GRAPHS, & DIAGRAMS

TIME LINES

MAPS

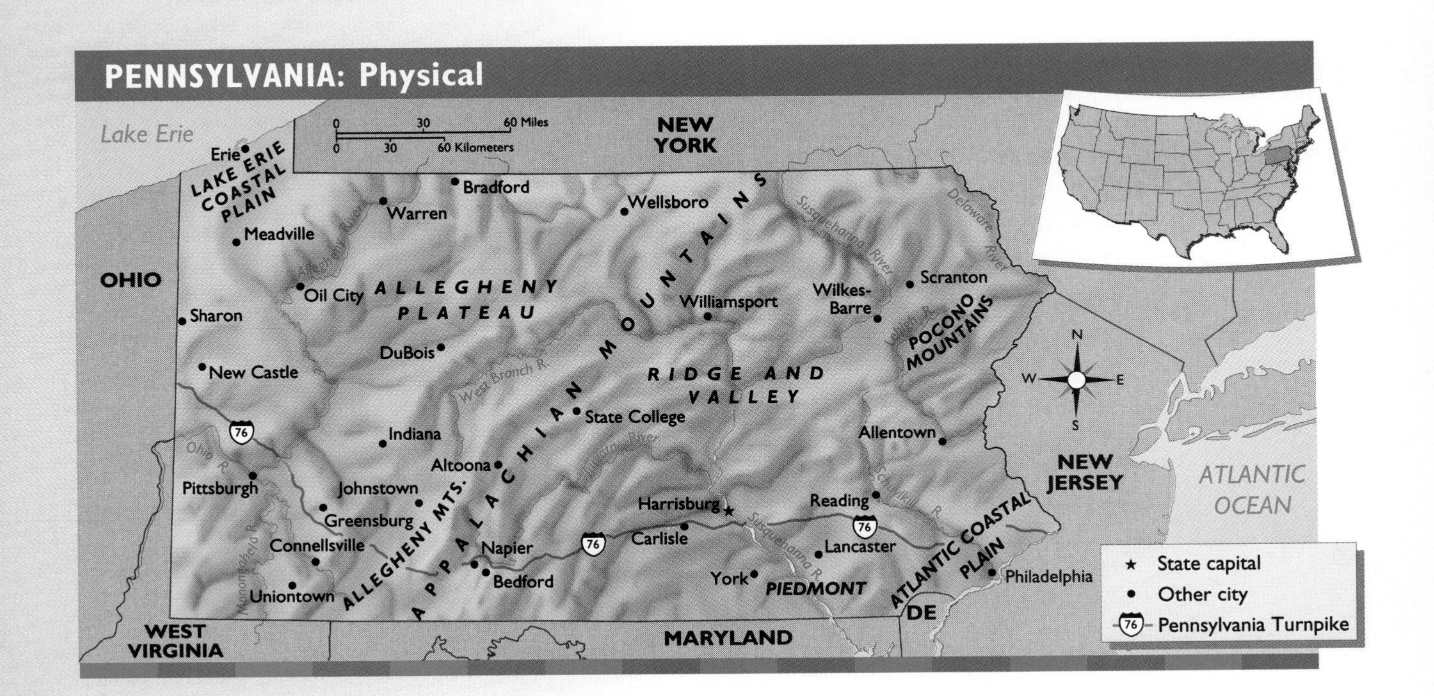

PENNSYLVANIA: Physical
Lake Erie
NEW YORK
OHIO
NEW JERSEY
WEST VIRGINIA
MARYLAND
DE
ATLANTIC OCEAN
LAKE ERIE COASTAL PLAIN
ALLEGHENY PLATEAU
APPALACHIAN MOUNTAINS
RIDGE AND VALLEY
POCONO MOUNTAINS
ALLEGHENY MTS.
PIEDMONT
ATLANTIC COASTAL PLAIN
Erie
Meadville
Warren
Bradford
Wellsboro
Oil City
Sharon
New Castle
DuBois
Williamsport
Wilkes-Barre
Scranton
State College
Indiana
Altoona
Johnstown
Pittsburgh
Greensburg
Connellsville
Uniontown
Napier
Bedford
Harrisburg
Carlisle
York
Lancaster
Reading
Allentown
Philadelphia
Allegheny River
West Branch R.
Susquehanna River
Delaware River
Lehigh R.
Juniata River
Schuylkill R.
Ohio R.
Monongahela R.
Susquehanna R.
0 30 60 Miles
0 30 60 Kilometers
N
S
E
W
State capital
Other city
Pennsylvania Turnpike
76

YOUR TEXTBOOK at a glance

Your book is called *Pennsylvania: Adventures in Time and Place*. It has eleven chapters. Each chapter has two or more lessons. There are also many special features for you to study and enjoy.

Movement
How can people travel from one place to another?

Place
What unique things make Pennsylvania different from other places?

▲ **Special pages bring you ideas in geography from National Geographic.**

LESSON 1

40,000 YEARS AGO — 1,000 YEARS AGO

HUNTERS AND GATHERERS

Focus Activity

READ TO LEARN
When and how did people first come to Pennsylvania?

VOCABULARY
Ice Age
glacier
prehistory
archaeology
artifact
hunter-gatherer

PLACES
Beringia
Bering Strait

READ ALOUD

"Each layer we uncovered was like a snapshot of that time." This is how Dr. James Adovasio described digging through layers of earth at Meadowcroft Rock Shelter near Pittsburgh in 1973. Dr. Adovasio and a team of scientists discovered objects made by Pennsylvanians nearly 18,000 years ago. Why might these objects be important to Pennsylvanians today?

THE BIG PICTURE

By studying objects like the ones found at Meadowcroft Rock Shelter, we can learn a lot about how the first Pennsylvanians lived. These early people left no written records. So scientists use objects like these to learn about life here thousands of years ago. But how did people first come to North America?

Many scientists believe that people first came to North America during the Ice Age. This was a time when glaciers (GLAY shurz), or huge sheets of ice, covered much of Earth's surface. Before the glaciers formed, large bodies of water separated Asia from North America. During the Ice Age the level of the oceans dropped because so much water became frozen into glaciers. For about 2,000 years a land bridge called Beringia (buh RIHN jee uh) connected Asia with North America. Today the land bridge is gone. The Bering Strait, a body of water 56 miles across, now separates North America from Asia.

58

colony. She became the only woman to lead one of the 13 English colonies. When Hannah Penn died in 1727, her three sons became the leaders of the colony.

In 1737, one son, Thomas Penn, had a treaty supposedly signed by his father and some Lenape chiefs. This treaty gave William Penn land west of the Delaware River as far "as a man can go in one day and a half." However, no one had ever made the walk for the land. So the Lenape agreed to let a walk take place.

On August 25, 1737, colonists

Links to MATHEMATICS
Mega Miles

The Lenape thought that the three colonists would walk only about 30 miles in 36 hours. The walkers traveled about 66 miles during that time. About how many miles per hour did the walkers travel?

EUROPEANS ARRIVE IN DELAWARE BAY

Cornelis Hendrickson, (kor NEEL yis HEN drik sun), a Dutch explorer from the Netherlands, a country in Europe, came to Delaware Bay in 1616. Hendrickson came to "trade with the [Native Americans for] furs, robes and other skins." Furs—especially beaver fur, which was used to make men's hats—could be sold for high prices in Europe.

In 1626, the Dutch set up two trading posts on the Delaware River near the mouth of the Schuylkill River. A trading post was a place where Native Americans could bring furs and trade them for goods. The Dutch traded such things as metal axes and cooking pots for furs.

New Sweden

The leaders of Sweden, a country in northern Europe, hired a Dutchman named Peter Minuit (MIN yoo wit) to set up a colony for them in 1636. A colony is a place ruled by another country. The Swedes named the colony New Sweden. It stretched into ... is now Pennsylvania.

DID YOU KNOW?

How did the Schuylkill River get its name?

In 1633, a Dutch trader named Arendt Corssen (ah RENT KOR suhn) sailed up the Delaware River. Some historians believe that he almost sailed past the mouth of another river because it was hidden by tall reeds. So Corssen named the river he almost missed the Schuylkill, which is Dutch for "hidden river."

SCHUYLKILL RIVER?

NEW SWEDEN, 1651

◀ **Some lessons have features called Links or Did You Know—activities to try and interesting information to share.**

Look for a variety of lessons and features. Infographics inform you with pictures and maps. You will build Skills, learn about Legacies that connect us to the past, and meet people who show what Citizenship is. ▶

Infographic

NATIVE AMERICANS OF PENNSYLVANIA

Each Native American group in Pennsylvania had its own culture, made and wore different kinds of clothing, and decorated objects in their own style. What can you learn about these groups from the photographs on these pages?

Iroquois

Susquehannock

In the early 1600s, the Susquehannock farmed and hunted in the Susquehanna Valley. They made this ceremonial mask and decorative comb.

West Branch · North Branch · Susquehanna River · Delaware River · Schuylkill River

Lenape

The Lenape lived near the Delaware River. Wampum belts, like this one, were used like money. This Lenape bag was used to carry many different things.

69

STUDYING THE PAST

We use the word *history* to describe the written story of the past. The period of time before people wrote down their history is known as **prehistory**. You will be able to understand the difference between these two words by remembering that *pre* means "before."

Archaeology (arh kee OL uh jee) is the study of prehistoric people. Archaeologists dig in places where prehistoric people lived. They may find pottery, clothing, or ashes from a campfire. These objects are called **artifacts**. Artifacts help archaeologists find out how people lived long ago. Special equipment is used to find out how old artifacts are. Bones of people and animals give clues about what they looked like. Where does Mel Higginson say that archaeologists look for artifacts?

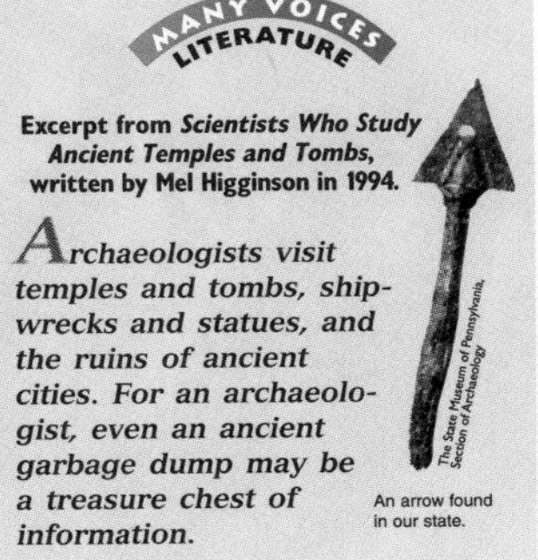

MANY VOICES LITERATURE

Excerpt from *Scientists Who Study Ancient Temples and Tombs*, written by Mel Higginson in 1994.

Archaeologists visit temples and tombs, shipwrecks and statues, and the ruins of ancient cities. For an archaeologist, even an ancient garbage dump may be a treasure chest of information.

An arrow found in our state.

The First Americans

No one knows when or how people came to North America. Some scientists believe that people crossed Beringia about 40,000 years ago. Look at the map below to see the routes they might have taken through North and South America.

The first Americans were the ancestors of the people now known as Native Americans. Many Native Americans, however, believe they have always lived in North and South America.

Some scientists believe that people first reached Pennsylvania about 18,000 years ago.

ROUTES OF THE FIRST AMERICANS

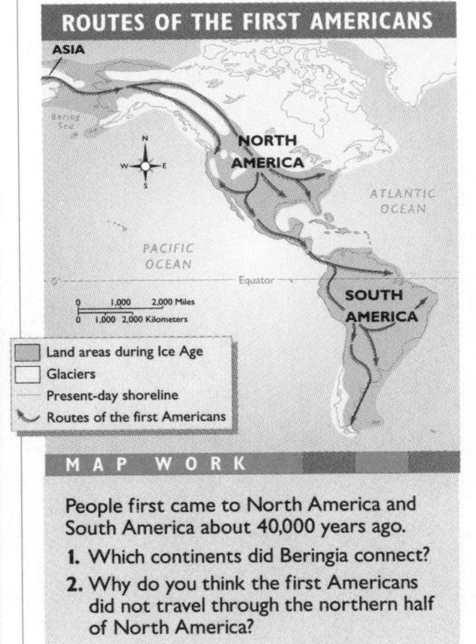

MAP WORK

People first came to North America and South America about 40,000 years ago.

1. Which continents did Beringia connect?
2. Why do you think the first Americans did not travel through the northern half of North America?

59

▲ **Lessons begin with a Read Aloud selection and The Big Picture. Study with the Read to Learn question and a list of words, people, and places. Enjoy Many Voices—writings from many sources.**

The end of your book has a Reference Section with many types of information. Use it to look up words, people, and places. ▼

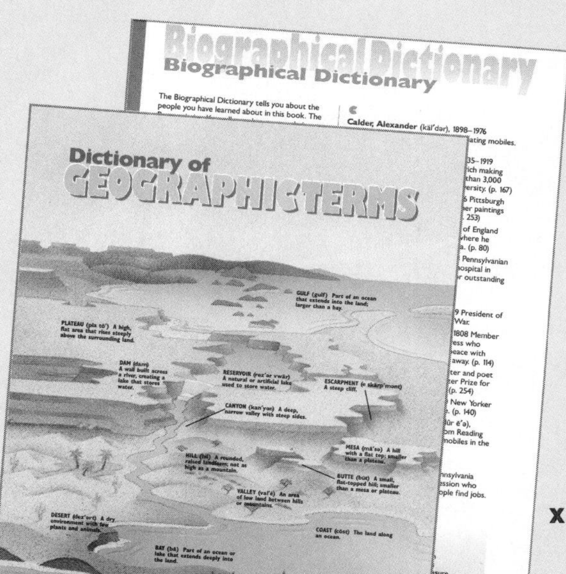

NATIONAL GEOGRAPHIC

A Look at Pennsylvania

Pittsburgh, the Steel City, guards the "Golden Triangle"—the junction of the Monongahela, Allegheny, and Ohio rivers.

Visiting a dairy farm in rural Pennsylvania can be a *mooving* experience!

The Liberty Bell is found in Philadelphia—the birthplace of the United States and our country's capital for ten years.

The fiery furnaces of the steel industry helped to make Pennsylvania one of the great manufacturing states of our nation.

At Valley Forge, poorly supplied Continental soldiers fought severe weather and disease and changed themselves into a well-trained army.

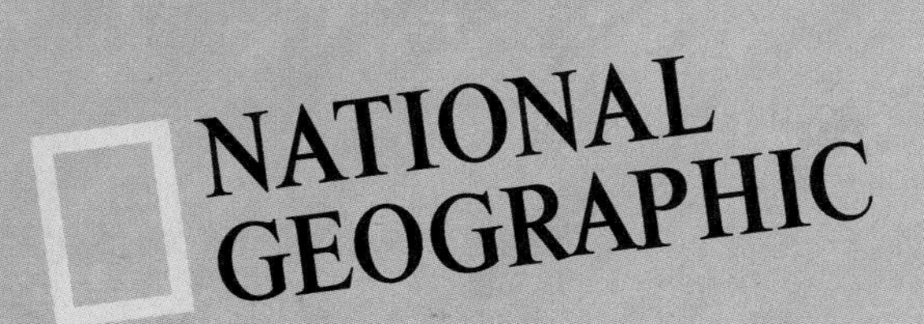

Five Themes of Geography

Movement
How can people travel from one place to another?

Place
What unique things make Pennsylvania different from other places?

Location
How do people know exactly where things are?

Region
What are some things that make Pennsylvania's regions special?

Human-Environment Interaction
How have people changed the landscape?

Reviewing
GEOGRAPHY SKILLS

PART 1
Using Globes

VOCABULARY
ocean
continent
hemisphere
equator

What does a globe show?

- A globe is a small copy of Earth. Like Earth, a globe is a round object, or sphere. A globe is a useful tool for showing what Earth looks like.
- Globes show the parts of Earth that are land and the parts that are water. Earth's largest bodies of water are called oceans. There are four oceans—the Atlantic, Arctic, Indian, and Pacific. Look at the globe on this page. What color is used to show oceans?
- Globes also show the seven large bodies of land called continents. The continents are Africa, Antarctica, Asia, Australia, Europe, North America, and South America. Find North America and South America on the globe below. Which oceans do you see bordering these continents?

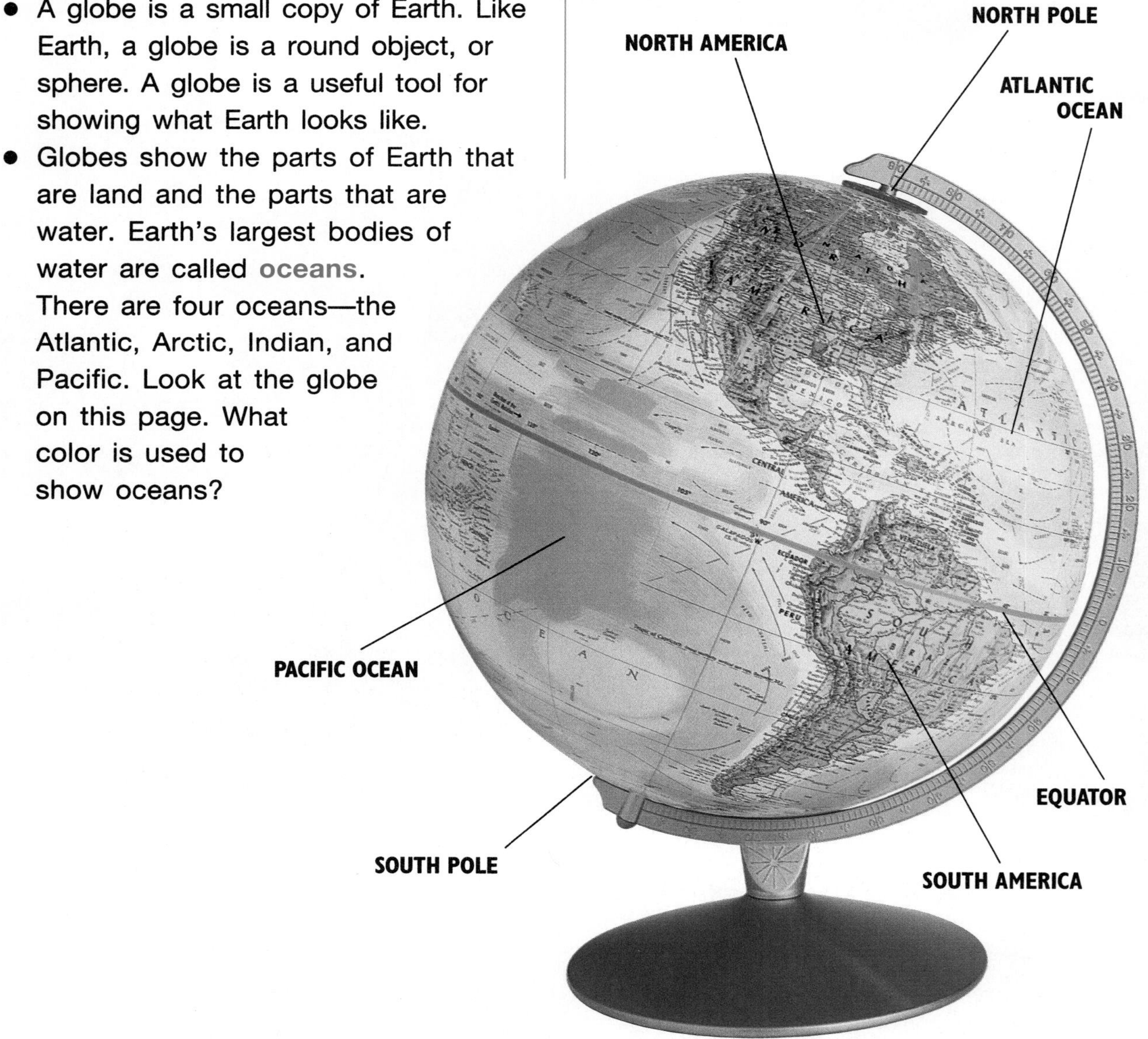

THE HEMISPHERES

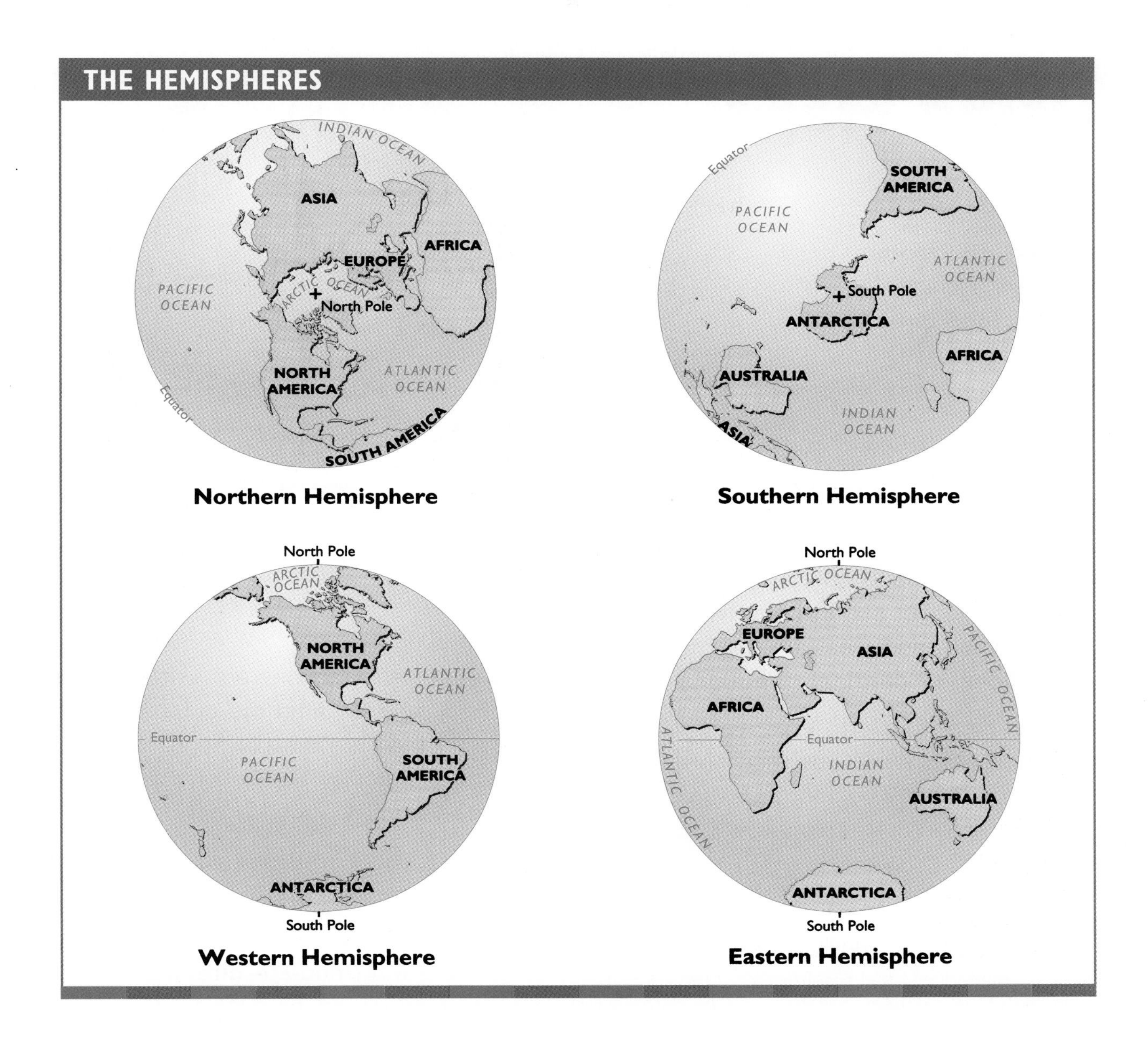

What are the four hemispheres?

- Look again at the globe on page G6. Can you see the whole globe? You can see only half of a globe from any one direction. A word for half a globe or sphere is **hemisphere**. The word *hemi* means "half." Geographers divide Earth into four different hemispheres.
- Earth is divided into the Northern Hemisphere and Southern Hemisphere by the equator. The **equator** is an imaginary line that lies halfway between the North Pole and the South Pole. Look at the maps of the hemispheres above. What continents are located on the equator? On which continent is the South Pole shown?
- Earth can also be divided into two other hemispheres. What are the names of these hemispheres? In which hemispheres do you live?

More Practice

There are more maps in this book that show the equator. For examples, see pages 18, 20, and 57.

PART 2
Using Maps

VOCABULARY

cardinal directions
compass rose
intermediate directions
symbol
map key
scale
locator

What are cardinal directions?

- Directions describe the way you face or move to get somewhere. North, east, south, and west are the main directions, or cardinal directions.
- If you face the North Pole, you are facing north. When you face north, south is directly behind you. West is to your left. What direction will be to your right?

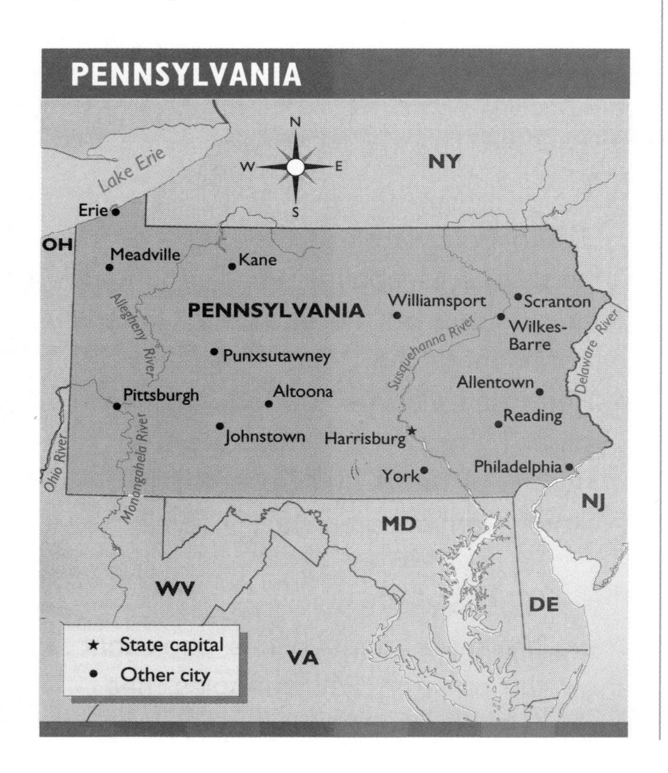

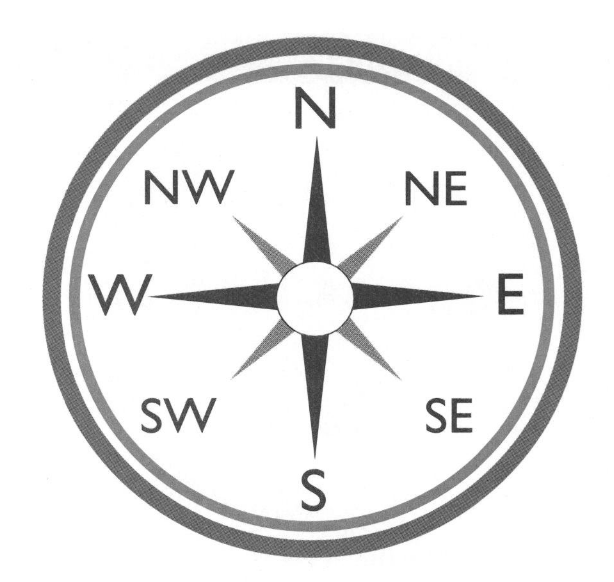

How do you use a compass rose?

- A compass rose is a small drawing on a map that can help you find directions.
- The cardinal directions are written as **N**, **E**, **S**, and **W**. Find the compass rose on the map on this page. In which direction is Reading from Wilkes-Barre?

What are intermediate directions?

- Notice the spikes between the cardinal directions on the compass rose. These show the intermediate directions, or in-between directions.
- The intermediate directions are northeast, southeast, southwest, and northwest. The direction northeast is often written as **NE**. What letters are used for the other intermediate directions? Which intermediate direction lies between south and east?

More Practice

You can practice finding directions using a compass rose on most maps in this book. For examples, see pages 92, 119, and 161.

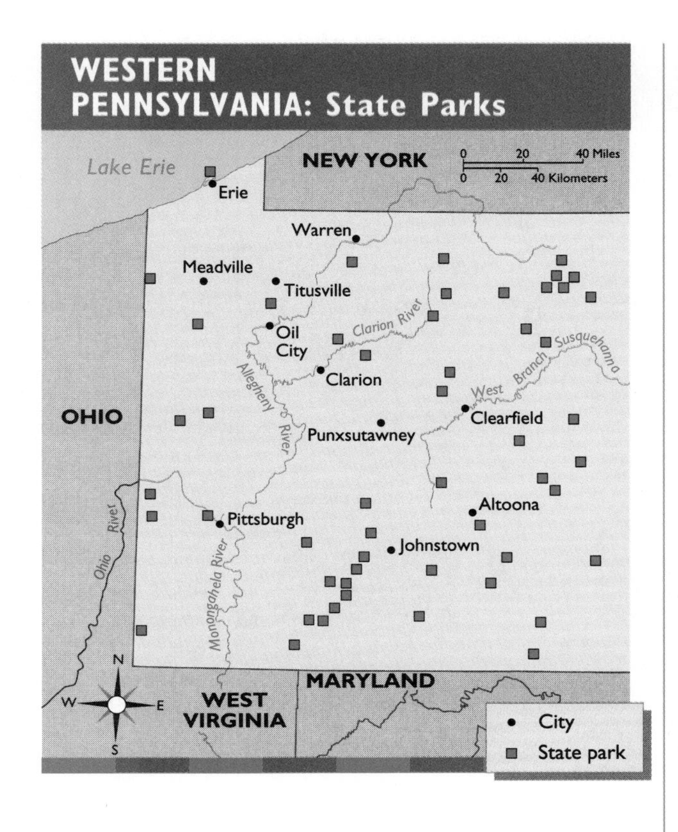

Why do maps have titles?

- When using a map, first look at the map title. The title names the area the map shows. It may also tell you the kind of information shown on the map. Look at the maps on this page. What is the title of each?

Why do maps include symbols?

- A **symbol** is something that stands for something else.
- On a map common symbols include dots, lines, stars, and colors. Many maps use the color blue to stand for water, for example. What do dots sometimes stand for?
- Maps also often use symbols that are small drawings of the things they stand for. A drawing of a tree, for example, might stand for a forest. What do you think an airplane might stand for?

How can you find out what map symbols stand for?

- Often the same symbol stands for different things on different maps. For this reason many maps include a **map key**. A map key gives the meaning of each symbol used on the map.
- When you look at a map, you should always study the map key. Look at the maps on this page. What symbol marks the state parks on the map of Western Pennsylvania? What does the same symbol stand for on the map of Harrisburg? What do the dots stand for on the map of Pennsylvania's state parks?

More Practice

There are many maps with symbols and map keys in this book. For examples, see pages 15, 65, and 217.

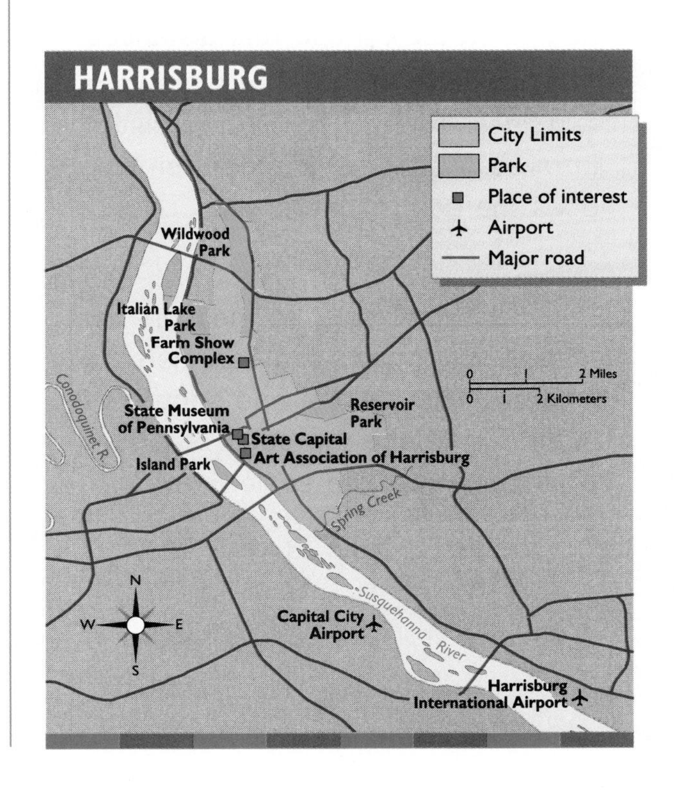

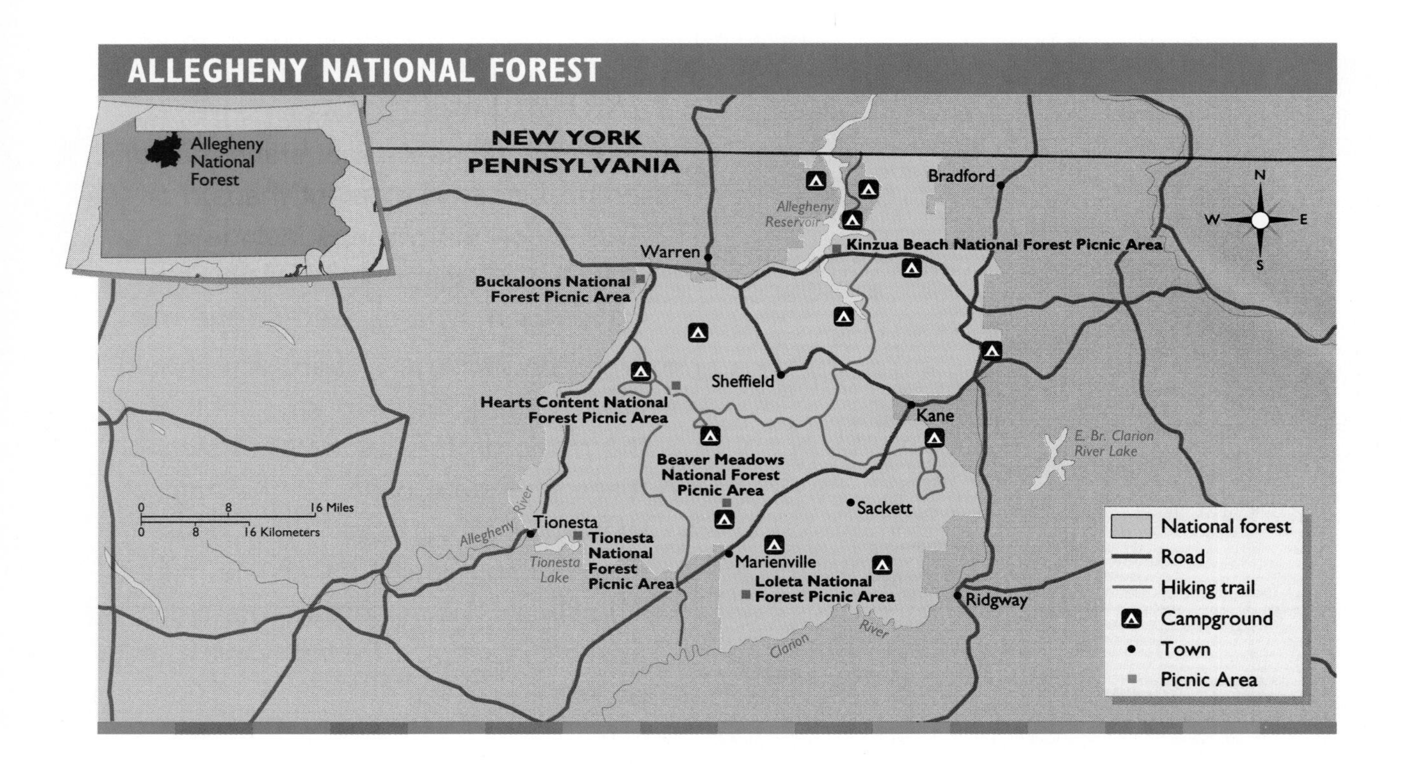

What is a map scale?

- All maps are smaller than the real area that they show. So how can you figure out the real distance between places? Most maps include a scale. The scale shows the relationship between distances on a map and real distances.
- The scales in this book are drawn with two lines. The top line shows distance in miles. What unit of measurement does the bottom line use?

How do you use a map scale?

- You can use a ruler to measure distances on a map. You can also make a scale strip like the one shown on this page. Place the edge of a strip of paper under the scale lines on the map above. Mark the distances in miles.

- Use your scale strip to measure the distance between the Kinzua Beach Picnic Area and Bradford. Place the edge of the strip under the two points. Line the zero up under the Kinzua Beach Picnic Area. What is the distance to Bradford in miles?

What do locators show?

- A locator is a small map set onto the main map. It shows where the area of the main map is located. Where on the map above is the locator?
- Most of the locators in this book show either the United States or Pennsylvania. Look at the map above. What area does the locator show?

More Practice

For examples of scales, see pages 7, 93, and R10. For examples of locators, see pages 77, 107, and 119.

PART 3
Different Kinds of Maps

VOCABULARY
political map
physical map
landform map
transportation map
historical map

What is a political map?

- A political map shows information such as cities, capital cities, states, and countries. What symbol is used to show state capitals on the map below? What city is the capital of our state? What is the symbol for our national capital?
- Political maps use lines to show borders. The states or countries are also shown in different colors. Look at the map below. What color is used to show our state? How many different colors are used to show the states? What countries are shown?

More Practice
There are other political maps in this book. For examples, see pages R4 and R8.

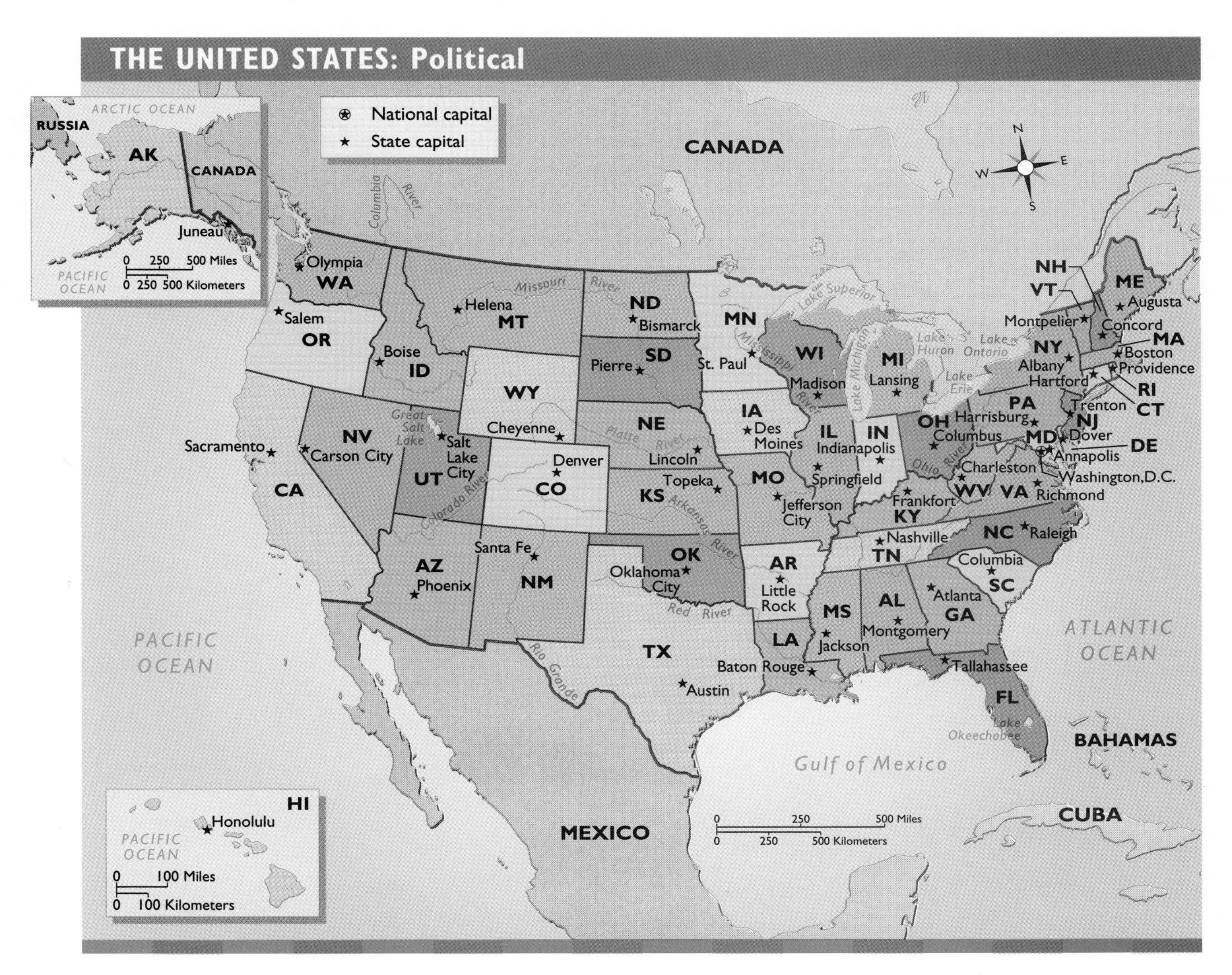

THE UNITED STATES: Political

What are physical maps?

- Maps that show the natural features of Earth are called **physical maps**. There are different kinds of physical maps in this book.
- One kind of physical map shows landforms, or the shapes that make up Earth's surface. These maps are called **landform maps**. Mountains, hills, and plains are all examples of landforms. Landform maps also show bodies of water such as lakes, rivers, and oceans.
- Look at the map below. What kinds of landforms are found in the United States? What is the name of the plains area that is to the east of the Rocky Mountains? What large bodies of water are shown? Which ocean borders the Coast Ranges?

What is a transportation map?

- A **transportation map** is a kind of map that shows you how you can travel from one place to another.
- Some transportation maps show roads for traveling by car, by bike, or on foot. Other transportation maps may show bus, train, ship, or airplane routes. What kinds of routes are shown on the map of Pittsburgh?

More Practice

There are other physical and transportation maps in this book. For examples of physical maps, see pages 7, R10, and R12. For examples of transportation maps, see pages 135 and 136.

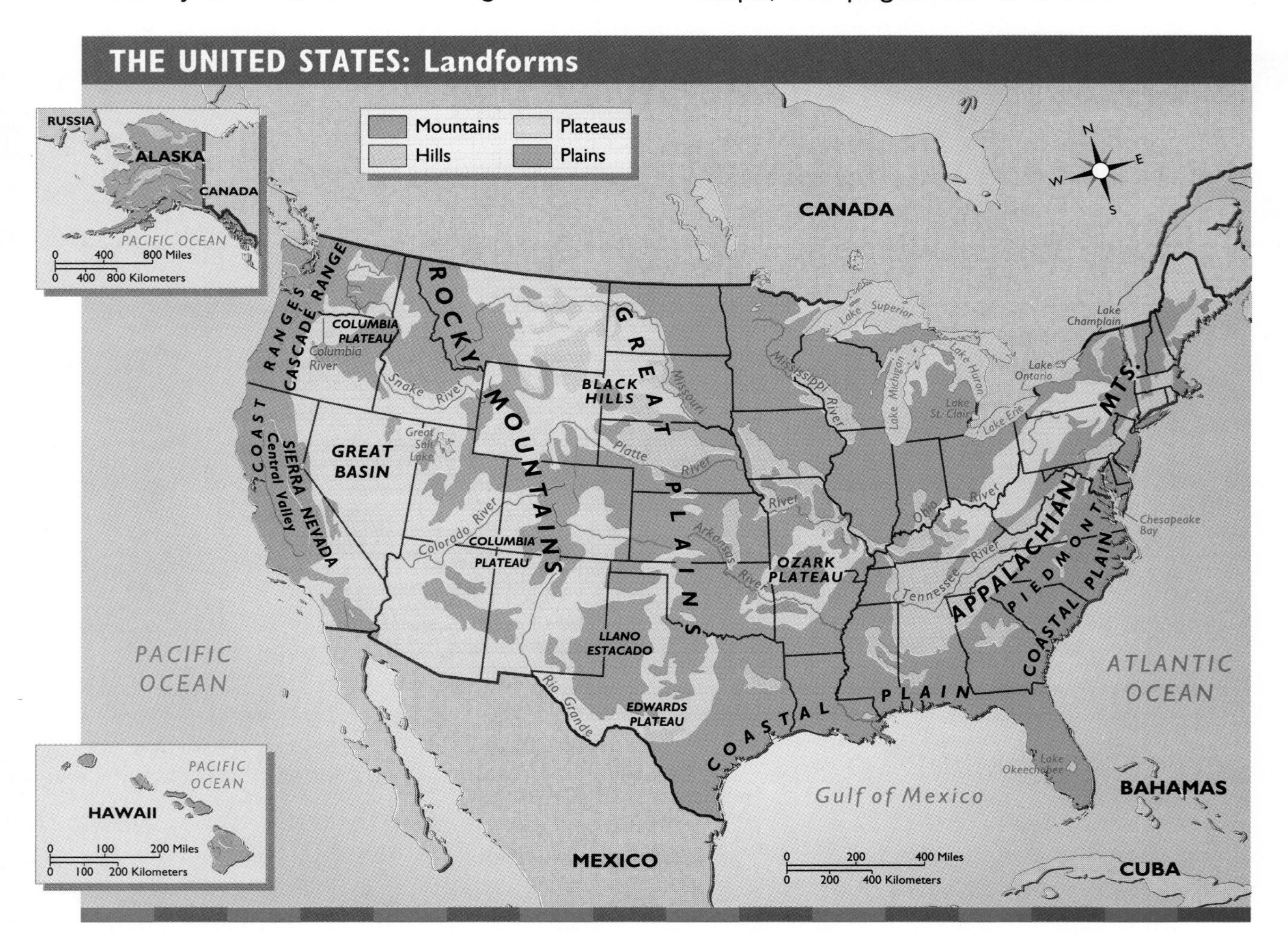

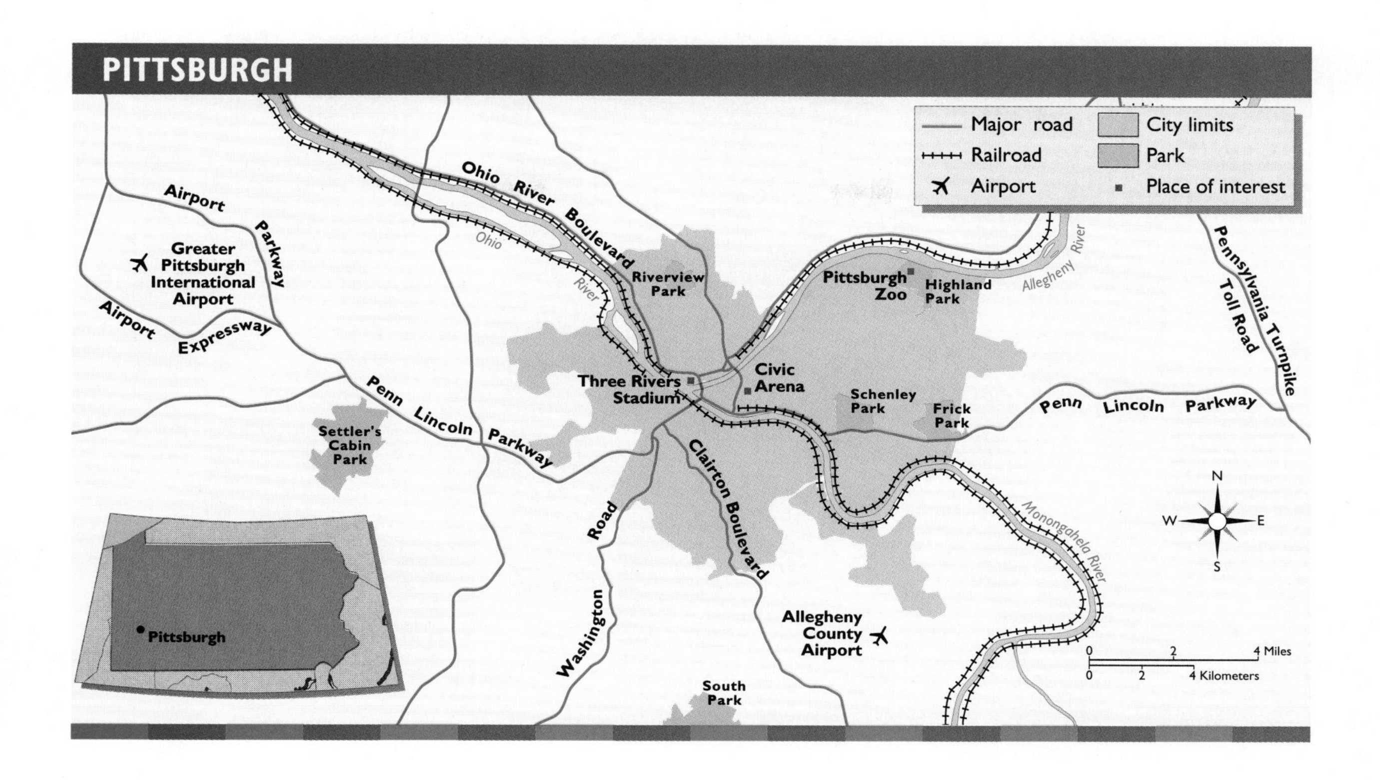

What is an historical map?

- An **historical map** is a map that shows information about past events and where they occurred.
- When you look at an historical map, first study the map title. What does it tell you about the historical map on this page?
- Historical maps often show dates in the title or on the map. Study the map on the American Revolution in Pennsylvania. What historical dates does it show?
- Next look at the map key. The map key tells you what the symbols stand for on the map. What is the symbol for a battle? Which symbol shows where British troops moved?

More Practice

There are other historical maps in this book. For examples, see pages 82, 95, and 161.

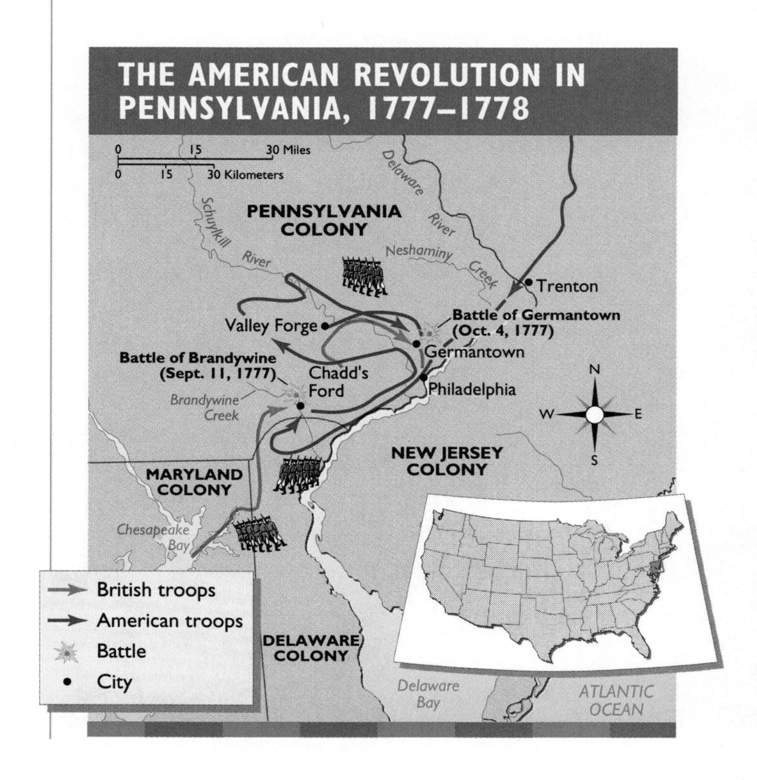

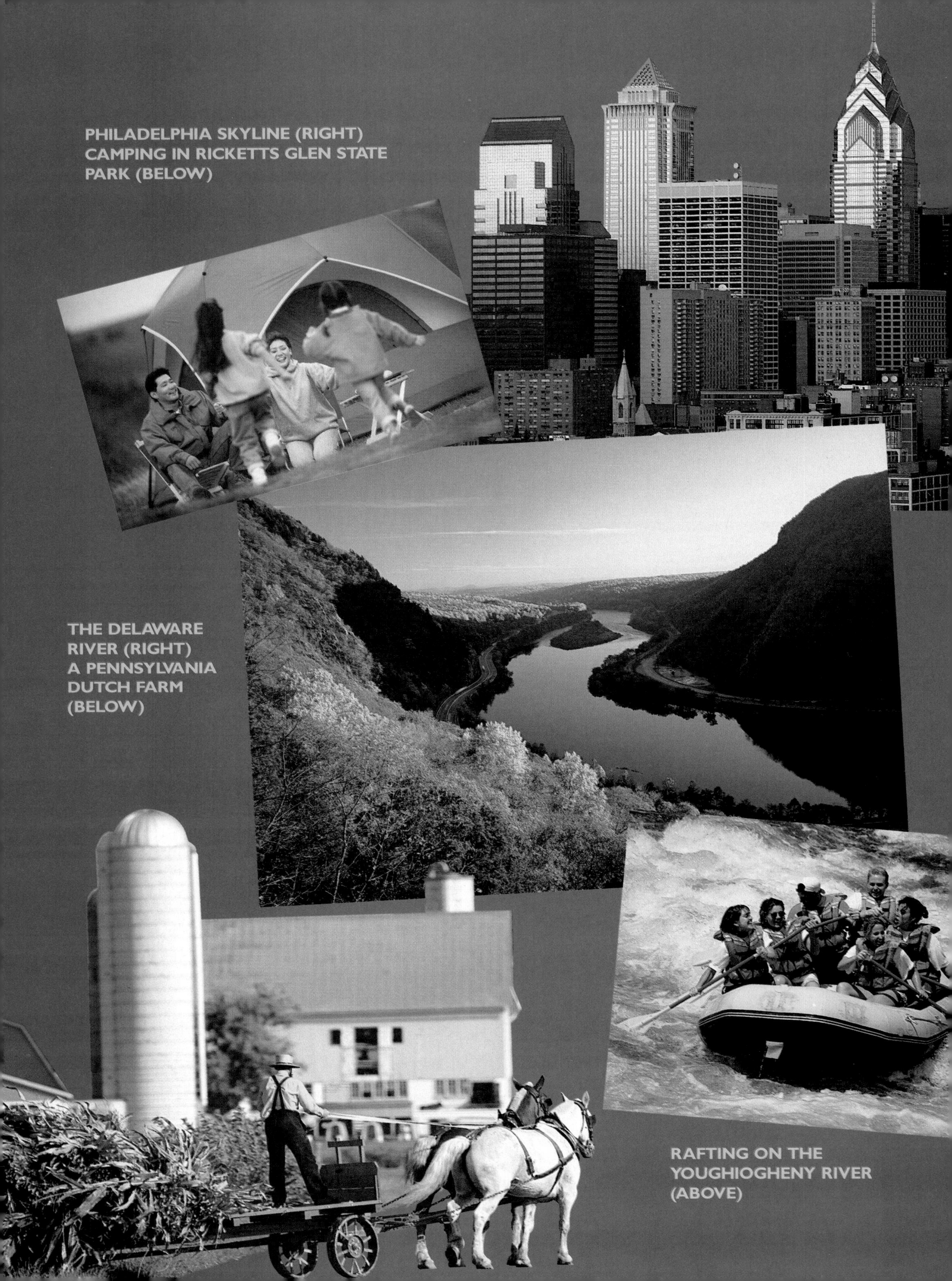

PHILADELPHIA SKYLINE (RIGHT)
CAMPING IN RICKETTS GLEN STATE PARK (BELOW)

THE DELAWARE RIVER (RIGHT)
A PENNSYLVANIA DUTCH FARM (BELOW)

RAFTING ON THE YOUGHIOGHENY RIVER (ABOVE)

UNIT ONE

The Geography of Pennsylvania

"this mountain region . . . is a garden"

Frances Trollope, visitor to Pennsylvania, early 1800s
See page 6.

WHY DOES IT MATTER?

Our state has the best of everything. It has high, rugged mountains and gently rolling hills. It has wide rivers and rushing mountain streams. Our state is also rich in resources, from farmlands to forests. Read on. Unit 1 introduces the geography and resources that make Pennsylvania the special place that it is.

MOUNTAIN LAUREL (TOP RIGHT)
WINTER IN THE ALLEGHENY FOREST (RIGHT)

CHAPTER 1

A Place Called Pennsylvania

THINKING ABOUT GEOGRAPHY

Pennsylvania has many different types of land, bodies of water, weather, and resources. Thousands of miles of rivers and streams flow through our state. Look at the photographs on the next page. Using the colored squares, match each photograph to its location on the map. What do they tell you about Pennsylvania?

Mt. Minsi

Winter can bring a lot of snow to our state's mountain areas.

Doe Run

Some of Pennsylvania's most beautiful and productive farmland lies in the southeastern corner of our state.

Kane

More than half of our state is covered in forests. In cities such as Kane, people turn some of these trees into furniture, paper, and other goods.

Pittsburgh

The city of Pittsburgh sits at the place where the Allegheny and Monongahela rivers come together to form the Ohio River.

Focus Activity

READ TO LEARN
What kind of land and water does Pennsylvania have?

VOCABULARY
border
geography
landform
plain
valley
ridge
plateau
river system
bay
tributary

PLACES
Lake Erie
Philadelphia
Pittsburgh
Atlantic Coastal Plain
Delaware River
Piedmont
Appalachian Mountains
Harrisburg
Allegheny Mountains
Allegheny Plateau
Delaware Bay
Susquehanna River

LAND AND WATER

READ ALOUD

Frances Trollope, an English visitor to Pennsylvania in the early 1800s, wrote about the beauty of the western part of our state: "The whole of this mountain region . . . is a garden. The . . . variety of plants, and the lavish [rich] profusion [plentiful amount] of their growth, produce an effect perfectly enchanting [delightful]."

THE BIG PICTURE

Suppose you wanted to tell a pen pal from another country where you live. You could tell your friend that Pennsylvania is one of the 50 states that make up the United States. You could also say that it is in the northeastern part of our country. The states of Ohio, West Virginia, Maryland, Delaware, New Jersey, and New York share Pennsylvania's borders. A border is an imaginary line that divides one place from another. Pennsylvania is also bordered by Lake Erie. Lake Erie is one of the five Great Lakes. The Great Lakes are the largest group of lakes in the world.

As you learn about Pennsylvania's geography (jee AHG ruh fee), you will be able to tell your friend about the beauty of the land and water in our state. Geography is the study of Earth and all the different things on it. Land and water, plant and animal life, and human activities are part of what geographers study. Earth's geography affects us all. It affects where we live and the way we live.

A TRIP ACROSS PENNSYLVANIA

One exciting way to learn about our state's geography is to drive across it. Suppose you and your family plan to take a trip from Philadelphia to Pittsburgh to visit friends. Look at the map below to find Philadelphia and Pittsburgh. It would take about 6 hours to drive that far on Interstate 76, also known as the Pennsylvania Turnpike.

You will see many landforms on your trip. Landforms are the shapes that make up Earth's surface. Hills, for example, are one kind of landform. Another is a plain, a large area of nearly flat land. What other landforms might you see on your trip?

Why is Pennsylvania called the Keystone state?

The stone at the top of an arch holds the other stones of the arch in place. This center stone is called the keystone. In the early days of the United States, Pennsylvania came to be called the "keystone state" because it lay in the middle between six northern and six southern states.

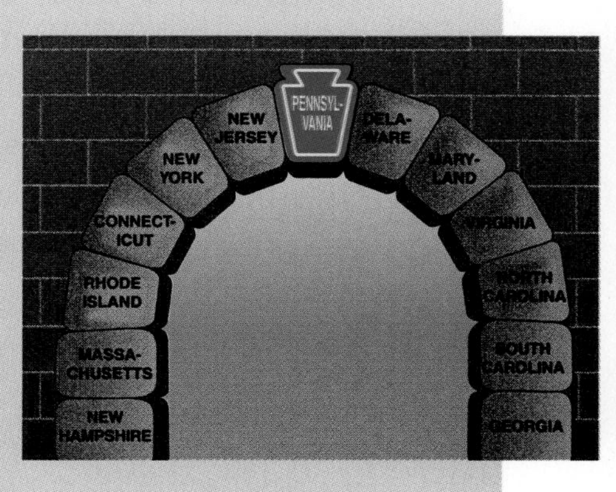

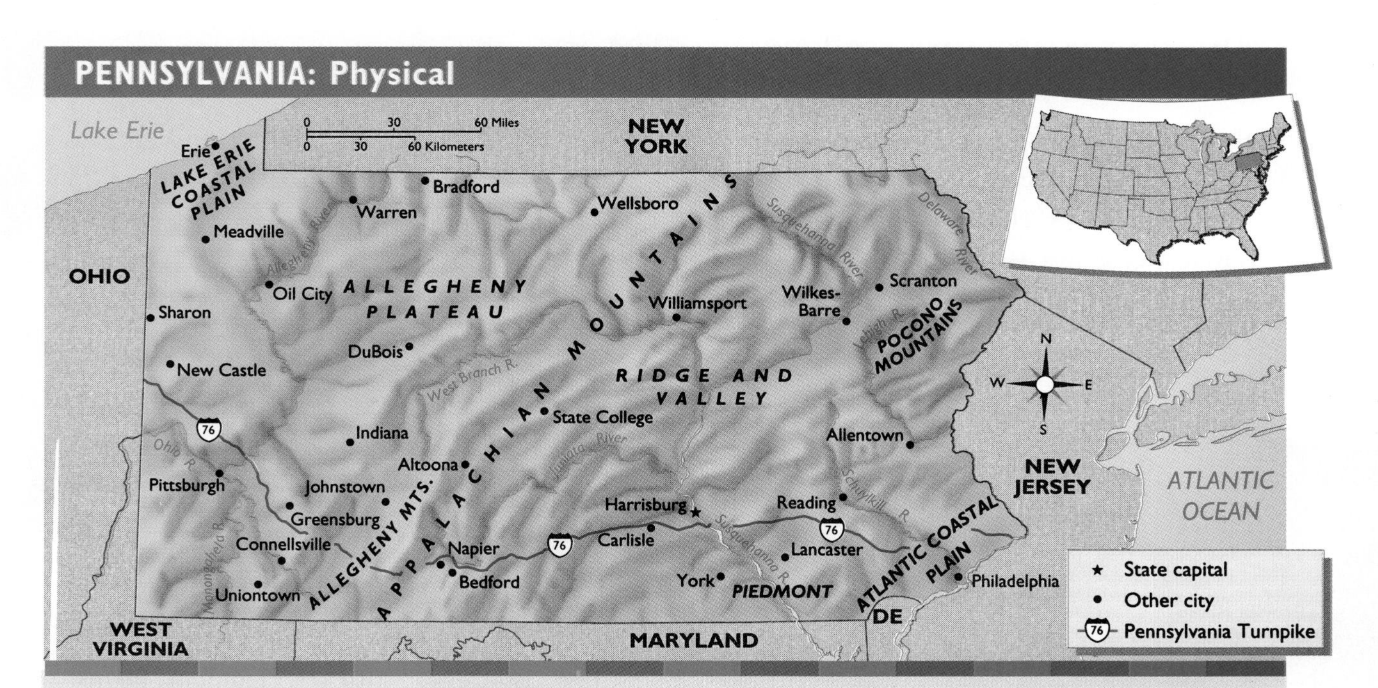

This map shows the physical features found in Pennsylvania.

1. What landform do you find along both the Delaware River and Lake Erie?
2. Where is the Allegheny Plateau?
3. What is similar about the locations of both Philadelphia and Pittsburgh?

PLAINS, HILLS, AND VALLEYS

You'll begin your drive in Philadelphia, our state's largest city. It is located in the eastern part of our state on the narrow **Atlantic Coastal Plain**. This landform is a sandy, flat lowland that lies along the **Delaware River**.

Just a few miles out of Philadelphia, you'll reach the **Piedmont** (PEED mahnt). Piedmont means "at the foot of the mountains." With its gently sloping hills and wide **valleys**, or low patches of land between the hills, this area has some of the richest farmland in the United States. In summer, you'll find corn growing in the fields.

The Highlands

Driving west you will see long, narrow chains of mountains, called **ridges**, one after the other. Can you imagine what it would be like to cross them on foot? Early westward travelers called them the "Endless Mountains." These ridges are separated by narrow valleys.

The rocky ridges are part of the **Appalachian** (ap uh LAY chee un) **Mountains**, one of the oldest mountain chains in the world. Over millions of years, wind, water, and ice have worn them down. The Appalachian Mountains stretch from Maine to Alabama.

By the time you reach our state's capital, **Harrisburg** (HAR is burg), you may notice that you are in a very

Philadelphia (left) lies along the flat Atlantic Coastal Plain. As you head into the Piedmont, farms like this one (above) are a common sight.

large valley surrounded by mountains. This valley, called the Cumberland Valley in Pennsylvania, is part of the larger Great Valley that runs all the way from New York to Georgia.

The Alleghenies

As you leave Harrisburg and continue west, you'll see the **Allegheny** (al uh GAY nee) **Mountains**. They are the highest part of the Appalachian Mountains in Pennsylvania. The Allegheny Mountains line the eastern edge of the **Allegheny Plateau**. A **plateau** is a high, flat area of land that rises steeply above the surrounding land. Over millions of years, this plateau has been shaped into rough, flat-topped hills and narrow valleys.

The plateau area covers more than half our state and has many sparkling lakes and shady forests. The huge Allegheny National Forest is in the northern part of this area.

As you near the end of your journey, you will see the skyline of busy downtown Pittsburgh. Pittsburgh is our state's second largest city. Its buildings and homes crowd the narrow valleys of the area.

The Lake Erie Coastal Plain

Our trip on the Pennsylvania Turnpike didn't take us across the northwestern corner of our state. This land along Lake Erie is called the Lake Erie Coastal Plain and is much like the Atlantic Coastal Plain. It slopes in large steps of land down from the Allegheny Plateau to the shores of the lake. The rich soil of this plain is good for growing fruits and vegetables.

Rivers and streams have cut through the Allegheny Plateau (above) over many years, making it hilly. Grapes (right) are an important crop on the Lake Erie Coastal Plain.

PENNSYLVANIA'S WATER

Pennsylvania is rich in water. Nearly 45,000 miles of rivers and streams wind across our state. It also has many lakes, especially in the mountain areas.

You have read that Pennsylvania borders Lake Erie. From Lake Erie, ships can travel through the other Great Lakes and the St. Lawrence Seaway to reach the Atlantic Ocean. Pennsylvania can ship goods all over the world from its Lake Erie coastline.

Links to **SCIENCE**

Ice is Nice!

Most of Earth's water is salt water. Very little of Earth's water is fresh water. People, plants, and animals need fresh water to stay alive. Most of the fresh water on Earth is in sheets of ice called glaciers (GLAY shurz). Look up the word *glacier* in an encyclopedia and find out where on Earth they can be found.

Our River Systems

Pennsylvania has three major **river systems**. A river system is made up of all the streams and rivers that flow into a larger river.

The Delaware River system lies in the eastern part of our state. The Delaware River itself forms the eastern border of Pennsylvania. Look at the map on page 7 and find the Delaware River. The river flows into **Delaware Bay** and out into the Atlantic Ocean. A **bay** is a part of an ocean that reaches into the land. The Delaware River system has long been an important shipping route for people in our state.

The Schuylkill (SKOOL kil) and Lehigh (LEE hī) rivers are **tributaries** (TRIH byoo tar eez) of the Delaware.

A tributary is a smaller river or stream that flows into a larger river.

In the central part of our state, the wide **Susquehanna** (suhs kwuh HAH nuh) **River** flows. The Susquehanna is 444 miles long. Its tributaries, the Juniata (JYOO nee ah tuh) River, the West Branch River, and their many creeks, make up the Susquehanna River system. Although the Susquehanna is a long river, it is not deep enough for large boats and ships. You will find only fishing boats and motor boats traveling on this river.

The **Ohio River** system in western Pennsylvania is our third river system. For hundreds of years, it has been used for moving people and goods. The Ohio's tributaries, the Allegheny and Monongahela (muh NON guh hee luh) rivers, are also heavily traveled.

The Allegheny and Monongahela rivers come together to form the Ohio River at Pittsburgh, one of our state's busiest cities.

WHY IT MATTERS

Our state has a great variety of landforms. It has beautiful, tall mountains covered with forests, as well as low coastal plains. Its many rivers and lakes are highways for moving people and goods. When we study our state's geography, we realize just how special Pennsylvania is.

Reviewing Facts and Ideas

SUM IT UP

- Geography is the study of Earth and everything on it.
- Landforms are the shapes that make up Earth's surface.
- Pennsylvania has several kinds of landforms, including plains, hills, mountains, and plateaus.
- Pennsylvania has three major river systems. They are the Delaware, Susquehanna, and Ohio river systems.

THINK ABOUT IT

1. Name the six states that border Pennsylvania.
2. What is a landform?
3. **FOCUS** Name three types of landforms found in Pennsylvania.
4. **THINKING SKILL** *Compare* and *contrast* the Lake Erie Coastal Plain with the Allegheny Plateau.
5. **GEOGRAPHY** Look at the physical map of Pennsylvania on page 7 and locate your city or the city nearest to where you live. Which of Pennsylvania's physical features are nearby?

GEOGRAPHYSKILLS

Reading Elevation Maps

VOCABULARY

elevation

WHY THE SKILL MATTERS

On your trip across Pennsylvania, you read that the Allegheny Mountains are part of the Appalachian Mountains. Did you know that the Appalachian mountain range stretches from Canada, in the north, to as far south in the United States as Alabama? Suppose you wanted to find out where the highest and lowest places in all of the Appalachian Mountains are. How would you know the height of the mountains?

You could use an elevation (el uh VAY shun) map to find out. Elevation is the height of the land above the level of the sea. Elevation at sea level is 0 feet.

How can a map tell you whether an area has a high or low elevation? An elevation map uses colors to show elevations. Look at the map key on this page. For example, all the places shown on the map in light green are between 650 feet and 1,000 feet above sea level.

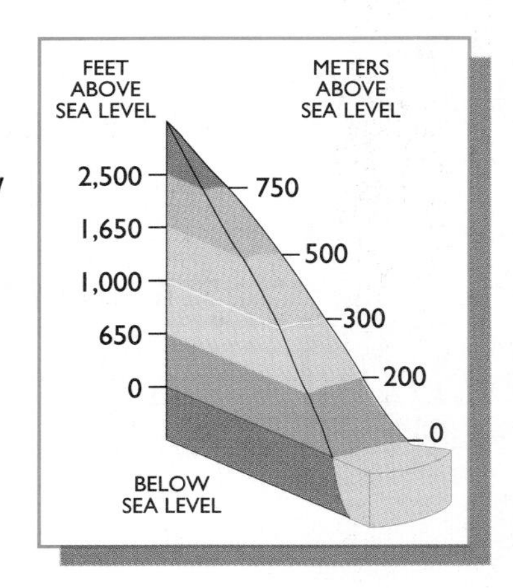

USING THE SKILL

Of course, elevation maps tell us about many things besides mountains and flat areas. For example, they give us important information about rivers.

Have you ever wondered why the water in a river flows? The answer is simple: because water runs downhill. Every river begins at a higher elevation than where it ends. Gravity pulls the water downhill toward a lower elevation.

Let's say the land slopes downhill toward the south. Then the river will flow from north to south. That's why an elevation map can help you understand a river's course.

Let's try using an elevation map to trace the path of a Pennsylvania river. The Susquehanna River begins in central New York. Locate the Susquehanna River on the map on the opposite page. What color is the area where the Susquehanna enters our state? Check the map key to find out what elevation this color represents. You can see that the Susquehanna first enters Pennsylvania at an elevation of 650 feet above sea level.

Follow the river's path. You can see that the Susquehanna flows through parts of New York and moves south into Pennsylvania. Through our state, the elevation along the river's path drops. Finally it reaches the border of Pennsylvania and flows through Maryland into the Chesapeake Bay. This is where the Susquehanna River finally reaches sea level.

TRYING THE SKILL

You have just used the map to trace the path of the Susquehanna. Now use the elevation map below to trace the path of the Allegheny River. The Allegheny starts in northern Pennsylvania, flows into New York, and then reenters our state.

At what elevation does the Allegheny River start? In which direction does it flow? What does that show you about the elevation in that direction? Trace the river's path with your finger. Into what other river does the Allegheny River flow?

HELPING Yourself

- **Elevation maps show you how high the land is above sea level.**
- **Study the map key to see which colors stand for different elevations on the map.**

REVIEWING THE SKILL

Now use the elevation map to answer the following questions. Use the Helping Yourself box for hints.

1. What is elevation?
2. How does an elevation map tell us which way a river flows?
3. What is the elevation of the highest mountain peak in Pennsylvania? Where is the lowest elevation found in Pennsylvania?
4. In what color would this map show a plateau that is 1,500 feet above sea level?
5. How does an elevation map help us learn about geography?

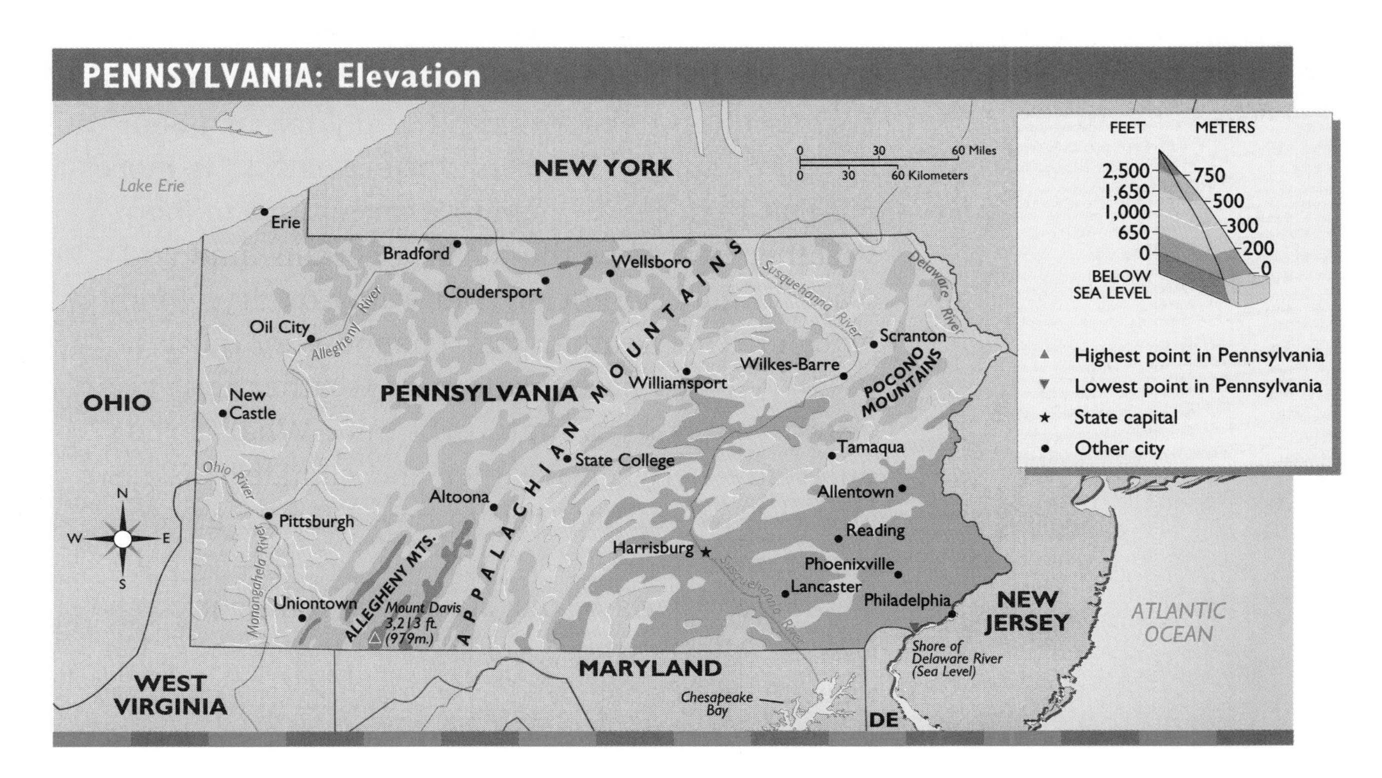

OUR STATE'S CLIMATE

Focus Activity

READ TO LEARN
Why do different parts of our state have different climates?

VOCABULARY
weather
climate
temperature
precipitation
hurricane
tornado

PLACES
Phoenixville
Tamaqua
Bradford
Wilkes-Barre

READ ALOUD

In 1990, The New Yorker *magazine reported the events on Groundhog Day in Punxsutawney, Pennsylvania. "At approximately 7:27 A.M. on the second of February, 1990, Punxsutawney Phil emerged from his burrow [hole]. . . . He . . . signaled . . . 'There is no shadow today.'" Every year thousands of people from all over the country gather to see whether Punxsutawney Phil will see his shadow. According to legend, if there's no shadow, spring will come sooner.*

THE BIG PICTURE

Groundhog Day is a lot of fun. But we know that a groundhog's shadow can't really tell us about the arrival of spring. Predicting the **weather** is more difficult than just watching a sleepy groundhog. Weather describes the air at a certain time and place. It may be hot or cold, rainy or dry, windy or calm. The weather may change very quickly.

Every place has a pattern of weather over many years. This is its **climate** (KLĪ mit). What is the difference between weather and climate? Weather affects how you live day to day. Climate affects long-range plans.

Different parts of our state have different climates. Climate affects where we live and the clothing we wear. It affects the foods we eat, how we enjoy ourselves, and the type of work we do.

TWO PARTS OF CLIMATE

What questions would you ask to find out about the climate of a certain place in Pennsylvania? You might start by asking, "How hot is the summer? How cold is the winter?" These questions are about **temperature** (TEM pur uh chur). Temperature is a measure of how hot or cold the air is. The map below tells you what temperatures you might expect in different parts of Pennsylvania in January. **Phoenixville** holds the record for the hottest temperature in Pennsylvania. On July 10, 1936, it was 111°F.

Another question you would want to ask is "How much **precipitation** (prih sihp ih TAY shun) falls?" Precipitation is the moisture that falls to the ground in the form of rain, snow, sleet, or hail. The precipitation map below shows you how much precipitation to expect during one year. The wettest place in our state is **Tamaqua**, which gets about 48 inches of precipitation per year.

Sometimes we get a lot of snow in the winter!

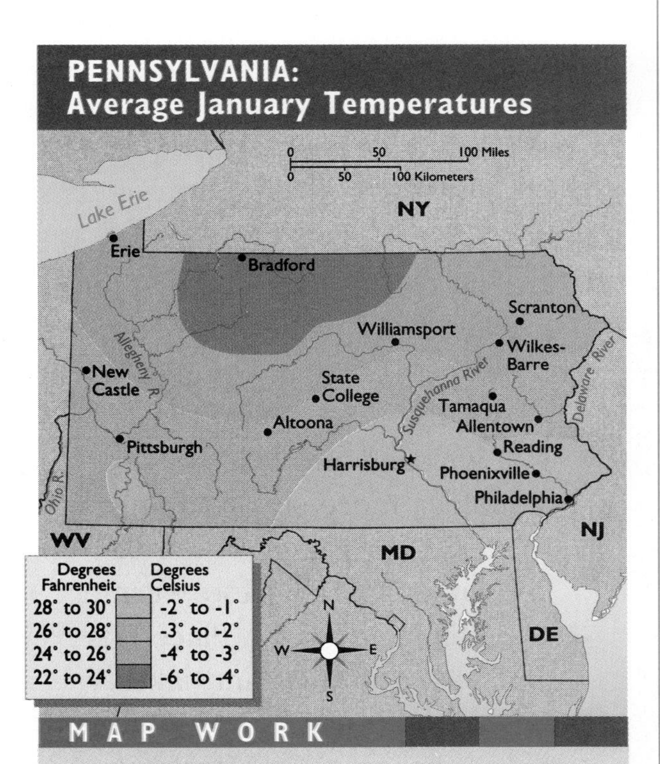

MAP WORK

January temperatures vary in Pennsylvania.

1. Which city is warmer in January, Pittsburgh or Scranton?
2. As you travel from Bradford to Harrisburg, would you notice a change in temperature? Why?

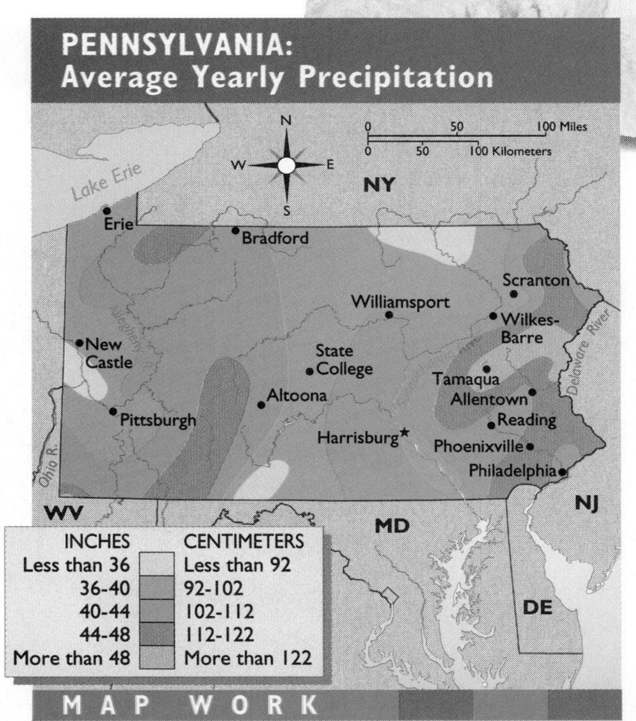

MAP WORK

Precipitation in our state varies greatly.

1. Which city on the map receives the most precipitation?
2. How much precipitation does Altoona receive?

INVESTIGATING CLIMATE

You have read about what it would be like to take a trip across Pennsylvania. On such a trip, you might notice changes in climate. Let's find out why.

How High?

Why is it cooler in the Allegheny Mountains? In the last skill lesson, you learned about elevation. Did you know that elevation also plays a role in climate? The higher a place is above sea level, the colder its climate usually will be. That's why you might feel chilly if you are driving in the Allegheny Mountains.

How Far from the Equator?

On the temperature map on page 15, you saw that the warmest January temperatures in our state are in the south. For example, the temperature in Philadelphia might be as high as 34°F on a particular day, but on that same day in **Bradford**, it might be only 18°F.

Why is the weather in Philadelphia and Bradford different? One reason is that Bradford is north of Philadelphia. This means that Bradford is farther from the equator. The farther from the equator you go, the cooler the climate will usually be.

How Far from an Ocean or Lake?

Did you ever go swimming on a hot summer day and find your teeth chattering? Water heats up in the spring and summer more slowly than air. So Lake Erie and the Atlantic Ocean stay cooler than the land all through the summer. Breezes from the water cool the land near the coast.

Oceans and lakes also get colder more slowly than the land. In winter, ocean or lake breezes bring warmer air to the land. Places far from oceans and lakes, however, do not feel these breezes. So Harrisburg, for example, tends to get hotter in the summer than Erie because it is farther from a body of water.

Pennsylvania's climate lets you play in the leaves in the autumn and go boating in the summer.

The Flood of '96 made driving impossible in some parts of our state.

Severe Weather

Sometimes our state gets heavy rains and strong winds from storms called **hurricanes** [HUR ih kaynz] that occur along the Atlantic coast.

Heavy rains often cause the rivers and streams of Pennsylvania to flood. The "Flood of '96," in January 1996, was very severe. Quickly melting snow and heavy rains caused unexpected flooding and much damage. Near **Wilkes-Barre**, the Susquehanna River rose more than six feet in just two hours! That's taller than the average adult!

Tornadoes [tawr NAY dohz] also affect Pennsylvania. A tornado is a swirling funnel of wind that moves quickly. The high speed winds of a tornado can destroy anything in its path. Thunderstorms often occur with tornadoes. The Piedmont in the southeastern part of our state gets more tornadoes than any other area in Pennsylvania. Our state gets about 10 tornadoes per year and 7 or 8 of those occur in the Piedmont.

WHY IT MATTERS

Elevation, distance from the equator, and distance from an ocean or lake affect the climate in different parts of our state in very different ways. As you continue to read about our state, think about how people learn to live in their surroundings.

Reviewing Facts and Ideas

SUM IT UP

- Climate is the pattern of weather a place has over a long period of time.
- Temperature and precipitation are two key parts of climate.
- Three factors that affect climate are distance from the equator, distance from an ocean or lake, and elevation.
- Severe weather that affects Pennsylvania includes hurricanes, floods, and tornadoes.

THINK ABOUT IT

1. What is the difference between climate and weather?
2. As you move away from the equator, what happens to the climate?
3. **FOCUS** Why do different parts of our state have different climates?
4. **THINKING SKILL** *Predict* which city on the maps on page 15 you think will get the most snow this January. Explain your prediction.
5. **WRITE** Write a description of the climate of your area. Include how the elevation, distance from the equator, and distance from a large body of water affect it.

GEOGRAPHYSKILLS

Using Latitude and Longitude

VOCABULARY

latitude
parallel
degree
longitude
prime meridian
meridian
global grid

WHY THE SKILL MATTERS

Suppose you have found an old, faded treasure map. An X marks the spot where the treasure is buried, but the map does not tell what city or town the treasure is near. Your only clues are some lines that crisscross the map like a tic-tac-toe grid. The X is printed where two of the lines cross. Every line has a number on it. If you knew what those numbers meant, you could find the treasure.

You discover that these are imaginary lines invented long ago by mapmakers. The lines describe the location of a particular place. They provide an "address" for every place on Earth—even places in the middle of an ocean.

Airline pilots use this same system of lines to keep track of where they are. Up among the clouds a pilot must be sure of a plane's location at all times. Pilots also need an exact way to explain where they are going.

The faded lines on the map will help you to find the treasure. You will use other imaginary lines on maps in this book and in many other books.

USING LATITUDE

Let's study these imaginary lines. Look at the map on this page and place your finger on the equator. This is the starting point for measuring latitude. Latitude is a measure of how far north or south a place is from the equator.

Geographers also call lines of latitude parallels because they are parallel lines. Parallel lines always remain the same distance apart.

Each line of latitude has a number. You can see that the equator is labeled 0°, meaning zero degrees. Degrees are

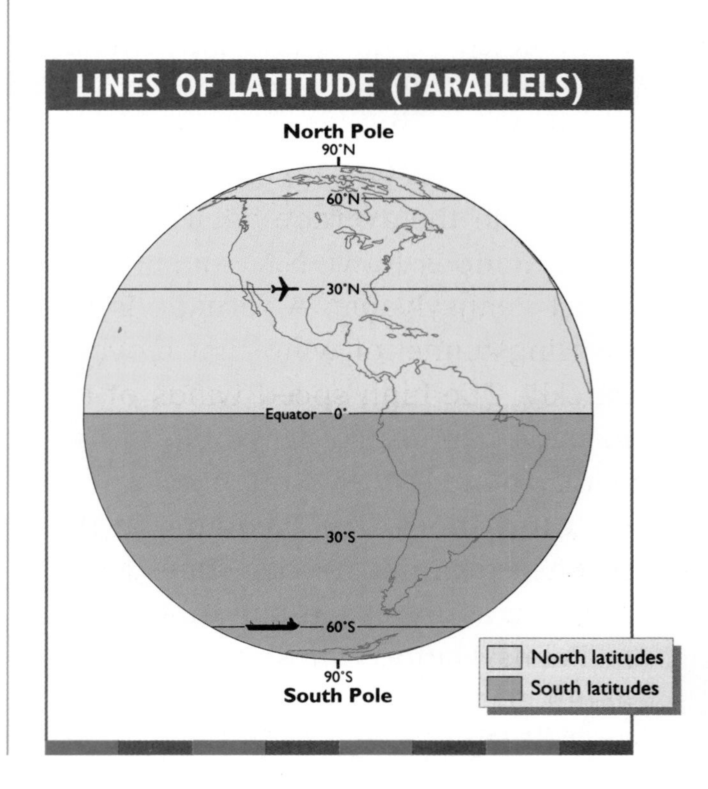

used to measure the distance on Earth's surface. The symbol ° stands for degrees. Look again at the map. What is the latitude of the equator?

Now look at the lines of latitude north of the equator. Notice that these parallels are labeled N for "north." The North Pole has a latitude, too, which is 90°N. The parallels south of the equator are labeled S for "south." The latitude of the South Pole is 90°S.

Find the ship on the map. The ship is sailing west. It is located at 60°S. Now find the small airplane on the map. Along which parallel is it flying?

USING LONGITUDE

Now look at the map on this page. It shows lines of **longitude**. Like parallels, these are imaginary lines on a map or globe. But instead of measuring distance north or south, they measure distance east or west of the **prime meridian**. Prime means "first." Lines of longitude are also called **meridians**. The prime meridian is the first line, or starting place, for measuring lines of longitude. That's why the prime meridian is marked 0° on the map. Put your finger on the prime meridian. It runs through the western parts of Europe and Africa.

Look at the meridians to the west of the prime meridian. These lines are labeled W for "west." The lines to the east of the prime meridian are labeled E for "east." Longitude is measured up to 180° east of the prime meridian and up to 180° west of the prime meridian.

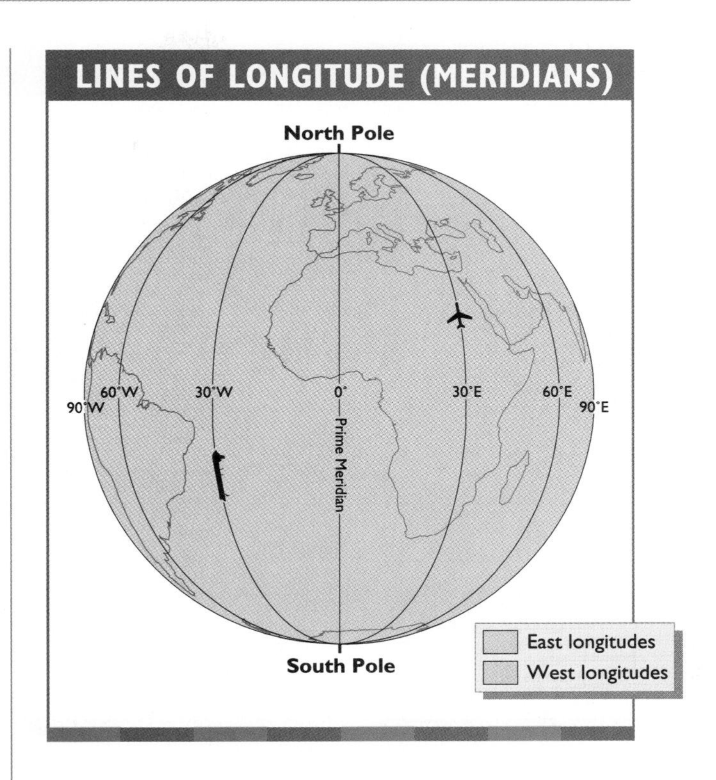

Since 180°E and 180°W fall on the same line, this line is marked neither E nor W. This line runs through the Pacific Ocean.

Unlike lines of latitude, meridians are not parallel to one another. Earth is round. Meridians divide Earth into pieces like the sections of an orange. Look at the map on this page again. As you can see, the meridians are far apart at the equator. They meet, however, at the North Pole and the South Pole.

Lines of longitude measure degrees east and west. Look at the ship on the map. It is sailing along the meridian known as 30°W. Now look at the airplane on the same map. It is flying over the continent of Africa. What meridian is it flying over? In which direction is the airplane traveling?

GEOGRAPHYSKILLS

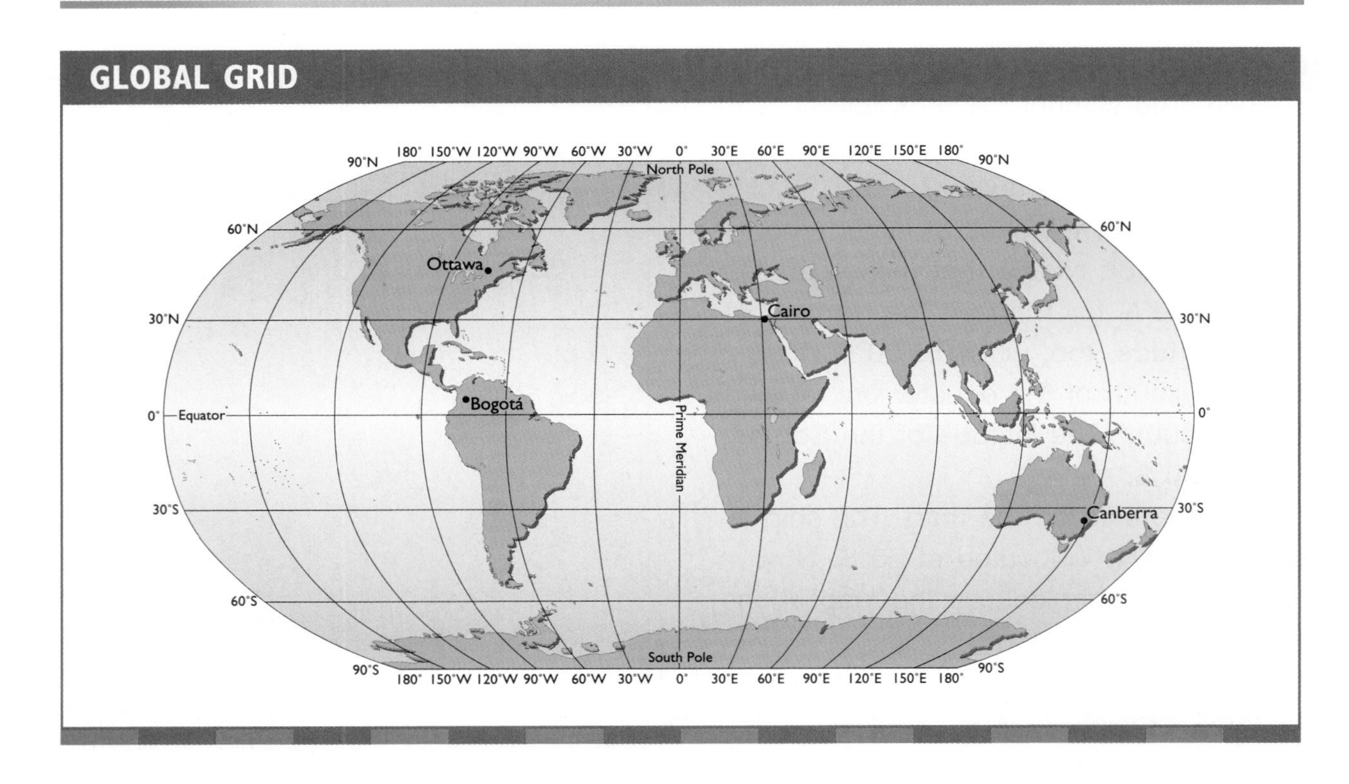

FINDING PLACES ON A MAP

In order to use latitude and longitude lines to find places, you must combine them on the same map. Look at the map of the world on this page. You can see that the lines of latitude and the lines of longitude cross to form a grid on the map. A grid is a set of crisscrossing lines.

The grid on this map is called a **global grid** because it covers Earth entirely. By using the global grid, you can locate the "address" of any place in the world.

Look at the map again. Find Canberra, Australia, and Bogotá, Colombia. Which of these two cities is closer to the equator? How can you tell?

Now find Ottawa, Canada. Is this city east or west of the prime meridian? Find Cairo, Egypt. Is Cairo east or west of the prime meridian? Is Cairo north or south of the equator?

Look at the latitude and longitude map of Pennsylvania on the opposite page. Find the city of Fredericktown. As you can see, it is located at the point where 40°N latitude and 80°W longitude cross on the map. So we say that the location, or "address," of the city of Fredericktown is 40°N, 80°W.

Remember that when you locate a place on a map, you must always give the latitude first and the longitude second. You also must remember to give north or south for the latitude, and east or west for the longitude. To describe a place that is not exactly at the point where two lines cross, you must use the closest lines.

TRYING THE SKILL

Try to find a city in Pennsylvania by its "address." This city is located at about 42°N, 80°W. What is the name of the city? Now describe the location of Anita, using latitude and longitude.

On your buried-treasure map are the following numbers: 41°N, 76°W. Do you understand what those numbers mean now? In what city is the treasure located? Start digging!

HELPING Yourself

- **Latitude is the distance north or south of the equator. Longitude is the distance east or west of the prime meridian.**
- **Follow the latitude line you are looking for on the global grid. Follow the line across until you reach the right longitude line.**

REVIEWING THE SKILL

Many maps include a grid of latitude and longitude. Use the map below to answer these questions.

1. What are lines of latitude and longitude? How can they be helpful?
2. Give the location of Erie, Pennsylvania, using latitude and longitude.
3. Name two cities in Pennsylvania that share the same line of latitude. Then name two cities that share the same line of longitude.
4. How did you find the answers to the last two questions?

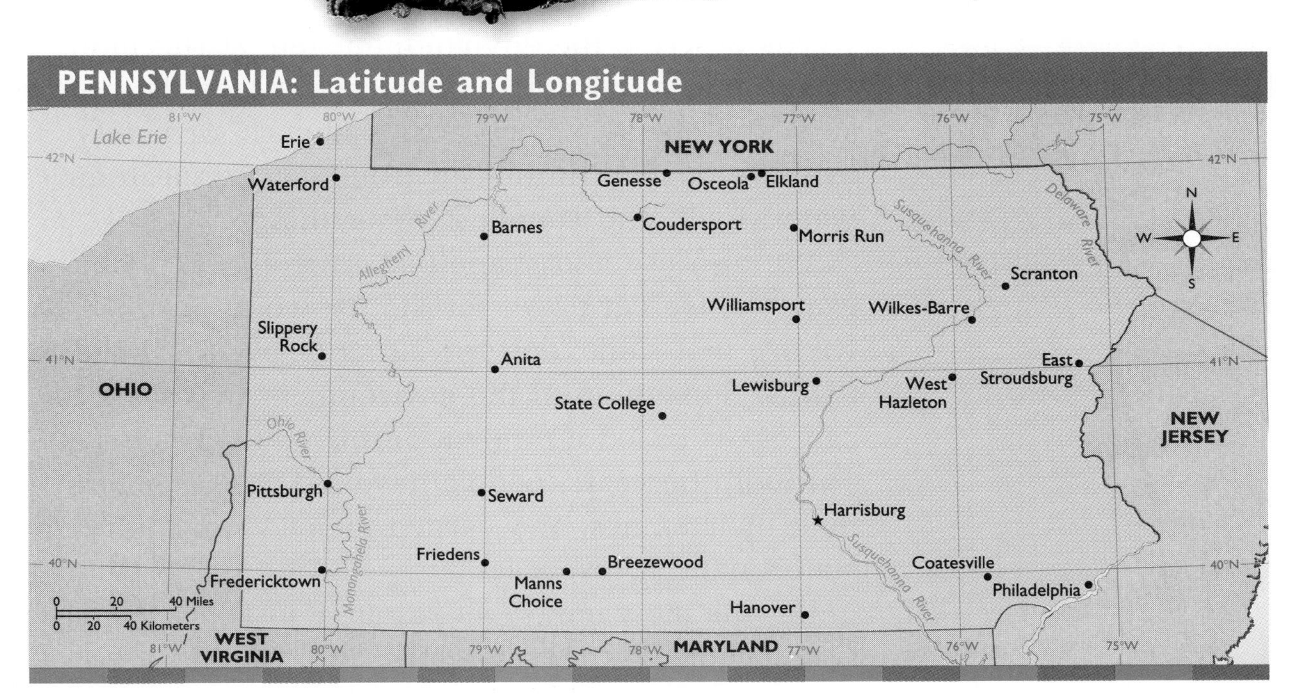

PENNSYLVANIA: Latitude and Longitude

Focus Activity

READ TO LEARN

In what ways are natural resources important to Pennsylvanians?

VOCABULARY

environment
natural resource
renewable resource
nonrenewable resource
fuel
mineral
economy
pollution
conservation
recycle

OUR STATE'S RESOURCES

READ ALOUD

"There are several sorts of grapes and strawberries plenty, . . . there are many sorts of wood, as black oaks, white oaks, red oaks. . . . We have turkeys wild in the woods, pheasants and partridges, with many other sorts of birds of diverse [different] colors." This is how George Haworth described what he found in Pennsylvania in a letter in 1699. Today, you can still see many of the same trees and birds in Pennsylvania.

THE BIG PICTURE

Though written nearly 300 years ago, Haworth's words describe the environment (en VĪ run munt) found in Pennsylvania today. Environment is the surroundings in which people, animals, or plants live. We depend on our environment for clean air, water, food, and countless other things.

We also use and shape our environment. For example, we cut down forests for wood. In time, we use that same land for farms or even to build towns. Something in the environment that people can use is called a natural resource (REE sors). Through the years, people have fed their families, built their homes, and earned their livings with our state's natural resources.

But the most important resource in Pennsylvania is its people. Farmers, doctors, and teachers are just a few of the people we need to keep things running.

RENEWABLE RESOURCES

Many different natural resources are found in our environment. Some of these are renewable resources. We can renew them. That is, we can replace them.

Forests

Trees, for example, are renewable resources because they can be replanted. More than 48 kinds of trees grow in the Allegheny National Forest in northwestern Pennsylvania. When a lumber company cuts down an area of forest, workers often plant new trees. Still, some trees take many years to grow. Because forests take time to be replaced, we need to use our forest resources carefully.

Soil

Pennsylvania farmers plant crops such as corn, soybeans, and tomatoes in the same soil over and over. Yet soil can become worn out from growing too many crops. Farmers renew soil by adding fertilizer that plants use up as they grow. So soil is also a renewable resource. Parts of our state have rich soil that can produce plenty of food for Pennsylvanians. Farmers must be careful that the soil does not get worn out.

Water

No one can live without water. Think about all the things you use it for. Drinking, washing, watering crops, and making electricity are all necessary to our lives. Every time it rains, water is returned to our state's land, rivers, and lakes. That means water also is a renewable resource.

What renewable resource is each person in the photographs making use of?

NONRENEWABLE RESOURCES

Some resources are **nonrenewable resources**. They are available in a limited supply. When we have used them up, they will be gone from our state forever. The Infographic on page 26 shows where some of our state's resources can be found.

Fuels

Fuels (FYOO ulz) that are found in the ground, such as coal, oil, and natural gas, are nonrenewable resources. We use fuels to make heat or energy. With fuels we heat our houses, power machinery that plows fields, and cook meals. They power buses, cars, trucks, and airplanes.

How is coal formed?

Hard, black coal comes from soft, green plants. When these plants died millions of years ago, they were covered with mud and sand. Over time, layers of dead plants, mud, and sand built up. Their weight squeezed the air and water out of the plants. What was left hardened, eventually becoming layers of coal.

Coal is a fuel that has long been an important resource in Pennsylvania.

Fuels for the Future

Scientists know that someday our nonrenewable fuels will be gone. So they are looking for new sources of energy. Solar power is one possibility. Solar power is the use of the sun's rays to make energy. Wind power and water power are other possible sources.

Nuclear power is a source for electricity. There are five nuclear power plants in Pennsylvania. Some people have raised questions about the safety of nuclear power. Because of these questions, fewer nuclear power plants are being built in our state today.

Minerals

Minerals are another kind of nonrenewable resource. A mineral is a natural substance that is found in the ground that does not come from plants or animals. Some important minerals found in our state are clay and limestone. Clay is used in making bricks. Limestone is used in building roads and making cement.

RESOURCES CREATE JOBS

Pennsylvania has many businesses that use natural resources. Some examples include coal mining, brick-making, and fishing. Can you name the natural resources these businesses use?

A Strong Economy

A state's **economy** is the way it produces and uses natural resources, goods, and services. Much of our state's economy uses our natural resources. These resources create many jobs. An important part of Pennsylvania's economy is farming. Without such natural resources as soil and water, farming would not be possible.

Cindy Rutter Johnson grew up on one of the oldest family farms in the United States. The Rutter family farm is located in York in southeastern Pennsylvania. It has been run by members of her family since 1747. Today, Johnson manages the dairy herd. Which of Pennsylvania's natural resources do you think are most important to her?

MANY VOICES PRIMARY SOURCE

Excerpt from an interview with Cindy Rutter Johnson, 1996

It's easy to understand why my family started farming in here in York 250 years ago. The rolling land and mild climate are perfect for raising dairy cows. We depend on the land to grow hay and corn to feed our cows. We also depend on the mild climate which makes it possible for our herd to graze in the pasture much of the year. Farming is a way of life for my family. I can't imagine living or working anywhere else.

Infographic

Where Are Pennsylvania's Resources?

Different parts of our state have different natural resources. Eastern Pennsylvania has rich soil and the best farmland in the state. Coal is an important resource found in many parts of Pennsylvania. What other resources are important in our state?

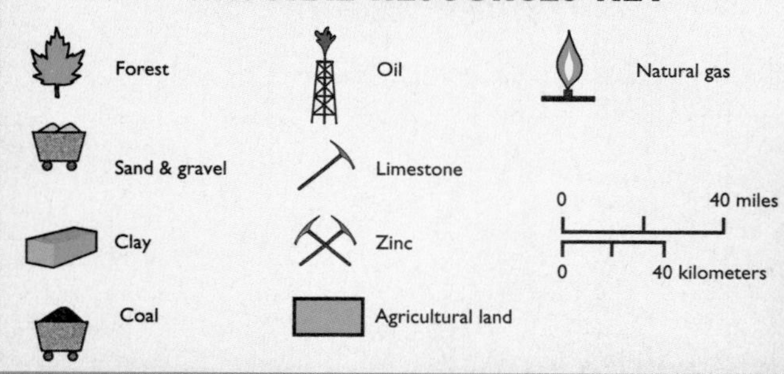

People

People are our state's most important resource.

Minerals

Limestone is one of Pennsylvania's mineral resources.

Fuel

We use fuel to make heat and energy. Oil wells like this one are used to get oil from the ground.

Soil

In the rich soil of the Piedmont, Pennsylvanians grow lots of corn.

Water

Water is both a resource and a home to another Pennsylvania resource—fish.

Forests

More than half of Pennsylvania is covered with forests. Besides providing homes for many kinds of animals, forests have other uses, too. People make products such as paper, fenceposts, and furniture from wood.

MAKING OUR RESOURCES LAST

Pennsylvania is rich in natural resources. People once thought our resources would last forever. Today we know that natural resources can be used up or damaged. Pollution (puh LOO shun) is the result of careless use of resources. Air, soil, or water become polluted as a result.

Conservation and Recycling

Conservation (kahn sur VAY shun) is the careful use of our natural resources. When people use only as much of a resource as they need, they are practicing conservation. When you turn off the water while brushing your teeth, you're conserving water. What other ways can you conserve our natural resources?

Another way to use our resources wisely is to recycle (ree SĪ kul). To recycle something is to use it again and again. Many Pennsylvanians recycle newspapers, aluminum, tin and steel cans, paper, glass, and some plastics.

WHY IT MATTERS

Pennsylvania's resources help make our lives comfortable. They have also created a strong economy in Pennsylvania. Our state's natural resources provide thousands of jobs for people here. As you read "River-keepers" on the next page, think about how it involves some of our state's natural resources.

Recycling is one way that you can help conserve Pennsylvania's resources.

Reviewing Facts and Ideas

SUM IT UP

- Natural resources are things in the environment that are useful to people. People are our state's most important resource.
- Renewable resources in Pennsylvania include forests, soil, and water.
- Nonrenewable resources include fuels and minerals. Conservation helps to protect our state's resources.

THINK ABOUT IT

1. Name three examples of natural resources found in Pennsylvania.
2. How do farmers renew soil when they plant crops?
3. **FOCUS** Why is it important for Pennsylvanians to protect the natural resources found in our state?
4. **THINKING SKILLS** *Compare* and *contrast* renewable and nonrenewable resources. Give two examples of each kind.
5. **WRITE** Which natural resource in Pennsylvania do you think is the most important? Write a paragraph explaining why you think so.

CITIZENSHIP
MAKING A DIFFERENCE

Riverkeepers

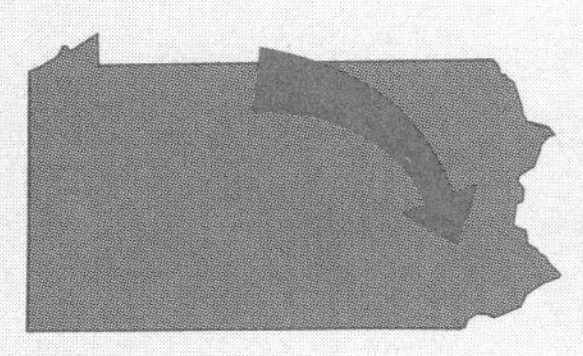

POTTSTOWN, PENNSYLVANIA—Why would a river need a keeper? And what would a riverkeeper do? Elisabeth Lynch is a good person to answer those questions. Since June of 1996, she has been a volunteer with the Schuylkill Riverkeepers. The Riverkeepers work to educate people about the value of the 130-mile Schuylkill River and teach them how to protect it. As a Riverkeeper volunteer, Lynch has worked hard to keep the Schuylkill clean and alive.

"A living river is a connection with nature," says Lynch. "For many years, factories, coal mines, farms, and communities have polluted the Schuylkill. This made it unsafe for swimming and fishing."

Schuylkill Riverkeepers trains volunteers like Elisabeth Lynch to test the water for pollution, to repair river banks, and to plant trees and shrubs. Volunteers also make sure that laws protecting the river are obeyed and warn people about fish that are not safe to eat.

Lynch and the other volunteers teach people how to keep the creeks and streams nearest their homes clean. "With a clean river, people can enjoy swimming, fishing, and boating. Hikers can walk along the river banks, and people who have homes along the river can enjoy the beautiful view."

Students can also become Riverkeeper volunteers. They join in special activities along the river such as trash clean-ups and canoe trips. Lynch is pleased that students are helping to preserve one of Pennsylvania's natural resources.

"I hope that everyone will experience what I have," Lynch says, "respect, interest, curiosity, and a great enjoyment of all life in the water and along the river's banks."

"A living river is a connection with nature."

CHAPTER 1 REVIEW

THINKING ABOUT VOCABULARY

Number a sheet of paper from 1 to 10. Next to each number write the word or phrase from the list that best completes the sentence.

environment	pollution
fuel	precipitation
geography	renewable resource
hurricane	tributary
landform	valley

1. A nonrenewable resource found in the ground that is used to make heat or energy is called a _____.
2. A _____ is a small river or stream that flows into a larger river.
3. _____ is the surroundings in which people, animals, or plants live.
4. Rain, snow, sleet, or hail are forms of _____, the moisture that falls to the ground.
5. The study of Earth and all the different things on it is called _____.
6. A _____ is a low patch of land between hills.
7. A type of natural resource that can be replaced is called a _____.
8. A _____ is a violent storm with very strong winds and heavy rains.
9. When people carelessly use resources, the result is _____.
10. A shape that makes up Earth's surface is called a _____.

THINKING ABOUT FACTS

1. Name four different landforms that are found in Pennsylvania.
2. Which areas of Pennsylvania have rich soil good for farming?
3. What are the three major river systems in our state?
4. What is the difference between weather and climate?
5. How does elevation affect the climate of an area?
6. What is a tornado?
7. Name three examples of renewable resources in our state.
8. Why is water an important natural resource?
9. Why are natural resources important to the economy of Pennsylvania?
10. Why are conservation and recycling important in our state?

THINK AND WRITE

WRITING A DESCRIPTION

Write a description of the area in which you live. Include landforms and information about climate in your description.

WRITING AN EXPLANATION

You have read how climate is affected by three factors. Write an explanation of how the climate in your area is affected by those three factors.

WRITING A POSTER

Suppose you wanted to start a conservation project in your school. Write and design a poster about conserving water or some other resource.

APPLYING GEOGRAPHY SKILLS

ELEVATION MAPS

Answer the following questions about the map on page 13 to practice your skill of reading elevation maps.

1. How do you know this is an elevation map?
2. What point in Pennsylvania has the highest elevation?
3. In what color would this map show a mountain that is 2,000 feet above sea level?
4. What is the approximate elevation of the city of Erie?
5. Why might it be useful to have an elevation map on a trip across Pennsylvania?

LATITUDE AND LONGITUDE

Answer the following questions about the map on page 21 to practice your skill at using latitude and longitude.

1. What do latitude and longitude lines on a map help you to do?
2. What city is located near 41°N, 80°W? How did you find it?
3. The capital of our state is closest to which line of latitude? To which line of longitude is the capital closest?
4. Give the approximate location of your own hometown, using latitude and longitude.
5. Why is it important to know how to use latitude and longitude?

Summing Up the Chapter

Use the following word map to organize information from the chapter. Copy the word map on a sheet of paper. Then write at least one piece of information in each blank circle. When you have filled in the maps, use them to write a paragraph that answers the question "How does your environment affect how you live?"

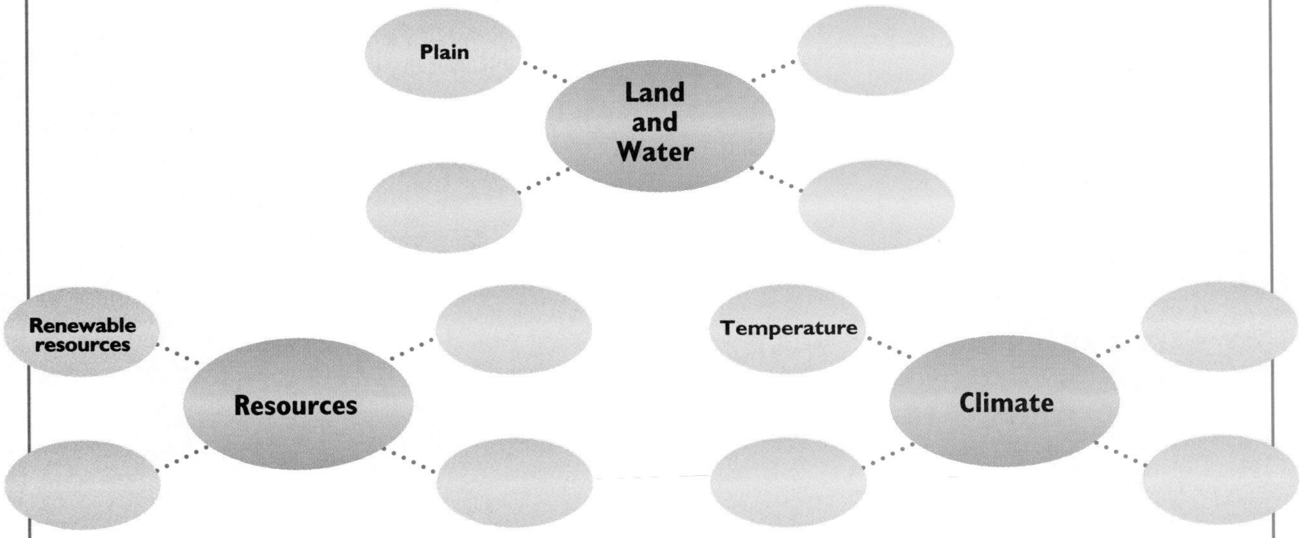

CHAPTER

2

The Regions of the United States and Pennsylvania

THINKING ABOUT GEOGRAPHY AND CULTURE

You already know about Pennsylvania's landforms. In this chapter, you will learn about the landforms of the United States. You will also learn about the different regions of Pennsylvania and of the United States. What makes each of these regions special? Find out as you read Chapter 2.

Philadelphia

A region can be defined by its history. Philadelphia has many statues, buildings, and parks that tell the story of Pennsylvania's past.

Near Lancaster

As you will learn, the Piedmont region is home to many people we call Pennsylvania Dutch. The families that live here often grow much of their own food.

Johnstown

Steel mills like this one in Johnstown in the Allegheny Plateau region help to make our state's economy strong.

Presque Isle State Park

The beaches along Lake Erie make the Lake Erie Coastal Plain region a popular vacation spot for many Pennsylvanians.

ONE COUNTRY, FIVE REGIONS

Focus Activity

READ TO LEARN
What is special about each region of the United States?

VOCABULARY
region
source
mouth
desert
rain shadow

PLACES
Mississippi River
Interior Plains
Central Plains
Great Plains
Rocky Mountains
Grand Canyon

READ ALOUD

In the late 1800s, the poet Walt Whitman celebrated America in a poem:

> ***Land of coal and iron! land of gold! land of cotton, sugar, rice!***
>
> ***Land of wheat, beef, pork! land of wool and hemp! land of the apple and the grape! . . .***
>
> ***Land of the ocean shores!***

THE BIG PICTURE

As Walt Whitman wrote, the United States is a country of great variety. Geographers find it useful to divide our country into five main **regions**. A region is an area with common features that set it apart from all other areas. Pennsylvania is in the Northeast. The other regions are the Southeast, the Middle West, the Southwest, and the West. Find these regions on the map on the next page.

These five regions have special features such as landforms, climate, and natural resources that set each apart from the other. Although the regions of the United States are different, Americans work together to make our nation strong.

In this lesson you will read about the regions and landforms of the United States. Use the Atlas map on page R10 to find the landforms of our country. Later in this chapter you will read about the regions of our state.

THE NORTHEAST

Can you find Pennsylvania on the map below? What other states are located in the Northeast? Many states of the Northeast are located on the Coastal Plain. You read about this low, flat landform in Chapter 1. It begins in Massachusetts and stretches south and west into Texas.

The Coastal Plain is home to many large cities, such as Philadelphia and Boston, Massachusetts. One reason cities have grown along the Coastal Plain is that it is much easier to build houses, stores, and factories on plains than on mountains. It is also easier to build highways on plains.

Four Seasons

In the Northeast, winter, spring, summer, and autumn bring different kinds of weather. Autumn is the favorite season of many Northeasterners. In the fall the days grow shorter and the temperature drops. These changes have an effect on the colors of the leaves of many trees.

For a few weeks, the leaves change from green to bright red, gold, and orange. Then the leaves drop off the branches. These trees are preparing for winter when there is less sunlight and lower temperatures.

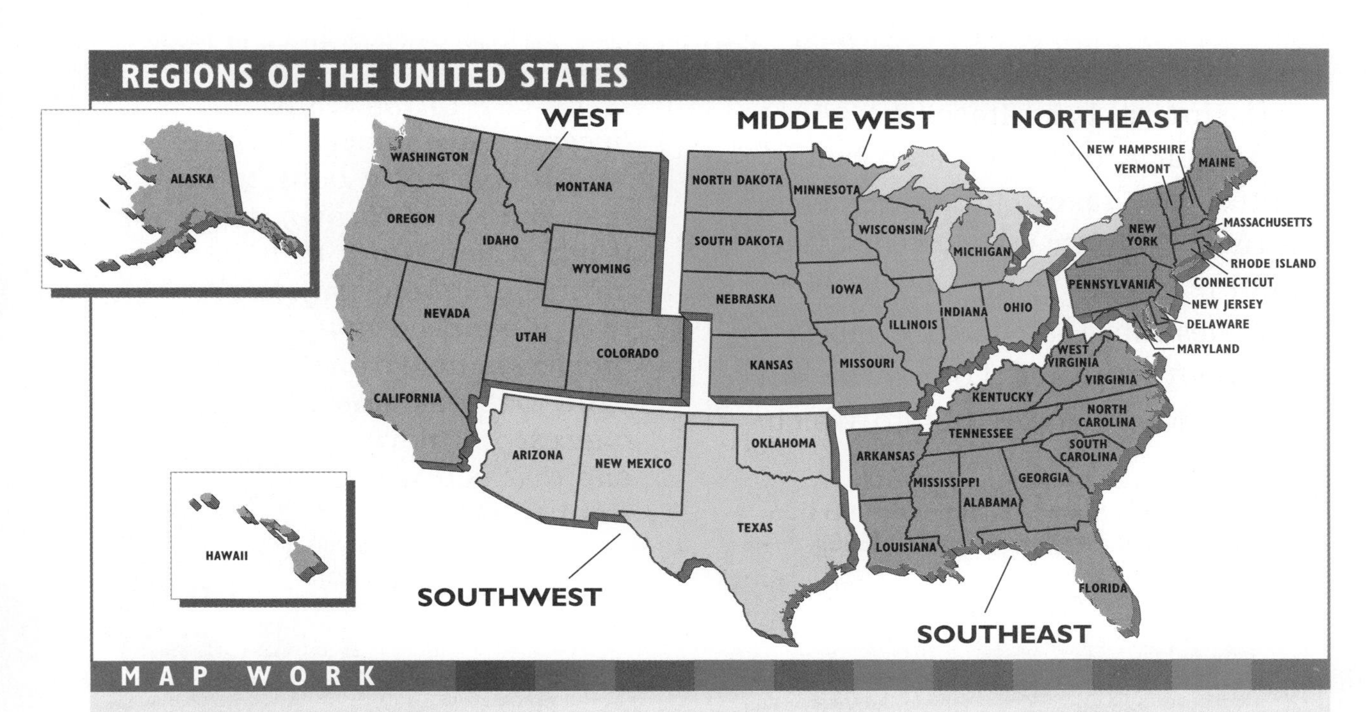

Pennsylvania is part of the Northeast **region**.

1. How many states make up the Northeast region?
2. Which two regions are closest to Pennsylvania?
3. Find Vermont. In which region is it?
4. Have you ever visited another state? What region is it in? What differences did you notice between that state and Pennsylvania?

THE SOUTHEAST

Like the Northeast, the Southeast is also part of the Coastal Plain of the United States. The Appalachian Mountains run through the Southeast too.

The Southeast is generally a warm region that is crisscrossed with rivers. Most rivers in the Southeast start in the Appalachian Mountains. The region's biggest river, though, is the **Mississippi River**. It begins in the Middle West.

The Mississippi River

Algonkian-speaking Native Americans named the Mississippi River. Their words *Misi Sipi* mean "big water" or "father of waters." The **source**, or starting point, of the Mississippi is Lake Itasca in Minnesota. A drop of water from this tiny lake takes 60 days to reach the river's **mouth** in Louisiana. The mouth of a river is the place where it empties into the ocean or another large body of water. Look at the Atlas map on page R10. Into which body of water does the Mississippi River empty?

At its source the Mississippi is hardly more than a shallow creek. The river grows broader and deeper as it flows south. Why? A major reason is that throughout its course the Mississippi River is fed by smaller tributaries.

The writer Mark Twain worked on a Mississippi riverboat in the 1850s. What does Mark Twain mean when he writes about "reading" the river like a book?

Excerpt from *Life on the Mississippi*, written by Mark Twain in 1863.

The face of the water . . . became a wonderful book. . . . And it was not a book to be read once and thrown aside, for it had a new story to tell every day. Throughout the long twelve hundred miles there was never a page that was ***void*** *of interest . . . never one that you would want to skip.*

void: empty

This paddleboat steamer is a modern version of the boat Mark Twain rode in the 1850s.

The corn grown on the Central Plains (left) and the wheat grown on the Great Plains (below) help feed our growing country.

THE MIDDLE WEST

The Middle West is part of a landform of the United States called the Interior Plains. There are really two parts to the Interior Plains. They are the Central Plains in the east and the Great Plains in the west. There is no sharp dividing line between them. Yet the geography of these two areas is different. Find them on the Atlas map on page R10.

Different Kinds of Plains

The Central Plains are low in elevation, not much higher than sea level in some places. Gently rolling hills cover much of the land. Corn is one of the main crops on the Central Plains. Farmers in Iowa can produce more than 900 million bushels of corn in a year. This amount is enough to give each person in the United States more than 100 quarts of corn! Can you imagine eating that much corn? Some of the corn is shipped to markets across the country and around the world.

The climate of the Middle West can be extreme. Writer Neal Peirce called the Great Plains "a land of fiercely cold winters and furnace-like summers." This region also experiences harsh storms and tornadoes, and the wind is often blowing.

The Great Plains are mostly dry grassland. Not enough rain falls for most trees to survive there.

Wheat is the major crop on the Great Plains. In fact, the drier climate is perfect for growing it. Kansas and North Dakota are the biggest wheat producers in the United States.

THE SOUTHWEST

The Southwest has only four states—Texas, Oklahoma, Arizona, and New Mexico. Except for Arizona, the states of the Southwest share the Great Plains of the Middle West.

Like the Northeast and the Southeast, the Southwest also is part of the Coastal Plain. But Texas is the only state of the Southwest that has this landform. Much of the Southwest is made up of high plateaus and plains.

As you move farther west, the geography changes suddenly. The Rocky Mountains appear. This mountain range stretches from Canada through many states of the United States, and into Mexico.

The climate of the Southwest is varied. The Coastal Plain in Texas is warm and rainy. High up in the Rocky Mountains, the temperature can drop far below the freezing mark. Much of the Southwest, however, is hot and dry. Many parts of the region are covered by deserts—dry land where little rain falls. A desert gets less than 10 inches of precipitation each year.

The Grand Canyon

One of the most famous landforms of the Southwest is the Grand Canyon. A canyon is a deep valley with steep sides.

The Grand Canyon was cut over centuries by the Colorado River and stretches 217 miles through northern Arizona. In some places this gigantic canyon is more than one mile deep! At its widest, the canyon measures 18 miles from one rim, or edge, to the other. If there were a footbridge across the canyon, it would take about six hours to walk across!

The Grand Canyon is vast—whether you are at the top looking down or riding into it.

The rain shadow helps explain why parts of the west are so dry. Why does more rain fall on one side of the mountain?

THE WEST

Among the different landforms in the West are mountains, plateaus, and valleys. The high elevations of the mountains affect temperature and precipitation. Look at the diagram above. The winds push the clouds up one side of the mountains. As the clouds rise, the temperature decreases. As the clouds cool, they drop most of their moisture in the form of rain or snow. Once the clouds have reached the top, most of the moisture is gone. Little water is left when the wind-driven air reaches the other side of the mountains. This eastern side of the mountains will stay much drier. The dry side lies in the rain shadow.

WHY IT MATTERS

Our country is one of the largest in the world. Each region has a great variety of landforms. In the next lesson, you will find out more about the regions of Pennsylvania.

Reviewing Facts and Ideas

SUM IT UP

- The five regions of the United States are the Northeast, the Southeast, the Middle West, the Southwest, and the West.
- The Coastal Plain is found in the Northeast, the Southeast, and the Southwest.
- Corn and wheat are the main crops of the Middle West.
- The mountains in the West have an effect on rainfall.

THINK ABOUT IT

1. Name the major landforms of the United States.
2. Describe how the rain shadow affects the climate of the West.
3. **FOCUS** What is different about each of our country's regions?
4. **THINKING SKILL** What *questions* would you ask someone to learn about his or her region?
5. **GEOGRAPHY** What landforms does Pennsylvania share with states in other regions of the United States?

THE REGIONS OF PENNSYLVANIA

Focus Activity

READ TO LEARN

What common features define the regions of Pennsylvania?

VOCABULARY

- urban
- rural
- history
- heritage
- ancestor
- ethnic group
- custom
- lake effect
- growing season

PLACES

- Scranton
- Presque Isle

READ ALOUD

Annie Dillard is a well-known nature writer who also wrote about her childhood in the 1950s: "It was a great town to grow up in, Pittsburgh. With one thousand other Pittsburgh schoolchildren, I attended free art classes in Carnegie Music Hall every Saturday morning for four years." Other things that make Pittsburgh special are tall buildings, many bridges, and lots of people. What makes the place where you live special? Are there farms or mountains? Perhaps there are sandy beaches or many trees. There may even be important buildings from our country's past.

THE BIG PICTURE

In the last lesson, you read about the regions and landforms of the United States. In addition to landforms, each region is defined by its past, its environment, its people, and its businesses.

Our state also has regions. Look at the map on page 41. What are the five regions in our state? In this lesson we will see how the features of each region make it special. For example, your region may have many busy **urban** areas. An urban area is a city and all the communities that surround it. Or it might be mostly **rural**. Rural means living in the countryside. Many farms and small towns are found in rural Pennsylvania. As you read this lesson, think about all the things that make your region of Pennsylvania special.

WHAT MAKES OUR REGIONS?

Our state is divided into the Atlantic Coastal Plain, the Piedmont, the Allegheny Plateau, the Lake Erie Coastal Plain, and the Ridge and Valley regions. You read about the landforms in these regions in Chapter 1. Now we will look at some of the other features of each region.

A Region's History

Although it is a small region, the Atlantic Coastal Plain is rich in **history**, which is the story of the past. This was the first part of our state that the Europeans came to. You will read more about these people in Chapter 4.

Today, visitors from around our country come to this region to see its historic cities and buildings. Philadelphia is one of the oldest cities on the Atlantic Coastal Plain. As you will read later, it played an important part in the creation of our country.

The Liberty Bell in Philadelphia is an important symbol in our state and country's history.

PENNSYLVANIA: Regions

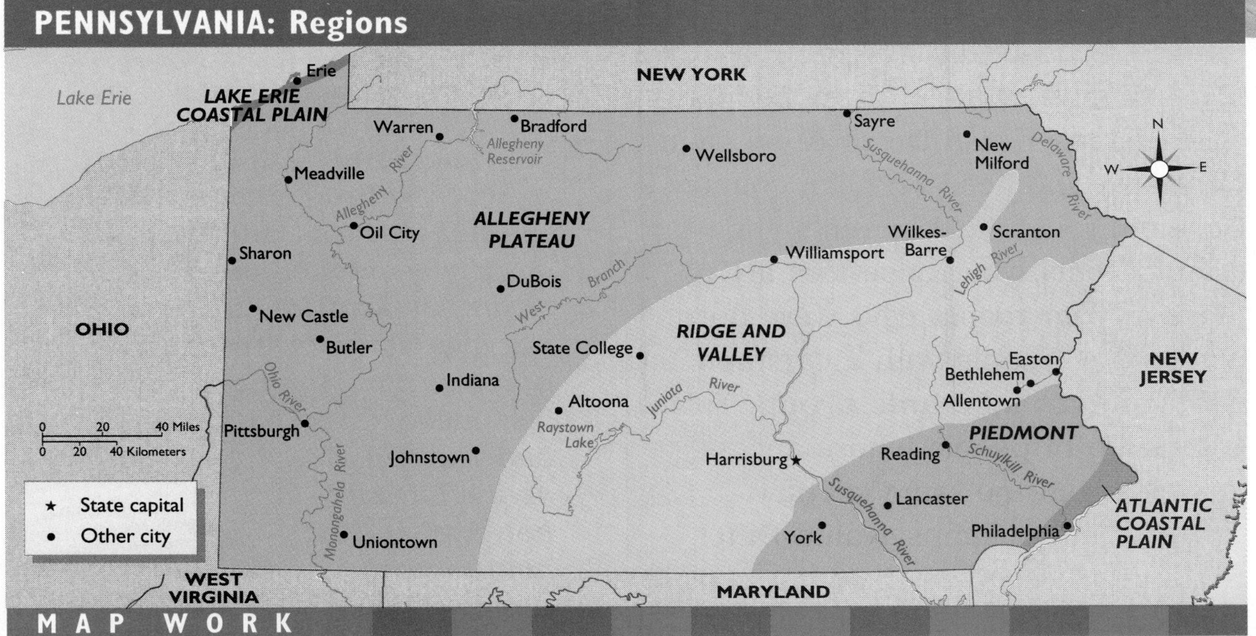

MAP WORK

Pennsylvania can be divided into five regions.

1. Which region covers most of our state?
2. Name and describe the region that covers the area where you live.

A REGION'S HERITAGE

Find the Piedmont region on the map on page 41. The ways of life the early settlers from Europe and Africa brought with them can still be seen here. Like all Pennsylvanians, the people of the Piedmont are proud of their **heritage** (HER ih tihj). Heritage is the history and way of life a group of people share.

The Pennsylvania Dutch

Much of the Piedmont is called Pennsylvania Dutch Country. This includes parts of Delaware, Chester, York, and Lancaster counties. The people who settled this region more than 300 years ago were not Dutch people from the Netherlands in Europe. Instead, the **ancestors** (AN ses turz) of most of the people called Pennsylvania Dutch came from Germany, another European country. Beginning with your parents and grandparents, your ancestors are all those in your family who were born before you. People with a common heritage form an **ethnic group**. This is a group of people whose ancestors are from the same country.

Today many Pennsylvania Dutch continue to carry on the **customs** of their ancestors. A custom is the special way a group of people does something. The language, crafts, and methods of farming of some Pennsylvania Dutch have changed little over the years. This is especially true of groups like the Amish.

The Amish are one of the groups of Pennsylvania Dutch. Most Amish are farmers. They are known for their hard work, plain clothing, and keeping to their own ways. Some Amish, for example, choose to live without electricity and cars. Like their ancestors, they use horses to pull farm machinery.

Read what Louise Stolzfus (STOLTS fus) wrote about her Amish grandmother. What kind of work does she describe her grandmother doing?

Excerpt from *Amish Women*, written by Louise Stoltzfus in 1986.

Grandmother Fannie loved to work with her hands. After the house, farm, and yard work were done, she would sit in her favorite chair by the coal stove or on the front porch in the summertime and make straw hats. She had learned wheat weaving as a child and, in her Amish way, made useful things—hundreds of men's straw hats.

DID YOU KNOW?

How did the Pennsylvania Dutch get their name?

The early Germans who settled in Pennsylvania called themselves "Deutsch" (DOITCH). *Deutsch* is the German word for "German." English-speaking people misunderstood and thought the Germans were calling themselves "Dutch."

The Pennsylvania Dutch use horse power for travel (opposite page) and for farm work (left). Families work together to prepare the food they grow (top left). Everyone in the community helps build a new barn (below).

OTHER TYPES OF REGIONS

The history and heritage of a region are important features defined by the region's people. Regions are sometimes defined by land. Did you know that minerals or climate could also define a region?

A Region's Businesses

Some regions are known for the natural resources and businesses that provide many jobs. The hills and mountains of Pennsylvania's largest regions—the Ridge and Valley and the Allegheny Plateau—are rich in minerals and forests.

Cities like Pittsburgh, in the Allegheny Plateau, and Scranton, in the Ridge and Valley region, grew as a result of coal. Not as much coal is mined today as in the past. However, coal is still used for the making of steel. Both cities use steel and iron to make machines, trains, and electrical equipment. Another valuable mineral, limestone, provides jobs for people in paper and glass-making businesses.

Lumber from the forests of the Allegheny Plateau has long been an important resource as well. The lumber business provides many jobs in these regions. People are needed to cut down the trees, saw the trees into boards, and turn the boards into houses, furniture, and other wooden objects.

A Region's Environment

Does your region have more rain than the rest of the state? Are its winters colder? Climate, as well as other parts of environment help to make a region special. One example is our state's smallest region, the Lake Erie Coastal Plain. Because this region is next to Lake Erie, it has a different climate than the rest of our state.

A worker (left) uses wood to create a new piece of furniture. Fishing (above) is a popular pastime in many of Pennsylvania's regions.

As winds blow across the lake from west to east, they have an effect similar to ocean breezes. In the summer they cool the land. In the winter they carry warmer air inland. This creates what is called the lake effect. The lake effect gives the region a long growing season. A growing season is the time of year when the weather is warm enough to grow crops in a certain place. Because it has a long growing season, the Lake Erie Coastal Plain is a good farming region.

Presque Isle (PRESK ĪL), a narrow strip of land that reaches out into Lake Erie, is on the Lake Erie Coastal Plain. Its beautiful beaches and wide variety of birds, fish, and other wildlife attract many visitors.

WHY IT MATTERS

As you have read, our state can be divided into five regions. Each region has features that make it special in its own way. Together they make our state a good place to live. In the next chapter you will learn about the first people who lived in Pennsylvania.

Reviewing Facts and Ideas

SUM IT UP

- Pennsylvania is divided into the Atlantic Coastal Plain, the Lake Erie Coastal Plain, the Piedmont, the Allegheny Plateau, and the Ridge and Valley regions.
- Each region has qualities that make it different from other regions. They include its history, heritage, businesses, and environment.

THINK ABOUT IT

1. What are urban and rural areas?
2. How does the lake effect create a long growing season on the Lake Erie Coastal Plain?
3. **FOCUS** What makes each region of Pennsylvania special?
4. **THINKING SKILL** *Compare* and *contrast* two of Pennsylvania's regions.
5. **WRITE** Write a letter to a friend describing the things that make the region where you live special.

A lighthouse on Presque Isle (left) warns ships at night to steer clear of the land.

THINKINGSKILLS

Some people choose to live in the busy city of Philadelphia (above), while others enjoy the quiet beauty of the Ridge and Valley region (right).

Decision Making

VOCABULARY
decision

WHY THE SKILL MATTERS

Decision making is a skill that you use every day. Making a decision is the same as making a choice. You have to make up your mind what to do. Decisions may be simple, like deciding what clothes to wear, or more difficult, like deciding where to live. To make a good decision, you have to know what your goal is.

New people move to Pennsylvania every day for many different reasons. Some come from other countries, some from other states. New people coming to Pennsylvania to live have to make many decisions. They have already made the important decision to leave their last home. When they arrive in our state, they have to decide where they want to live. That decision isn't always easy.

USING THE SKILL

Newcomers to Pennsylvania have many choices. They can decide to live in any one of our state's five regions. Of course, most people live where they can find work. Let's read about one recent newcomer who is deciding where to live.

Larry Bukaty has arrived in Pennsylvania from Colorado. He is staying with relatives in Philadelphia while he makes his plans. His relatives want him to remain in Philadelphia to be near them. But Larry has never lived in a flat area before. He misses the mountains of Colorado. He is thinking about moving to the Ridge and Valley region. But that would mean he would be living many miles away from his relatives in Philadelphia.

Here are some possible results of each choice.

- Larry may find it difficult to adjust in a new location where he has no family.
- Larry may learn to like living in Philadelphia.
- Larry may continue to miss the landscape that he prefers.

If your goal were to find a good place to live, what decision would you make?

HELPING Yourself

- **A decision is a choice about what to do.**
- **Identify the choices you can make, and predict the results of each choice.**
- **Make the choice that helps you reach your goal.**

TRYING THE SKILL

Suppose your family is planning to take a summer vacation. Your family must choose a place to go camping. Your choices are in different regions of our state.

The first is Presque Isle State Park on Lake Erie. Here your parents can relax and lie in the sun. Presque Isle would be a good place to see many kinds of birds. There are also nature walks and special programs for children. You could not camp there though. You would have to stay in a rented cottage.

The other choice is Allegheny National Forest, which is located in the north central part of the state. It is a forest, but there's a lot more to see than just trees. There are many wild animals, including white-tailed deer and beavers. There are even black bears! You will also be able to take your tent and camp in the wilderness.

Each member of your family has one vote. You will have to decide which location to choose. Use the Helping Yourself box hints. What is your goal for the vacation? What do you think the results of either choice might be?

REVIEWING THE SKILL

1. What is a decision?
2. Look at the section called Trying the Skill. If your goal were to learn how to set up a tent, how would you have voted?
3. How will predicting possible results help you to make a good decision?
4. Why is it important to know how to make a good decision?

Legacy

LINKING PAST AND PRESENT

Pennsylvania's State Parks

Have you ever visited one of the state parks in Pennsylvania? If so, you may have seen some of the scenery shown on these pages. Pennsylvania's state parks are lands our state government has set aside to protect wildlife and plant life. They are a legacy for all Pennsylvanians to enjoy. A legacy is something we have received from the past that we want to pass on to the future.

People go to state parks to explore natural wonders and to watch birds and other wildlife. They also visit state parks to picnic, camp, and enjoy sports.

As you look at the photographs on these pages, think about what nature means to you. Thanks to our state parks, you have the chance to visit some of these special places yourself!

In French, *Presque Isle* means "almost an island." Presque Isle State Park is on a peninsula, or land with water on three sides. It stretches from the city of Erie out into Lake Erie. Swimming and fishing are the main activities at this popular vacation spot.

World's End State Park, near Laporte, contains the beautiful Loyalsock Creek Canyon. The park's unusual name comes from an early road that was cut through the steep canyon. At one point, the road dropped sharply from view, giving travelers the feeling that they had come to the end of the world.

The beautiful and wild Youghiogheny River roars through Ohiopyle State Park near Uniontown in southeast Pennsylvania. The "Yough" (YOCK), as the river is known, provides an exciting ride for people in rafts or canoes. The park also has 41 miles of hiking trails, as well as cross-country skiing in the winter.

Hiking, fishing, bird watching, and canoeing are just some of the fun things to do at Black Moshannon State Park near Philipsburg. Black Moshannon Lake is at the center of the park. Overnight visitors to Black Moshannon can stay in tents or cabins.

CHAPTER 2 REVIEW

THINKING ABOUT VOCABULARY

Number a sheet of paper from 1 to 10. Beside each number write **C** if the underlined word or phrase is used correctly. If it is not, write the word or phrase that would correctly complete the sentence.

1. Custom is the story of what happened in the past.
2. An area with features that set it apart from other areas is called a region.
3. The special way a group of people does something is called heritage.
4. A rain shadow is the starting point of a river.
5. A growing season is the time of the year when the weather is warm enough for crops to grow in a certain place.
6. The side of a mountain that is usually dry because precipitation falls on the other side is called the desert.
7. An ethnic group area is a city and all the communities that surround it.
8. Ancestor is the history and way of life a group of people share.
9. An area that includes small towns and farms is called a rural area.
10. A mouth of a river is the place where it empties into the ocean or another large body of water.

THINKING ABOUT FACTS

1. What major landform is found in three regions of the United States? What are the three regions?
2. Where does the Mississippi River begin?
3. Into which two areas can the Interior Plains be divided? How are they different?
4. How does the climate vary in the Southwest region?
5. Why is autumn the favorite season of Northeasterners?
6. Why is the heritage of the people of the Piedmont region special?
7. How do the Pennsylvania Dutch, especially the Amish, carry on the customs of their ancestors?
8. What are the two largest regions in Pennsylvania, and what landforms would you find there?
9. Some of the businesses of Pittsburgh and Scranton use coal and limestone to make what types of products?
10. Name at least two reasons many people visit the Lake Erie Coastal Plain.

THINK AND WRITE

WRITING A REPORT
Suppose you are a scientist studying the rain shadow in the West. Write a report explaining how the mountains of this region affect temperature and precipitation.

WRITING A POEM
Write a poem about riding on a boat down the Mississippi River.

WRITING A SUMMARY
You have read about the Lake Erie Coastal Plain. Write a summary about how the lake affects the climate and growing season of this area.

APPLYING THINKING SKILLS

DECISION MAKING
Suppose that you and your friends are riding bikes in your neighborhood. You notice a dog with a broken chain attached to its collar. What do you do about the dog? Answer the following questions to practice your skill at making decisions.

1. What goal do you set for yourself?
2. What are the choices you have to reach your goal?
3. What might the results of each choice be?
4. Which choice will you make?
5. Do you think you made a good decision? Why?

Summing Up the Chapter

Use the table below to organize information from the chapter. Complete the table by writing down geography words that apply to each main topic. Use the table to write a paragraph that answers the question: "How does the geography of our state compare to the rest of the United States?"

UNITED STATES	ATLANTIC COASTAL PLAIN	PIEDMONT	RIDGE AND VALLEY	ALLEGHENY PLATEAU	LAKE ERIE COASTAL PLAIN
canyon	coast	sloping hills	ridges	plateau	plain

UNIT 1 REVIEW

THINKING ABOUT VOCABULARY

Number a sheet of paper from 1 to 10. Beside each number write **C** if the underlined word is used correctly. If it is not, write the word that would correctly complete the sentence.

1. Dry land where little rain falls is called a desert.
2. A rain shadow is an imaginary line that divides one place from another.
3. Something in the environment that people can use is a natural resource.
4. Minerals are examples of renewable resources.
5. Weather is a description of the air at a certain time and place.
6. The effect of Lake Erie on the climate of the Lake Erie Coastal Plain is called lake effect.
7. The source of a river is the place where it empties into the ocean or another large body of water.
8. A hurricane is a swirling funnel of wind that moves very quickly.
9. A river system is a smaller river or stream that flows into a larger river.
10. A group of people with ancestors from the same country is called an urban.

THINK AND WRITE

WRITING A LETTER

Write a letter to a newspaper about why you think our renewable resources are important. Suggest ways we can conserve our soil, water, forests, or other resources.

WRITING A BROCHURE

Choose a region of our state. Write and illustrate a travel brochure describing why it would be a fun and interesting place to visit.

WRITING A LIST

Write a list of five vocabulary words from Unit 1. Then write a paragraph with five sentences, using each of the vocabulary words in a sentence.

BUILDING SKILLS

1. **Elevation maps** Using the map on page 13, find the approximate elevation of the area where you live. Name a city that has an elevation of 650 feet or less.
2. **Elevation maps** How would an elevation map be useful if you were planning a bicycle trip across the state?
3. **Latitude and longitude** Look at the map on page 21. Between which two lines of longitude does Pennsylvania lie?
4. **Decision making** What is a good first step to take when making a decision? Describe one decision you have made today. What steps did you take to make it?
5. **Decision making** Why do you think it is important for you to learn how to make good decisions?

YESTERDAY, TODAY & TOMORROW

People used to think that our natural resources would last forever. Now we know that many of these resources can be used up or polluted. Do you think that conservation efforts will be able to preserve our state's resources? Why or why not?

READING ON YOUR OWN

These are some of the books you could find at the library to help you learn more.

WEATHER FORECASTING
by Gail Gibbons
This book shows how weather forecasters track the weather and make predictions.

THE PENNSYLVANIA DUTCH: CRAFTSMEN AND FARMERS
by Eva Deutsch Costabel
Read what life is like for a traditional Pennsylvania Dutch family.

RESOURCES
by Brian Knapp
Explore the history of natural resources such as coal and water.

UNIT PROJECT

Make a Geography Mobile

1. List three of Pennsylvania's natural resources and landforms.
2. Cut three different shapes from construction paper. On the shapes, draw and color pictures of your three resources. Punch a hole in the top of each shape. On the back of each one, write a sentence to explain the picture.
3. Cut a 12-inch by 4-inch rectangle out of cardboard. Write "Pennsylvania's Landforms and Resources" on it.
4. Punch three equally spaced holes along the top and bottom of your rectangle. Thread a 2-foot piece of string through each top hole. Tie all the loose ends together.
5. Thread a 12-inch piece of string through each bottom hole in the rectangle and then through each shape. Tie the ends of each string.
6. Take turns sharing the information on your mobiles before hanging them up in the classroom.

BENJAMIN AND DEBORAH FRANKLIN (LEFT)
SUSQUEHANNOCK BEADS (BELOW)

LENAPE VILLAGE (RIGHT)
SPINNING WHEEL (BELOW)

CONESTOGA WAGON

Early Pennsylvania

"[They] lived in three or four cabins built close together."

from the journal of Rhoda Barber
See page 94.

WHY DOES IT MATTER?

Who were the earliest people living in what is now Pennsylvania? When did the first European settlers arrive? Who else came to Pennsylvania over the years?

Read on. You will find out how the first people may have arrived in North America. You will learn about early Pennsylvanians and how they used the land and resources around them. You will also read about the relationships among all the people who lived in what is now Pennsylvania.

WILLIAM PENN

CHAPTER 3

The First Pennsylvanians

THINKING ABOUT GEOGRAPHY AND HISTORY

How did people first arrive in Pennsylvania? According to many historians, the first people in North America may have walked over land from Asia 40,000 years ago. As people spread out through North America, they began to live in different ways. Read on to find out what Pennsylvania was like long, long ago.

18,000 years ago

MEADOWCROFT ROCK SHELTER

Hunter-gatherers around a campfire

1000

LOCK HAVEN

Native American women planting corn

1600

SUSQUEHANNA RIVER

Susquehannock building a longhouse

CANADA
Lake Erie
PENNSYLVANIA
Lock Haven
Meadowcroft
Rock Shelter
Susquehanna
River
Delaware River
UNITED
STATES
ATLANTIC
OCEAN
1650
DELAWARE RIVER
Lenape drying fish

LESSON 1

40,000 YEARS AGO — 1,000 YEARS AGO

HUNTERS AND GATHERERS

Focus Activity

READ TO LEARN
When and how did people first come to Pennsylvania?

VOCABULARY
Ice Age
glacier
prehistory
archaeology
artifact
hunter-gatherer

PLACES
Beringia
Bering Strait

READ ALOUD

"Each layer we uncovered was like a snapshot of that time." This is how Dr. James Adovasio described digging through layers of earth at Meadowcroft Rock Shelter near Pittsburgh in 1973. Dr. Adovasio and a team of scientists discovered objects made by Pennsylvanians nearly 18,000 years ago. Why might these objects be important to Pennsylvanians today?

THE BIG PICTURE

By studying objects like the ones found at Meadowcroft Rock Shelter, we can learn a lot about how the first Pennsylvanians lived. These early people left no written records. So scientists use objects like these to learn about life here thousands of years ago. But how did people first come to North America?

Many scientists believe that people first came to North America during the **Ice Age**. This was a time when **glaciers** (GLAY shurz), or huge sheets of ice, covered much of Earth's surface. Before the glaciers formed, large bodies of water separated Asia from North America. During the Ice Age the level of the oceans dropped because so much water became frozen into glaciers. For about 2,000 years a land bridge called **Beringia** (buh RIHN jee uh) connected Asia with North America. Today the land bridge is gone. The **Bering Strait**, a body of water 56 miles across, now separates North America from Asia.

STUDYING THE PAST

We use the word *history* to describe the written story of the past. The period of time before people wrote down their history is known as **prehistory**. You will be able to understand the difference between these two words by remembering that *pre* means "before."

Archaeology (arh kee OL uh jee) is the study of prehistoric people. Archaeologists dig in places where prehistoric people lived. They may find pottery, clothing, or ashes from a campfire. These objects are called **artifacts**. Artifacts help archaeologists find out how people lived long ago. Special equipment is used to find out how old artifacts are. Bones of people and animals give clues about what they looked like. Where does Mel Higginson say that archaeologists look for artifacts?

Excerpt from *Scientists Who Study Ancient Temples and Tombs*, written by Mel Higginson in 1994.

Archaeologists visit temples and tombs, shipwrecks and statues, and the ruins of ancient cities. For an archaeologist, even an ancient garbage dump may be a treasure chest of information.

An arrow found in our state.

The First Americans

No one knows when or how people came to North America. Some scientists believe that people crossed Beringia about 40,000 years ago. Look at the map below to see the routes they might have taken through North and South America.

The first Americans were the ancestors of the people now known as Native Americans. Many Native Americans, however, believe they have always lived in North and South America.

Some scientists believe that people first reached Pennsylvania about 18,000 years ago.

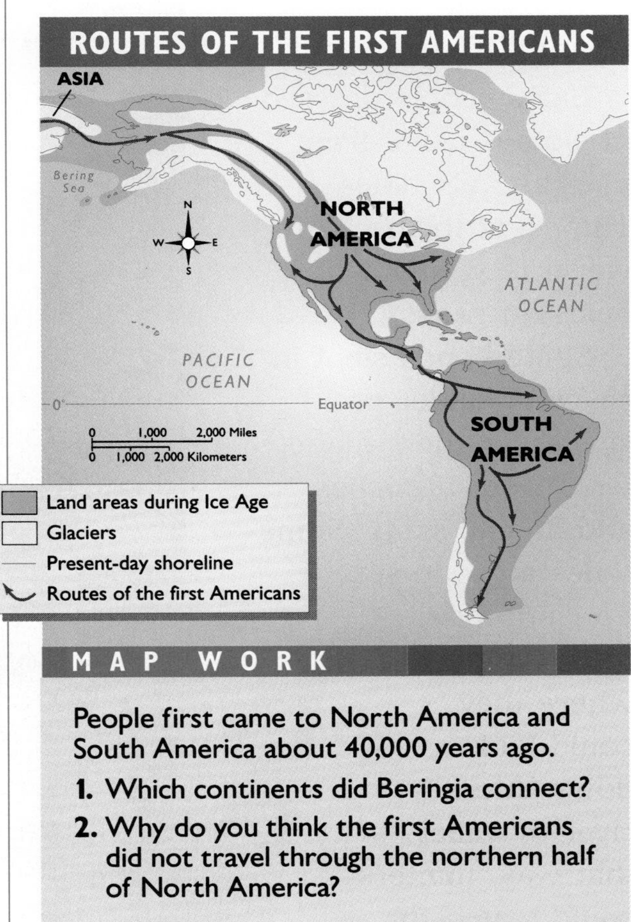

MAP WORK

People first came to North America and South America about 40,000 years ago.

1. Which continents did Beringia connect?
2. Why do you think the first Americans did not travel through the northern half of North America?

LIFE ON THE MOVE

Think of the feeling of being the first person in a new place. About 18,000 years ago, people came to the place we now call Pennsylvania. It must have been exciting but dangerous. These early Pennsylvanians had no idea what they would find across the river or over the next hill or mountain. Was the sound they heard in the forest made by a falling branch—or a wild animal? They had to stay alert to stay alive. They never seemed to stay in one place very long. Bands, or groups, moved from place to place in search of food.

Living Off the Land

Early people dressed in clothes made from deer and elk hides. They kept themselves warm in winter with bearskin robes.

Some bands slept in caves or under rock shelters. Others made tents from branches and animal skins. Sometimes a group set up camp on top of a hill where they could look down into a river or valley. In that way, hunters could watch for animals that might pass by. Hunters carried wooden spears with sharp stone tips.

Hunting was not the only way early Pennsylvanians got their food. They also gathered plants, fruit, and nuts from the forests. Pennsylvania's forests offered plenty of walnuts, hickory nuts, black cherries, berries, and seeds. From the rivers early people gathered shellfish. Because both hunting and gathering food were very important parts of their lives, we call these people **hunter-gatherers**.

Pennsylvania's rivers held plenty of clams (left), fish, and turtles.

THE WOODLAND INDIANS

About 3,000 years ago Native Americans who lived in the Northeast region of our country began to settle along rivers and lakes. They lived in small villages. These Native Americans began to burn down trees in order to farm the land. The ashes from the burnt wood made the soil rich for growing crops. Archaeologists call these people the Woodland Indians. Some of these Woodland Indians became the first farmers in our state.

The Woodland Indians learned to grow a number of crops, including corn, beans, and squash. "At Meadowcroft," said Dr. Adovasio, "we even found a kind of popcorn that was over 2,000 years old!" Corn 1,000 years old has also been found at a site in Lock Haven.

As they farmed the land, the Woodland Indians no longer moved from place to place in search of food. Farming allowed these people to have a regular food supply.

WHY IT MATTERS

By studying artifacts, archaeologists know how the early people of Pennsylvania used the natural resources around them. Over time, Native Americans became farmers and settled in villages. In the next lesson you will get a closer look at the daily life of these early Pennsylvanians.

These artifacts made by the Woodland Indians were found by archaeologists in Pennsylvania.

Reviewing Facts and Ideas

SUM IT UP

- Some scientists think that people crossed Beringia from Asia to North America about 40,000 years ago.
- Archaeologists use artifacts to learn about people who lived thousands of years ago.
- About 3,000 years ago people in Pennsylvania began to farm the land.

THINK ABOUT IT

1. What is the difference between history and prehistory?
2. How do archaeologists learn about the past?
3. **FOCUS** When and how did the first people come to Pennsylvania?
4. **THINKING SKILL** What *decisions* might have led early Pennsylvanians to become farmers?
5. **GEOGRAPHY** Give two reasons why people of the Woodlands might have settled near rivers and lakes.

THINKING SKILLS

Identifying Cause and Effect

VOCABULARY

cause

effect

WHY THE SKILL MATTERS

You read in the last lesson about how some scientists think that people crossed Beringia about 40,000 years ago. This land bridge appeared when the water level in the ocean fell. The fall in the level of the ocean was a **cause**. A cause is something that makes something else happen. The appearance of the land bridge was an **effect**. An effect is what happens as a result of something else.

Understanding cause and effect allows you to put facts together in a meaningful way. It helps explain *why* things happen. It shows connections between one event and another. Use the Helping Yourself box for some word clues that may help you find causes and effects.

USING THE SKILL

As you read the passage below, look for a cause and an effect. Try to find some clue words that can help you identify the effect.

> *About 3,000 years ago, some Woodland Indians in Pennsylvania stopped moving from place to place to hunt. They learned how to farm the land, and they grew crops such as corn, squash, and beans. As a result, these Native Americans started to build and live in permanent villages. Farming allowed people to have a regular food supply. Therefore, they stayed in one place for longer periods of time.*

Farming the land was the cause of the Woodland Indians living in permanent villages. Building permanent villages was the effect of staying in one place for longer periods of time. Some of the clue words that helped you tell the effect were *as a result* and *therefore*.

People crossing Beringia were probably following the animals they hunted for food.

HELPING Yourself

- **A cause is an event that makes something happen. An effect is what happens because of it.**
- **Look for clue words that show causes—*because, since, as a result*.**
- **Look for clue words that show effects—*so, therefore, as a result*.**

TRYING THE SKILL

Now read this passage. Look for any causes and effects. Remember to watch for word clues.

> *Early Native Americans in what is now Pennsylvania hunted animals with spears. They made the spears go farther and faster by using a special throwing stick called an atlatl (aht LAHT uhl).*
>
> *About 2,000 years ago, Native Americans learned how to make bows and arrows. They found that arrows shot with bows were more accurate than spears thrown with an atlatl. As a result, they stopped using spears and atlatls.*

What was the cause of Native Americans no longer using spears and atlatls? What was the effect of using a bow and arrow? How do you know?

REVIEWING THE SKILL

1. What is a cause? What is an effect?
2. Was the coming of people to North America a cause or an effect of the appearance of Beringia?
3. How were permanent villages an effect of farming?
4. How might identifying cause and effect help you understand history?

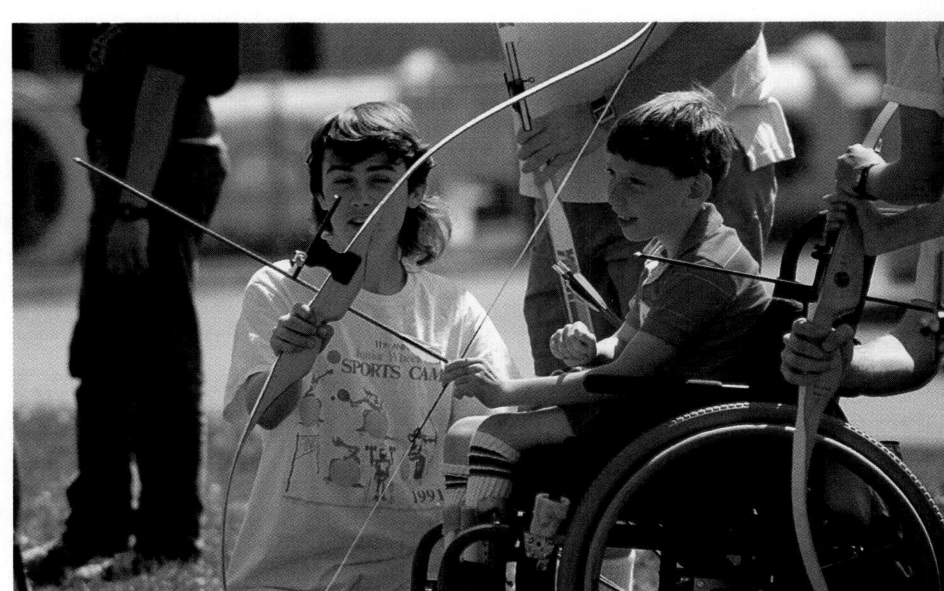

This drawing (above, right) shows how the atlatl was used. Many people today learn to use the bow and arrow for sport (right).

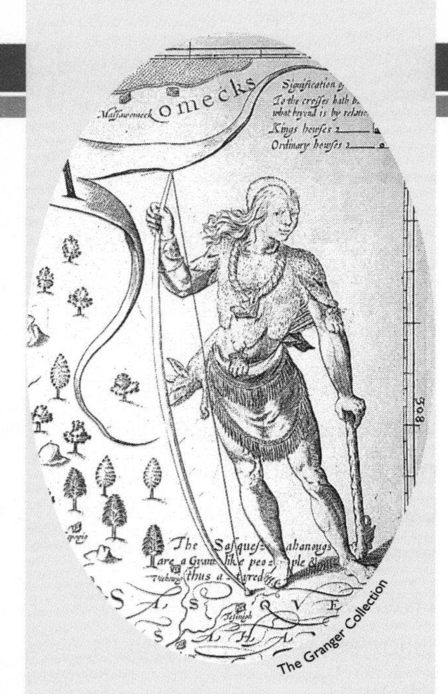
The Granger Collection

NATIVE AMERICANS OF THE 1600s

Focus Activity

READ TO LEARN

What was life like for Pennsylvania's Native Americans in the 1600s?

VOCABULARY

culture
nation
longhouse
clan
wigwam
council
descendant

READ ALOUD

In 1608, an Englishman met with a group of Native Americans in Pennsylvania. Some years later he described this meeting. He wrote, "Sixty of these giant-like people came down, with presents of venison (deer meat), tobacco pipes three foot in length, baskets, targets, bows and arrows."

THE BIG PICTURE

Archaeologists have learned about some Native American groups who lived in our state from writings and drawings by European sailors. However, we have to be careful when we read these records. Most Europeans did not speak Native American languages. They probably did not understand some of what they saw.

Each Native American group had its own culture, or way of life. Culture includes many things people share, such as beliefs, languages, art, music, and even food. In the early 1600s there were about five different groups of Native Americans living in our state. You can read about these groups in the Infographic on page 68. In this lesson you will read about the Susquehannock (suhs kwuh HAN nuk) and the Lenni Lenape (LE nee le NAH pay).

ONE PEOPLE, MANY NATIONS

The Susquehannock and the Lenape were two different **nations**. A nation is a group of Native Americans who share the same culture. Look at the map on this page and find where these two nations lived in our state.

The Susquehannock

The Susquehannock were farmers who lived in villages near the Susquehanna River. As many as 1,700 people might live in one village. The Susquehannock built a high wooden fence around each village. This protected them from other Native American groups who sometimes fought with them.

Farming was at the center of Susquehannock life. They grew large crops of corn, beans, and squash. They also gathered nuts and berries, hunted animals, and fished in the Susquehanna River.

The Susquehannock built long buildings made of poles and covered with sheets of bark. These were called **longhouses**. Each house was about 20 feet wide and up to 100 feet long. That's about the size of a parking lot for 25 cars! Seven or eight families often lived in one longhouse.

Archaeologists think that the families who lived together in one longhouse belonged to one **clan**. A clan is a group of families who share the same ancestor. The head of each clan was a woman who was called the clan mother.

Susquehannock women had a great deal of power. They decided how the land would be used and who would use it. They owned the longhouses and everything in them. No important village decision could be made without the permission of the clan mothers.

Around 1600, there were about 5,000 Susquehannock living in what is now Pennsylvania. Many were killed in wars with other Native Americans or Europeans. Others died from diseases brought by European traders and settlers. By the 1750s most Susquehannock had moved from Pennsylvania.

THE SUSQUEHANNOCK AND THE LENAPE IN PENNSYLVANIA, 1600s

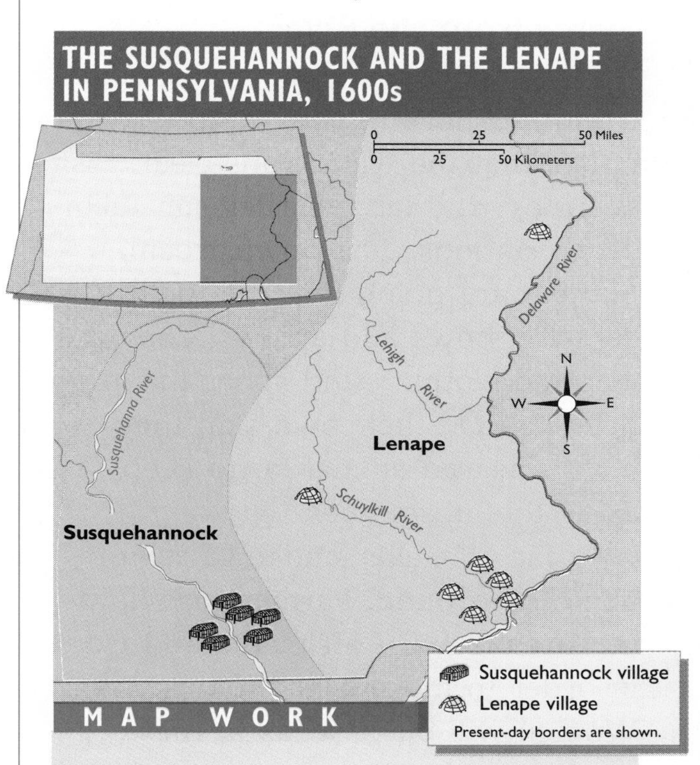

MAP WORK

The Susquehannock and the Lenape once lived in the eastern part of our state.

1. Near what river did the Susquehannock live?
2. Why do you think the Susquehannock and the Lenape chose to live near rivers?

THE LENAPE

The Lenape lived in small farming villages near Delaware Bay. One early Dutch visitor described them like this:

> *slender around the waist, broad-shouldered; all having black hair and brown eyes; they are very nimble [lively], . . . well adapted to travel on foot and to carrying heavy burdens.*

What was daily life like for the Lenape in the early 1600s? If you could step back in time and take a canoe trip down a river, what do you think you would see?

Sights from the River

It is summer, and as you push off from the shore in your canoe, you notice that the water runs clear. Fish swim by, and large turtles sun themselves on logs. Just downstream, hunters are going into the forest carrying bows and arrows. They are wearing clothing and shoes made of deerskin. On their own skin they have smeared animal fat to keep away the mosquitoes.

In far-off fields smoke is rising from the ground. Farmers are lighting fires to burn off plants and trees in order to make space for gardens. Women will plant seeds in these gardens with digging sticks. In some of the fields, corn rises above beans and squash. Elsewhere women pick grapes and wild plums. In the spring they collected sap from maple trees to make syrup and sugar. The sugar is mixed with corn meal to make breakfast cereal.

In a Lenape Village

As you near a Lenape village, you see a number of one-room wigwams and longhouses. A wigwam is a house made of poles covered with bark, animal skins, or grass. There are two or three different shapes, but all have holes in their roofs to let out the smoke from the fire inside. An animal skin hangs over the doorway. Inside are beds built of tree limbs. On the floor are clay pots and other cooking tools. The spoons are made from wood or clamshells, the knives from stone. Dried food is hanging from above.

Have you ever cooked a hot dog on a stick over an open fire? That is how the Lenape are cooking small

This Lenape village has been recreated to show people today how the Lenape lived in the 1600s.

pieces of meat. Because it is summer, they are cooking and eating their food outside. When winter comes they will cook their food and eat it inside their wigwams.

Lenape Children

In the village you see a mother with her baby. The baby is strapped to a stiff board to protect it. The mother can carry the baby with her—even hang it in a tree—while she works in the garden.

Young boys dress like their fathers, wearing breechcloths in the summer. A breechcloth is a piece of deerskin worn between the legs and held up by a belt. Young girls wear short deerskin skirts. In winter everyone will wear deerskin leggings, fur robes, and feather cloaks.

Lenape children have many chores. Girls help their mothers in the fields. Boys are given small bows and arrows so they can learn how to fish and hunt.

Village Leaders

Near a large tree there is a small group of men and women having a meeting. This is the village **council**. A council is a group of people who make decisions. This council is meeting with the village leader. They are helping the leader to choose the person to take his place after he dies.

The Big House Ceremony

You are invited to take part in an important ceremony. It takes place in a large meeting house. Everyone has put on their best clothes and they sit in special places. They sing songs and dance to show how thankful they are for everything their god has given them.

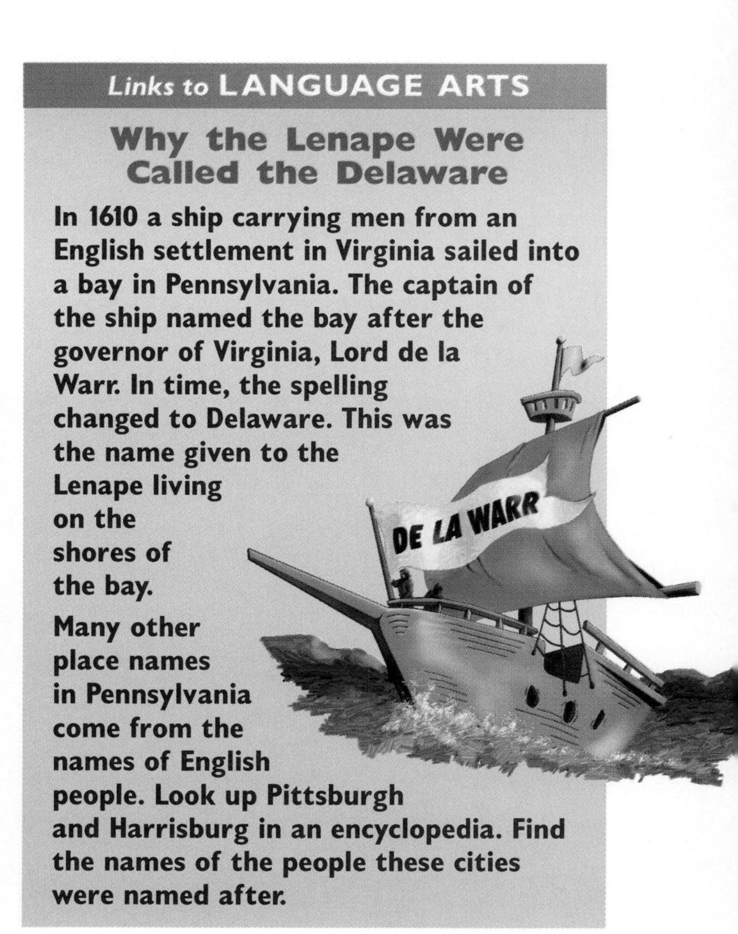

Links to **LANGUAGE ARTS**

Why the Lenape Were Called the Delaware

In 1610 a ship carrying men from an English settlement in Virginia sailed into a bay in Pennsylvania. The captain of the ship named the bay after the governor of Virginia, Lord de la Warr. In time, the spelling changed to Delaware. This was the name given to the Lenape living on the shores of the bay.

Many other place names in Pennsylvania come from the names of English people. Look up Pittsburgh and Harrisburg in an encyclopedia. Find the names of the people these cities were named after.

Infographic

NATIVE AMERICANS OF PENNSYLVANIA

Each Native American group in Pennsylvania had its own culture, made and wore different kinds of clothing, and decorated objects in their own style. What can you learn about these groups from the photographs on these pages?

Buffalo Museum of Science

Iroquois

The Iroquois lived for a time in north central Pennsylvania. This wooden bowl and beaded sash were made by them.

Thaw Collection, Fenimore House Museum, Cooperstown, N.Y., Photo by John Bigelow Taylor, N.Y.C.

Erie

The Erie lived along the shore of Lake Erie. They were driven out of Pennsylvania in the 1600s by the Iroquois. They made this vase and these pipes.

Thaw Collection, Fenimore House Museum, Cooperstown, N.Y., Photo by John Bigelow Taylor, N.Y.C.

Buffalo Museum of Science

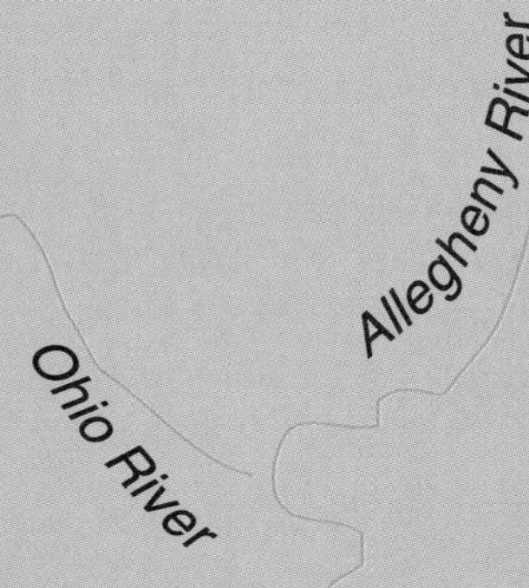

Shawnee

Pennsylvania was one of the many states where the Shawnee lived. They made these gold armbands and leather moccasins.

The Ohio Historical Society

National Museum of the American Indian, Smithsonian Institution

Susquehannock

In the early 1600s, the Susquehannock farmed and hunted in the Susquehanna Valley. They made this ceremonial mask and decorative comb.

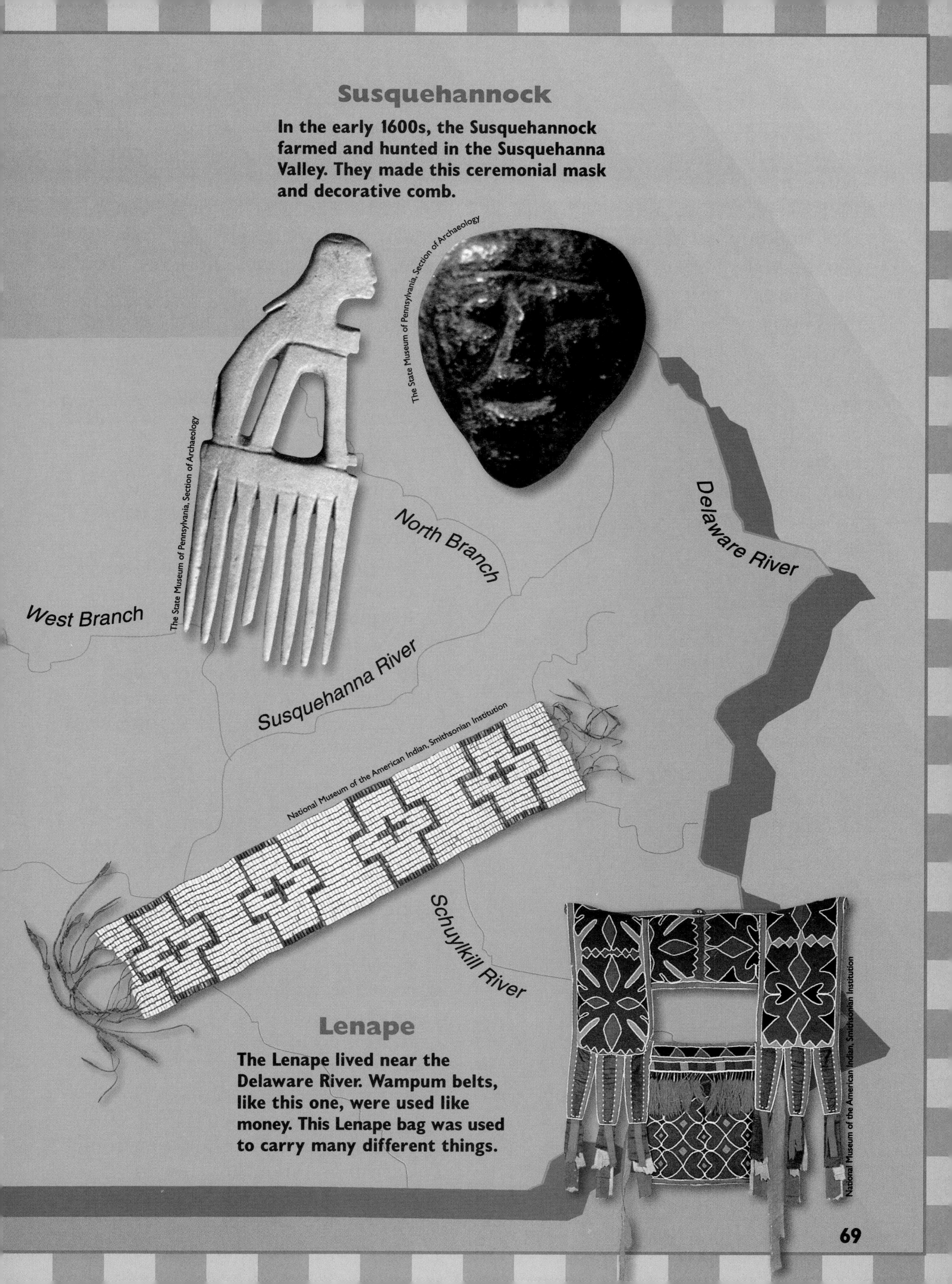

Lenape

The Lenape lived near the Delaware River. Wampum belts, like this one, were used like money. This Lenape bag was used to carry many different things.

THE LENAPE TODAY

Most of the Lenape remained in Pennsylvania until 1763. Some were living in Pennsylvania as late as 1778. Newcomers to Pennsylvania kept building on Lenape land. The Lenape were forced to move farther west. Today their **descendants**, or the people who came after them, live in Pennsylvania, Oklahoma, Wisconsin, and Ontario, Canada. Many Lenape today celebrate their heritage by taking part in traditional Lenape customs. In Making a Difference on page 71, you will read about how some people are helping to preserve Lenni Lenape culture and history in our state.

Descendants of the Lenape sometimes wear traditional dress for special celebrations.

WHY IT MATTERS

The Susquehannock and the Lenape were just two of the Native American groups who lived in what is now Pennsylvania. Most of them lived in small farming villages. They raised corn, beans, squash, and other crops. Before long, however, their lives would change greatly. New people were coming to Pennsylvania.

Reviewing Facts and Ideas

SUM IT UP

- By the 1600s about five Native American groups lived in Pennsylvania.
- The Susquehannock were farmers who lived in villages along the Susquehanna River. Their homes were called longhouses.
- The Lenape were farmers who lived in villages near Delaware Bay. Their homes were longhouses and wigwams.

THINK ABOUT IT

1. What natural resources were important to the Susquehannock?
2. What is a wigwam?
3. **FOCUS** What were the ways of life of the Susquehannock and the Lenape?
4. **THINKING SKILL** List two ways in which your life is the *same* as and *different* from the Lenape way of life.
5. **WRITE** Suppose a Lenape artifact was found near your school. Write a paragraph telling how you could learn more about it.

CITIZENSHIP
MAKING A DIFFERENCE

Saving Lenni Lenape Culture

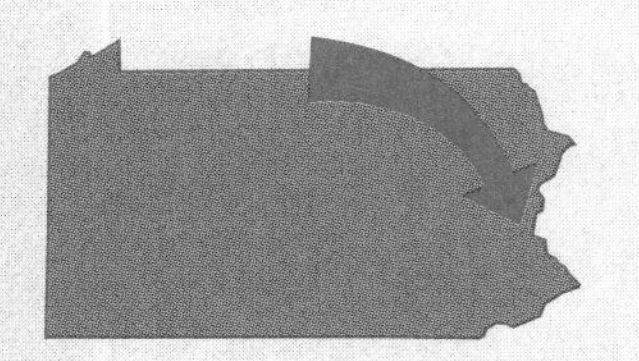

ALLENTOWN, PA—Today fewer than 1,000 descendants of the Lenape live in Pennsylvania. Carla Messinger has Lenape ancestors. She is one of the founders of the Lenni Lenape Historical Society. Members of the Society wanted a place where people could learn about Lenape history and culture. "Native cultures are living cultures," says Messinger. So in 1983, the Society opened the Lenni Lenape Museum of Indian Culture in Allentown.

Today the museum has many exhibits. Most of them are about Lenape family life during the 1600s and 1700s. Visitors can see tools, baskets, toys, food, and crafts that were an important part of Lenape culture.

Many of the objects on display were donated by Dorothy Schiavone, Carla Messinger's mother. One shell necklace belonged to Schiavone's grandmother. There is a basket that belonged to her great-grandmother. In Lenni Lenape culture every girl had a basket in which to keep her personal belongings.

Children are especially welcome at the museum. They are allowed to touch and even smell some of the museum's pieces. Messinger and the other volunteers would like visitors to experience the everyday life of the Lenape during the 1600s and 1700s.

Carla Messinger and Dorothy Schiavone are just two of the many volunteers who work to make the museum an interesting place for visitors. Because of their efforts, thousands of people—some from around the world—have learned about Lenape history and culture. Messinger says, "We hope that by showing such exhibits we will keep the culture alive not only for today's Lenape, but for all people."

CHAPTER 3 REVIEW

THINKING ABOUT VOCABULARY

Number a sheet of paper from 1 to 10. Next to each number write the word or phrase that best matches the definition.

archaeology	glacier
artifact	hunter-gatherer
clan	longhouse
council	prehistory
culture	wigwam

1. A group of people who meet to talk and make decisions
2. A small hut covered with bark, animal skins, or grass
3. A huge sheet of ice
4. The study of ancient people that uses artifacts to learn about the past
5. A person who travels from place to place in search of food
6. A group of families who share the same ancestor
7. An object that is found in a place where prehistoric people lived
8. The way of life of a group of people
9. The period of time before people wrote down their history
10. A long building made of poles and covered with sheets of bark

THINKING ABOUT FACTS

1. What is the Bering Strait? What was Beringia?
2. Why is it difficult for archaeologists to learn much about Pennsylvania's ancient people?
3. Name three places where an archaeologist might look for artifacts.
4. When did the earliest people first reach Pennsylvania? How do scientists believe they got here?
5. What kinds of foods did the early hunter-gathers eat?
6. Why did the Woodland Indians burn down trees?
7. Describe how the Susquehannock protected themselves from danger.
8. How many Susquehannock families could live in one longhouse?
9. What types of homes did the Lenape build? How were their homes different from the homes built by the Susquehannock?
10. Describe some of the chores Lenape children did.

THINK AND WRITE

WRITING A SUMMARY
Write a summary about life in a Lenape village in the 1600s.

WRITING A JOURNAL
Suppose you are an archaeologist working at Meadowcroft Rock Shelter. Write a journal entry describing some of the things you find at the rock shelter.

WRITING A COMPARISON
Write a paragraph comparing the lives of the earliest people of Pennsylvania to the lives of Woodland Indians.

APPLYING THINKING SKILLS

CAUSE AND EFFECT
1. What is a cause? What is an effect?
2. What caused the disappearance of Beringia?
3. Was learning about farming by Pennsylvania's Native Americans a cause or an effect of their need to hunt less?
4. What do you think was an effect of modern archaeologists' discovering the Meadowcroft Rock Shelter?
5. How does studying cause and effect help you understand history?

SUMMING UP THE CHAPTER

Use the following cause-and-effect chart to organize information from the chapter. Fill in the blank spaces and use the information to write a paragraph answering the question "How did Pennsylvania's Native Americans lives change from prehistory to the 1600s?"

CAUSE	EFFECT
Woodland Indians learn to grow crops	
Native Americans burned down trees to clear the land	
	The Susquehannock built high wooden fences around their villages
	The Lenape are forced to move further west

CHAPTER 4

Colonial Pennsylvania

THINKING ABOUT GEOGRAPHY AND HISTORY

For thousands of years only Native Americans lived in Pennsylvania. In the 1600s something happened that would change the lives of these people and of others around the world. Europeans came in ships to the Americas. Read Chapter 4 to find out how this contact changed life in Pennsylvania forever.

1609

DELAWARE BAY

Henry Hudson sails into the Delaware Bay

1682

PHILADELPHIA

William Penn begins planning Philadelphia

1732

PHILADELPHIA

Benjamin and Deborah Franklin run a printing business in Philadelphia

CANADA
Lake Erie
PENNSYLVANIA
Raystown
Philadelphia
Delaware Bay
UNITED
STATES
ATLANTIC
OCEAN
1753
RAYSTOWN
Pioneers move to the
Pennsylvania frontier

The Historical Society of Pennsylvania

LESSON 1

1550 1609 1655 1700 1750

EUROPEAN EXPLORATION AND SETTLEMENT

Focus Activity

READ TO LEARN

Which Europeans explored and settled in what is now Pennsylvania?

VOCABULARY

explore
Northwest Passage
trading post
colony

PEOPLE

Johan Printz
Henry Hudson
Cornelis Hendrickson
Peter Minuit
Peter Stuyvesant
Johan Rising

PLACES

New Sweden
Fort Christina
Tinicum Island
New Gothenburg
New Netherland

READ ALOUD

Johan Printz, leader of the Swedish settlement at Delaware Bay in 1643 wrote, "I wish . . . to report that this is a very lovely country, with everything a person can wish himself on this earth."

THE BIG PICTURE

Johan Printz (YO hahn PRINTS) was describing the rich natural resources found in North America. These resources included land, forests, and fur-bearing animals. By 1643, many European explorers had already sailed to North America. To explore is to travel in unfamiliar places in order to find out about them. These explorers had followed Henry Hudson, an English sailor working for a Dutch company.

Hudson was searching for a Northwest Passage in 1609. Explorers thought the Northwest Passage was a water route through North America to Asia. Instead Hudson came upon Delaware Bay. Hudson did not think the water in the bay was deep enough for his ship to sail into. However, his report of the bay interested the rulers of European countries. They sent explorers to claim land in North America. Some of these explorers had sailed up the Delaware Bay and learned about some of the natural resources there.

EUROPEANS ARRIVE IN DELAWARE BAY

Cornelis Hendrickson, (kor NEEL yis HEN drik sun), a Dutch explorer from the Netherlands, a country in Europe, came to Delaware Bay in 1616. Hendrickson came to "trade with the [Native Americans for] furs, robes and other skins." Furs—especially beaver fur, which was used to make men's hats—could be sold for high prices in Europe.

In 1626, the Dutch set up two trading posts on the Delaware River near the mouth of the Schuylkill River. A trading post was a place where Native Americans could bring furs and trade them for goods. The Dutch traded such things as metal axes and cooking pots for furs.

New Sweden

The leaders of Sweden, a country in northern Europe, hired a Dutchman named Peter Minuit (MIN yoo wit) to set up a colony for them in 1636. A colony is a place ruled by another country. The Swedes named the colony New Sweden. It stretched into what is now Pennsylvania.

In 1638, Swedish colonists built a fort on the land Minuit had bought from the Susquehannock and the Lenape. It was where Wilmington, Delaware, is now located. Minuit named the settlement Fort Christina after the queen of Sweden. Find this fort on the map on this page.

How did the Schuylkill River get its name?

In 1633, a Dutch trader named Arendt Corssen (ah RENT KOR suhn) sailed up the Delaware River. Some historians believe that he almost sailed past the mouth of another river because it was hidden by tall reeds. So Corssen named the river he almost missed the Schuylkill, which is Dutch for "hidden river."

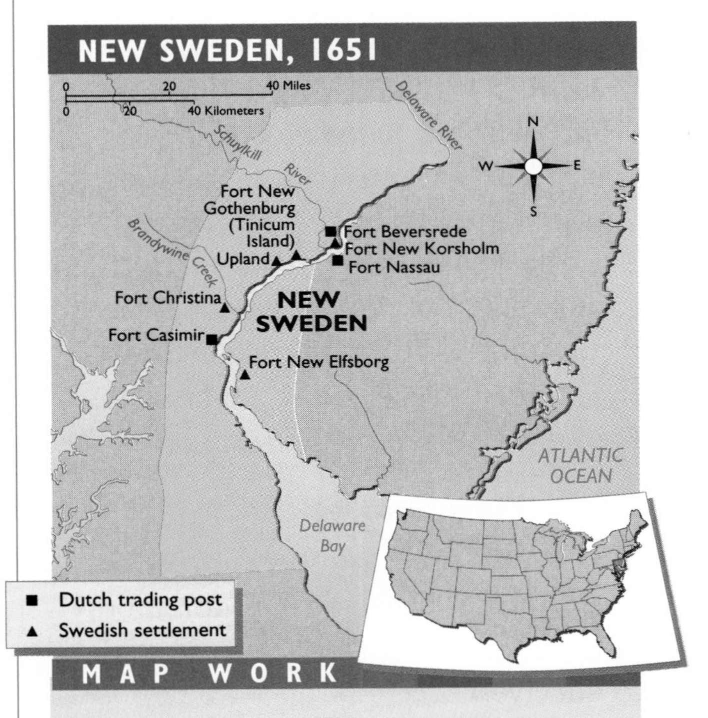

MAP WORK

The Swedish and the Dutch were the first Europeans to settle along the Delaware Bay.

1. Which Dutch fort was located opposite the mouth of the Schuylkill River?
2. How do you think the Dutch and Swedes traveled from fort to fort?

BUILDING NEW SWEDEN

Most Swedes did not want to make the long trip across the Atlantic Ocean to New Sweden because of stormy seas and a lack of fresh food and water. So the leaders of Sweden sent soldiers to help build the colony. The leaders also sent some Finns who were living in Sweden. Finns are people from Finland, a country that borders Sweden. At this time Finland was ruled by Sweden.

A New Leader

In 1642, Johan Printz, a former Swedish soldier was made the leader of New Sweden. In order to increase Swedish trade with Native Americans, Printz was friendly toward them and treated them with respect. Some Swedes learned to speak Native American languages.

After Printz arrived in New Sweden in February 1643, he decided to build a new settlement on **Tinicum Island** in the Delaware River near present-day Philadelphia. He named it **New Gothenburg**.

Life in New Sweden

Life was not easy for the settlers. They had to hunt and fish for food, clear land, and build homes in order to survive.

The Swedes were very skilled in building log cabins. The only tool needed to build a log cabin was an ax. After chopping down trees, the Swedes cut off the branches. Then they stacked the logs, criss-crossing them at the corners, to build the cabin walls. The thick log walls kept people warm during winter.

In 1653, there were only about 200 men, women, and children living in New Sweden. Some settlers wanted to leave. Printz had written several letters to the leaders of Sweden asking them to send more farmers and skilled workers. The leaders did not answer Printz because Sweden was at war in Europe. Printz became upset with the way things were going, so he returned to Sweden in 1654.

The Dutch Take Over

At the same time that Sweden was building its colony in North America, the Dutch were building their colony of **New Netherland** nearby. The leader of New Netherland was **Peter Stuyvesant** (STĪ vuh suhnt). New Netherland had built a fort on Delaware Bay.

American Swedish Historical Museum, Philadelphia, Pennsylvania

Johan Rising, was sent to replace Printz. He arrived in New Sweden in May 1654. Rising was told to drive the Dutch off land belonging to New Sweden. He immediately sent his soldiers to capture the Dutch fort, Casimir, which was located just south of Fort Christina.

This attack made Peter Stuyvesant angry. He and his soldiers went from New Netherland to New Sweden. In September 1655 they captured Fort Christina. New Sweden now became a part of New Netherland.

The Swedish settlers were allowed to stay in their settlements, but they now had to obey the laws of New Netherland.

Courtesy of the Friends of the Swedish Cabin

This tapestry (left) shows life in New Sweden. The Swedes were the first to build log cabins (above) in North America.

WHY IT MATTERS

The discovery of rich land and natural resources in North America led many European countries to begin colonies there. The Dutch and Swedes began settlements in what is today Pennsylvania. In the next lesson you will read about the other European colonists who followed these groups to Pennsylvania.

Reviewing Facts and Ideas

SUM IT UP

- In 1626, the Dutch built the first trading posts along the Delaware River.
- In 1636, the colony of New Sweden, part of which was in present-day Pennsylvania, was founded.
- In 1655, Peter Stuyvesant of New Netherland captured the colony of New Sweden.

THINK ABOUT IT

1. Why did European countries want to build colonies in North America?
2. Why were animal furs so valuable in Europe?
3. **FOCUS** List three Europeans who helped settle or explore the Delaware Bay area.
4. **THINKING SKILL** Was Peter Stuyvesant's attack on New Sweden a *cause* or an *effect* of the capture of Fort Casimir?
5. **WRITE** Write a paragraph explaining why the Swedes are important to Pennsylvania history.

1550 1600 1650 1664 1737 1750

WILLIAM PENN AND ENGLISH SETTLEMENT

Focus Activity

READ TO LEARN
How did William Penn build the colony of Pennsylvania?

VOCABULARY
Great Law
treaty
Great Treaty
Walking Purchase

PEOPLE
King Charles II
William Penn
Tamenend
Hannah Penn
Thomas Penn
Lappawinzoe

PLACE
Philadelphia

READ ALOUD

It was the year 1682, and the word was out. Many people in Europe were reading William Penn's advertisements for a colony in North America called Pennsylvania. These ads promised that "the Air is sweet and clear." Who was William Penn? Could his ads really be believed?

THE BIG PICTURE

By 1664 the English had already established seven colonies along the east coast of North America. They were Massachusetts, Virginia, Maryland, New Hampshire, Connecticut, Rhode Island, and Carolina. In 1664 King Charles II of England wanted to make New Netherland an English colony. He sent a large army to North America to attack the Dutch. The Dutch quickly gave up, and the English easily took control of the Dutch and Swedish settlements.

In 1681 King Charles II granted some of this captured land to an Englishman named William Penn who wanted to start a colony there. The king was paying back a debt he owed to Penn's father. King Charles II wanted the colony to be named after William Penn's father. But Penn wanted to call it *Sylvania,* which means "woods." This is how they came to agree upon the name *Pennsylvania.*

A HOLY EXPERIMENT

William Penn was a Quaker. The Quakers are a Christian religious group also known as the Society of Friends. The Quakers did not worship in churches or have ministers. Most lived a simple life and believed that all people should be treated fairly. English law said that English people had to follow the Church of England. If they didn't, they were treated badly and sometimes put in jail. William Penn was put in jail many times for his Quaker beliefs.

Penn's plans for his colony in America were based upon Quaker beliefs. He wanted a place where Quakers and people of other religions could live and worship without fear. He called Pennsylvania his "holy experiment."

Penn and the Earliest Settlers

Before leaving England to go to the new colony, Penn sent a letter to the Swedes and the Dutch already living in the area. He explained that "it has pleased God . . . to put you in my . . . care. . . . You shall be governed by laws of your own making." He wanted the colonists to know that he would try to be fair with everyone who lived in the new colony.

Unlike most other English colonists, William Penn also wanted to be fair with the Native Americans living in his colony. So he wrote a letter to them too, saying, "the Indians [of Pennsylvania] shall have liberty to do all things . . . that any of the planters [colonists] shall enjoy." He told them he wanted them to "always live together as neighbors and friends."

In keeping with his Quaker belief in fairness, Penn paid the Dutch, the Swedes, and the Lenape for their land. The leaders of other English colonies often chose not to do this because it was not required by English law.

The Historical Society of Pennsylvania

Penn looks at the land in his new colony (below). This Indian Peace Medal shows the friendship Penn and the Native Americans shared.

SETTING UP THE COLONY

Before Penn came to Pennsylvania, he wrote the **Great Law**, a set of laws to rule his colony. For example, one law said that no one could work on Sundays. Another law set up care for poor people and orphans.

The City of Brotherly Love

In April 1681 Penn sent his cousin to Pennsylvania to choose a place for the colony's main settlement. It was named **Philadelphia**, which means "city of brotherly love" in the Greek language.

Penn arrived in Philadelphia in October 1682. He worked hard to make it a nice place to live. He mapped the streets in a grid pattern to make it easy for colonists to get around the town. The streets running from east to west were named after trees. The streets running from north to south were numbered. This was just one reason colonists liked living in Philadelphia.

Penn's street plan for Philadelphia was later copied by many others who planned towns.

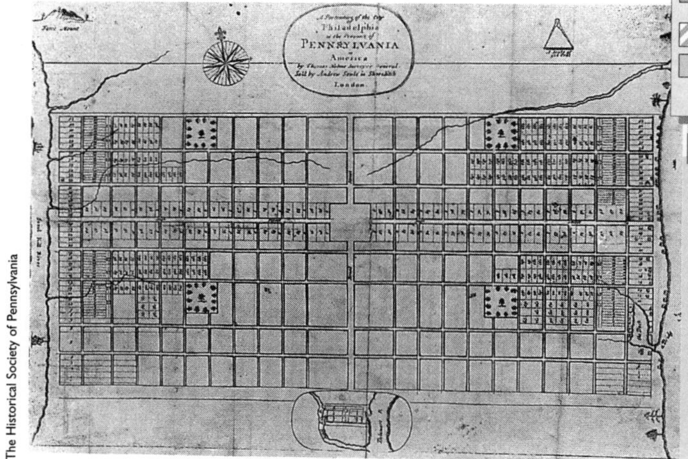

The Historical Society of Pennsylvania

Penn and the Native Americans

Soon after he arrived, William Penn signed several **treaties** with the Lenape. A treaty is a formal agreement between countries or peoples. Some historians think that Penn signed a **Great Treaty** of friendship with the Lenape chief, called **Tamenend** [TAM uh nend]. We do not know this for sure. However, the colonists and the Lenape kept the peace as long as both Penn and Tamenend lived.

The Walking Purchase

After William Penn died in 1718, **Hannah Penn**, his wife, ruled the

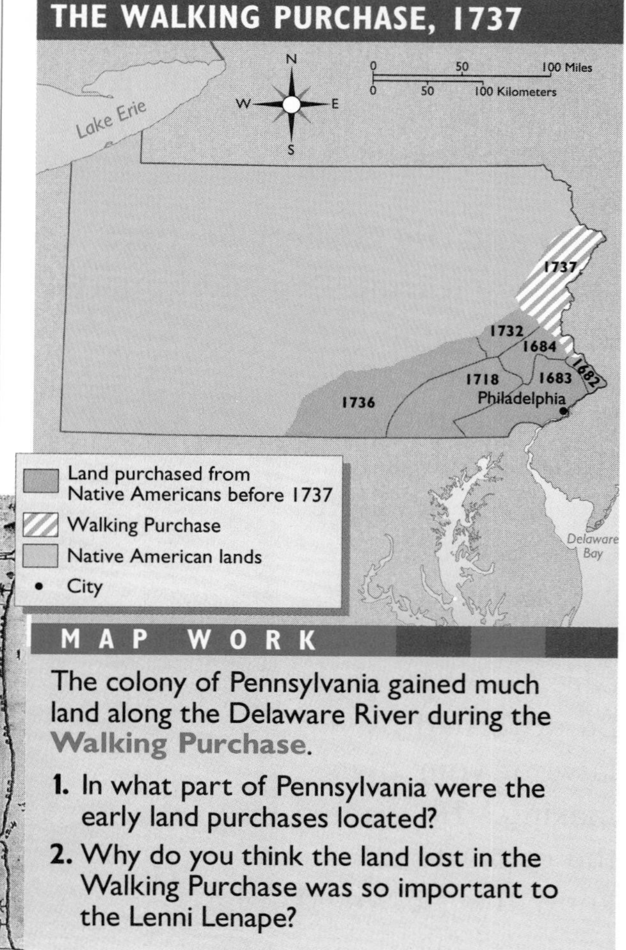

MAP WORK

The colony of Pennsylvania gained much land along the Delaware River during the **Walking Purchase**.

1. In what part of Pennsylvania were the early land purchases located?
2. Why do you think the land lost in the Walking Purchase was so important to the Lenni Lenape?

colony. She became the only woman to lead one of the 13 English colonies. When Hannah Penn died in 1727, her three sons became the leaders of the colony.

In 1737, one son, **Thomas Penn**, had a treaty supposedly signed by his father and some Lenape chiefs. This treaty gave William Penn land west of the Delaware River as far "as a man can go in one day and a half." However, no one had ever made the walk for the land. So the Lenape agreed to let a walk take place.

On September 19, 1737, colonists cheered as three walkers set off. Soon they began to run. This angered the Lenape because they realized they were being cheated. One Lenape chief, who was called **Lappawinzoe** [LAP pah wihn zoh], later complained that "the walkers should have walked for a few miles and then have sat down . . . and not have kept upon the run, run all day." The map on page 82 shows how much land the Lenape lost. The **Walking Purchase** hurt the friendship between the colonists and the Lenape forever.

WHY IT MATTERS

William Penn worked hard to make Pennsylvania a good place for everyone to live. Pennsylvanians had a good relationship with the Native Americans until the Walking Purchase of 1737. In the next lesson, you will read about life in the new colony.

Links to **MATHEMATICS**

Mega Miles

The Lenape thought that the three colonists would walk only about 30 miles in 36 hours. The walkers traveled about 66 miles during that time. About how many miles per hour did the walkers travel?

Reviewing Facts and Ideas

SUM IT UP

- William Penn founded Pennsylvania as a colony where people of different religions could live together peacefully.
- Before coming to Pennsylvania, Penn wrote the Great Law, a set of laws to rule his colony.
- The colonists' relations with Native Americans remained friendly until the Walking Purchase of 1737.

THINK ABOUT IT

1. Why was Pennsylvania called a "holy experiment"?
2. What was the Great Law?
3. **FOCUS** What did William Penn do to help the colony of Pennsylvania to grow?
4. **THINKING SKILL** What <u>effect</u> did William Penn's Quaker beliefs have on the laws of the colony?
5. **GEOGRAPHY** Look at the map on page 82. Where was the land gained by Pennsylvania?

STUDYSKILLS

Reading Time Lines

VOCABULARY
time line

WHY THE SKILL MATTERS

In Lesson 2 you read that William Penn arrived in America in 1682. This was just one event in Penn's life. You also read that Penn mapped the streets for the city of Philadelphia. This was another event.

To understand history, you need to know when events happened. You also need to know in which *order* they happened. Penn came to America. He also got married. And he sailed back to England twice.

In what time order did he do these things? To help answer these questions, you can use a **time line**. A time line is a diagram that shows when events took place. It shows the amount of time that passed between events. The way a time line is drawn helps to give a sense of sequence, or order, to history. The time line below shows important events in the life of William Penn.

USING THE SKILL

Look at the time line. As you can see, the name of each event appears below or above the date it happened. The earliest event—the birth of William Penn—is on the left side. The most recent event—the death of William Penn—is on the right.

Like most time lines, this one is divided into equal parts. Each part represents

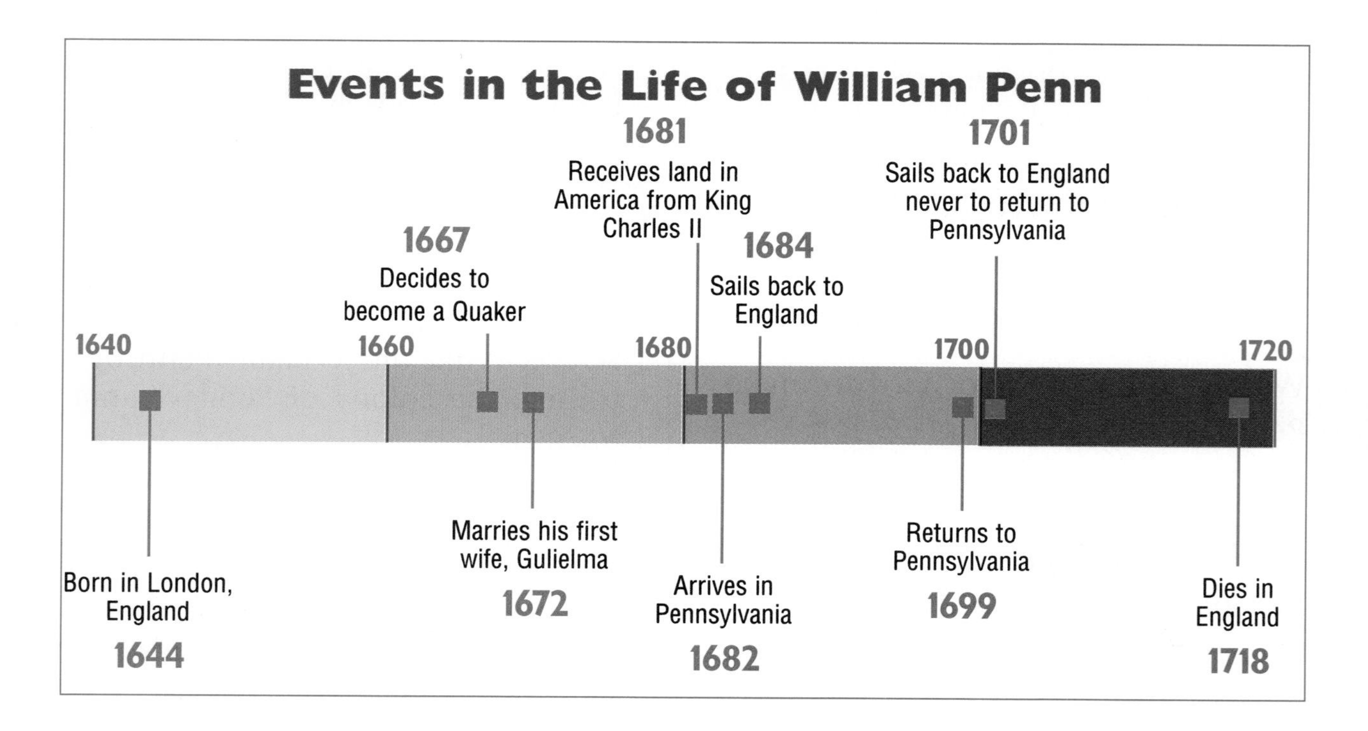

a certain number of years. Each part of Penn's time line represents 20 years.

Now read the time line from left to right. Which event took place *between* 1700 and 1718?

HELPING Yourself

- **A time line is a diagram that shows when historical events took place.**
- **Note how much time is represented by each part of the time line.**
- **Read the events from left to right.**

TRYING THE SKILL

Now read the time line of Events in the American Colonies. Use the Helping Yourself box for hints.

What period of history does the time line cover? Which event on the time line happened first? When was the colony of New Jersey settled? What event happened in 1704? Was the colony of North Carolina settled before or after New Jersey?

REVIEWING THE SKILL

Look again at the time line of Events in the American Colonies. Use it to answer the following questions.

1. How does a time line help you to place events in the right order?
2. Which event took place in 1719?
3. How much time passed between Stuyvesant becoming leader of New Netherland and Penn receiving land from King Charles?
4. Did Peter Stuyvesant become leader of New Netherland before or after the colony of New Jersey was settled?
5. In what other subjects would a time line be useful?

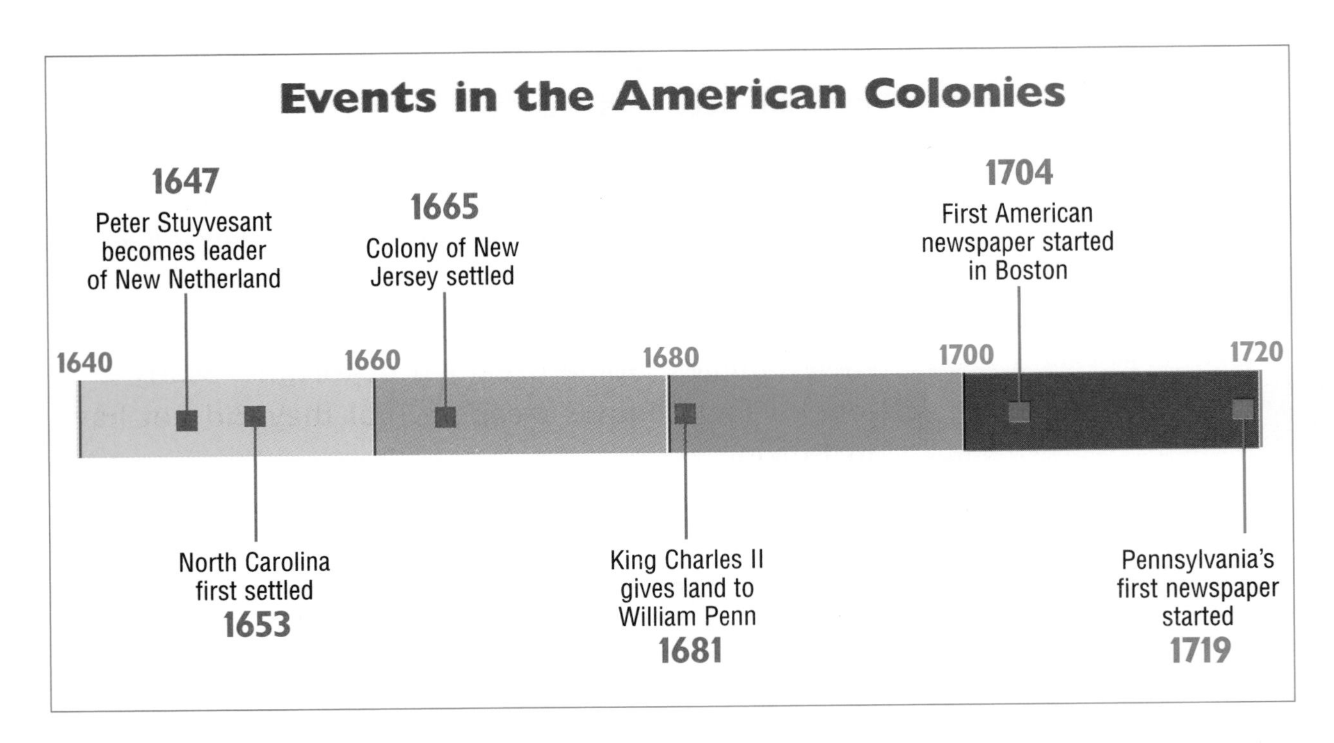

Poor Richard, 1733.

AN

Almanack

For the Year of Chrift

1733,

Being the Firft after LEAP YEAR:

And makes fince the Creation	Years
By the Account of the Eaftern *Greeks*	7241
By the Latin Church, when ☉ ent. ♈	6932
By the Computation of *W.W*	5742
By the *Roman* Chronology	5682
By the *Jewifh* Rabbies	5494

Wherein is contained

The Lunations, Eclipfes, Judgment of the Weather, Spring Tides, Planets Motions & mutual Afpects, Sun and Moon's Rifing and Setting, Length of Days, Time of High Water, Fairs, Courts, and obfervable Days

Fitted to the Latitude of Forty Degrees, and a Meridian of Five Hours Weft from *London*, but may without fenfible Error, ferve all the adjacent Places, even from *Newfoundland* to *South-Carolina*.

By *RICHARD SAUNDERS*, Philom.

PHILADELPHIA:
Printed and fold by *B. FRANKLIN*, at the New Printing Office near the Market.

The Third Impreffion.

Focus Activity

READ TO LEARN

What was life like in colonial Pennsylvania?

VOCABULARY

immigrant
indentured servant
slavery
manufacture
port

PEOPLE

Benjamin Franklin
Jane Hoskens
Thomas Rutter
Wilhelm Rittenhausen
Deborah Franklin
Sybilla Masters

PLACES

Germantown
Lancaster
Bethlehem
Pottstown
Ephrata

LIFE IN COLONIAL PENNSYLVANIA

READ ALOUD

"Early to bed and early to rise, makes a man healthy, wealthy, and wise." Have you heard this saying? Thousands of people in the 1700s read Benjamin Franklin's **Poor Richard's Almanac.** ***An almanac is a reference book that contains information about the weather and other topics. Pennsylvanians loved Franklin's funny sayings, which are still popular today.***

THE BIG PICTURE

In the 1700s many people in Pennsylvania took Benjamin Franklin's saying to heart. Making a new life here was hard work for colonists from Europe. Yet thousands of people were willing to try.

Men, women, and children had risked their lives crossing the dangerous waters of the Atlantic Ocean. Why would anyone make such an uncertain journey? They came in search of a better life for their families. Some dreamed of fortune. Many longed for religious freedom that they did not have in Europe.

These immigrants came from countries such as Ireland, Germany, Switzerland, and England. An immigrant is a person who comes to live in a new land from another place. Some of these immigrants might have been your ancestors.

NEW IMMIGRANTS ARRIVE

Immigrants came to the Pennsylvania colony in large numbers. Each group brought its own language, customs, and beliefs. Among those who came to find religious freedom were Roman Catholics from Ireland and Germany, Jews from Portugal, and Protestants from France.

German Settlers

The first German settlers also came to the Pennsylvania colony in search of religious freedom. The Mennonites [MEH nuh nits] were a group with beliefs similar to the Quakers. Unlike the Quakers, though, Mennonites chose to live separate from other colonists. They settled in Germantown in 1683 and in Lancaster in 1710. The Amish came from Germany and Switzerland and settled around Lancaster beginning in 1737.

Indentured Servants

Many immigrants who had little or no money came to Pennsylvania as indentured servants. An indentured servant is a person who agreed to work for someone in the colonies for a fixed amount of time to pay for their trip. Some indentured servants worked clearing land. Others learned trades such as printing and watch-making.

Jane Hoskens, an indentured servant, arrived in Philadelphia from Plymouth, England in 1719. How did she feel about her job as a teacher?

Excerpt from the Autobiography of Jane Hoskens, published in 1837.

The [heads] of four families living in Plymouth, who had several children, agreed to procure a . . . young woman, as a school-mistress to instruct them in reading. . . . I bound myself to them by indenture for three years, and went cheerfully with them. . . . The children learned very fast, which afforded comfort to me and satisfaction to their parents.

The Granger Collection

procure: get
afforded: gave

African Captives

Thousands of Africans were taken by force from their homes in West Africa. German, Scottish, Irish, and even Quaker traders brought these captives to the American colonies to be sold into slavery. Slavery is the practice of making one person the property of another.

In the Pennsylvania colony, enslaved Africans often became house servants or skilled craft workers. By the 1750s there were about 8,000 enslaved Africans in Pennsylvania. There were few free Africans at this time.

A GROWING COLONY

Immigrants helped the Pennsylvania colony to grow. Family-owned farms in the southeast raised so much corn and wheat that Pennsylvania was called the "Breadbasket of America."

Craft shops and small factories were started in many towns. Germantown was known for **manufacturing** cloth. To manufacture is to make goods by machine. **Bethlehem** had a wagon shop and craft shops that made glass and pottery.

In 1716 **Thomas Rutter** started manufacturing iron on Manatawny [man uh TAW nee] Creek near **Pottstown**. Iron was used to make wire, nails, and tools. By 1750 Pennsylvania was the leading manufacturer of iron in the colonies.

Wilhelm Rittenhausen [VIL helm RIH tin hah sun] built the first paper mill in the colonies in Germantown in 1690. **Ephrata** [eh FRAY tuh] had a mill to grind wheat, a sawmill, and a large printing shop.

The City of Philadelphia

By 1775 Philadelphia was the largest city in the 13 English colonies with 35,000 people. Wagons and carts clattered over the wide stone streets. Sometimes they got tangled in traffic jams. Most houses were two stories high and built of red brick.

Because ships could travel from the Atlantic Ocean through the Delaware Bay to Philadelphia, it became an important **port**. A port is a place where ships load and unload goods. Philadelphia's businesses shipped wheat, lumber, furs, iron, and beef to other colonies and to Europe.

Benjamin Franklin

Born in Boston, Benjamin Franklin ran away to Philadelphia at the age of 17. In 1730 when he was 24, he started his own printing business and became the publisher of the *Pennsylvania Gazette*. From 1732 to 1751 Franklin also published *Poor Richard's Almanac*, filled with his jokes and sayings. You read one of his sayings in the Read Aloud on page 86. Franklin was also a scientist and an inventor. You can see some of his inventions in the Legacy on page 90.

Doctors, lawyers, and business owners from many different countries lived in early Philadelphia (below). Deborah Franklin (right) ran much of the printing business her husband started.

The man at a colonial village (above) is showing how people made baskets in the colonies.

The Granger Collection

Women in Colonial Pennsylvania

In the Pennsylvania colony, women worked on farms and in businesses their husbands owned. Deborah Franklin, Benjamin Franklin's wife, ran much of his business. She also took care of their children and a busy household.

Some women started their own businesses. Sybilla [SIH buh luh] Masters, a Philadelphia businesswoman, may have been the first American woman inventor. One of the things she made was a machine for cleaning corn.

WHY IT MATTERS

Many immigrants came to Pennsylvania hoping for a better life. Indentured servants from Europe and captives from Africa helped the colony grow. Philadelphia became an important port, and farming and manufacturing made the colony wealthy. In the next lesson you will read about people moving west.

Reviewing Facts and Ideas

SUM IT UP

- Many immigrants came to Pennsylvania to find a better life and religious freedom.
- Indentured servants from Europe and African captives also came to colonial Pennsylvania.
- Manufacturing and farming helped Pennsylvania to grow, and Philadelphia became an important port.

THINK ABOUT IT

1. Give two reasons why Europeans came to colonial Pennsylvania.
2. Name two of the groups that came to Pennsylvania looking for religious freedom.
3. **FOCUS** Describe life in colonial Pennsylvania.
4. **THINKING SKILL** *Compare* and *contrast* indentured servants with enslaved persons.
5. **WRITE** Suppose you are a young person who wants to move to the colony of Pennsylvania from Europe. Write a letter to your parents explaining your reasons.

Legacy

LINKING PAST AND PRESENT

Benjamin Franklin and Colonial Philadelphia

As you read in the last lesson, Benjamin Franklin was one of the people who helped Philadelphia grow. He became well-known throughout the colonies as a printer, writer, inventor, and scientist. As a scientist, Franklin is best known for his experiments with electricity. Look at the photographs on these pages to see some other things for which Franklin became known. Do you recognize some of the things he made that are still used today?

In addition to publishing *Poor Richard's Almanac,* Franklin started the city's first public library and helped found its first hospital. In 1740, he founded Pennsylvania's first college, which later became the University of Pennsylvania. It is one of the oldest colleges in the United States. Franklin also helped to start a school for African Americans in the late 1700s. Franklin's inventions and contributions to colonial life are a legacy that is still an important part of our life today.

Franklin invented bifocal eyeglasses with two types of lenses that help people see both close up and far away. We still use these today.

Franklin's printing business made newspapers and pamphlets available to many colonists.

Franklin started the world's first volunteer fire department, called the Union Fire Company.

Franklin improved the fireplace with his wood-burning, cast-iron stove called the Franklin stove, or the "Pennsylvania Fireplace."

With his famous kite experiment, Franklin showed that lightning was a kind of electricity.

The Metropolitan Museum of Art, Rogers Fund, 1922

GEOGRAPHYSKILLS

Using Map Scales

VOCABULARY
scale

WHY THE SKILL MATTERS

Suppose you are a colonist trading goods in Pennsylvania and the other colonies in 1755. How can you find out how far you have to travel between cities? **Scale** on a map can tell you the answer. Scale is the relationship between the distance shown on a map and the real distance. A map has a scale because it is not the same size as the area it represents.

Look at the map of the 13 English colonies on this page. It is marked Map A. Then look at the map of the Pennsylvania colony and surrounding area on the facing page. It is marked Map B. The two maps are drawn to different scales.

Why are the two maps here drawn to different scales? Some maps need to include many details. To show many details, a map cannot include a very large area. A very detailed map that shows every street, tree, and building might cover an area of only a few blocks. If less detail is necessary, a map can show a much larger area.

USING THE SKILL

Look again at Map A on this page. Find the map scale. The top line shows how many miles on Earth are shown by one inch on the map. One inch stands for 400 miles. The bottom line shows how many kilometers on Earth are shown by one and one-half centimeters.

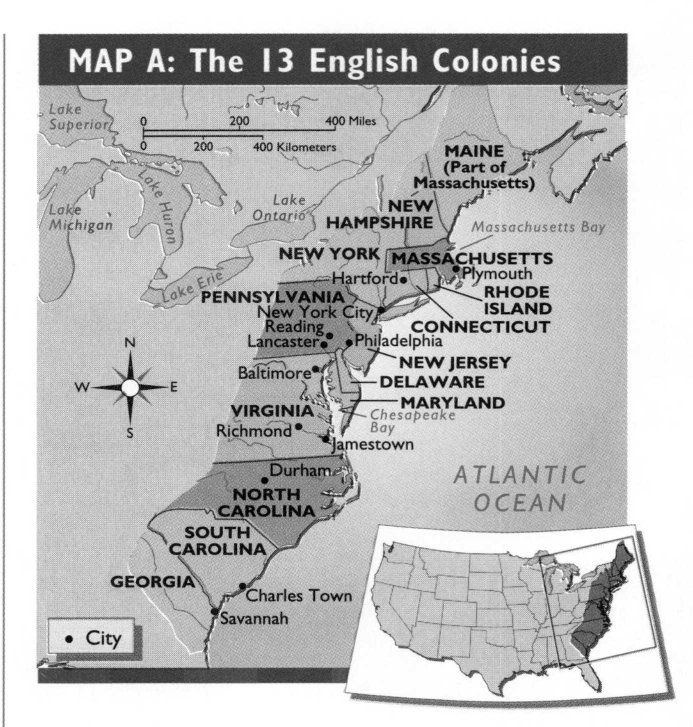

Suppose you wanted to measure the distance from Lancaster to Jamestown. You could guess by looking at the map scale, but you could make a more accurate measurement by using a scale strip.

Use the scale on Map A above to make a scale strip. Place a piece of paper below the scale and mark the distances. Move the paper along and continue marking distances. Your scale strip should look like this:

Place the edge of the scale strip between the symbols for the two cities. Make sure the zero is directly below Lancaster, Pennsylvania. Then read the numbers beneath Jamestown, Virginia. You can see that the distance between the cities is about 200 miles. How far is Savannah, Georgia from Lancaster, Pennsylvania? What is the distance in inches on the map?

HELPING Yourself

- **Different scales allow maps to show either more detail or a greater area.**
- **Study the scale on the map.**
- **You can make a scale strip to find out the real distance between points on a map.**

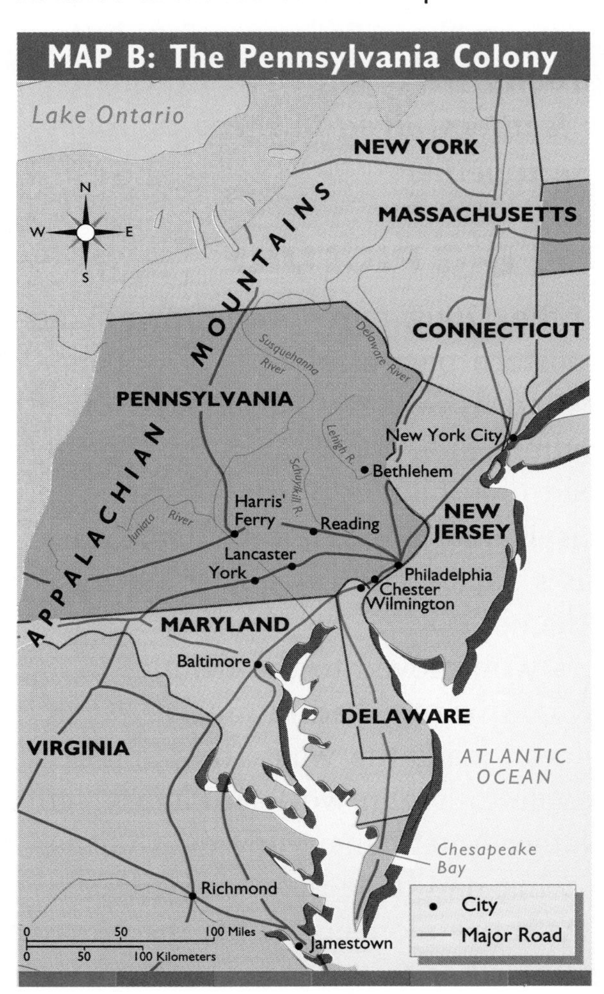

TRYING THE SKILL

Now look at Map B on this page. This map shows some of the same area of land as Map A. As you can see, however, the maps are different sizes. If you compare the two map scales, you will see that they are different. On which map does one inch stand for a greater distance? Which map shows more detail? Use the Helping Yourself box for hints.

Make a scale strip for Map B. Measure the distance between Reading, Pennsylvania, and Richmond, Virginia. What is the distance in miles? On Map A, the two cities are about 1/2 inch apart. On Map B they are about 2 inches apart. On which map does one inch stand for a smaller distance?

REVIEWING THE SKILL

1. What information does a map scale give us about a map?
2. How does using a scale strip help make accurate measurements?
3. Which map would you use to find the distance between Bethlehem and Philadelphia? What is the distance between the two cities in miles? In kilometers?
4. What information is shown on Map B that is not shown on Map A?
5. When might it be helpful to use maps drawn to different scales?

1550 1600 1650 1700 1742 1754

Pennsylvania Historical and Museum Commission

LIFE ON THE PENNSYLVANIA FRONTIER

Focus Activity

READ TO LEARN

What was life like on the Pennsylvania frontier?

VOCABULARY

frontier
pioneer
Conestoga wagon
subsistence farming

PEOPLE

Daniel Boone
Conrad Weiser
John Shikellamy

PLACES

Reading
Scotland
Ireland
Cumberland Valley
Carlisle
Bedford

READ ALOUD

A colonist named Rhoda Barber wrote down her memories of an early Pennsylvania town: "Not far from Columbia [on the Susquehanna River] was a place called Smoke Town. . . . A little stream wound among the hills, and a few little spots of level ground were sometimes farmed. The inhabitants [settlers] lived in three or four cabins built close together."

THE BIG PICTURE

By the middle of the 1700s, most of the towns and cities along the eastern part of what is now Pennsylvania were owned by wealthy farmers. Colonists and many new immigrants could not afford to buy land there. Instead they began to travel further west to the Pennsylvania **frontier**. Frontier is the word that colonists used to describe land on the edge of their settlement.

The newcomers who moved to the frontier in western Pennsylvania were called **pioneers**. A pioneer is a person who leads the way. The pioneers were the first people to live in western Pennsylvania who were not Native Americans. They built farms and towns from what had once been only forests and mountains. As more pioneers came, the frontier moved farther and farther west.

MOVING WEST

The pioneers had a difficult time traveling west. Rough mountains and thick forests made their journey dangerous. Most pioneers had a guide for the trip. Trappers, who were usually the first pioneers on the frontier, found many of the trails.

Daniel Boone

Daniel Boone was one of the best known trappers. Born near Reading, he grew up exploring the woods. Boone followed trails built by Native Americans and became an excellent guide. He helped build new trails and led thousands of pioneers west.

Scots-Irish Pioneers

Many of the pioneers who settled on the Pennsylvania frontier were Scots-Irish immigrants. During the 1700s, the Scots-Irish arrived in the colony by the tens of thousands. They had lived in Scotland and Ireland before moving to the colonies. Many had left Scotland because they were forced off the land they rented. When they moved to Ireland, they faced high rents and poor harvests. They came to Pennsylvania with their families in search of land and a new life.

By 1742 pioneers had crossed into the Cumberland Valley. The town of Carlisle was planned in 1751. During the 1750s the town of Bedford grew out of a trading post called Raystown. Find Bedford on the map to the right.

Daniel Boone, Pennsylvania's most famous pioneer, explored Kentucky and Missouri.

SETTLEMENT IN PENNSYLVANIA, 1754

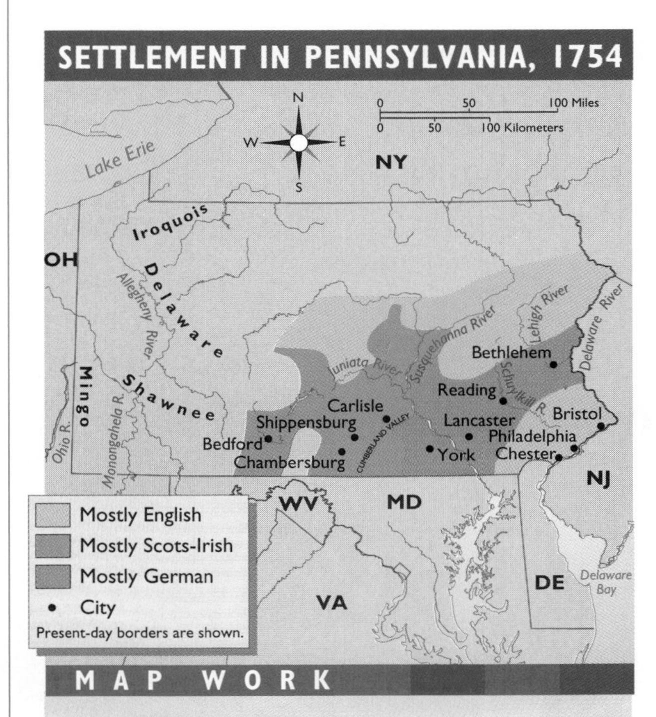

MAP WORK

The English, Germans, and Scots-Irish were the three main European groups to settle in Pennsylvania in the early 1700s.

1. What Native American groups lived west of the frontier?
2. Why do you think these European groups settled close to one another?

SETTLING THE FRONTIER

Pioneers often moved west in Conestoga [kahn uh STOH guh] wagons. English and German wagon makers in the Conestoga Valley near Lancaster first built these huge, canvas-covered wagons to carry crops to market. They were 11 feet high and weighed over 3,000 pounds, which is about the same as a minivan. Besides carrying a family's belongings, the wagon was a home on wheels that protected its passengers from rain and snow.

Pioneer Living

Pioneer life was difficult. When a pioneer family found their land, the first job was to clear it. They chopped down the trees and burned the logs in the field.

Once the field was cleared, the pioneers planted corn. The land in Pennsylvania was often rocky and uneven. This is not good for farming. Pioneers grew only the food they needed, with nothing extra to sell. This kind of farming is called subsistence [suhb SIHS tihns] farming.

Pioneers usually built a one-room log cabin for their first home. Moss and straw mixed with mud filled the cracks between the logs. There was no running water. Besides the fireplace, a burning candle or piece of cane soaked in grease was often the only light.

Pioneer Children

Like their parents, children on the frontier worked hard. Both boys and girls helped cook, feed the animals, and carry water. As they grew older, boys learned to hunt and fish for food. Girls became skilled at spinning, weaving, and knitting clothing.

Unrest on the Frontier

As pioneers moved to the Pennsylvania frontier, they often settled on Native American land. This land is where the Lenape, the Shawnee [Shaw NEE], and the Seneca [SEN ih cuh] lived. The Lenape had moved farther west because the early Pennsylvania colonists had either bought or taken much of their land. The Shawnee and Seneca, an Iroquois people, had also recently moved onto the Pennsylvania frontier.

These Native Americans needed land for hunting in order to survive. As pioneers settled on their hunting grounds, the Native Americans became angry.

By the 1700 the Iroquois controlled the Native Americans in the Pennsylvania colony. **Conrad Weiser** [VĪ ser], a German immigrant, had lived with the Iroquois in New York as a boy and learned their language and customs. He traveled to the Iroquois homeland in New York five times in order to strengthen Pennsylvania's friendship with them. The Iroquois made **John Shikellamy** [Shi KELL a mee], who spoke English, the chief of the Native American groups in Pennsylvania. Weiser and Shikellamy often worked together to keep the peace.

Pioneers had to make many things themselves. The picture (far left) shows a frontier woman making soap. This rocking horse (left) was a toy for pioneer children.

WHY IT MATTERS

As the Pennsylvania colony grew, new immigrants began moving to the frontier in search of land. Many of these pioneers were Scots-Irish. Even though life was difficult, pioneers built farms and towns.

Unrest between Native Americans and pioneers grew as the Europeans settled on Native American land.

Reviewing Facts and Ideas

SUM IT UP

- The frontier is the edge of a settled area.
- Many pioneers from the Pennsylvania colony were Scots-Irish immigrants.
- Many pioneers were subsistence farmers.
- Pioneers who moved west often settled on Native American land.

THINK ABOUT IT

1. Why did settlers move to the frontier?
2. Why was the Conestoga wagon often used to travel west?
3. **FOCUS** What was life like on the Pennsylvania frontier?
4. **THINKING SKILL** What *effect* did the pioneers moving west have on the Lenape, the Shawnee, and the Seneca people?
5. **WRITE** Suppose you are a pioneer in western Pennsylvania in 1740. Write a letter to a friend in your home town in Europe describing your new life.

CHAPTER 4 REVIEW

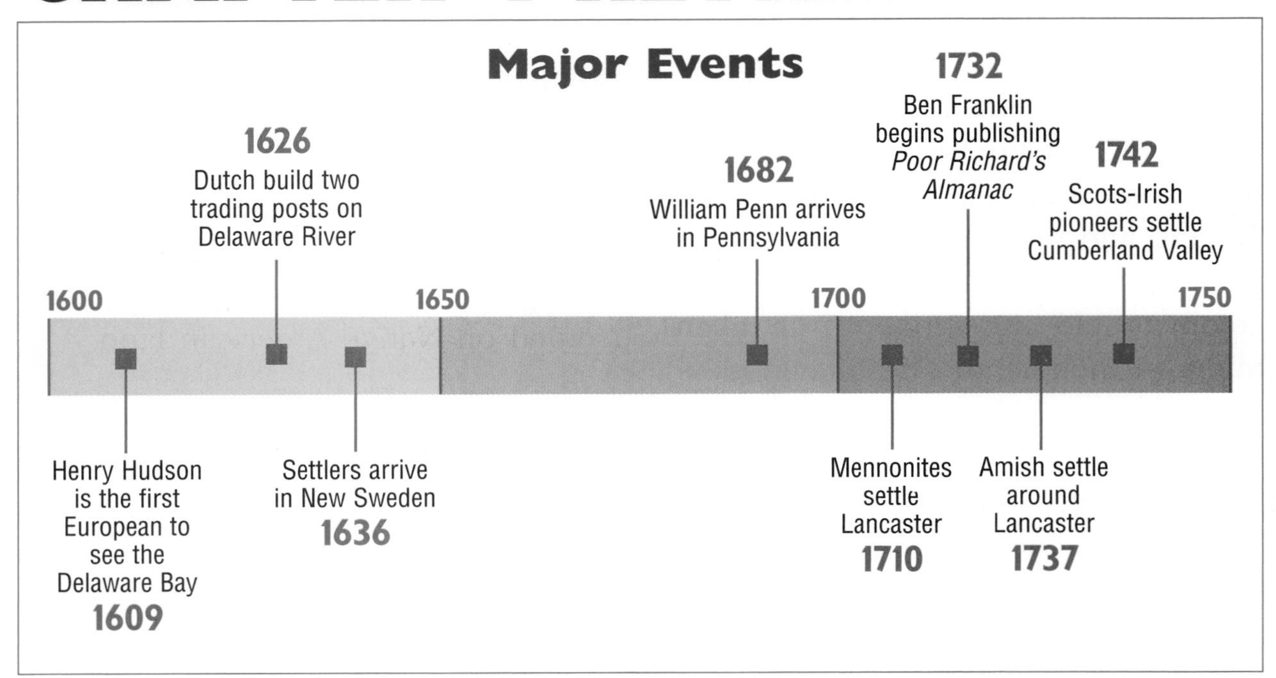

THINKING ABOUT VOCABULARY

Number from 1 to 5 on a sheet of paper. Next to each number write the word or term from the list below that best matches the statement.

explore **slavery**
frontier **treaty**
port

1. A place where a ship can load and unload goods
2. A formal agreement between countries or peoples
3. The practice of making one person the property of another
4. Traveling in unfamiliar places in order to find out about them
5. Land on the edge of a settlement

THINKING ABOUT FACTS

1. What two European countries first sent people to Pennsylvania?
2. What was the Walking Purchase?
3. List some of the goods manufactured in the Pennsylvania colony.
4. Who was Benjamin Franklin?
5. Explain why problems arose between Native Americans and pioneers.

THINK AND WRITE

WRITING A SUMMARY
Write a summary describing the settlement of Pennsylvania by Europeans.

WRITING AN ADVERTISEMENT
Write an advertisement telling people why they should move to Penn's colony.

WRITING A DESCRIPTION
Write a description of the relationship between settlers and Native Americans in early Pennsylvania.

APPLYING STUDY SKILLS

READING TIME LINES

Use the Major Events time line on the opposite page to answer the following questions.

1. How many years does the time line cover?
2. When did William Penn arrive in his new colony?
3. How many years later did the Scots-Irish settle the Cumberland Valley?
4. Did the Dutch build trading posts on the Delaware River before or after settlers arrived in New Sweden?
5. How are time lines useful for studying history?

APPLYING GEOGRAPHY SKILLS

USING MAP SCALES

Refer to the map on page 93 to answer the following questions.

1. What is a map scale?
2. How does a scale strip help you to measure distances accurately?
3. Use a scale strip to measure the distance between New York City and Philadelphia. About how many miles is it from Lancaster to Philadelphia?
4. Which cities are closer—Richmond and Philadelphia, or Baltimore and New York City?
5. Why is it useful to have maps drawn at different scales?

Summing Up the Chapter

Use the following word maps to organize information from the chapter. Copy the word maps on a sheet of paper. Then write at least one piece of information in each blank box. When you have filled in the maps, use them to write a paragraph that answers the question, "How did these immigrants help Pennsylvania to grow?"

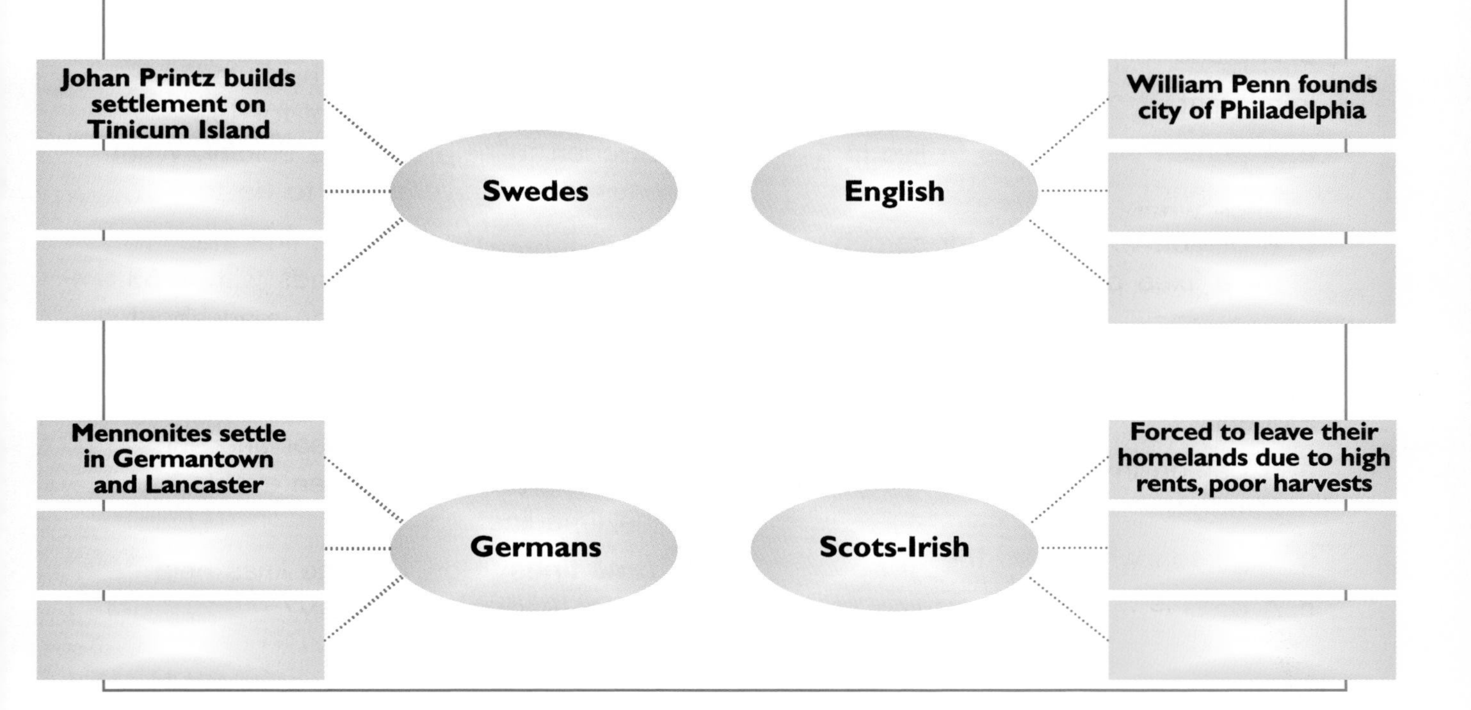

UNIT 2 REVIEW

THINKING ABOUT VOCABULARY

Number a sheet of paper from 1 to 5. Next to each number write the letter of the definition that best matches the word.

1. Ice age
- **a.** A time before there were any people
- **b.** A time when glaciers covered much of Earth's surface
- **c.** A cold winter after the arrival of European colonists in Pennsylvania

2. Descendants
- **a.** The people who come after you
- **b.** The people who come before you
- **c.** The people who live with you

3. Colony
- **a.** A place people leave in search of new lands
- **b.** A place discovered by an explorer
- **c.** A place ruled by another country

4. Immigrant
- **a.** A person who comes to live in a new land
- **b.** A person who works for someone for a fixed period of time
- **c.** A person who is the property of another person

5. Pioneer
- **a.** A person in search of religious freedom
- **b.** A person who leads the way
- **c.** A person who runs a trading post

THINK AND WRITE

WRITING A DESCRIPTION
In this unit you have read about shelters. Write a description of the different kinds of shelters lived in by Native Americans.

WRITING AN EXPLANATION
History tells us about past events that were preserved in written records. Write an explanation telling how we have learned about prehistory.

WRITING A NEWSPAPER ARTICLE
Suppose you are a newspaper reporter for the *Susquehannock Times*. William Penn arrives in your village for the first time. Write an article for the newspaper describing his visit.

BUILDING SKILLS

1. **Identifying cause and effect** What are some of the clue words that show cause and effect?
2. **Identifying cause and effect** You read in Chapter 4 that the Swedish government sent soldiers to New Sweden to help built the colony. What caused the government to do this?
3. **Time lines** Draw a time line that begins with 1600 and ends with 1753. Place five events that you read about in Unit 2 on the time line.
4. **Time lines** Draw a time line that begins with your birth year and ends with this year. Place three events on the time line.
5. **Time lines** How do time lines help you to understand history?

YESTERDAY, TODAY & TOMORROW

Native Americans depended on many natural resources to survive. How do we use these resources differently from the early Native Americans? Would you like to go back in time to the way Native Americans used natural resources? Can you think of ways we can use natural resources more wisely in the future?

READING ON YOUR OWN

These are some of the books you could find at the library to help you learn more.

THE STORY OF WILLIAM PENN
by Aliki
Read about William Penn, the founding father of Pennsylvania and Philadelphia.

WHAT'S THE BIG IDEA, BEN FRANKLIN?
by Jean Fritz
This biography of the 18th century printer, inventor, and statesman shows the important role he played in the history of our country.

THE DELAWARE
by Jay Miller
This book traces the incredible history and culture of the Delaware Indians.

UNIT PROJECT

Write a Historical Diary

1. Suppose you are one of the following people:
   - a Lenape in the 1600s
   - an English explorer in early Pennsylvania
   - an early Pennsylvania settler from Europe
2. Gather information from your textbook and your school library about the person you chose.
3. Write a diary page that might have been written by that person. You may write about your home life, family, or thoughts on the new or changing world around you.
4. Trade papers with a partner. Challenge your partner to guess which person from the list wrote the diary.

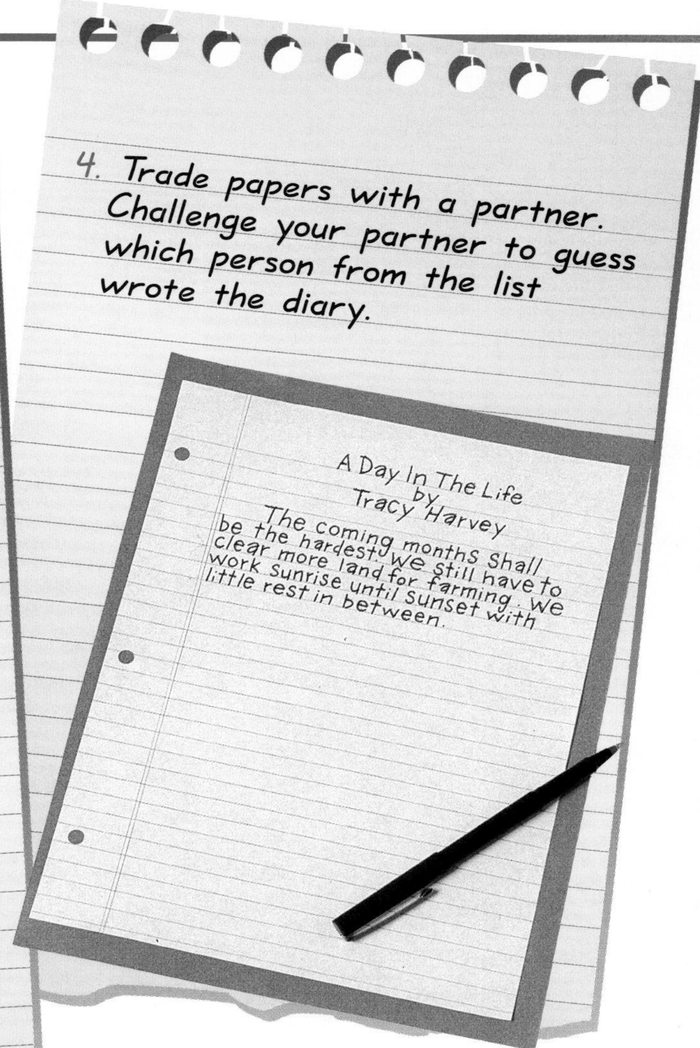

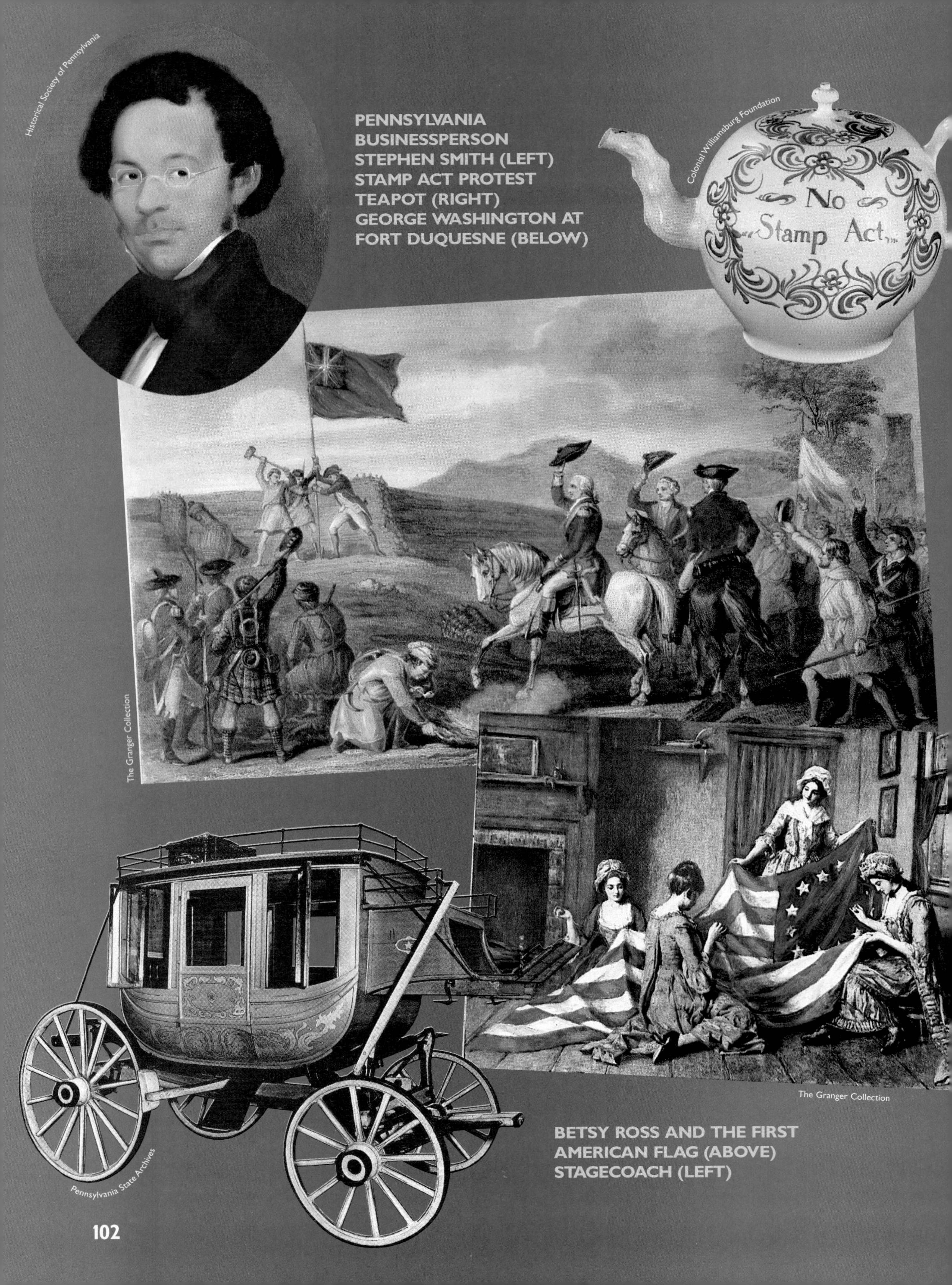

Historical Society of Pennsylvania

Colonial Williamsburg Foundation

PENNSYLVANIA BUSINESSPERSON STEPHEN SMITH (LEFT)
STAMP ACT PROTEST TEAPOT (RIGHT)
GEORGE WASHINGTON AT FORT DUQUESNE (BELOW)

The Granger Collection

The Granger Collection

Pennsylvania State Archives

BETSY ROSS AND THE FIRST AMERICAN FLAG (ABOVE)
STAGECOACH (LEFT)

UNIT THREE

Forming a New Country

"... we have become a nation ..."

from a statement by Dr. Benjamin Rush, 1788
See page 128.

WHY DOES IT MATTER?

In the 1600s, the area that is today Pennsylvania was claimed first by the Swedes, then by the Dutch, and then the English. How did Pennsylvania become part of the United States of America? What role did Pennsylvania play in the creation of a government for the new country? How did our state put its resources to work as the young United States grew?

Read on. As you do, you will discover more of the fascinating and exciting story that is the history of our state.

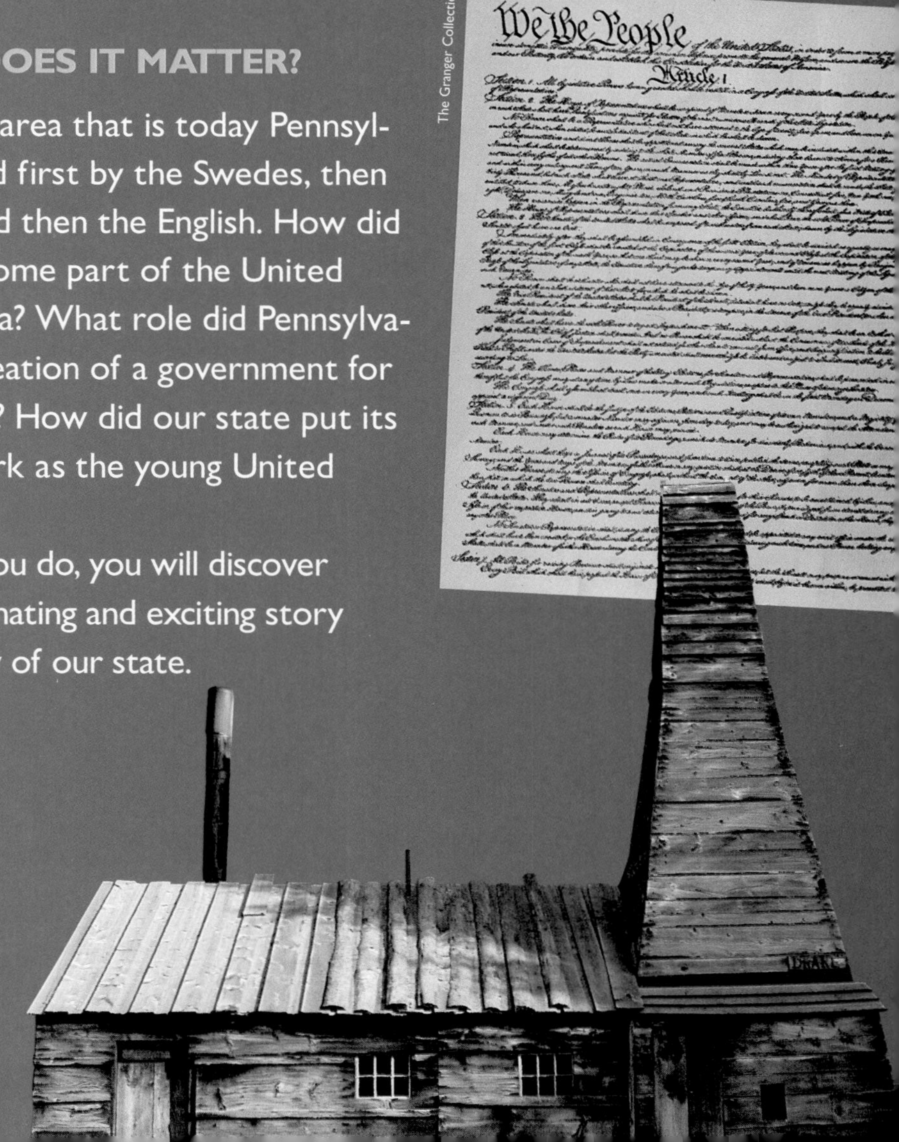

The Granger Collection

UNITED STATES CONSTITUTION (ABOVE RIGHT)
DRAKE OIL WELL (RIGHT)

CHAPTER 5

Birthplace of Independence

THINKING ABOUT GEOGRAPHY AND HISTORY

As more and more Europeans came to Pennsylvania, settlers pushed even further west into the colony. Conflict then arose between the British settlers and the Native Americans and French who also claimed the western lands. When this conflict was finally settled, American colonists began to argue with Great Britain about their rights and freedoms. Read on to discover what part Pennsylvania played in the making of the United States.

1755

PITTSBURGH

Braddock and his army are defeated near Fort Duquesne

1770

PITTSBURGH

The settlement around Fort Pitt grows

1776

PHILADELPHIA

Members of the Second Continental Congress sign the Declaration of Independence

CANADA
Lake Erie
PENNSYLVANIA
Pittsburgh
Valley Forge
Philadelphia
UNITED STATES
ATLANTIC OCEAN
1777
VALLEY FORGE
The Continental Army spends winter at Valley Forge

The Granger Collection

1740 1750 1753 1772 1780

THE FRENCH AND INDIAN WAR

Focus Activity

READ TO LEARN

How did the French and Indian War affect Pennsylvania?

VOCABULARY

French and Indian War
ally
Treaty of Paris

PEOPLE

George Washington
Half King
Edward Braddock
William Pitt
John Forbes
Henry Bouquet

PLACES

Pittsburgh
Fort Duquesne
Great Meadows
Fort Necessity
Fort Pitt
Bushy Run

READ ALOUD

In 1753 a 21-year-old young man from the Virginia colony traveled to western Pennsylvania to deliver a message. The message was given to the commander of a French fort in northwestern Pennsylvania. It asked for the "peaceable departure [leaving]" of French soldiers and trappers from British lands. The French refused to leave. They said that British claims on this land were "sheer imagination, for it belongs to us."

THE BIG PICTURE

By the middle 1700s, both Great Britain and France claimed the land that is today western Pennsylvania. Until that time the Native Americans who lived there had kept both the French and the British from settling near the Ohio River. Then, after fighting amongst themselves and with British settlers, some Native Americans sold their land to the British colonists. To protect their claim to lands in the west, the French built three forts between Lake Erie and the Ohio River. These were named Fort Presque Isle, Fort LeBoeuf (le BOOF), and Fort Machault (ma SHOL). You can find these three forts on the map on the next page.

THE STRUGGLE OVER LAND

George Washington was the 21-year-old Virginian in the Read Aloud. When the French refused to leave, Washington traveled back to Virginia. While crossing the Allegheny River in December 1753, his raft ran into ice. Washington fell into the river and nearly drowned.

Washington had visited the area that is now Pittsburgh. He described it as "extremely well [located] for a fort, as it has the absolute [complete] command of both rivers." British soldiers immediately set out to build a fort there. In April 1754, French soldiers forced them to stop working and head back to Virginia.

Fort Duquesne and Fort Necessity

The French built Fort Duquesne (doo KAYN) at the place where the Allegheny and Monongahela rivers come together. In May 1754, Washington and 120 soldiers set out to capture this fort. They defeated a small group of French soldiers near the fort. However, a larger group of French soon made Washington and his forces flee.

Fort Duquesne (below) was located where Pittsburgh is today.

At a place called Great Meadows, Washington's troops built a small wooden fort called Fort Necessity. A Seneca chief named Half King, who was a guide for the British, called Fort Necessity "that little thing upon the meadow." He saw that it was not strong enough to last through an attack. So Half King and the other Native Americans left before the French arrived. On July 3, 1754, the French attacked Fort Necessity. Washington was forced to surrender in only eight hours.

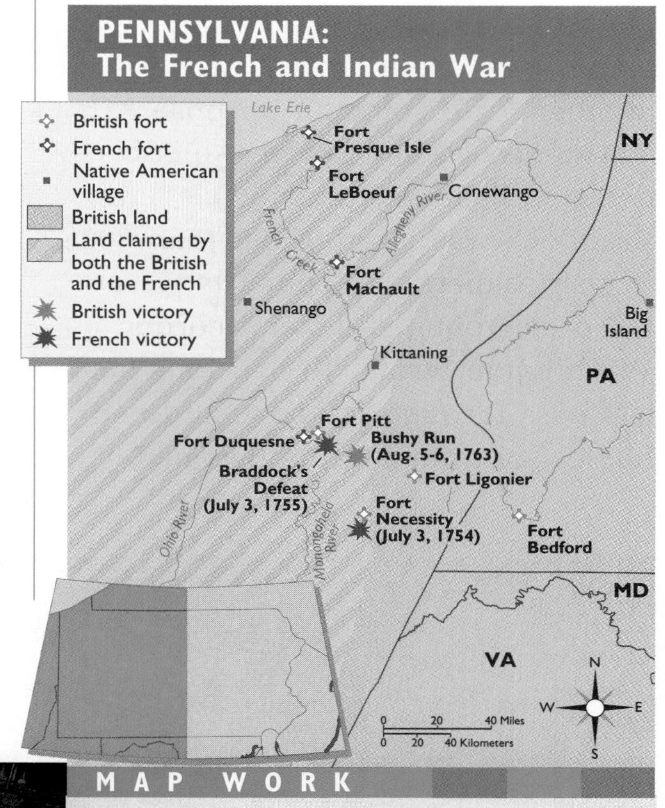

MAP WORK

Both the British and the French built forts in what is today western Pennsylvania.

1. What is the westernmost European settlement shown on the map?
2. How are the sites of Fort Machault and Fort Duquesne similar?

FRANCE AND GREAT BRITAIN AT WAR

The short battle at Fort Necessity in 1754 marked the beginning of the French and Indian War. The war was named for the two groups who fought against the British.

General Braddock's Defeat

In 1755, the British sent another army to capture Fort Duquesne. General Edward Braddock commanded about 2,000 British soldiers and colonists. As part of this army neared Fort Duquesne, the French and their Native American allies attacked it. An ally is a person, country, or group united with another for a common purpose.

The French and Native Americans defeated Braddock's army. General Braddock was killed. More than 800 British soldiers and colonists were killed or wounded. Later George Washington wrote "[I] had four bullets pass through my coat, and two horses shot out from under me."

Britain Wins the War

For several years the war went badly for Britain. Then in 1757, William Pitt became a leader in Great Britain. He sent a powerful army to the colonies to capture Fort Duquesne in 1758. When the British, led by General John Forbes, reached Fort Duquesne, they found it burned to the ground. Outnumbered by the British army, the French soldiers had burned the fort and fled. By 1763, the British declared victory over the French and Indians. The French were forced to sign the Treaty of Paris, giving up all their land in North America.

The Battle of Bushy Run

The British built Fort Pitt at the place where Fort Duquesne had stood. Colonists moved west and began to settle near this new fort.

While the French had been driven from the area, the Native Americans had not. In 1763, Shawnee and Lenape groups who had moved out of Pennsylvania, attacked settlements on the Pennsylvania frontier. Settlers around Fort Pitt were forced to seek protection inside the fort. In July 1763, British troops led by Colonel Henry Bouquet (bo KAY)

General Braddock, shown riding on the cart, was wounded in the battle near Fort Duquesne. He died several days later and was buried in the road his army had created.

set out from Carlisle to aid the settlers at Fort Pitt. On August 5th and 6th, Bouquet's soldiers defeated the Native Americans in a battle at Bushy Run, about 25 miles east of the fort. For many years afterward the Pennsylvania frontier remained peaceful.

Early Pittsburgh

When the Native American attacks on the Pennsylvania frontier ended, thousands of colonists moved west. By 1770, about 5,000 colonists settled south of Fort Pitt.

The settlement at the fort became an important trading post. There was so much trade that one company needed 600 horses to carry goods to and from the east. In 1772, British soldiers left Fort Pitt. The town that grew there became known as Pittsburgh.

WHY IT MATTERS

The French and Indian War ended French claims to lands in western Pennsylvania. After the Battle of Bushy Run, Native Americans no longer kept colonists from settling the area. In the next lesson you will read about the conflict between the colonists and their British rulers.

Historical Artist, Robert Griffing

Thaw Collection, Fenimore House Museum, Cooperstown, N.Y., Photo by John Bigelow Taylor, N.Y.C.

Native Americans came to Fort Pitt to trade. They traded for items such as the metal head of this tomahawk.

Reviewing Facts and Ideas

SUM IT UP

- In the French and Indian War, the British fought against the French and Native Americans.
- In the Treaty of Paris, the French gave up all their lands in North America.
- After the Battle of Bushy Run, Native Americans ended their attacks on settlers on the frontier.

THINK ABOUT IT

1. What two countries claimed land in western Pennsylvania?
2. What are the rivers that came together at Fort Duquesne?
3. **FOCUS** How did the French and Indian War change Pennsylvania?
4. **THINKING SKILL** What *effect* did the Battle of Bushy Run have on the settlement of Pittsburgh?
5. **WRITE** Suppose you are a British leader in 1753. Write a letter for George Washington to deliver to the French in western Pennsylvania asking them to leave.

STUDYSKILLS

Using Reference Sources

VOCABULARY

reference source
dictionary
guide word
encyclopedia
CD-ROM

WHY THE SKILL MATTERS

In the last lesson you read about George Washington, General Edward Braddock, the Treaty of Paris, and the French and Indian War. You might like to find out more about any of these topics—let's say, the French and Indian War.

You could find the information you want in **reference sources**. These are books and other sources that contain facts about many different subjects. They can be found in a special part of the library called the reference section.

USING A DICTIONARY

To begin, you might want to know the exact meaning of the word *treaty*. To find out, you would look in a **dictionary**. A dictionary gives the meanings of words. It shows how to pronounce and spell each word. Sometimes a dictionary explains where a word comes from, or uses it in a sentence. Some dictionaries also provide synonyms, or words with similar meanings.

The words in a dictionary are arranged in alphabetical order. To make your work faster, you can refer to the **guide words**. These appear at the top of each page of the dictionary. They tell you the first and last words that are defined on that page.

Look at the guide words on the sample dictionary page. According to them, what is the last word to be defined on the page? Find the word *treasure*. What does this word mean? Now find the word *treaty*. What does this word mean?

treadmill/trial

treadmill A device turned by animals or persons walking on moving steps or on a belt formed into a loop. Treadmills produce motion to run machines, raise water from wells, and perform other tasks.
tread·mill (tred′mil′) *noun, plural* **treadmills.**

treason The betraying of one's country by helping an enemy. Giving the army's battle plans to the enemy was an act of *treason*.
trea·son (trē′zən) *noun.*

treasure Money, jewels, or other things that are valuable. A chest of gold coins was part of the pirates' *treasure. Noun.*
—To think of as being of great value or importance; cherish. We *treasure* the memory of our grandparents. *Verb.*
treas·ure (trezh′ər) *noun, plural* **treasures;** *verb,* **treasured, treasuring.**

treasurer A person responsible for taking care of the money of a club or business.
treas·ur·er (trezh′ər ər) *noun, plural* **treasurers.**

treasury **1.** The money or other funds of a business, government, or other group. The club paid for a party out of its *treasury*. **2. Treasury.** A department of the government in charge of the country's finances.
treas·ur·y (trezh′ə rē) *noun, plural* **treasuries.**

treat **1.** To behave toward or deal with in a certain way. The principal *treated* the student fairly. **2.** To talk or write about; consider or discuss. The Sunday paper *treats* the week's sports events in detail. **3.** To give medical care to. The doctor *treated* my burned hand with an ointment. **4.** To subject to a process. You can *treat* cloth with a chemical to make it waterproof. **5.** To pay for the entertainment of another person. I will *treat* you to the movie. *Verb.*
—Something that is a special pleasure. Going to the circus was a *treat. Noun.*
treat (trēt) *verb,* **treated, treating;** *noun, plural* **treats.**

treatment **1.** The way something or someone is treated. That scratched record has had rough *treatment*. **2.** The care or medicine used to help cure a sick or injured person. Rest was the recommended *treatment*.
treat·ment (trēt′mənt) *noun, plural* **treatments.**

treaty A formal agreement between countries. A *treaty* was signed to end the war.
trea·ty (trē′tē) *noun, plural* **treaties.**

tree A plant with a single main stem or trunk that is made up of solid, woody tissue. Trees have branches and leaves at a distance above the ground. *Noun.*
—To chase up a tree. The dog *treed* the squirrel. *Verb.*
tree (trē) *noun, plural* **trees;** *verb,* **treed, treeing.**

trellis A frame of crossed strips of wood or metal for a plant to grow on.
trel·lis (trel′is) *noun, plural* **trellises.**

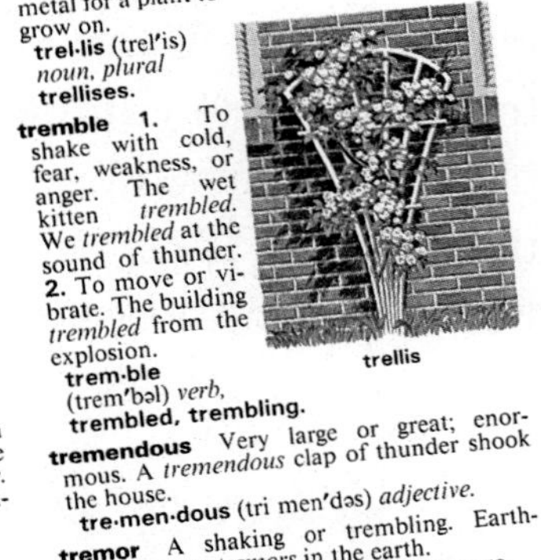
trellis

tremble **1.** To shake with cold, fear, weakness, or anger. The wet kitten *trembled*. We *trembled* at the sound of thunder. **2.** To move or vibrate. The building *trembled* from the explosion.
trem·ble (trem′bəl) *verb,* **trembled, trembling.**

tremendous Very large or great; enormous. A *tremendous* clap of thunder shook the house.
tre·men·dous (tri men′dəs) *adjective.*

tremor A shaking or trembling. Earthquakes cause *tremors* in the earth.
trem·or (trem′ər) *noun, plural* **tremors.**

trench A long, narrow ditch. The soldiers fought from *trenches* in the battlefield.
trench (trench) *noun, plural* **trenches.**

trend A direction or course that seems to be followed; tendency. There is a *trend* toward higher prices in this country.
trend (trend) *noun, plural* **trends.**

trespass To go on another person's property without permission. The swimmers *trespassed* on the private beach. *Verb.*
—A sin. *Noun.*
tres·pass (tres′pəs *or* tres′pas′) *verb,* **trespassed, trespassing;** *noun, plural* **trespasses.**

trestle A framework used to hold up a railroad bridge or other raised structure.
tres·tle (tres′əl) *noun, plural* **trestles.**

tri- A *prefix* that means having or involving three. A *triangle* is a figure with three sides.

trial **1.** The examination of a person accused of a crime in a court of law. **2.** A trying or testing of something. **3.** A test of someone's strength, patience, or faith; hardship. The cold winter was a *trial* for the Pilgrims.
tri·al (trī′əl) *noun, plural* **trials.**

764

USING AN ENCYCLOPEDIA OR A CD-ROM

Another useful reference book is the encyclopedia. This book or set of books gives information about people, places, things, and events. Like a dictionary, the topics in an encyclopedia are arranged in alphabetical order. Most encyclopedias also use guide words.

Let's say you want to learn more about the history of forts. You would look in the volume, or book of the set, with *F* on the spine. Which volume would you look in to learn about Edward Braddock?

A newer kind of reference source is the CD-ROM. This is a compact disc that you "read" with the aid of a computer. Like an encyclopedia, a CD-ROM contains facts about many subjects. It also may include sounds, music, and even short movies! Your teacher or librarian will help you use this type of reference source.

HELPING Yourself

- **Reference sources have information about many subjects.**
- **A dictionary gives the meanings of words. An encyclopedia gives information on people, places, things, and events.**
- **Look up a subject using a key word or title.**

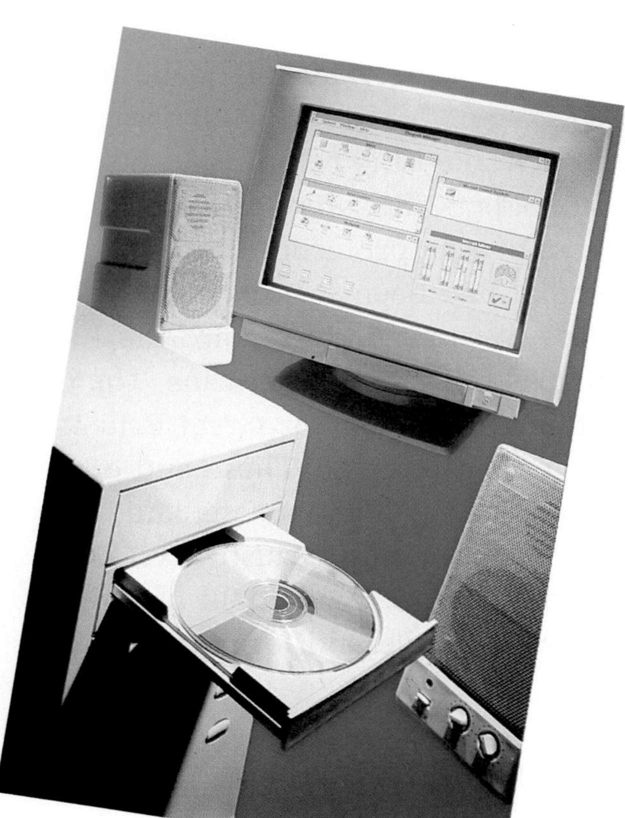

One CD-ROM can contain an entire set of encyclopedias.

TRYING THE SKILL

You have practiced using reference sources. Now suppose that you want to write a report on George Washington. Which reference sources would you use? How would you find the information you need? Use the Helping Yourself box before you begin your report.

REVIEWING THE SKILL

1. What is a reference source?
2. Which reference source or sources would you use to find the meaning of the word *ally*?
3. Some encyclopedias have guide words on their spine instead of letters. Suppose you had a volume covering everything from *automobile* to *button*. Would this volume contain an article about Bushy Run?
4. When are reference sources useful?

1740 1750 1760 1765 1776 1780

PROBLEMS WITH GREAT BRITAIN

Focus Activity

READ TO LEARN

What led the colonies to separate from Great Britain?

VOCABULARY

- tax
- Stamp Act
- boycott
- First Continental Congress
- minuteman
- American Revolution
- Second Continental Congress
- Continental Army
- Declaration of Independence

PEOPLE

- John Dickinson
- King George
- Thomas Paine
- Thomas Jefferson

PLACES

- Carpenters' Hall

READ ALOUD

In 1775 Nicholas Cresswell, an English visitor to western Pennsylvania, wrote, "the people here are liberty [freedom] mad, and nothing but war is thought of."

THE BIG PICTURE

Nicholas Cresswell was writing about a possible war between Great Britain and the American colonies. Since the French and Indian War, problems had been growing between the colonies and Great Britain. Great Britain had spent a great deal of money to send British soldiers to North America to fight in the war. Now it wanted the colonists to help pay for the cost of the war. This made the colonists angry.

Great Britain also wanted the colonists to help pay for the British soldiers that were now in the colonies. These troops were protecting the land along the frontier that had been won from the French. The soldiers were needed to guard the settlers against attacks by Native Americans. The colonists did not think it was fair for Great Britain to make them pay for these things. These and other problems would soon lead Pennsylvanians and other colonists to fight against the new British laws. Some colonists even began to think about breaking away from Great Britain's rule and forming a brand new country.

TAXES AND PROTESTS

To raise money, Great Britain wanted the colonists to pay new taxes. A tax is money people pay to a government. In 1765 Britain passed the Stamp Act. It placed a tax on everything made of paper that was sold in the colonies. This made the colonists angry. They attacked tax offices, burned papers, and destroyed items belonging to tax collectors. Some tax collectors were captured by the colonists. The colonists poured hot, sticky tar over them and then covered the collectors with feathers.

The angry colonists decided that Great Britain could not tax them without their permission. They demanded an end to the Stamp Act, or they would continue to protest, or fight against, it. In 1766 Great Britain ended the Stamp Act.

American colonists fought the Stamp Act by attacking tax collectors' offices.

The Granger Collection

Turning Back the *Polly*

Great Britain continued to put a tax on goods sold in the colonies. In 1767 it placed a tax on tea, paper, and objects made of glass. Pennsylvanians and other Americans decided to boycott these goods. To boycott is to join with others in refusing to buy a product.

In November 1773, the British ship *Polly* sailed up the Delaware River with a shipment of tea. Philadelphians sent a letter to the ship's captain. They warned him that "your arrival here will most assuredly [surely] bring you into hot water [trouble]." When the captain saw thousands of angry colonists in Philadelphia, he decided to sail the ship back to Britain.

The First Continental Congress

On September 5, 1774, leaders from nearly all the 13 English colonies met at Carpenters' Hall in Philadelphia. They wanted to talk about their problems with Great Britain. This meeting is called the First Continental Congress. A congress is a formal meeting to discuss a matter of common interest.

The 56 men who met agreed to stop trade with Britain. They also demanded that the colonies be allowed to make their own laws. To prepare for possible conflict with Britain, the leaders of the colonies decided to ask minutemen to defend the cities. Minutemen were colonists who promised to be ready for battle at a minute's notice.

THE AMERICAN REVOLUTION BEGINS

On April 19, 1775, minutemen and British soldiers fought battles in the Massachusetts colony. This began the American Revolution. A revolution is a sudden, violent, or very great change. You will read about Pennsylvania in the American Revolution in the next lesson.

The Second Continental Congress

In May 1775, leaders of the colonies met again. The Second Continental Congress met at the Pennsylvania State House in Philadelphia. They chose George Washington to lead a new army called the Continental Army.

The congress tried one last time to make peace with Britain. Pennsylvanian John Dickinson wrote a letter to King George. He asked the king to solve their differences. King George refused to read the letter. Angry colonists prepared to break away from Britain.

Thomas Paine

An Englishman named Thomas Paine met Benjamin Franklin in London. The two became friends. Franklin helped Paine get a job as a writer in Philadelphia. In January 1776, Paine published *Common Sense*. This pamphlet gave reasons why the colonies should break away from Britain. "Tis time to part,"

John Dickinson (below, left) wanted the colonies and Britain to work together. *Common Sense* (right) convinced many colonists to break away from Britain. Can you find Ben Franklin at the Second Continental Congress (below)?

COMMON SENSE:
ADDRESSED TO THE
INHABITANTS
OF
AMERICA,
On the following interesting
SUBJECTS.
I. Of the Origin and Design of Government in general, with concise Remarks on the English Constitution.
II. Of Monarchy and Hereditary Succession.
III. Thoughts on the present State of American Affairs.
IV. Of the present Ability of America, with some miscellaneous Reflections.
Written by an ENGLISHMAN.

Man knows no Master save creating HEAVEN,
Or those whom choice and common good ordain.
Thom[illegible]

PHILADELPHIA, Printed
And Sold by R. BELL, in Third-Stre[illegible]

The Granger Collection

Paine wrote, because it made no sense for "a continent to be . . . [ruled] by an island."

The Declaration of Independence

In June 1776, members of the Second Continental Congress decided to write a statement declaring their independence from Britain. They formed a committee to write the Declaration of Independence. Ben Franklin and Thomas Jefferson of Virginia were two committee members. Jefferson was a good writer. He wrote the Declaration of Independence in two days.

Not all members of the congress were ready to be free from British rule. John Dickinson said that declaring independence "would be like destroying our house in winter . . . before we have got another." Most of the other leaders, though, were ready to form a new country. The congress approved the Declaration on July 4, 1776. Those who signed it were breaking British law. Benjamin Franklin joked, "We must all hang together, or [else], we shall all hang separately."

WHY IT MATTERS

On July 8, 1776, the Declaration of Independence was read to the public for the first time in Philadelphia. Today we celebrate Independence Day, July 4th, as the birth of our country. In Philadelphia people dress as colonists and read the Declaration outside Independence Hall.

What was the Pine Creek Declaration of Independence?

On July 4, 1776, settlers along Pine Creek near the present-day town of Avis held a meeting under a huge old elm tree. At the meeting, they declared their own independence from Great Britain. They did not know that on the same day, the Declaration of Independence was being approved in Philadelphia.

Reviewing Facts and Ideas

SUM IT UP

- Colonists fought against the Stamp Act of 1765.
- The First and Second Continental Congresses tried to solve their problems with Great Britain.
- The Declaration of Independence was approved by the Second Continental Congress on July 4, 1776.

THINK ABOUT IT

1. What is a tax?
2. Why did Great Britain want the colonists to pay more taxes?
3. **FOCUS** Why did colonists want to break away from Great Britain?
4. **THINKING SKILL** *Predict* what might have happened if King George had tried to solve Britain's differences with the colonists.
5. **WRITE** Suppose you are on the British ship *Polly*. Write about what happened when you tried to deliver tea to Philadelphia.

CITIZENSHIP VIEWPOINTS

1776: HOW DID PENNSYLVANIANS FEEL ABOUT REBELLING AGAINST GREAT BRITAIN?

The Granger Collection

Many Americans decided they would go against British rule. Here a colonist replaces a British flag with a flag of the thirteen colonies.

In the struggle over British rule in the 13 colonies, colonists in Pennsylvania had different points of view. Some favored rebelling, or resisting Great Britain's control over them. They were known as Patriots. Sarah Morris Mifflin, a Patriot from Philadelphia, believed that rebelling to gain freedom from Britain was worthwhile.

Other Pennsylvanians sided with the British. They were called Loyalists. Many Loyalists had family or friends in Great Britain or were shopkeepers or traders with strong business ties there. Joseph Galloway was an important member of the Pennsylvania government before the American Revolution. He felt, however, that the actions of the Patriots were destroying the rights that the colonists enjoyed.

Some Pennsylvanians did not want to take sides in the rebellion. Deeply-held religious beliefs against the violence of war made Quakers like John Pemberton feel they could not take part in the rebellion. Read the three viewpoints on this issue. Then answer the questions that follow.

Three DIFFERENT Viewpoints

1

JOSEPH GALLOWAY
Pennsylvania lawyer and politician
Excerpt from a pamphlet titled *Candid Examination of the Mutual Claims of Great Britain*, 1775.

[In the colonies there is] freedom of speech [limited], the liberty . . . of the press destroyed, the voice of truth silenced; a lawless power established throughout the Colonies, . . . [and] the Colonies . . . pushing on with . . . madness, in the high-road of . . . rebellion.

2

SARAH MORRIS MIFFLIN
Wife of General Thomas Mifflin of the Continental Army
Excerpt from a letter to a friend in Boston, 1776.

I know this, that as free I can die but once; but as a slave I shall not be worthy of life. I have the pleasure to assure you that these are the [feelings] of my sister Americans. They have sacrificed [gatherings], parties of pleasure, tea-drinkings and finery, to that great spirit of patriotism which [moves] . . . people throughout this . . . country.

3

JOHN PEMBERTON
Quaker church official
Excerpt from a document released by the Quaker church, 1776.

The setting up and putting down [of] Kings and Government is God's [right] . . . and it is not our business to have any hand . . . therein.

BUILDING CITIZENSHIP

THINKING ABOUT VIEWPOINTS

1. What was the viewpoint of each person? How did each one support his or her views?
2. In what ways are some of the viewpoints alike? How are they different?
3. What other viewpoints might colonists have had on this issue?

SHARING VIEWPOINTS

Suppose you and your classmates were colonists in Pennsylvania at the start of the American Revolution. Discuss what you agree with about these viewpoints. Then, as a class, write three statements that all of you could have agreed with about rebelling against Great Britain.

1740 1750 1760 1770 1776 1781

THE AMERICAN REVOLUTION

READ ALOUD

"These are the times that try men's souls." Thomas Paine wrote these words in his pamphlet, "The Crisis," in December 1776. He was talking about the difficult times facing the American Patriots.

THE BIG PICTURE

The American Revolution, also called the Revolutionary War, was not going well for the Americans near the end of 1776. The Continental Army had lost several major battles. Supplies were low. Many American soldiers had only worn-out clothes and shoes. General Washington was afraid that his men would simply quit fighting and go home.

Then Washington came up with a plan. On December 25, 1776, American soldiers crossed the icy Delaware River near New Hope, Pennsylvania. They landed at Trenton, New Jersey. There they surprised a group of German soldiers, called Hessians. The Hessians had been hired by Britain to fight in America. The attack captured hundreds of Hessian soldiers, who had not expected an attack on Christmas. The Battle of Trenton was a complete success for the Americans. It helped keep the war effort in America alive. In this lesson you will read about Pennsylvania's important part in the war.

Focus Activity

READ TO LEARN

What role did Pennsylvania play in the American Revolution?

VOCABULARY

Battle of Trenton
Battle of Brandywine
Battle of Germantown
Great Runaway

PEOPLE

William Howe
Martha Washington
Baron Von Steuben
Mary Hays
Betsy Ross
Haym Salomon
Anthony Wayne
James Forten

PLACES

New Hope
Trenton
Brandywine Creek
Valley Forge

THE WAR IN PENNSYLVANIA

Philadelphia was the capital of the thirteen colonies. In the summer of 1777, British General William Howe decided to attack Philadelphia. Howe brought his troops to Maryland by boat. Then he marched his troops north toward Philadelphia. Washington and the Continental Army were waiting along Brandywine Creek, near Chadds Ford. On September 11, both armies fought in the Battle of Brandywine. Washington's troops lost the fight. The British then marched into Philadelphia on September 26.

On October 4, 1777, at the Battle of Germantown, Washington hoped to drive the British out of Pennsylvania. Again, the American troops were beaten. They then fled to their winter camp at Valley Forge.

Many soldiers in the Continental Army had not been properly trained before fighting in the Battle of Brandywine.

The British in Philadelphia

Once Howe's troops entered Philadelphia, they stopped chasing the American army. British officers enjoyed the city's horse races, dances, and parties. When Benjamin Franklin was told that General Howe had captured Philadelphia, he disagreed. "No," Franklin said, "Philadelphia has captured Howe." Philadelphia's Loyalists even threw a giant party for Howe when the general was called back to Britain in April 1778. The party included soldiers dressed as knights, marching bands, and fireworks.

THE AMERICAN REVOLUTION IN PENNSYLVANIA, 1777–1778

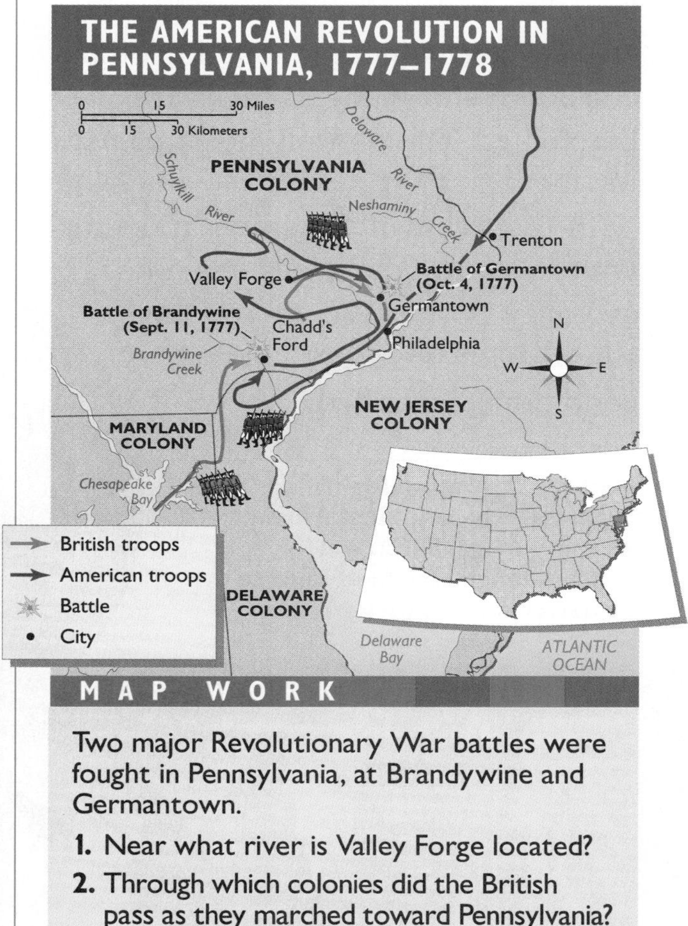

MAP WORK

Two major Revolutionary War battles were fought in Pennsylvania, at Brandywine and Germantown.

1. Near what river is Valley Forge located?
2. Through which colonies did the British pass as they marched toward Pennsylvania?

VALLEY FORGE

The soldiers who marched to Valley Forge were hungry and cold. Washington wrote, "You might have tracked the army . . . by the blood of their feet."

A Bitter Winter

When the troops arrived at Valley Forge, George Washington ordered them to pitch their tents. Then he had them cut down trees and build log huts in which 12 men could sleep. Some soldiers used their tents as blankets. Others cut the tents into strips and wrapped their bare feet and legs with them.

When Martha Washington came to Valley Forge she wrote, "The poor soldiers are without [enough] clothing and food, and many of them are barefooted. Oh how my heart pains for them."

In the following passage, a doctor with the army describes the food at Valley Forge. Would you have stayed with the army under the conditions described?

Excerpt from the diary of Connecticut Doctor Albigence Waldo, in December 1777.

December 21 [1777]. . . . A general cry through the camp this evening among the soldiers, "No meat! No meat!". . . .

"What have you for your dinner, boys?"

*"Nothing but **fire cake** and water, sir."*

fire cake: thin bread made of water and flour

Martha Washington (right) supported the Continental Army. At Valley Forge, Baron von Steuben taught the Americans to be better soldiers (below).

The Granger Collection

Help from Europe

To make the Americans better soldiers, Washington called upon Baron Friedrich Wilhelm August von Steuben (STOO buhn). Von Steuben was a skilled soldier from Prussia, a country that is now part of Germany. At Valley Forge, he taught the Americans how to use their weapons and fight better.

The Americans also received help from France. Ben Franklin traveled to France to ask French leaders to send troops and money to help fight the British. In the spring of 1778, the French agreed.

PENNSYLVANIA'S ROLE IN THE REVOLUTION

Pennsylvania did much to help the Americans during the war. Many Pennsylvanians joined the Continental Army. Some African Americans from the colony fought on the Patriot side. Enslaved blacks were promised their freedom if they joined the army. Other African Americans fought for the British, who made the same promise. Most of the colony's Quakers did not join in the war. Their religious beliefs did not allow fighting. You can read about some Pennsylvania Patriots in the Infographic on page 122.

Resources for the Soldiers

Pennsylvania's rich resources were especially needed by the Continental Army. Iron from the colony was used to make cannons and cannonballs. This resource was so important that captured Hessian soldiers were forced to work in the iron mines. Lead, mined near what is today Altoona, was used to make rifle balls. German craftspeople from Lancaster and York made Pennsylvania rifles. And Pennsylvania farmers grew much of the wheat that fed the American troops.

The War on the Pennsylvania Frontier

After the battles of Brandywine and Germantown, no more major battles were fought between the British and the American troops in Pennsylvania. However, fighting did continue in northern and western Pennsylvania between Native Americans and settlers. The Native Americans helped the British and Loyalist soldiers in return for gifts and weapons.

In the summer of 1778, some Delaware and Seneca joined Loyalists from the New York colony. They attacked the Wyoming Valley, near what is today Wilkes-Barre. Scared settlers fled south, taking only what they could carry. This flight is known as the "**Great Runaway**."

In the summer of 1779, an American army headed north from Pennsylvania into New York. It destroyed 40 villages of Native Americans who had attacked the Wyoming Valley. Washington told the army to "ruin their [the Native Americans'] crops now in the ground and prevent their planting more." The New York Indians did not make another major attack into Pennsylvania during the rest of the war.

Revolutionary War cannons like this one were made with iron mined in Pennsylvania.

Infographic

Pennsylvania Patriots

Many Pennsylvanians, both men and women, played important roles in the American Revolution. Thousands of Pennsylvanians became soldiers and fought for freedom. How else did Pennsylvanians take part in the war?

The Granger Collection

The Granger Collection

Mary Hays of Carlisle became known as "Molly Pitcher" because she carried water to the soldiers during the Battle of Monmouth in New Jersey in June, 1778. During this battle, her husband, William, was wounded and Mary took his place on the battlefield loading and firing a cannon.

Carlisle

Haym Salomon was a Polish Jew who became a banker in New York and then Philadelphia. He loaned his personal fortune to the Continental Congress to help in the war.

General Anthony Wayne was born near Paoli. He earned the nickname, "Mad Anthony," for his bravery in battle. When Wayne was hit in the head by a bullet in battle he called out, "Carry me up to the fort, boys. Let's go forward."

Betsy Ross of Philadelphia is believed to have helped design and sew the first American flag for George Washington.

James Forten was a free African American in Philadelphia. After being captured by the British, Forten was offered freedom in Britain. He refused, saying "No, I'm a prisoner for my country, and I'll never be a traitor [cheater] to her."

WHY IT MATTERS

After the battles in Pennsylvania, much of the fighting of the American Revolution moved to the southern colonies. In 1781 the war finally ended. Pennsylvania became part of a new country—the United States of America. Now the 13 states had to create a plan for their new government which would run the country.

Reviewing Facts and Ideas

SUM IT UP

- American losses at the battles of Brandywine and Germantown in 1777 allowed the British forces to capture Philadelphia.
- The Continental Army spent the cold winter of 1777–1778 at Valley Forge training and resting.
- Pennsylvania supplied resources to the Patriots during the war, including iron, lead, and wheat.

THINK ABOUT IT

1. What was the "Great Runaway"?
2. Describe what the winter of 1777–1778 was like for the troops at Valley Forge.
3. **FOCUS** How did Pennsylvania help in the American Revolution?
4. **THINKING SKILL** Why did General Washington <u>decide</u> to cross the Delaware River with the Continental Army?
5. **GEOGRAPHY** Look at the map on page 119. Why do you think the Americans chose to fight at Brandywine Creek in September 1777?

CHAPTER 5 REVIEW

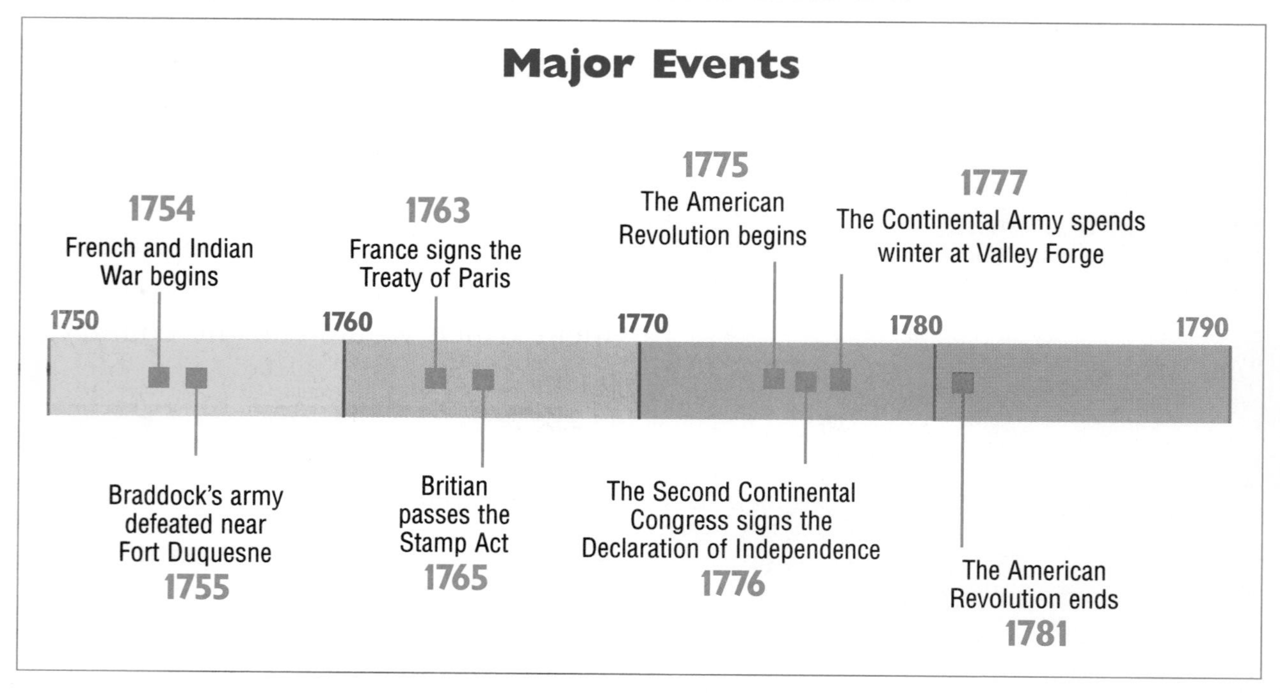

THINKING ABOUT VOCABULARY

Number a sheet of paper from 1 to 5. Beside each number write the word or term from the list below that best completes the sentence.

ally
Battle of Trenton
boycott
Declaration of Independence
Treaty of Paris

1. To _______ is to join with others in refusing to buy a product.
2. In 1763 the French were forced to sign the _______.
3. On July 4, 1776, the members of the Second Continental Congress signed the _______.
4. The Continental Army crossed the Delaware River and won the _______ in New Jersey.
5. An _______ is a person, country, or group united with another for a common purpose.

THINKING ABOUT FACTS

1. What was the importance of the battle at Fort Necessity in 1754?
2. Who took part in the Battle of Bushy Run, and how did the battle affect the Pennsylvania frontier?
3. Why did the British government tax the American colonists following the French and Indian War?
4. What happened to the British ship *Polly*?
5. What did the American colonists think about the Stamp Act?
6. What problems were discussed at the First Continental Congress in 1774?
7. Why did British General William Howe stay in Philadelphia?
8. What did Washington's troops do at Valley Forge?
9. Why was Baron Von Steuben important to the Continental Army?
10. What was the Great Runaway?

THINK AND WRITE

WRITING A NEWSPAPER ARTICLE

Suppose you are a reporter during the French and Indian War. Write a newspaper article describing the battles.

WRITING A LETTER

Write a letter from the colonies to King George explaining why you think the Stamp Act of 1765 is unfair.

WRITING A LIST

Write a list of some of the resources from Pennsylvania that were needed by American soldiers. Then explain how each one was used to help the army.

APPLYING STUDY SKILLS

USING REFERENCE SOURCES

1. What are reference sources? Name three different kinds.
2. Which reference source would you use to learn more about Half King?
3. Suppose the guide words on a dictionary page are *floor* and *flounder*. Would the word *flute* be found on the page?
4. Suppose you wanted to listen to and watch a re-creation of the winter at Valley Forge. Which kind of reference would you use?
5. How might reference sources be helpful when you are studying history?

Summing Up The Chapter

Use the following time line to organize information from the chapter. Copy the time line on a piece of paper. Then fill in a major event from our state's history for each date on the time line. When you have filled in the time line, use the information to write an answer to the question,"What were some of the important events in Pennsylvania that led to the independence of the United States?"

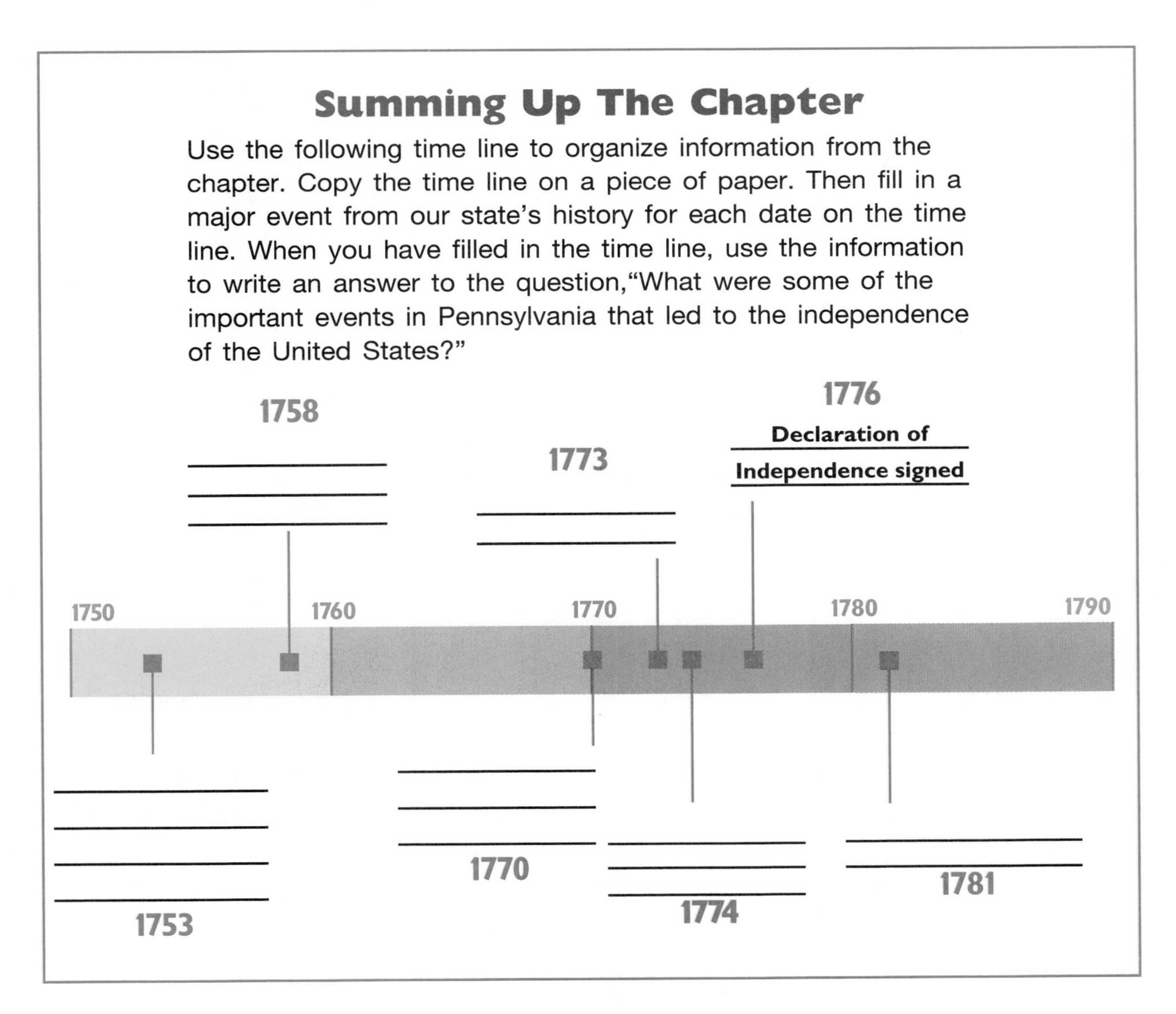

CHAPTER

6

Pennsylvania and the New Country

THINKING ABOUT GEOGRAPHY AND HISTORY

You have read how the American Revolution was won and the United States became an independent country. In this chapter you will learn about Pennsylvania's role in forming our country's government. You will also read about the early growth of our state's industry, farming, and transportation.

1787

PHILADELPHIA

A new government for the United States is created at the Constitutional Convention

1829

CARBONDALE

The *Stourbridge Lion* is the first steam locomotive to run on tracks in the United States

1840

CARLISLE

The McCormick reaper is used for the first time in Pennsylvania

CANADA
Lake Erie
Titusville
Carbondale
PENNSYLVANIA
Carlisle
Philadelphia
UNITED STATES
ATLANTIC OCEAN
1859
TITUSVILLE
The country's first successful oil well is drilled

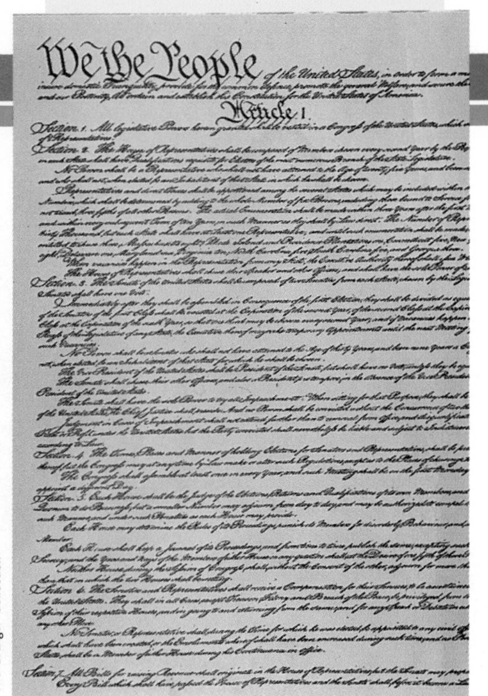
We the People
Article. I.

The Granger Collection

A NEW GOVERNMENT

READ ALOUD

"'Tis done, we have become a nation." When Dr. Benjamin Rush of Philadelphia wrote this in 1788, he did not mean only that the United States had won independence from Great Britain. He meant that the 13 new states had agreed on a plan of government to unite them.

Focus Activity

READ TO LEARN

How was Pennsylvania important in the creation of the Constitution of the United States?

VOCABULARY

Constitution
Constitutional Convention
delegate

PEOPLE

Robert Morris
James Madison
Eliza Powel
Gouverneur Morris

PLACES

Philadelphia
Washington, D.C.

THE BIG PICTURE

The years just after the American Revolution were exciting for our new country. The 13 colonies had won freedom and independence from Great Britain. They were now states. With this freedom came new responsibilities. In the beginning, each state worked mainly on its own government. Some Americans soon decided that a stronger government was needed for the whole country.

In 1787, a meeting was held at the Pennsylvania State House in Philadelphia. The group that met there talked about how the United States government should work. They wrote our country's plan of government, or Constitution. This historic event became known as the Constitutional Convention.

MEETING IN PHILADELPHIA

Each state was invited to send delegates, or representatives, to the "Grand Convention," which was to begin May 14. Many delegates did not arrive by that date. It was a rainy spring, and the roads were muddy, making travel slow. George Washington was a delegate from Virginia. When he arrived, there were parades and celebrations. While in Philadelphia, Washington stayed in the three-story, brick house of Robert Morris. Morris was a Pennsylvania delegate and a friend of Washington's from the Revolutionary War.

On May 25, the convention finally began. Twenty-nine delegates from seven states had arrived. All of Pennsylvania's delegates, except Benjamin Franklin, were there. Franklin's poor health forced him to miss some of the meetings.

The Constitutional Convention

The delegates met each day in the Pennsylvania State House to discuss their plans for a new government. Virginia delegate James Madison took notes of everything that was said. He wrote later: "I chose a seat in front. . . . In this favorable position for hearing all that passed, I noted what was read from the chair or spoken by members." This was a great task, as the delegates spoke from May to September.

How did Benjamin Franklin travel to the Constitutional Convention?

Most delegates to the Convention arrived by coach or on horseback. At 81, Ben Franklin was the oldest delegate to the meeting. Although he lived in Philadelphia, his age and health made it difficult for him to get around. So he traveled in a special chair that he had brought back from a visit to Paris. This chair had glass windows and was carried on long poles. Four men carried the chair, with Franklin inside, from his home to the meeting room. Philadelphia had never seen anything like it.

Robert Morris was one of eight Pennsylvania delegates to the Constitutional Convention.

The Granger Collection

CREATING A NEW GOVERNMENT

The delegates to the convention decided to keep their talks secret. The doors and windows to the Statehouse were kept closed. The delegates were not allowed to tell anyone about what was said. They couldn't even write letters home about the convention to their families.

Some Philadelphians tried to make the delegates more comfortable. Eliza Powel, wife of Philadelphia leader Samuel Powel, held parties for the delegates. In the following excerpt, children's author Jean Fritz describes what Philadelphia was like for the delegates. Would you like to have been part of the convention?

Excerpt from *Shh! We're Writing the Constitution* written by Jean Fritz in 1987.

Meanwhile the people in Philadelphia did their best to keep the delegates happy. They entertained them, provided musicals, and so they could work in peace and quiet, they covered the cobblestone street in front of the State House with gravel. Now carriages made less noise when they rolled past.

But there were some things Philadelphians couldn't change. The heat for instance.

The Constitution

While all of the delegates agreed that a new government was needed for the country, they did not agree on how it should work. Arguments during the convention grew very heated. Some delegates feared the meeting would break up. By September, however, the disagreements had been solved. Gouverneur Morris, another delegate from Pennsylvania, is believed to have written the Constitution. On September 17, the delegates signed the document.

In June 1788, nine states had approved the Constitution. The new government would now be able to start. On the Fourth of July, Philadelphia held a gigantic celebration in honor of the government that had been created there. A parade one and a half miles long included an American warship set on wheels. Seventeen thousand people attended a picnic following the parade.

The Granger Collection

Philadelphia: National Capital

Pennsylvanians were honored that the Constitutional Convention was held in Philadelphia. Philadelphia had been the capital during the American Revolution. Several years later, in 1790, Philadelphia was honored again. Our country's capital, which had been located in New York, was returned to Philadelphia for ten years. In 1800, the United States built a new capital along the Potomac River, which we now call **Washington, D.C.**

In the Legacy on page 132, you will read about how much of the history of Philadelphia has been saved for us to learn about.

The Granger Collection

Benjamin Franklin and George Washington were among the famous Americans present at the Constitutional Convention (left). Philadelphia (above) was a large busy city when it served as our country's capital in the 1790s.

WHY IT MATTERS

The plan of government written by the delegates to the Constitutional Convention in 1787 is the same one that we use in the United States today. You will read more about how our state and country's governments work in Chapter 10. In the next lessons, you will read about the growth of our state's economy in the early 1800s.

Reviewing Facts and Ideas

SUM IT UP

- The Constitutional Convention was held in Philadelphia in 1787.
- Delegates from different states worked together to write a plan of government for our country.
- The Constitution is still our plan of government today.
- The United States built Washington, D.C. in 1800 to be our country's new capital.

THINK ABOUT IT

1. Where did the Constitutional Convention take place?
2. How was Philadelphia honored in 1790?
3. **FOCUS** What role did Pennsylvania play in the creation of the Constitution of the United States?
4. **THINKING SKILL** *Predict* what might have happened if all of the delegates had refused to work together and had gone home.
5. **WRITE** Write a newspaper article describing the opening of the Constitutional Convention in Philadelphia.

Legacy

LINKING PAST AND PRESENT

PHILADELPHIA RESTORED

As you know, history is the study of the past. The restored buildings at Independence National Historical Park in Philadelphia are a living history for all to visit.

During the 1940s, people noticed that many historic buildings in Philadelphia were in poor condition. Some, like the Pennsylvania State House where both the Declaration of Independence and Constitution were signed, were nearly 200 years old. People thought that if the buildings disappeared, part of our history would disappear with them. So in 1948 the United States government decided to restore and protect some important buildings. Carpenters, painters, and other workers made the buildings look almost new.

Today Independence Hall, as the Pennsylvania State House was renamed, is the centerpiece of the park. In all, the park has 26 sites. Perhaps you will visit them someday and explore our state's important part in the making of our country.

The Second Continental Congress met in what is now called Independence Hall. It was here that the Declaration of Independence was adopted on July 4, 1776.

Philadelphia was the capital of the United States from 1790 to 1800. At the time part of the country's government met in this room in Congress Hall to take care of United States business.

George Washington sat in this chair during the Constitutional Convention in 1787. Benjamin Franklin thought that the carving of a rising sun on the back of the chair stood for the future of the United States.

This silver inkstand was used at the signing of both the Declaration of Independence and the Constitution of the United States.

1765 1852 1860

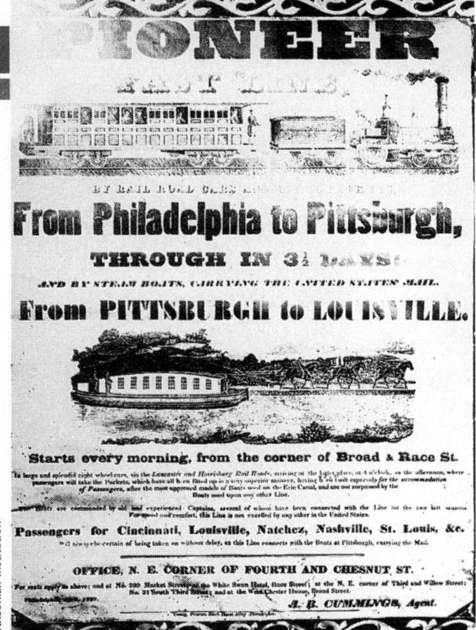

Smithsonian Institution

STEAMBOATS, CANALS, TURNPIKES, AND RAILROADS

Focus Activity

READ TO LEARN

How did new forms of transportation change life in Pennsylvania?

VOCABULARY

transportation
steamboat
canal
turnpike
Stourbridge Lion

PEOPLE

John Fitch
Robert Fulton

PLACES

Wrightsville
Carbondale
Honesdale

READ ALOUD

In 1842 English writer Charles Dickens traveled across Pennsylvania by canal and railroad. He wrote later about part of his railroad trip: "It was very pretty traveling thus, at a rapid pace along the heights of the mountain . . . , to look down into a valley full of light and softness; catching glimpses, through the tree tops, of scattered cabins."

THE BIG PICTURE

As our state grew larger, people needed better **transportation**. Transportation is a way to move goods and people from one place to another. By the early 1800s new means of transportation were making travel much easier.

In 1787 on the Delaware River, **John Fitch** ran the first **steamboat** in Pennsylvania. A steamboat had a large paddle wheel. It was powered by a steam engine. Steamboats could travel against the flow of a river's current. By 1788, steamboats took people from Philadelphia to several cities in New Jersey, including Burlington and Trenton.

STEAMBOATS AND CANALS

Robert Fulton was born in 1765 in Little Britain near Lancaster. He went to Europe to earn a living as a painter, but he failed. Fulton then decided to build a steamship.

When Fulton returned to America, he got right to work. "I now have shipbuilders, blacksmiths, and carpenters," he wrote, building "my steamboat." Fulton completed his first boat in 1807. In 1811 one of his ships, the *New Orleans*, became the first steamboat in Pittsburgh. Soon it was running up and down the Ohio and Mississippi rivers.

Canals

During the early 1800s, several canals were built in our state. A canal is an inland waterway built for transportation. Canals saved people a lot of money. They also shortened the travel time from Philadelphia to Pittsburgh from 23 days to 4 days.

To build a canal, the land had to be cleared of trees and rocks. The road also had to be flattened. Then a channel wide and deep enough for a boat to travel was dug. When the canal was finished, it was filled with water from a nearby river.

Canal boats were not powered by steam or sail. They were pulled by mules or oxen. These animals walked along a path at the side of the canal.

In 1834, the Pennsylvania Main Line was finished. Look at the map to see what cities it connected.

PENNSYLVANIA CANALS, 1840

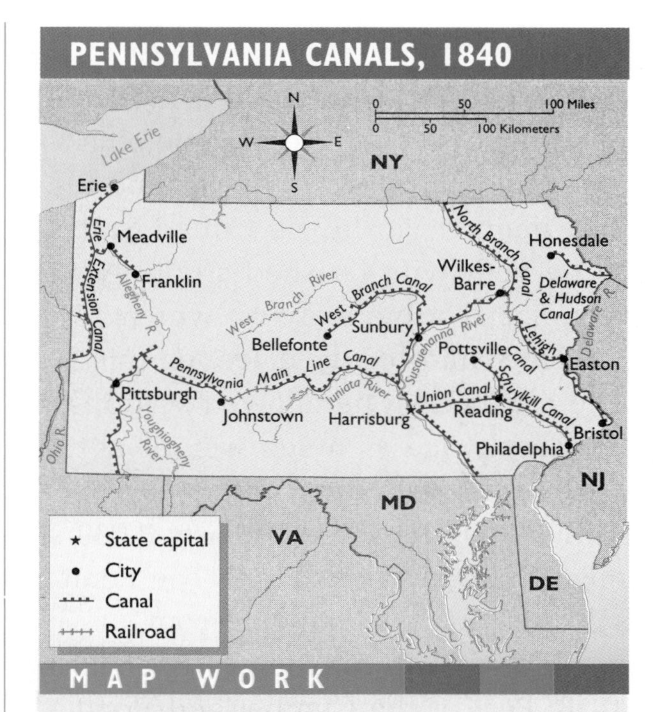

MAP WORK

By the 1840s, Pennsylvania had nearly 1,000 miles of canals.

1. Which canal ran to Lake Erie?
2. Which canal would you have traveled to get from Philadelphia to Pittsburgh?
3. Why do you think few canals were built in northern Pennsylvania?

To get over our state's mountains, canal boats were pulled out of the water and put on rail cars.

Pennsylvania State Archives

TRAVEL OVERLAND

Early roads were made out of hardened dirt. In 1794 the Philadelphia and Lancaster **Turnpike** became the first major road in the United States to be built with crushed stone. A turnpike is a highway on which travelers had to pay a fee, or toll. The crushed stone allowed wagons to carry twice as much weight as they could on a dirt road.

By 1830, there were nearly 3,000 miles of road in our state. The Pennsylvania Road, which ran from **Wrightsville** to Pittsburgh, opened in 1818. Part of the Cumberland Road, which ran from Cumberland, Maryland, to Illinois, cut through western Pennsylvania. On that road, a toll of four cents was charged for a horse and rider. A wagon could be charged as much as 18 cents. It cost 12 cents to move 20 cattle along the road. Look at the map and find the Cumberland Road.

PENNSYLVANIA TURNPIKES, EARLY 1800s

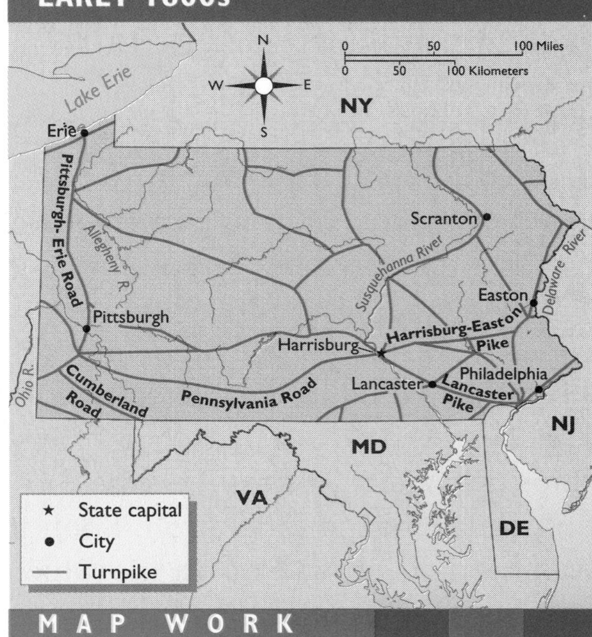

MAP WORK

By the 1830s, most major Pennsylvania towns were connected by roads.

1. Which road connected Philadelphia and Lancaster?
2. Name one road that ran west from Harrisburg.
3. Which road do you think carried the most traffic in the early 1800s? Why?

Links to MATHEMATICS

Paying the Toll!

On the Cumberland Road, moving 20 sheep or hogs cost 6 cents. Use this information, along with that given in the text above, to figure out the following problem about a farmer taking his animals to market.

A farmer on his horse is moving 60 cattle, 100 hogs, and 20 sheep on the Cumberland Road. What will be his toll?

Railroads

On August 8, 1829, the first steam train to travel on rails in the United States was run in Pennsylvania. The English-built *Stourbridge Lion* made its test run between the towns of **Carbondale** and **Honesdale**. Horatio Allen, the driver and only person on the train, later remembered, "When the cheers of the onlookers died out as I left them on the memorable trip, the only sound to greet my ears until my safe return, in addition to that of the exhaust steam, was that of the creaking of the [wooden rails]." The *Stourbridge Lion* never made another trip. It was too heavy for the tracks then being used.

Within a few years, railroads were begun in several parts of our state and all along the eastern part of the United States. Railroads were important because they made journeys faster. They also created jobs for people.

In some places, railroads put canals out of business. In 1852 it took only 15 hours to travel by train between Pittsburgh and Philadelphia. The train followed the same route as the Pennsylvania Main Line Canal, which took four days. Canal boats could not compete with the speed of trains.

The Horseshoe Curve was built in the mid-1800s near Altoona to help trains climb our state's mountains.

WHY IT MATTERS

In the early 1800s, new forms of transportation made it possible to travel greater distances more quickly. They also lowered the cost of transportation. As you will read in the next lesson, transportation helped industry in our state to grow.

Reviewing Facts and Ideas

SUM IT UP

- John Fitch and Robert Fulton built some of the earliest steamboats that ran in Pennsylvania.
- The invention of steamboats in the late 1700s aided water travel on some Pennsylvania rivers.
- The Pennsylvania Main Line Canal shipped goods cheaper and faster than overland.
- The Philadelphia and Lancaster Turnpike and the Pennsylvania Road improved travel by road.
- The *Stourbridge Lion* was the first steam train to run on rails in our country in 1829.

THINK ABOUT IT

1. How did the steamboat improve transportation in our state?
2. What is a canal?
3. **FOCUS** How did new transportation change life in Pennsylvania?
4. **THINKING SKILL** *Compare* and *contrast* the building of canals and railroads in Pennsylvania.
5. **GEOGRAPHY** Look at the maps of Pennsylvania's canals and roads. Why do you think some of the routes on both are similar?

The Granger Collection

LESSON 3

1780 1800 1860

GROWTH OF PENNSYLVANIA'S INDUSTRY

READ ALOUD

In 1800, Englishman John Bernard was visiting Pittsburgh. He described the city as: "A cloud of smoke hung over it in an exceedingly [very] clear sky, ... Instead of wood they here use coal, mines of which are plentiful in the neighborhood."

Focus Activity

READ TO LEARN

What industries grew in Pennsylvania after the American Revolution?

VOCABULARY

industry
bituminous coal
coke
anthracite coal
boom town
textile
population

PEOPLE

Samuel Kier
Edwin L. Drake
Stephen Smith

PLACES

Titusville

THE BIG PICTURE

The smoke that hung over Pittsburgh was from the burning of coal in the town's homes and factories. Coal was used to heat homes. It was also used to run the machinery in Pittsburgh's growing **industries**. An industry is all the businesses that make one kind of goods. Following the American Revolution, industries grew all over Pennsylvania. One reason for that growth was our state's plentiful supply of coal. Coal could be burned to power steam engines. That meant that factories no longer needed to be located near running water to run their machinery. The improvements in transportation that you read about in the last lesson also helped industries to grow. Goods could now be shipped all over our country more easily.

KING COAL

Pennsylvania was rich in coal. A visitor to our state in 1803 wrote, "The whole region [is filled with] coal, which lies almost on the surface. The banks of the river opposite to Pittsburgh, and on each side . . . appear to be one entire body of coal."

Black Diamonds

Pennsylvania had two types of coal. **Bituminous** [bi TOO mih nus] **coal**, also known as soft coal, was found mostly in western Pennsylvania. When burned in an open fire, it produces much smoke. Soft coal could be heated in an oven that has very little air in it to make a gray-black solid fuel called **coke**. Coke is needed to make iron, so many iron mills opened in western Pennsylvania near the coal mines.

Anthracite [AN thruh sit] **coal**, or hard coal, was mostly found in eastern Pennsylvania. When burned, it makes a very hot fire with very little smoke. Industries that needed great heat, such as glass-making and brick-making, began to use anthracite coal.

Coal was also used in Pennsylvania homes. In Pittsburgh in 1808, two dollars bought enough coal to keep two fires, one for heat and one for cooking, burning constantly for a month. In 1831, a Philadelphia newspaper reported that $4.50 worth of coal would last for the winter. Firewood for the winter cost $21.00.

Coal was so valuable in Pennsylvania that it was sometimes called "black diamonds." Before 1860, our state produced almost all of the anthracite and about half of the bituminous coal in the United States.

Anthracite coal was dug from this coal mine near Summit Hill.

OIL AND OTHER INDUSTRIES

For many years, Pennsylvanians had seen oil seeping up from the ground, but no one knew what to do with it. In the 1850s, **Samuel Kier** of Pittsburgh found a way to change oil so it could be burned in lamps to light homes. People then realized that oil could be valuable.

It's a Gusher!

In 1859, New Yorker **Edwin L. Drake** hired workers to dig a well near **Titusville**. One morning, he saw some black liquid around the well. "What's that?" Drake asked. "That's your fortune!" a worker answered as a fountain of oil, or gusher, spouted from the ground.

Almost overnight, oil towns such as Oil City and Petroleum Center sprang up all over the northwest corner of Pennsylvania. Towns like these, which grow quickly, are called **boom towns**.

Other Important Industries

The **textile**, or clothmaking, industry was also important in Pennsylvania. Steam-powered machines for making yarn and thread and for weaving cloth and carpets increased production. The very first carpet factory in the United States was built in Philadelphia. Even with the new machinery, the factories still needed thousands of workers. They hired mostly women and children who worked up to twelve hours a day, six days a week.

From the collection of the Drake Well Museum

The Drake oil well near Titusville was the first of many wells in northwest Pennsylvania.

In addition to textiles, Philadelphia was a leader in shipbuilding. By 1860, Pennsylvania led the country in the production of textiles, iron, leather, and lumber.

Pennsylvania's Workers

The growth of industries brought large numbers of immigrants to Pennsylvania. Between 1820 and 1860, the state's **population** nearly tripled from one million to about three million people. Population is the number of people who live in a place or area. Many of the immigrants during this period were from Ireland and Germany. They filled many new jobs.

Few of these new jobs in industry were given to African Americans. However, African Americans became skilled workers, like barbers, shoemakers, hat makers, bakers, and builders. Others worked as day laborers, waiters, and sailors. Some African Americans ran their own businesses selling food on the street. They sold oysters, clams, pepperpot soup, and other food items.

Still other African Americans went into business buying and selling lumber and coal. **Stephen Smith** made his fortune in this way. By 1860 he was one of the wealthiest people in the town of Columbia. Smith gave a lot of money to charities, including $250,000 to a home for older African Americans.

Lumber merchant Stephen Smith may have been the richest African American in the United States during his time.

The Historical Society of Pennsylvania

WHY IT MATTERS

During the early 1800s, coal helped industry in our state to grow rapidly. New forms of transportation made it possible to bring natural resources to factories and finished goods from factory to market. In the next chapter, you will read about how Pennsylvanians worked to improve life for our state's growing population.

Reviewing Facts and Ideas

SUM IT UP

- Pennsylvania mined large amounts of bituminous and anthracite coal. Coal helped industries within our state grow rapidly.
- After Samuel Kier learned how to make oil usable in lamps, the oil industry in our state boomed.
- By 1860, Pennsylvania led the nation in the production of textiles, iron, and leather.
- Pennsylvania's population increased in the first half of the 1800s, with many new immigrants from Ireland and Germany.

THINK ABOUT IT

1. What is an industry?
2. Why did Pennsylvania's population grow in the early 1800s?
3. **FOCUS** What were some important Pennsylvania industries in the early 1800s?
4. **THINKING SKILL** *Compare* and *contrast* the uses of bituminous coal and anthracite coal.
5. **GEOGRAPHY** Why do you think iron mills were located in areas near coal mines?

STUDYSKILLS

Reading Circle and Line Graphs

VOCABULARY
graph
circle graph
line graph

WHY THE SKILL MATTERS

In the last lesson you read about immigration to Pennsylvania in the early 1800s. One way to understand who the different groups of immigrants were is to read a graph. Graphs are special diagrams that show a lot of information in a clear way. They can help you make conclusions. By presenting facts in a picture, they tell you a lot with only a few words.

USING A CIRCLE GRAPH

Look at the graph on this page. It is a circle graph. This kind of graph can show you how the parts of something make up or fit into the whole. A circle graph is sometimes called a pie graph or pie chart because each part may look like a slice of pie.

Read the title of the graph. The circle graph shows the number of immigrants who lived in Pennsylvania in 1850.

The "slices" show the number of people from different countries. You can tell that the largest number of immigrants to Pennsylvania came from Ireland because this is the largest "slice" on the graph.

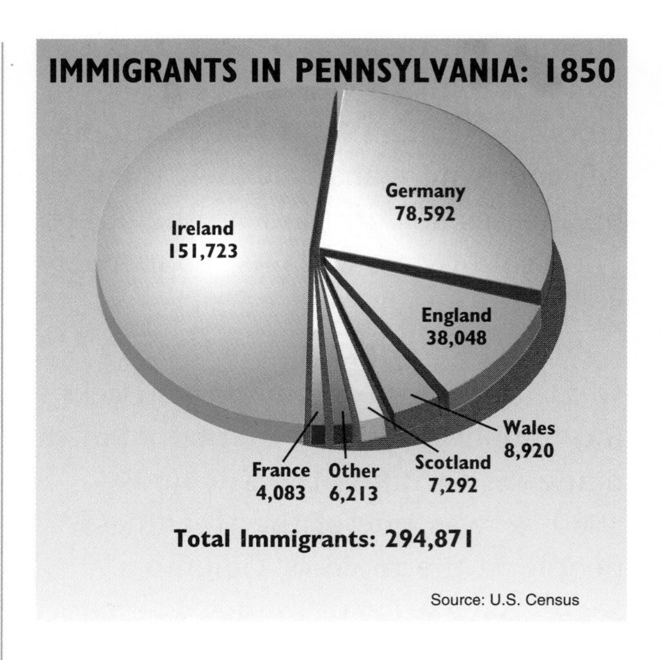

USING A LINE GRAPH

Unlike a circle graph, a line graph shows you how a piece of information changes with time. A line graph often shows an increase or decrease in number.

Look at the line graph on page 143. Start by reading the title. The title tells you that this is a graph which shows the total number of people in Pennsylvania from 1800 to 1850.

Read the label at the left side of the graph. This gives you the number of people. The dates at the bottom of the graph tell you the years during which the number of people were measured.

Trace the line with your finger. Each dot on the line stands for the number of people who were living in Pennsylvania during a particular year. As you can see, the population of Pennsylvania was smallest in 1800.

TRYING THE SKILL

Now study the circle graph of immigrants in Pennsylvania in 1850. Use the Helping Yourself box for hints. What country sent the second-largest number of immigrants to Pennsylvania? Which country sent the smallest number?

Now look at the line graph of the population of Pennsylvania from 1800 to 1850. How many people lived in Pennsylvania in the year 1830? How many lived in our state in the year 1850?

HELPING Yourself

- **Circle graphs** show you how the parts fit into the whole.
- **Line graphs** show how a piece of information changes over time.
- **Study the title and the labels.**
- **Use the graphs to compare facts and figures.**

REVIEWING THE SKILL

1. Did more immigrants come to Pennsylvania from France or Scotland? How did you get your answer?
2. What can you conclude from the line graph about the number of people in Pennsylvania between 1800 and 1850?
3. How do line and circle graphs differ? How do graphs make it easier for you to understand information?

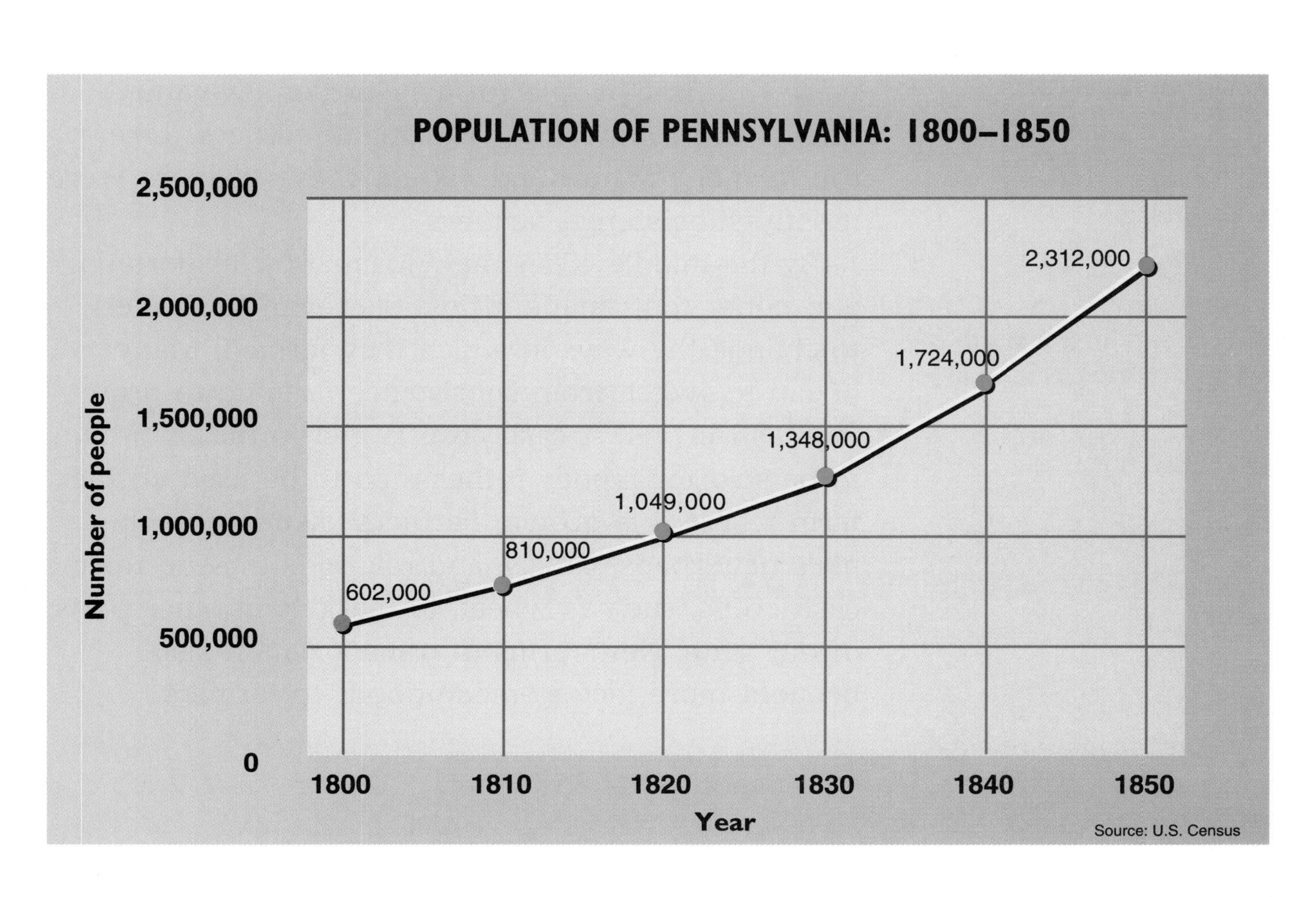

LESSON 4

1800 1860

THE CHANGING FARMS OF PENNSYLVANIA

The Granger Collection

Focus Activity

READ TO LEARN
How did farming in Pennsylvania change after the American Revolution?

VOCABULARY
cash crop
crop rotation
reaper

PEOPLE
Robert and Joseph Smith
Cyrus McCormick

PLACES
Columbia
Carlisle

READ ALOUD

In the late 1700s, a farmer in western Pennsylvania wrote that, except for paying taxes, he did not spend "more than 10 dollars a year, which was for salt, nails and the like; nothing to wear, eat or drink was purchased, as my farm provided all."

THE BIG PICTURE

As you have already read, Native Americans were the first people to farm in Pennsylvania. They were followed by European settlers. Like the farmer in the Read Aloud, these farmers were mostly subsistence farmers.

By the middle 1800s, new forms of transportation and better tools made it possible for most farmers to change the ways in which they farmed. Many began to switch from subsistence farming to growing **cash crops**. A cash crop is a crop that is grown to be sold for money rather than to be used on the farm where it is grown. Farmers used Pennsylvania's new roads, canals, and railroads to send their cash crops, such as wheat, to markets in other parts of our state. New forms of transportation also brought more factory-made goods to farmers.

THE PENNSYLVANIA FARMER

In the early 1800s, the farmers of southeast Pennsylvania continued to be successful. Wheat remained an important crop in that region, even though new states like Ohio and Indiana also produced large amounts of this crop. Because Pennsylvania's population was growing, more wheat was used in the state. **Columbia**, which lay along the Susquehanna River and the Lancaster Pike, became an important town in the wheat trade. One man remembered that "About 100,000 barrels of flour, 300,000 bushels of wheat, [and a large] quantity of . . . beef and pork [came through Columbia]. . . . The flour is chiefly sent to Philadelphia, [and] the wheat is bought for the Lancaster and Chester . . . mills."

More western Pennsylvania crops also began to move east on the canals and railroads. Before, most crops from that area had been sent down the Ohio and Mississippi rivers to other states and countries.

The Carnegie Museum of Art

This painting by Edward Hicks shows a southeastern Pennsylvania farm in the late 1700s.

Life on the Farm

Life on our state's farms changed very little from colonial times to the early 1800s. Farm work remained hard. Farmers plowed the soil, planted the seeds, and harvested the crops. Every family member and hired hand helped with these chores during busy times in the spring and autumn. Women worked hard all year as well. John Culbertson was born on a farm in southern Pennsylvania in 1841. He later remembered the work his mother did:

> *In addition to such household cares as cooking, sweeping, scrubbing, washing, and ironing, she made the soap, milked the cows, fed the pigs and calves, cared for the chickens, ducks, turkeys, . . . and geese; with the feathers of the (geese) she filled her downy pillows and mattresses.*

Although there was little time for play on the farm, singing was a favorite family activity. The song in the Many Voices on the next page was a popular lullaby among German families in Pennsylvania. What farm chores are mentioned in the song?

Sleep, My Baby, Sleep (Schloof, Bubbeli, Schloof)

A well-known traditional lullaby still sung in Pennsylvania.

The Granger Collection

By 1860, most larger farms in our state depended upon the McCormick reaper.

CHANGES ON THE FARM

Farming methods improved greatly during the early 1800s. Most Pennsylvania farmers began to use crop rotation. This is a method of farming in which a different crop is planted in the same soil each year. Crop rotation helps keep the soil healthy. It is still practiced by farmers around the world.

New machinery also improved farming. Robert and Joseph Smith of Pineville made an iron plow in 1800. Earlier plows were made of wood and were not as strong. A mechanical horse-drawn reaper made by Cyrus McCormick of Virginia helped farmers cut and gather their grain. The sharp cutting blades of the McCormick reaper harvested as much grain as 10 to 12 people harvesting by hand. The McCormick reaper was first used in Pennsylvania in 1840 on a farm near Carlisle.

WHY IT MATTERS

Changes in transportation and farming methods and machinery made life better for Pennsylvania farmers. Many were able to change from subsistence farming to growing cash crops. With the money they earned they could buy manufactured goods, such as clothes and farm tools, that were made in distant places and brought to them on the canals and railroads.

Reviewing Facts and Ideas

SUM IT UP

- In the early 1800s, Pennsylvania farmers changed from subsistence farming to growing cash crops.
- New farming methods, such as crop rotation, and new machinery, such as the iron plow and McCormick reaper, helped farmers grow more crops.

THINK ABOUT IT

1. What is a cash crop?
2. Why is crop rotation important?
3. **FOCUS** What changed on Pennsylvania farms in the early 1800s?
4. **THINKING SKILL** Was the growing of cash crops by Pennsylvania farmers a cause or effect of improvements in our state's transportation?
5. **WRITE** Write a song about life on an early 1800s Pennsylvania farm.

CHAPTER 6 REVIEW

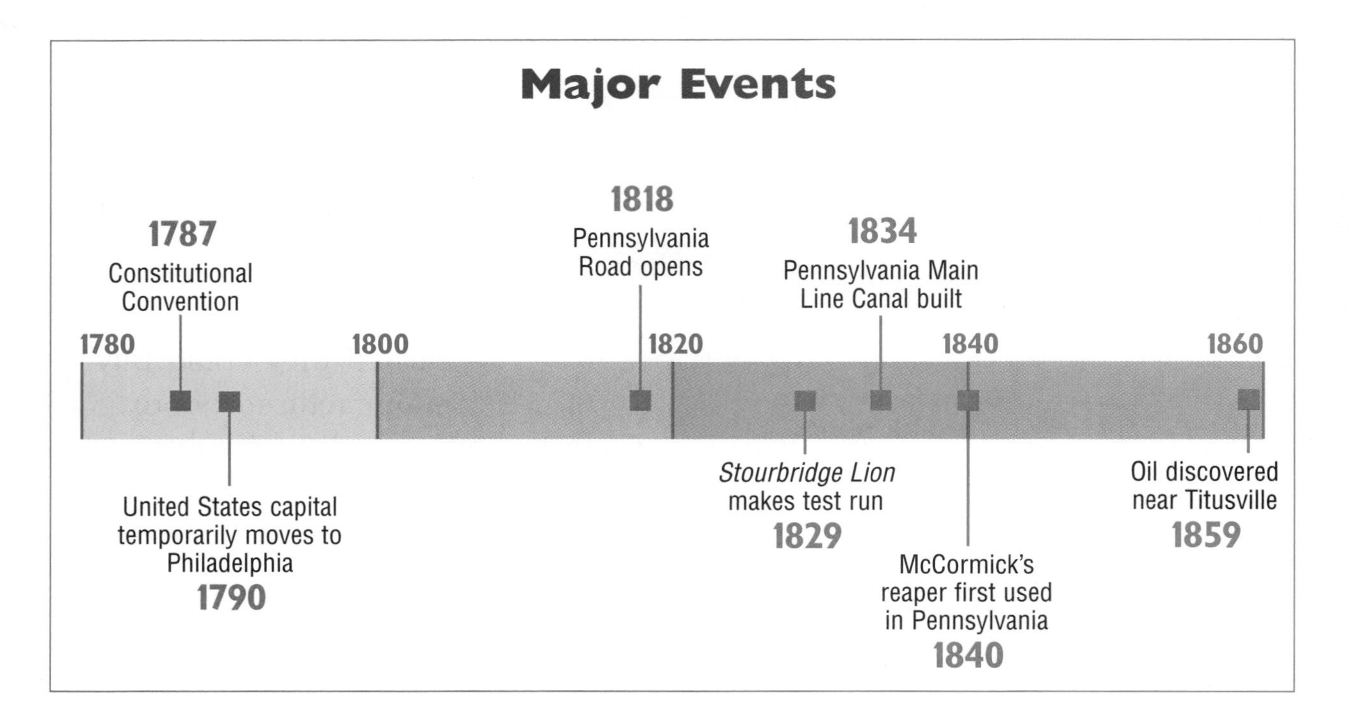

THINKING ABOUT VOCABULARY

Number a sheet of paper from 1 to 10. Next to each number write the word or term from the list below that best matches the statement.

boom town	Constitutional Convention
canal	delegate
cash crop	industry
coke	population
Constitution	turnpike

1. A highway on which travelers have to pay a fee
2. A person chosen to represent a group
3. An inland waterway built for transportation
4. A town which grows quickly, such as Titusville
5. Our country's plan of government
6. A gray-black solid fuel made from bituminous coal used to make iron
7. Food sold for money instead of being used where it is grown
8. The meeting held in Philadelphia in 1787 to talk about how the United States government should work
9. The number of people living in an area
10. All the businesses that make one kind of good

THINKING ABOUT FACTS

1. How was Gouverneur Morris important to the Constitutional Convention?
2. Why did railroads put canals out of business in some places?
3. How did new forms of transportation affect industry and agriculture in Pennsylvania?
4. Why did Pennsylvania's population nearly triple between 1820 and 1860?
5. How did the McCormick reaper change farming?

THINK AND WRITE

WRITING A SUMMARY
Reread Lesson 1 in Chapter 6, which describes the start of our country's government. Then write a summary of the information you have read in the lesson.

WRITING A LIST
Suppose you were able to interview Benjamin Franklin about what happened during the Constitutional Convention. List three questions you would ask him. Then write answers he might give.

WRITING A COMPARISON
Write a paragraph comparing bituminous coal and anthracite coal. Describe how each type of coal is used differently and the industries that used them.

APPLYING STUDY SKILLS

READING CIRCLE AND LINE GRAPHS

1. How are circle and line graphs different?
2. Look at the circle graph on page 142. Which group made up the largest part of the population?
3. Look at the line graph on page 143. About how many people lived in Pennsylvania in 1820?
4. Which kind of graph, circle or line, would you use to show how the temperature in Pittsburgh changes from August to December?
5. How do graphs make some information easier to understand?

Summing Up the Chapter

Use the following word maps to organize the information from Chapter 6. Copy the word maps on a sheet of paper. Then write at least one piece of information in each blank circle. When you have filled in the maps, use them to write a paragraph that answers the questions "How did Pennsylvania respond to the challenges following the American Revolution?"

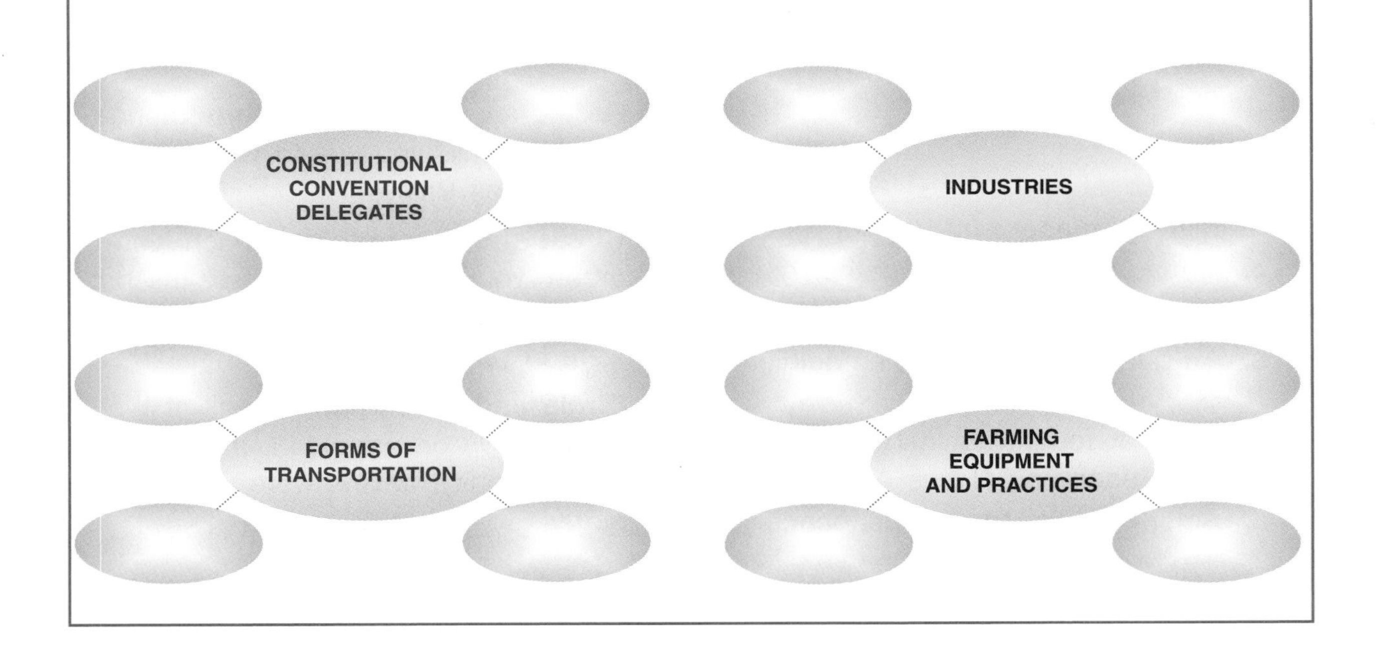

UNIT 3 REVIEW

THINKING ABOUT VOCABULARY

Number a sheet from 1 to 5. Next to each number write the letter of the definition that best matches the word or phrase.

1. Great Runaway
   - **a.** The first steam train in the United States
   - **b.** Scared settlers who fled south in 1778
   - **c.** A highway on which travelers pay a fee
2. Stamp Act
   - **a.** A tax on paper goods sold in the colonies
   - **b.** A statement declaring the colonies' independence from Britain
   - **c.** Our country's plan of government
3. First Continental Congress
   - **a.** Leaders who met at Carpenters' Hall in Philadelphia
   - **b.** Colonists who promised to be ready for battle at a minute's notice
   - **c.** The army of the American colonies
4. textile
   - **a.** Hard coal
   - **b.** Material made from yarn or thread
   - **c.** A machine to cut and gather grain
5. Battle of Trenton
   - **a.** An attack against Hessian soldiers by Americans
   - **b.** The war fought against Britain by the French and Native Americans
   - **c.** America's war for independence

THINK AND WRITE

WRITING A POSTER

Suppose you lived in Pennsylvania in 1776. Write and design a poster to get people to join the Continental Army.

WRITING AN INTERVIEW

Suppose you were able to interview Robert Fulton. Write three questions you would ask him. Then write the answers he might give.

WRITING AN EXPLANATION

Suppose you were one of the people who decided to build a canal in Pennsylvania. Write a paragraph explaining some of the reasons why a canal would be useful.

BUILDING SKILLS

1. **Reference sources** Which reference source would you use to find the meaning of the word *bituminous*?
2. **Reference sources** How are reference books different from other types of books?
3. **Reference sources** Which reference source would you use to write a report on Thomas Paine?
4. **Circle and line graphs** Which kind of graph would you use to show the proportion of American colonists who were Loyalists in 1776?
5. **Circle and line graphs** Look at the circle graph on page 143. In 1850 how many Pennsylvanians were English by birth?

YESTERDAY, TODAY & TOMORROW

In the 1800s the people living in Pennsylvania were mainly European settlers, their descendants, and African Americans. Try to find out about the groups of people that make up Pennsylvania today. In what ways do you think they might change in the future?

READING ON YOUR OWN

Here are some of books you might find at the library to help you learn more.

SILVER FOR GENERAL WASHINGTON: A STORY OF VALLEY FORGE
by Enid LaMonte Meadowcroft
This story of the Continental Army's winter in Pennsylvania is told through the eyes of children.

SHH! WE'RE WRITING THE CONSTITUTION
by Jean Fritz
Take a trip back in time to learn about how our government was formed.

CANALS AND WATERWAYS
by Chris Oxlade
Read how canals and waterways work and the ways in which they are made.

UNIT PROJECT

Write a Historical Newspaper

1. Suppose you are a writer for your own historical newspaper. Take a look at a present-day newspaper to see what type of articles it includes.
2. Working in a group, choose a name for your paper and three news items from the following list to write about:
   - the French and Indian War
   - Revolutionary War
   - the winter at Valley Forge
   - Philadelphia landmarks
3. After you decide what articles your group will write, group members should gather information from your textbook and the school library. Remember to report the facts.
4. You may also want to include illustrations, editorials, comic strips about Pennsylvania, and advertisements for historical Pennsylvania products.
5. Present your newspaper to the rest of the class.

Pennsylvania Gazette

The French and Indian War

Philadelphia Landmarks

The Winter at Valley Forge

Franklin Memorial

MANUFACTURING ADVERTISEMENT (LEFT) ANDREW CARNEGIE (RIGHT)

HENRY "BOX" BROWN (RIGHT) CIVIL WAR SWORD (BELOW) CIVIL WAR REENACTORS (BOTTOM)

SUFFRAGISTS (RIGHT)

The Granger Collection

UNIT FOUR

Challenge and Growth

"... forever free ..."

from the Emancipation Proclamation, announced by President Lincoln in September 1862
See page 165.

WHY DOES IT MATTER?

In the 1840s, many Pennsylvanians sought equal rights for all Americans. This was a difficult time in our country's history. Just twenty years later, the Civil War would split our country apart. When the war was over, our state would face new challenges. There would also be new opportunities for Pennsylvanians in our growing state.

What role did Pennsylvania play in the Civil War? How did life change for different groups of people living in our state? When the war was over, how did our state continue to grow?

Read on. You will learn about many major events that changed the state and people of Pennsylvania.

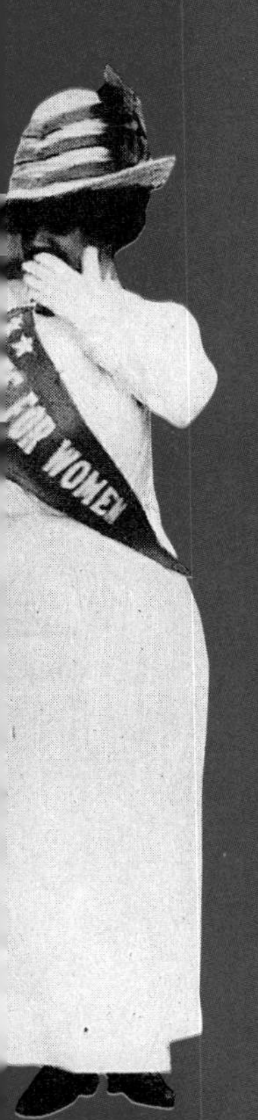

The Ohio Historical Society

The Granger Collection

WORLD WAR I ARMY POSTER (ABOVE RIGHT)
WORLD WAR II SOLDIERS (RIGHT)

CHAPTER 7

The Civil War Era

THINKING ABOUT GEOGRAPHY AND HISTORY

Chapter 7 begins at a time in our country when women and African Americans struggled to gain their rights as Americans. The story of this struggle continues, telling of a brave journey from slavery in the South to freedom in the North. During and after the war that ended slavery in the United States, Pennsylvania's industry and economy grew greatly. Follow these events on the time line below. You will learn much more about them as you read Chapter 7.

1840s

NEW BRIGHTON

Quakers help enslaved people escape on the Underground Railroad

1850

PHILADELPHIA

The Women's Medical College of Pennsylvania opens

1863

GETTYSBURG

The Battle of Gettysburg is fought

CANADA
Lake Erie
PENNSYLVANIA
New Brighton
Braddock
Gettysburg
Philadelphia
UNITED STATES
ATLANTIC OCEAN
1875
BRADDOCK
Andrew Carnegie opens J. Edgar Thomson Works steel mill
STEEL WORKS

Friends Historical Library, Swarthmore College

Focus Activity

READ TO LEARN

Who led the struggle for the rights of women and abolition in Pennsylvania?

VOCABULARY

abolition
Underground Railroad

PEOPLE

Lucretia Mott
Thaddeus Stevens
Ann Preston
James Forten
Robert Purvis
William Lloyd Garrison
Harriet Tubman
William Still
J. Miller McKim

PLACES

Oxford
New Brighton

LESSON 1

1820 1860 1880 1900

ABOLITION AND EQUAL RIGHTS

READ ALOUD

Francis Ellen Watkins Harper was an African American poet who lived in Philadelphia in 1854. She opposed slavery and worked for the rights of women. In one of her poems, she wrote about Lucretia Mott, who started the Female Anti-Slavery Society of Philadelphia in 1833.

Nor let it be said that we forgot
The women who stood with Lucretia Mott
The women faithful, true, and brave;
Who came to the rescue of the slave.

THE BIG PICTURE

As you read in Chapter 4, some early Quakers had been slave traders. Yet other Quakers were among the first people in favor of **abolition**, or the ending of slavery. Abolitionists were members of other religious groups as well. As a result of their efforts, Pennsylvania became one of the first states to make slavery against the law in 1780. Other states in the North soon followed.

Many African Americans who escaped to the North worked to end slavery. They described how their children were sold and taken away forever. They also told about being whipped and put in chains. These stories angered black and white Pennsylvanians alike. They worked harder to bring about an end to slavery in the United States.

THE NEED FOR CHANGE

Lucretia Mott was a Philadelphia Quaker. She and other Pennsylvanians wanted many changes in our state. Two of the most important changes were education and the rights of women.

Education

Few children went to school regularly in the 1800s. In the cities, parents who had enough money sent their children to private schools. In rural areas, neighbors sometimes got together to hire teachers. Classes were held in homes or in small school buildings built by parents. In the 1820s African Americans in Philadelphia opened schools for black children. Only a few other schools, such as those run by Quakers, allowed African Americans to attend.

In 1834 Pennsylvanians began paying for public schools with taxes. The schools were free and open to all children, both black and white. Thaddeus Stevens, a lawmaker from Gettysburg, said, "the blessing of education shall be carried home to the poorest child." Public schools usually had just one room and one teacher.

During the 1800s many colleges were started in Pennsylvania. In 1854 the Ashmun Institute, now called Lincoln University, opened in Oxford. This school is the oldest African American college in the United States still in operation.

Rights for Women

You have read that women in the Pennsylvania colony had few rights. This was still true in the early 1800s. A married woman could not own property. If she had a job, her husband could demand her pay. Even the children in a family belonged to the husband. Women who worked outside the home usually held low-paying jobs such as servants or factory workers.

Lucretia Mott and other women worked hard to make their lives better. Some women began to study and train for jobs that only men had held. In 1850 the Women's Medical College of Pennsylvania opened in Philadelphia. It was the first medical college in the United States for women. One of the first students was Ann Preston of West Grove.

Courtesy of the Archives and Special Collections on Women in Medicine, Allegheny University of the Health Sciences

Courtesy of the Archives and Special Collections on Women in Medicine, Allegheny University of the Health Sciences

Ann Preston (left) became a professor at the Women's Medical College (below), which helped many women to become doctors.

VOICES AGAINST SLAVERY

Wealthy African Americans, such as James Forten and Robert Purvis of Philadelphia, played an important part in the move to end slavery. In 1830 they helped organize the first national African American anti-slavery meeting in Philadelphia.

William Lloyd Garrison, a famous abolitionist from Boston, met three years later in Philadelphia with abolitionists from eleven states to form the American Anti-Slavery Society. However, not all Philadelphians were for abolition. In 1838 an angry group of white Philadelphians burned down an abolitionist meeting place only three days after it opened. Yet this did not stop the abolitionists from continuing to meet.

How did Henry "Box" Brown get his nickname?

One enslaved African American, Henry Brown, had himself mailed in a large wooden box from Richmond, Virginia, to Philadelphia. When the crate was opened, he stood up and cried, "Great God, am I a free man?" Henry Brown gained his freedom and a new nickname. For the rest of his life he was known as "Box" Brown.

The Underground Railroad

In the 1840s an enslaved woman named Harriet Tubman escaped to Pennsylvania. There she began to help other abolitionists on the Underground Railroad. The Underground Railroad was a system of secret routes that those escaping slavery followed to freedom. Many routes went on to Canada.

Underground Railroad workers used a secret code. Men and women who helped enslaved people escape

Harriet Tubman (right) was a very successful "conductor" on the Underground Railroad. By helping enslaved people escape on the Underground Railroad (below), "conductors" risked going to jail.

The Granger Collection

The Granger Collection

were called "conductors." Enslaved "passengers" were led by conductors from one "station," or hiding place, to another.

Pennsylvania was an important part of the Underground Railroad. Quakers in New Brighton, for example, became well known for their many hiding places. These included a cave and an island in the Beaver River.

Tubman and other abolitionists, such as African American William Still and the Quaker J. Miller McKim, helped people escape from slavery. Between 1830 and 1860, more than 9,000 African Americans escaped through Philadelphia. Read the following letter to William Still. How you would describe the type of person that became a conductor?

Excerpt from a letter by Hiram Wilson to William Still in 1858.

"I am happy to inform you that Mrs. Jackson and her interesting family of seven children arrived safe and in good health. . . . With sincere pleasure I provided for them comfortable ***quarters*** *till this morning, when they left for* ***Toronto****. . . . My wife gave them all a good supply of clothing before they left us."*

quarters: rooms
Toronto: a city in Canada

WHY IT MATTERS

By the 1850s many Pennsylvanians were fighting for better education, women's rights, and an end to slavery. Our state became an important part of the Underground Railroad. Yet the issue of slavery began to divide the people of the United States. In the next lesson you will read how these differences led to war.

Reviewing Facts and Ideas

SUM IT UP

- In the 1800s, Pennsylvanians worked to improve education and the rights of women and to end slavery.
- Abolitionists helped many enslaved African Americans escape to freedom on the Underground Railroad.

THINK ABOUT IT

1. How did education in our state improve in the early 1800s?
2. What was the Underground Railroad?
3. **FOCUS** How were Pennsylvanians involved in the struggle for the rights of women and abolition?
4. **THINKING SKILL** Place the following in the correct *sequence*: escaping on the Underground Railroad, being enslaved, freedom in Canada.
5. **WRITING** Suppose you are a "conductor" on the Underground Railroad. Write a letter to William Still telling him about how you helped a family of runaways escape to Canada.

Focus Activity

READ TO LEARN

What role did Pennsylvania play in the Civil War?

VOCABULARY

states' rights
secede
Union
Confederacy
Civil War
regiment
Battle of Gettysburg
Gettysburg Address
Emancipation Proclamation

PEOPLE

James Buchanan
Abraham Lincoln
Jefferson Davis
Alexander Kelly
Mary Owens
Robert E. Lee
George Meade
Ulysses S. Grant
John Wilkes Booth

PLACES

Fort Sumter
Camp William Penn
Gettysburg
Chambersburg
Appomattox

A DIVIDED COUNTRY

READ ALOUD

"A house divided against itself cannot stand. I believe this government cannot endure [last] permanently half slave and half free. It will become all one thing or all the other." These words were spoken by Abraham Lincoln in 1858, two years before he became President. Lincoln believed that our country would not last if it remained divided into two opposite ways of life.

THE BIG PICTURE

By 1860 three and one-half million African Americans were held in slavery in the South. Their work helped Southern farmers grow two-thirds of the world's cotton.

The North and South argued about slavery and **states' rights**. States' rights means that states should be able to make their own laws. Many white Southerners thought states should make their own laws about slavery. President **James Buchanan**, a Pennsylvanian, tried to calm the fears of white Southerners by supporting the rights of slave owners.

When **Abraham Lincoln** became President in 1861, he was strongly against the spread of slavery. Although he did not say that slavery should be ended, many white southerners believed that Lincoln would try to free those in slavery.

THE SOUTH BREAKS AWAY

After Lincoln became President of the United States in 1861, eleven states **seceded**, or left, the **Union**. The word Union describes the states that make up the United States. The eleven states that seceded joined to form the Confederate States of America, or the **Confederacy**. Look at the map to find the Confederate states. **Jefferson Davis** was chosen President of the Confederacy.

The Civil War Begins

In April 1861 Confederate soldiers fired at **Fort Sumter**, a Union fort in South Carolina. This started the bloodiest war in United States history. It was called the **Civil War**, or the "War Between the States." Look again at the map to find Fort Sumter.

Pennsylvania Goes to War

When war broke out, Lincoln asked the Northern states for volunteers to form a Union Army. Pennsylvania sent many soldiers to protect our country's capital, Washington, D.C. Horace Binney was a volunteer from Pennsylvania who said, "There is among us but one thought . . . one end, one symbol—the Stars and Stripes."

As the war dragged on, not enough Northerners volunteered. In March 1863, President Lincoln drafted, or selected, men for the Union army. Coal miners near Pottsville, Wilkes-Barre, and other towns stopped working to protest. However, Lincoln sent soldiers to force the miners back to work.

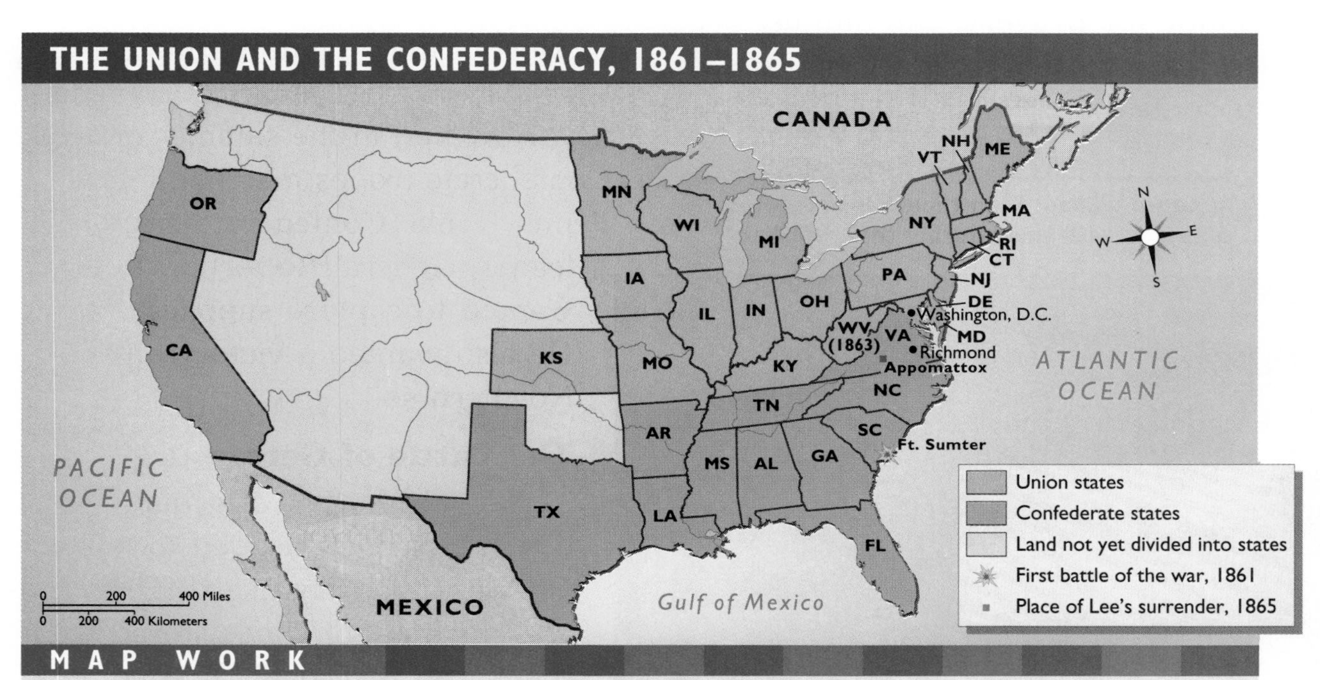

MAP WORK

During the Civil War, the United States split into two separate countries.

1. In what state did the first battle of the Civil War take place?
2. Why did much of the western land belong to neither the Union nor the Confederacy?
3. How were the Union and the Confederacy divided geographically?
4. Looking at the map, why do you think Pennsylvania joined the Union?

PENNSYLVANIANS VOLUNTEER

There were 337,936 Pennsylvanians who fought for the Union. More than 8,000 were African Americans. Many of these African Americans trained at Camp William Penn just outside Philadelphia.

Nine hundred fifty soldiers served in the all-African American Sixth Regiment (REJ ih ment) during the Civil War. A regiment is a military unit. Many of the regiment's soldiers were former slaves. Black soldiers knew that if they were captured by the Confederates, they could be sold into slavery or killed.

One soldier in the Sixth Regiment was Pennsylvanian Alexander Kelly. He was given the Medal of Honor for bravery, the highest award the government can give to soldiers.

At Camp William Penn thousands of troops were trained during the Civil War.

Historical Society of Pennsylvania

Life in Wartime Pennsylvania

Our state's businesses helped supply the Union during the war. Factories in Pittsburgh, Reading, and Phoenixville made guns, bullets, swords, cannons, and wagons. Philadelphia mills wove cloth for uniforms, blankets, and bandages. Western Pennsylvania coal was used to run Union trains and ships. To feed Union soldiers, farmers from our state grew large amounts of crops.

Pennsylvania women also played an important role during the war. Though they were not allowed to fight, some women became nurses in army hospitals. Others donated money and supplies to the Union army. Some, such as Mary Owens of Danville, even disguised themselves as men and fought in battle.

Most of the fighting during the Civil War took place in the Confederacy. However, in the summer of 1863, Confederate troops marched into Pennsylvania. Confederate army leader, General Robert E. Lee, wanted to capture supplies. He also wanted a victory on Northern soil.

The Battle of Gettysburg

On July 1, 1863, a group of Lee's soldiers headed for Gettysburg. They heard there was a supply of shoes stored there, and they badly needed shoes. Instead of shoes they found Union soldiers. Neither army had planned to fight there. Yet the Battle of Gettysburg soon began.

In a short time there were 75,000 Confederate soldiers and 88,000 Union soldiers. The Union soldiers were led by Pennsylvania General George Meade. Both armies fought fiercely for two days. On the third day, the Confederate Army made what became known as Pickett's Charge. Confederate soldiers attacked the Union troops, and failed.

In three days over 22,000 Confederate soldiers were killed or wounded. More than 3,000 Union soldiers were killed, and 14,000 were wounded. The Union army had won. Gettysburg was the turning point of the Civil War. You can read more about the Battle of Gettysburg in the Infographic on page 164.

Four months after the battle, President Lincoln traveled to Gettysburg to declare part of the battlefield a national cemetery. Lincoln gave his Gettysburg Address on November 19, 1863. Though it lasted only two minutes it became known as one of the greatest speeches ever given. "This nation, under God," he said "shall have a new birth of freedom." Lincoln also promised that "government of the people, by the people, for the people, shall not perish [disappear] from the earth."

The Burning of Chambersburg

After Gettysburg, the war was not over for our state. Confederate soldiers were angry because Union troops had stolen property and burned homes in Virginia. As a result, Confederate soldiers marched to the city of Chambersburg on July 30, 1864. They demanded the city give them $100,000 in gold or $500,000 in United States dollars. When they didn't receive the money, the soldiers began burning the buildings. After the fires had gone out, two-thirds of the town had been burned down.

The Granger Collection

The Granger Collection

General George Meade (left) led the Union army to victory at the Battle of Gettysburg. This uniform (center) was worn by a Confederate general at Gettysburg. The telescope (far left) was used by Union soldiers during the Civil War.

Infographic

The Battle of Gettysburg

Before July 1863, Gettysburg was a quiet little-known town in south central Pennsylvania. Then, over a three-day period, Union and Confederate armies fought in and around the town. Thousands of lives were lost. Today, over a million visitors a year come to visit this historic site.

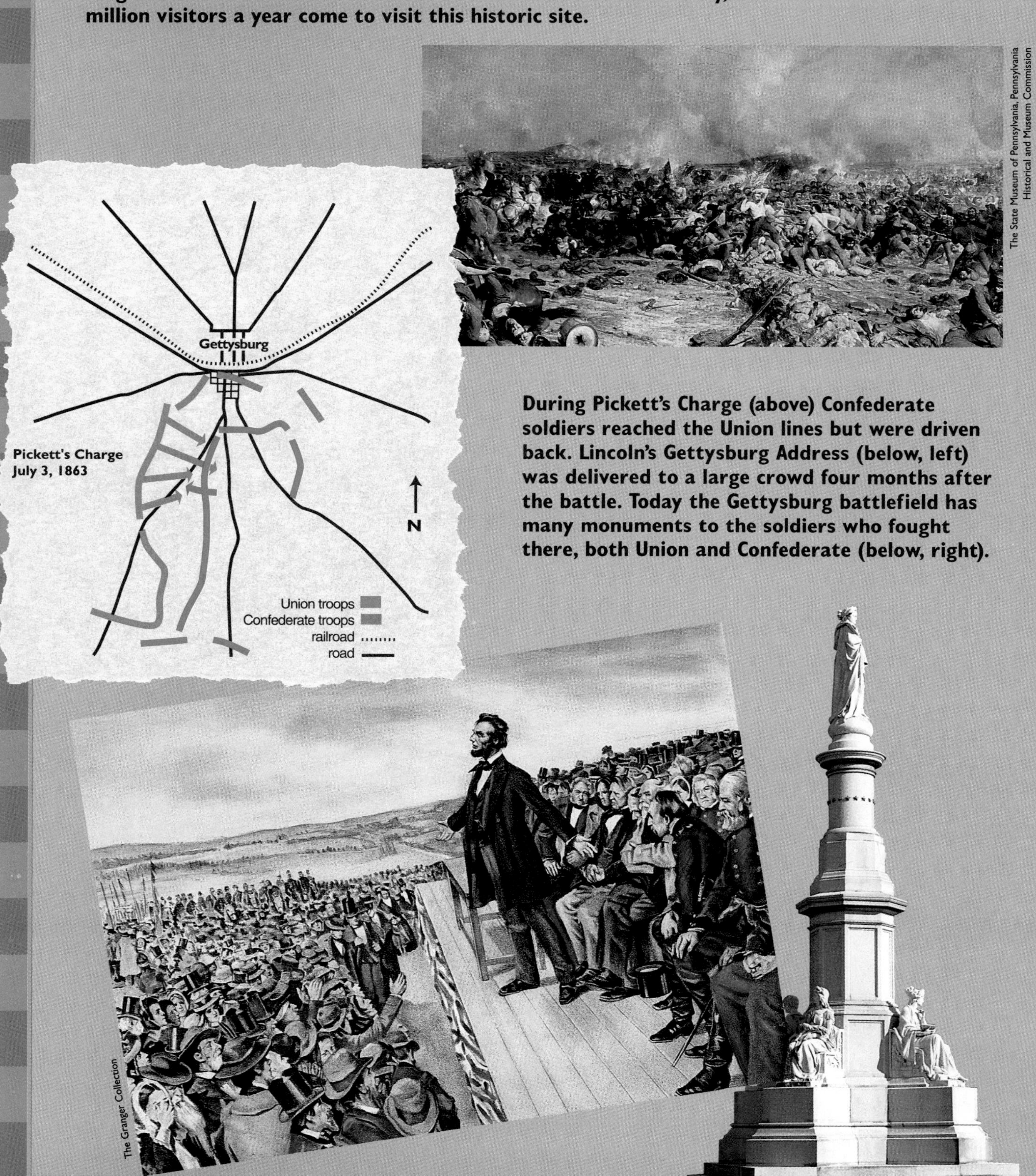

The State Museum of Pennsylvania, Pennsylvania Historical and Museum Commission

During Pickett's Charge (above) Confederate soldiers reached the Union lines but were driven back. Lincoln's Gettysburg Address (below, left) was delivered to a large crowd four months after the battle. Today the Gettysburg battlefield has many monuments to the soldiers who fought there, both Union and Confederate (below, right).

The Granger Collection

THE END OF SLAVERY AND THE CIVIL WAR

President Lincoln announced the **Emancipation Proclamation** (ee man suh PAY shun prahk luh MAY shun) in September 1862. Emancipation means freedom. This official announcement said that on January 1, 1863, all enslaved people in the Confederate states would be "forever free." People throughout the North celebrated. Yet many enslaved African Americans in the South did not learn of their freedom for more than two years.

On April 9, 1865, Confederate General Robert E. Lee surrendered to Union General **Ulysses S. Grant** at **Appomattox**, Virginia. Look back at the map on page 161 and find Appomattox. After four long years, the Civil War was over and more than 600,000 people had died.

The Confederacy was defeated, and the Union had survived. President Lincoln was not able to help the country heal, however. He was killed by an angry supporter of the South, **John Wilkes Booth**, only five days after the end of the war.

WHY IT MATTERS

The cost of the Civil War was huge. Of the 600,000 who died, 33,183 were Pennsylvanians. The South and some of the North lay in ruins. Soon after the war, slavery was outlawed everywhere in the United States. However, in both the North and the South, African Americans still did not have the same rights and freedoms that other Americans had. In the next lesson, you will read about some of the changes that took place in Pennsylvania after the war.

Reviewing Facts and Ideas

SUM IT UP

- The issues of slavery and states' rights divided our country.
- Eleven states seceded from the Union in 1861 to form the Confederacy.
- Pennsylvanians provided many soldiers and supplies to the Union army.
- The Battle of Gettysburg was the turning point of the Civil War.
- General Robert E. Lee surrendered to General Ulysses S. Grant in April 1865, ending the Civil War.

THINK ABOUT IT

1. Why did eleven states secede and form the Confederacy?
2. What was the Gettysburg Address?
3. **FOCUS** What role did Pennsylvania play in the Civil War?
4. **THINKING SKILL** Was the burning of Chambersburg a *cause* or an *effect* of what Union soldiers had done in Virginia?
5. **WRITE** Suppose you were asked to make supplies for the Union army during the Civil War. Write a paragraph describing what you would make, and explain why they would be important.

1820 1840 1860 1865 1914

CHANGES AFTER THE WAR

Focus Activity

READ TO LEARN

What changes took place in Pennsylvania after the Civil War?

VOCABULARY

food processing
technology
invention
union
strike
Johnstown Flood
dam

PEOPLE

Andrew Carnegie
Henry Clay Frick
Henry J. Heinz
John Wanamaker
Frank W. Woolworth
George Westinghouse
George Skinner
Clara Barton

PLACES

Braddock
Homestead
Lake Conemaugh

READ ALOUD

Upon seeing in Europe a quick, new way of making steel from iron, Andrew Carnegie said, "Farewell, then, Age of Iron; all hail King Steel!" This Scottish immigrant to Pittsburgh later became a millionaire in the steel industry.

THE BIG PICTURE

From 1865 to 1914, Pennsylvania became a leader in industry. As you have read, coal was one of our state's most important natural resources. It is used to make steel.

New immigrants from Europe came to work in the steel factories that were opening throughout our country. Coal miners and their families filled the once quiet towns. Cities grew even larger as people poured in to fill new jobs.

By 1910, 7.6 million people lived in Pennsylvania. More than half of the people in our state lived in cities and in towns instead of rural areas. Our state was no longer just a farming state. Industry had become an important part of the economy, and its effect was being felt all over our state.

Commonwealth of Pennsylvania, Division of Archives and Manuscripts

THE GROWTH OF INDUSTRY

Following the Civil War, steel and coke became some of the most important industries of our state's growing economy. Both industries depended on the rich supply of coal found throughout Pennsylvania.

Andrew Carnegie

As you have read in the Read Aloud, Andrew Carnegie became rich making steel. He thought that steel would become more important than iron. In 1875, Carnegie opened a huge steel mill, the J. Edgar Thomson Works, in Braddock. Steel was used to make train rails, bridge supports, and beams for buildings. By the end of the century, Andrew Carnegie controlled about one fourth of all the iron and steel that was made in the United States. You will read more about Carnegie in the Legacy on page 172.

Although much of our state's steel came from Pittsburgh, other Pennsylvania cities such as Bethlehem, Steelton, Johnstown, and Scranton also had large steel mills.

The coke industry boomed as the steel industry grew. Coke was used to make steel. One of the largest coke companies in the world was owned by Henry Clay Frick of West Overton. Frick worked closely with Andrew Carnegie to make steel.

By 1885, Henry Clay Frick (bottom, right) owned four-fifths of all the coke ovens (below) in Pennsylvania. With the opening of Carnegie's J. Edgar Thomson Works (bottom, left), the Age of Steel had begun.

Pennsylvania State Archives

The Granger Collection

FACTORIES AND NEW IDEAS

Besides steel and coke, other industries and businesses became important around our state. Factories made new food products, and larger stores for shopping opened.

Food Processing

As people moved from farms to cities, the **food processing** industry grew. It supplied food for busy urban families. Food processing is any of hundreds of ways of turning raw food into different kinds of products. After a new process of canning food was discovered in 1872, food processing grew even more rapidly.

An important leader in the food processing industry was **Henry J. Heinz** of Pittsburgh. Starting in 1869, Heinz built a huge industry that canned and sold meat, fruits, and vegetables. Today, the Heinz name is known all over the world.

New Ways to Shop

Before the Civil War, Pennsylvanians bought food and clothing in small stores. In 1876, **John Wanamaker** opened our country's first department store in Philadelphia. For the first time, people could shop for many kinds of goods in one place.

In 1879 **Frank W. Woolworth** opened the first of his "Five and Dime" stores in Lancaster. At Woolworth's, customers could buy anything from squirt guns to lipstick all for under ten cents.

New Technology

New **technology** also led to the start of new Pennsylvania businesses. Technology is the use of skills, ideas, and tools to meet people's needs. In 1868 in Pittsburgh, **George Westinghouse** invented a new brake that made trains much safer. The railroad brake and some of his 400 other **inventions** were made at his factories in Pittsburgh. An invention is a newly created product.

Ketchup was just one of the many food products made by the Heinz company of Pittsburgh (above). The first of Frank W. Woolworth's "Five and Dime" stores opened in Lancaster in 1879 (right).

NEW IMMIGRANTS

As you have read, immigrants from Europe came to our state after the Civil War to find work. Many Austrians, Hungarians, Italians, Russians, and other groups arrived in the late 1800s and early 1900s.

As cities became overcrowded, many immigrants faced terrible living and working conditions. Sometimes as many as twelve people in one family lived in a one-room apartment. They shared a bathroom with 30 other families living in the same building.

The Rise of Unions

People who had jobs in steel mills and coal mines worked 12 hours a day, six days a week. They braved dangerous conditions with few safety rules. Many died in accidents. Women worked over 70 hours a week in clothing factories. Children worked 15 to 18 hours a day in factories and coal mines. At this time, no laws protected workers' rights.

In the late 1800s, many **unions** were started in Pennsylvania. A union is an organization formed by workers. These workers joined together to ask for better pay and better working conditions.

Strikes in Pennsylvania

In 1892 workers went on **strike** at a steel mill in **Homestead** owned by Andrew Carnegie and Henry Frick. A strike is the stopping of work by workers in order to get higher pay or better working conditions. Frick sent people to end the strike. Fighting broke out, and twenty steelworkers were killed.

Strikes helped bring the problems of workers to the notice of the public. During the next 20 years, laws were passed to improve working conditions for all. A law passed in 1893 made it against the law for children under 12 to work.

Other laws made coal mines and steel mills provide doctors for workers. In 1903, after many strikes, miners made more money, and their work days were reduced to 8 or 9 hours. In the Many Voices on the next page, you will read a mining song from Pennsylvania. What does it tell you about the conditions in the mines?

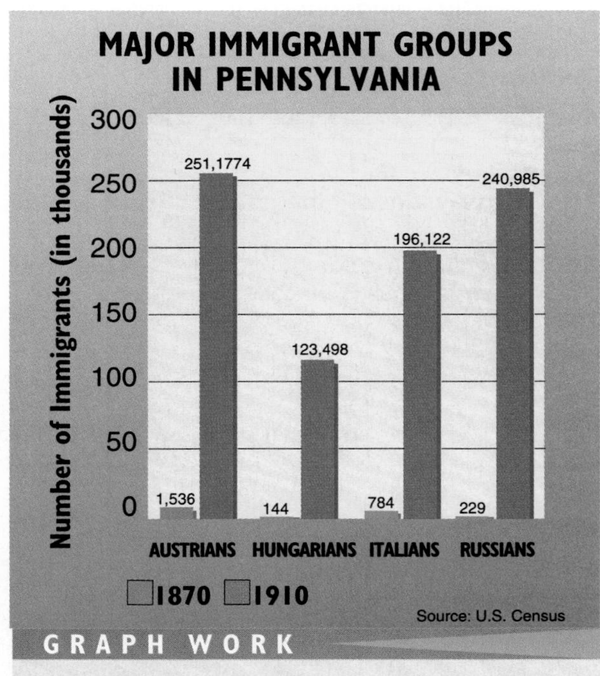

GRAPH WORK

The graph shows immigration to Pennsylvania.

1. Which immigrant group was the largest to come to Pennsylvania by 1910?
2. What do you think a graph of other European immigrant groups for the same time would look like? Why?

Down in a Coal Mine

Excerpt from a traditional mining song popular in eastern Pennsylvania and published in 1872.

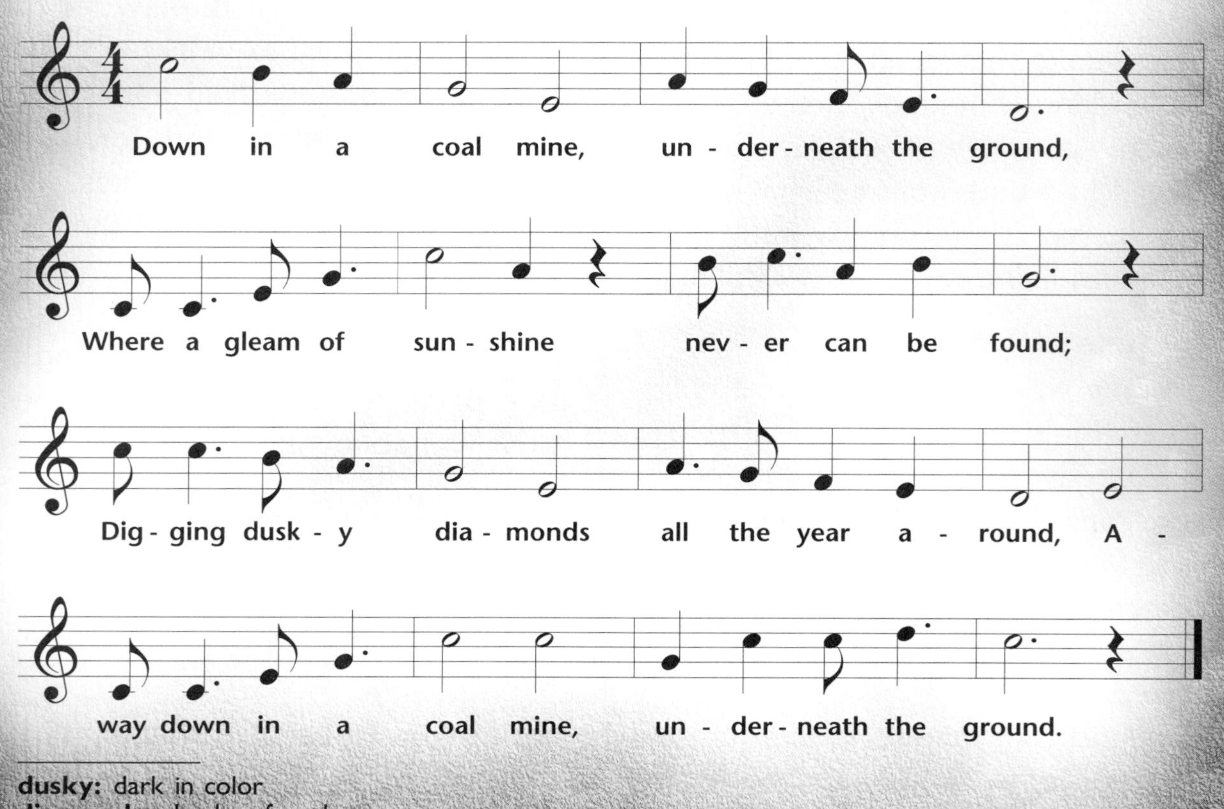

dusky: dark in color
diamonds: chunks of coal

THE JOHNSTOWN FLOOD

The **Johnstown Flood** of 1889 was one of the worst floods in United States history. East of the city was an 80-foot-high **dam** on **Lake Conemaugh** built in 1852. A dam is a wall built to hold back flowing water. A group of wealthy Pennsylvanians, including Andrew Carnegie and Henry Clay Frick, owned the land around the lake. The dam needed repairs. However, no one bothered to make them.

On May 31, 1889, during a heavy rainfall, the dam burst. A wall of water 75 feet high came crashing down on Johnstown, washing away everything in its path. The city was destroyed, and 2,209 people died.

Many people worked quickly to help the victims of the flood. African American **George Skinner** worked at a nearby hotel. He became famous for saving the life of a young girl. **Clara Barton**, a nurse who founded the American Red Cross, brought medical aid to the victims. It was five months before the city was rebuilt.

Clara Barton and her American Red Cross helped out at the Johnstown Flood and many other disasters.

WHY IT MATTERS

After the Civil War our state became a leader in industry and business. Cities and towns grew as new immigrants arrived to fill jobs in mines and factories. Workers formed unions to get better pay and working conditions. In the next lesson, you will read about how this new growth affected our state.

Reviewing Facts and Ideas

SUM IT UP

- Andrew Carnegie made steel an important industry in our state.
- Henry J. Heinz was a leader in the food processing industry. John Wanamaker and Frank W. Woolworth opened new kinds of stores.
- Pennsylvanians formed unions to improve their pay and working conditions.

THINK ABOUT IT

1. How did steel become an important industry in our state?
2. From which countries did immigrants come to Pennsylvania after the Civil War?
3. **FOCUS** What are some ways that life in Pennsylvania changed after the Civil War?
4. **THINKING SKILL** What three *questions* might you *ask* Clara Barton to learn more about the Johnstown Flood?
5. **WRITE** Suppose you are the head of a Pennsylvania mining town in 1880. What would you do to improve the way that mining families work and live?

THINKINGSKILLS

Making Conclusions

VOCABULARY

conclusion

WHY THE SKILL MATTERS

In Lesson 1 you read about slavery and the Underground Railroad. Abolitionists in Pennsylvania and other states worked together to help enslaved African Americans escape to freedom. You might conclude that many Pennsylvanians wanted to end slavery throughout the United States.

When you make a **conclusion**, you put together several pieces of information and decide what they mean. A conclusion does not repeat specific facts. Instead, it adds up these facts and tells how they are connected.

USING THE SKILL

In the last lesson you read about coal in Pennsylvania. Now read these statements:

- Pennsylvania's railroads made money moving coal.
- Many new Pennsylvania industries used steam engines powered by burning coal.
- Coke made from soft coal was used in the process to make steel.

First ask yourself, "What do all these statements have in common?" All of these statements give information about coal. Now put together these different pieces of information. A conclusion you might make is, "Many industries in Pennsylvania needed coal." This conclusion connects all three statements. It finds a common idea behind the statements and describes it in a sentence. Like all good conclusions, this one is based on facts.

The Historical Society of Schuylkill County

Pennsylvania railroads were very important to the coal industry. They moved coal from place to place.

TRYING THE SKILL

You have practiced making a conclusion about industries in our state that needed coal. Now you are ready to make a conclusion on your own. Read the following statements about the working and living conditions of coal miners and their families in the late 1870s. Then make a conclusion from the statements. Use the Helping Yourself box for hints.

- Mine workers worked 10–12 hour days.
- There was little fresh air in the mines, and workers often became very sick.
- Sometimes mines caved in, and miners were hurt or killed.
- Mining companies gave miners and their families tiny, run-down houses without running water in which to live.

HELPING Yourself

- **When you make a conclusion you "add up" several facts or statements to see how they are connected.**
- **Skim through the information for a common idea.**
- **State this meaning in your own words.**

What common theme or meaning did you find in all four statements? How do they "add up" to a conclusion? What conclusion can you make about the life of a mine worker in the late 1870s?

REVIEWING THE SKILL

1. How did you reach your conclusion? Is your conclusion based on facts?
2. What did the four statements suggest about the lives of coal miners and their families? How do you know?
3. How might making conclusions help you learn about history?
4. Name some occasions in school when you might find it useful to make conclusions.

Miners often worked deep beneath the surface of the earth in poor conditions.

Legacy

LINKING PAST AND PRESENT

Andrew Carnegie

In the last lesson you read about steel king, Andrew Carnegie. As a young Scottish immigrant in Pennsylvania, Carnegie improved his education by reading as much as he could. When he became a millionaire, he gave away millions of dollars to help others. He once said, "He who dies rich dies disgraced." What do you think he meant by this statement? If you had millions of dollars to help others, how would you do it? The photographs on these pages show some of the many ways in which Carnegie used his money to help others.

Andrew Carnegie donated, or gave, money to build more than 3,000 public libraries around the world.

In 1895 Carnegie opened his Carnegie Institute in Pittsburgh. This includes a library, art gallery, music hall, and museum. Perhaps you have also heard about the Carnegie Mellon University in Pittsburgh, which he founded in 1900.

Today, more than 75 years after his death, Andrew Carnegie's legacy is still helping to educate the world.

Carnegie Mellon University

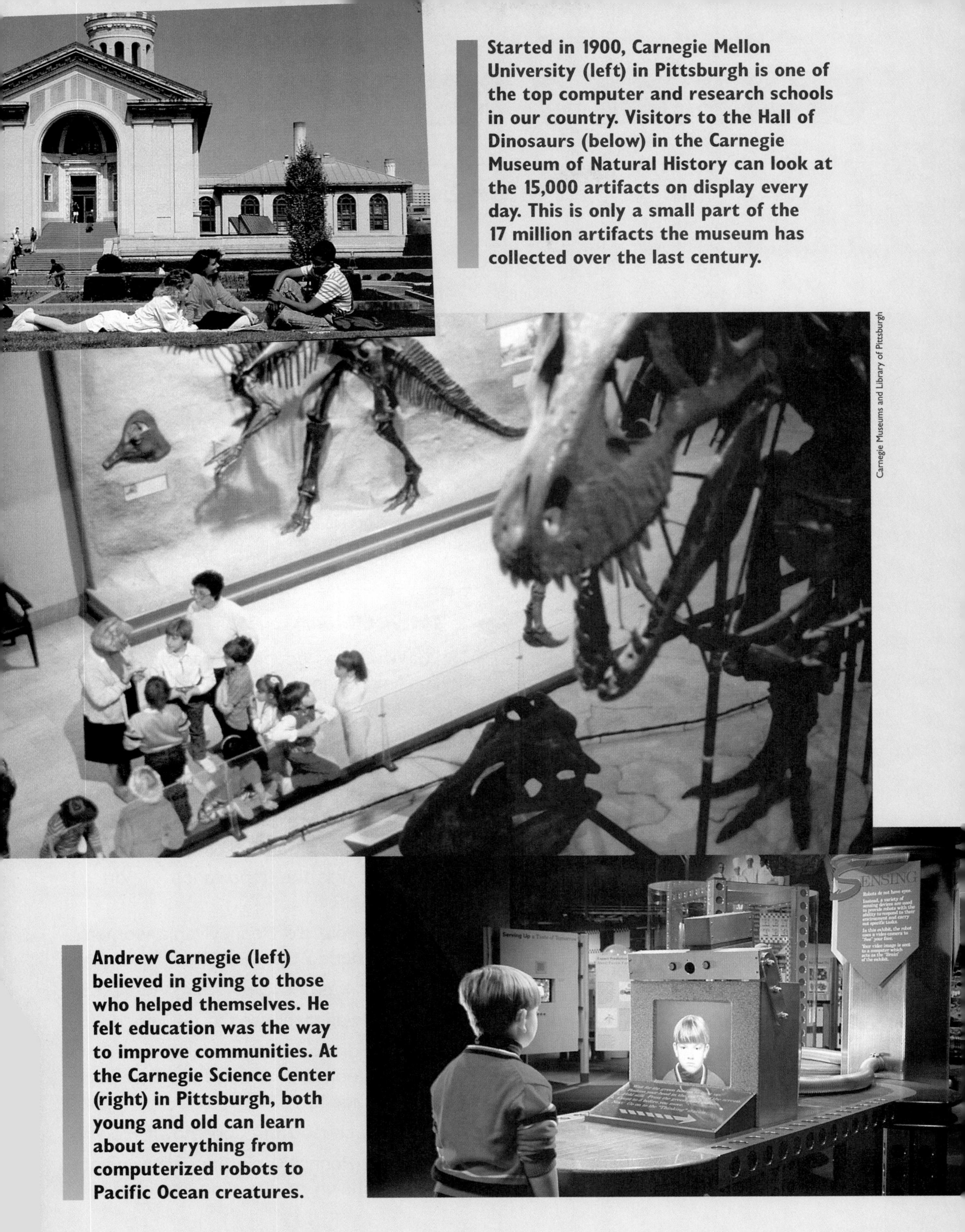

Started in 1900, Carnegie Mellon University (left) in Pittsburgh is one of the top computer and research schools in our country. Visitors to the Hall of Dinosaurs (below) in the Carnegie Museum of Natural History can look at the 15,000 artifacts on display every day. This is only a small part of the 17 million artifacts the museum has collected over the last century.

Carnegie Museums and Library of Pittsburgh

Andrew Carnegie (left) believed in giving to those who helped themselves. He felt education was the way to improve communities. At the Carnegie Science Center (right) in Pittsburgh, both young and old can learn about everything from computerized robots to Pacific Ocean creatures.

CHAPTER 7 REVIEW

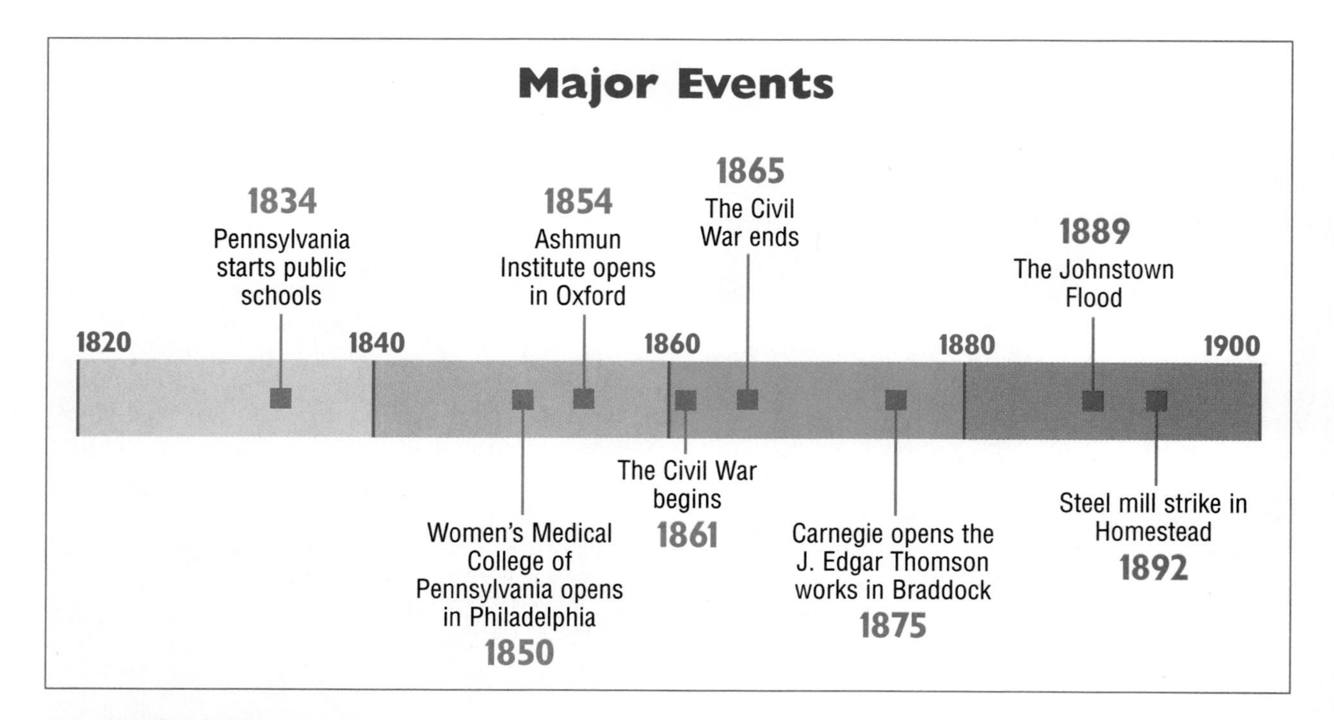

THINKING ABOUT VOCABULARY

Number a sheet of paper from 1 to 5. Next to each number write the term from the list that best fits the description.

abolition
Emancipation Proclamation
secede
technology
union

1. To withdraw or leave an organization such as a government
2. A group of workers organized to get better pay and better working conditions
3. Ending completely; often used in reference to slavery
4. The announcement by President Lincoln in 1863 that all enslaved people living in Confederate states were free
5. The use of skills, ideas, and tools to meet people's needs

THINKING ABOUT FACTS

1. What was education for African Americans in Pennsylvania like in the early 1800s?
2. Why did many women in Pennsylvania work hard to better their lives in the early 1800s?
3. Name several Pennsylvanians who fought to abolish slavery.
4. What was the importance of Fort Sumter?
5. What role did Pennsylvania women play during the Civil War?
6. What was the Gettysburg Address?
7. How was steel used in the late 1800s?
8. How did John Wanamaker and Frank W. Woolworth change the way people shopped?
9. What caused the Johnstown Flood?
10. What Pennsylvania education events are shown on the time line above?

THINK AND WRITE

WRITING A SPEECH

Suppose you are an abolitionist in Pennsylvania in the early 1800s. Write a speech saying why you think slavery should be abolished.

WRITING A POEM

You have read about the Battle of Gettysburg in Lesson 2. Write a poem describing the events and importance of the battle.

WRITING A SUMMARY

Reread the section in Lesson 3 titled "Factories and New Ideas." Then write a detailed summary of the changes in Pennsylvania business and industry you read about.

APPLYING THINKING SKILLS

MAKING CONCLUSIONS

1. What is meant by making a conclusion?
2. What steps should you follow when making a conclusion?
3. Read the sections under "Voices Against Slavery" on pages 158–159. What conclusion could you make about people escaping slavery using the Underground Railroad?
4. Read the sections under "New Immigrants" on page 169. What conclusion could you make about life as a new immigrant in Pennsylvania?
5. Why is it important to make conclusions about what you read?

Summing Up the Chapter

Copy the following cause-and-effect chart on a sheet of paper. Fill in the blank spaces on the chart. Then use the information to write a paragraph that answers the question: "How did life change in Pennsylvania during the Civil War era?"

CAUSE	EFFECT
	Pennsylvania outlaws slavery in 1780.
Confederate soldiers fire at Fort Sumter.	
Booming industries in Pennsylvania need many workers.	
	Workers form unions.

CHAPTER 8

A New Century

THINKING ABOUT GEOGRAPHY AND HISTORY

The twentieth century brought good times and hard times to Pennsylvania. The steel industry brought new wealth and new jobs. New inventions such as the radio and automobile made staying in touch and transportation easier. As proud citizens of the United States, Pennsylvanians fought alongside other Americans in two world wars. In Chapter 8 you will read about all of these events in our state's history and more.

CANADA
Lake Erie
Scranton
PENNSYLVANIA
Pittsburgh
Indiantown
Gap
Levittown
UNITED
STATES
ATLANTIC
OCEAN
1950s
LEVITTOWN
Families start moving from
the cities to the suburbs

1900 1929 1950 1975 2000

The Ohio Historical Society

WAR AND GROWTH

Focus Activity

READ TO LEARN
How did Pennsylvania change in the early 1900s?

VOCABULARY
World War I
Allied Powers
Central Powers
Great Migration
war bond
Roaring Twenties
suffrage
amendment

PEOPLE
William S. Sims
Daisy Lampkin
Jim Thorpe
Charles Duryea
J. Frank Duryea
Lucretia Blankenburg

PLACES
Austria-Hungary
Chester
Reading
Carlisle

READ ALOUD

In 1928 President Herbert Hoover exclaimed proudly: "We in America today are nearer to the final triumph over poverty than ever before in the history of any land." During much of the 1920s, many Americans would have agreed with what he said.

THE BIG PICTURE

Throughout the United States, the years between 1900 and 1914 were a time of steady growth. Plumbing moved indoors. An automobile might pass by. In Pennsylvania, of course, the steel industry was changing business and our way of life.

For most Americans the time was peaceful. The future seemed full of promise. Then a gunshot rang out in Europe, and the world changed. In June 1914 Archduke Francis Ferdinand, a noble in line to rule the empire of Austria-Hungary, was killed. This event triggered the start of what became known as World War I. For the first time in history, countries around the world would be at war with each other.

In 1917 the United States entered the war on the side of the Allied Powers. The Allied Powers included Great Britain, France, and Russia. The opposing countries were known as the Central Powers. The Central Powers included Germany, Austria-Hungary, and Italy.

WORLD WAR I

At first most Americans wanted to stay out of World War I. But attacks by German submarines on ships carrying United States passengers began to make people angry. Finally the United States joined the Allied Powers on April 6, 1917.

Pennsylvania at War and at Home

About 371,000 Pennsylvania men served as soldiers, sailors, and marines during the war. Most fought in France. The American naval forces in Europe were led by **William S. Sims** of Orbisonia.

At home, our state's steel industry became important to the war effort. Steel from Pittsburgh factories was used to make guns, tanks, and ships. In Philadelphia and **Chester**, shipyards boomed, and Pennsylvania became the top shipbuilding state.

To meet the demand for factory workers, many African Americans from the Southeast moved to the Northeast and the Middle West. This was known as the **Great Migration**. A migration is the movement of people from one place to another.

Although women were not allowed to fight in the war, hundreds served as nurses. Women worked in machine shops, post offices, and other workplaces left by men who went to war. African American community leader **Daisy Lampkin** of **Reading** helped raise more than 2 million dollars in **war bonds**. A war bond is a written promise by the government to pay back money that has been loaned to help pay for the war.

The war pulled Pennsylvanians together. Yet it also led to conflicts. Some German Americans were treated as possible enemies and were not trusted. The German language was outlawed in many schools.

Fisk University Library

The Granger Collection

Daisy Lampkin (above) helped raise money for the war. As thousands of men left Pennsylvania to fight in the war, many women took jobs in our state's factories (right).

THE ROARING TWENTIES

The Allied Powers defeated the Central Powers in 1918, ending World War I. During the next 10 years there were a number of exciting changes. Pennsylvanians, like all Americans, were happy the war was over. More people than ever had jobs. The 1920s became known as the Roaring Twenties.

Sights and Sounds

On November 2, 1920, in Pittsburgh, radio station KDKA made the first commercial radio broadcast in the United States. Now Pennsylvanians could turn on a radio and listen to the news, music, and sports. They could hear about football great, Jim Thorpe, a Native American athlete from Carlisle.

At the same time, movies were becoming popular. Every city had its "picture palaces," where people watched silent movies.

Links to **LANGUAGE ARTS**

The Original Nickelodeon

The Nickelodeon was the name of our country's first movie theater. It opened in Pittsburgh in 1905. *Nickel* comes from the original cost to get into the theater, five cents. *Odeon* is the Greek word for "a theater or concert hall." Look up the word *nickelodeon* in the dictionary. How is this word used today?

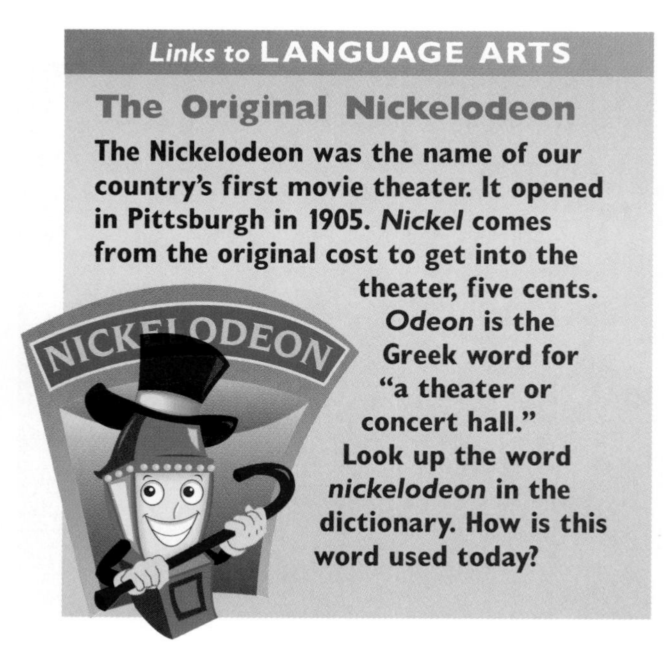

New Inventions

Inventions of the time were changing the way Americans lived. The radio and telephone helped Pennsylvanians to stay in touch with each other and the world. Perhaps the invention that led to the biggest change in our way of life in the early 1900s was the automobile.

In their Reading factory in 1896, the brothers Charles and J. Frank Duryea began building some of the first automobiles in the United States. Yet in Pennsylvania, the railroads were still very popular. The Duryeas only sold a few automobiles. However, by the 1920s, cars had become very popular throughout our country. By 1927 there were more than 1.5 million vehicles on Pennsylvania roads.

Jim Thorpe (below) was an early football star in our country. In the early 1900s, women took part in marches to gain the right to vote (right).

EQUAL RIGHTS FOR WOMEN

Until 1920 women in our country could not vote. The struggle for **suffrage** (SUF rijh), or the right to vote, lasted for many years.

Pennsylvania women such as **Lucretia Blankenburg** of Philadelphia were members of groups working for suffrage. Blankenburg was president of the Pennsylvania Women's Suffrage Association.

Support for women's suffrage increased during World War I, when women took over many men's jobs. In 1920 the Nineteenth **Amendment** to the United States Constitution gave women the right to vote. An amendment is an addition to our constitution.

WHY IT MATTERS

The first 30 years of the 1900s were a time of both pain and excitement for Pennsylvanians and all Americans. New inventions changed the way Pennsylvanians lived, worked, and played. Women also gained the right to vote. In the next lesson you will learn that these "good times" would not last forever.

Reviewing Facts and Ideas

SUM IT UP

- The United States entered World War I in 1917. Many Pennsylvanians fought overseas or helped at home.
- The Roaring Twenties brought excitement and change to the lives of many Americans.
- The Nineteenth Amendment gave women the right to vote.

THINK ABOUT IT

1. Name the Allied Powers in World War I.
2. How did Pennsylvanians help the war effort at home?
3. **FOCUS** How did Pennsylvania change in the early 1900s?
4. **THINKING SKILLS** What *effect* do you think the increased use of cars had on road building?
5. **WRITE** Suppose that you were living during the 1920s. Write a letter to a friend describing the effect of one new invention on your life.

LESSON 2

1900 | 1929 1945 | 1950 | 1975 | 2000

THE GREAT DEPRESSION AND WORLD WAR II

Focus Activity

READ TO LEARN
How did the Great Depression and World War II affect Pennsylvanians?

VOCABULARY
stock
Great Depression
New Deal
Little New Deal
World War II
Axis Powers
Allies

PEOPLE
Franklin D. Roosevelt
Gifford Pinchot
George Earle
George C. Marshall
Frances Coble

PLACES
Indiantown Gap
Camp Reynolds

READ ALOUD

Many Americans were suffering in 1931. One Pennsylvania man sent a letter to Governor Gifford Pinchot saying, "Help me. I have six little children to take care of. I have been out of work for over a year and a half. . . . Oh what will I do . . . ?"

THE BIG PICTURE

The Roaring Twenties were good years for the stock market. **Stocks** are shares, or parts, of ownership in a company. In the 1920s many Americans bought stocks. They hoped to make money as stock prices rose. In October 1929 many stockholders grew worried because prices began to fall.

On October 29, 1929, people across the country rushed to sell their stocks. This caused prices to fall to rock bottom. The stock market had "crashed," or broken down.

This marked the start of hard times for the entire country. Many people took loans from banks but did not have enough money to pay them back. As a result, many banks failed. People could not afford to buy things, so companies needed fewer workers. Many Pennsylvanians lost their jobs as factories, steel mills, and mines shut down. The **Great Depression** of the 1930s had begun. A depression is a time when business is slow and people are out of work.

THE DEPRESSION IN PENNSYLVANIA

The Great Depression hit hard in our state. From 1929 to 1933, one fourth of our state's workers lost their jobs. In towns like Scranton, steelmaking fell to one fifth of normal production. Hundreds of businesses shut down.

The Government Responds

In 1932 Americans chose a new President, Franklin D. Roosevelt. FDR, as he was called, started government programs to help struggling Americans get back on their feet. Roosevelt called his new program the New Deal. Some New Deal programs helped farmers and banks. Others put people to work improving their communities.

Men in the Civilian Conservation Corps, or the "CCC Boys," planted trees and worked in national parks. The Works Progress Administration, or WPA, and other government agencies put artists, writers, and teachers to work across our country. In the Many Voices, what are the people in the painting doing?

Clearing the Land
painted by Lorin Thompson in the 1930s.

Government projects helped many artists find jobs. This mural, or painting, was made on the wall of a Mercer post office.

National Archives

Little New Deal

In Pennsylvania, Governors Gifford Pinchot and George Earle also began programs to help the people of our state find jobs. These programs became known as the Little New Deal. Little New Deal workers helped to build the Pennsylvania Turnpike, as well as thousands of miles of roads in our state during the 1930s.

President Franklin D. Roosevelt created the New Deal to help Pennsylvanians and other Americans survive the Great Depression.

WORLD WAR II BEGINS

In 1939, while Americans were still struggling though the Great Depression, another world war broke out. World War II was started by the Axis Powers led by Germany, Italy, and Japan. They fought against the Allies, led by Great Britain, France, and later the Soviet Union.

The United States at first tried to stay out of this conflict. Then, on December 7, 1941, Japanese planes bombed the United States naval base at Pearl Harbor, Hawaii, in a surprise attack. The next day Congress declared war on Japan. Germany and Italy, in turn, declared war on the United States.

Pennsylvanians in World War II

More than a million men and women from our state served in the armed forces during World War II. Five-star general George C. Marshall of Uniontown was the commander of United States forces during the war. Frances Coble from Dubois was the chief nurse of an army hospital in North Africa. For her outstanding service to our country, Coble was honored with the Army Commendation Medal.

Thousands of African Americans from Pennsylvania served in the war. However, most were separated from white troops.

The War at Home

Pennsylvanians at home worked hard to support the war effort. Communities collected scrap metal and old tires for military supplies. Because so many men were away fighting the war, women took over many of their jobs. Others sold war bonds, which helped pay for the war.

The war brought many changes to our state. At Indiantown Gap near Harrisburg, hundreds of thousands

By the end of World War II, there were more than 6 million African American men and women in the armed forces (left). Some Pennsylvanians planted "victory gardens" (above) to grow food for the war effort.

Posters urged Americans, even children, to help in the war effort.

of soldiers trained for the war. The biggest change was that the war effort finally brought the Great Depression to an end. Our state provided one third of our country's steel and coal and one fourth of its ships during the war.

The government built three prisoner of war camps in Pennsylvania. **Camp Reynolds** near Greenville was set up to hold 90,000 prisoners. Yet the camp held only 1,800 German soldiers by the war's end.

Unlike German Americans, Japanese Americans were sent to "relocation" camps. Victims of fear and distrust, most of the Japanese Americans were taken from their homes in California. They were forced to live in the government camps until the war ended. No relocation camps were built in Pennsylvania. In 1988, the United States made an official apology for these actions.

WHY IT MATTERS

In Pennsylvania and the United States, the Great Depression ended the Roaring Twenties. New Deal programs helped people through the hardships. Still, the economy did not fully recover until World War II.

In 1945, both Germany and Japan surrendered to the Allies. Pennsylvanians, like other Americans, then began to get on with their lives.

Reviewing Facts and Ideas

SUM IT UP

- In 1929, the stock market crashed, and the Great Depression began.
- President Roosevelt's New Deal and Pennsylvania's Little New Deal programs helped many people in our state find jobs.
- The United States entered World War II in 1941. The war ended the Great Depression.
- World War II ended in 1945.

THINK ABOUT IT

1. What was the stock market crash?
2. How did the New Deal try to help the people of our state?
3. **FOCUS** How did the Depression and World War II affect Pennsylvanians?
4. **THINKING SKILLS** Make a *conclusion* about how World War II helped Pennsylvania recover from the Great Depression.
5. **GEOGRAPHY** Look at the Atlas map on page R4. Why do you think the United States was able to stay out of World War II until 1941?

THINKINGSKILLS

Identifying Fact and Opinion

VOCABULARY
fact
opinion

WHY THE SKILL MATTERS

In the last lesson, you saw a picture of a victory garden. Suppose someone told you that people planted victory gardens to help the war effort during World War II. This statement is a **fact**. You can check that it is true by looking up the information in a reference source, such as an encyclopedia. A fact is a statement that can be proven.

Suppose, however, that somebody told you that the best thing to do with your backyard is plant a victory garden. This statement is an **opinion**. An opinion expresses one person's belief or feeling. Another person might believe that backyards should have playground equipment instead. Still another might prefer to plant roses.

Facts and opinions are very different kinds of statements. You must be able to tell them apart because the decisions you make should be based on facts. Use the Helping Yourself box to guide you in identifying these two kinds of statements.

USING THE SKILL

Read the following passage about the Pennsylvania Turnpike. Then identify the statements that are facts and those that are opinions.

> *The Pennsylvania Turnpike was built during the Great Depression with money from a New Deal program. It was first opened on October 1, 1940. Some people think more work should be done on the Pennsylvania Turnpike today to make it wider. They believe traffic will increase greatly in the next fifty years.*

Which statements in the passage are facts? Which are opinions? The first two sentences are facts. They can be proven. You can check the information in a reference source.

The last two sentences are opinions. They contain word clues that often appear in opinions: *think*, *should*, and *believe*. Opinions do not always have word clues, however.

HELPING *Yourself*

- **Facts are statements that can be proven.**
- **Opinions are beliefs or feelings.**
- **Opinions can sometimes be recognized by such word clues as *think*, *believe*, or *should*.**

TRYING THE SKILL

You have practiced identifying facts and opinions in a passage about the Pennsylvania Turnpike. Now read this passage about Gifford Pinchot. As you read the passage, watch for word clues that indicate when the writer is giving an opinion.

Gifford Pinchot cared deeply about our country's environment, and he became chief of the United States Division of Forestry in 1898. He was elected governor of Pennsylvania in 1922 and again in 1930. Pinchot was the best governor in Pennsylvania's history. Some people believe he was also President Theodore Roosevelt's best friend.

Which statements do you think could be proven true? How? Which statements do you think are opinions? What did you do to identify the facts and the opinions?

REVIEWING THE SKILL

1. How is a fact different from an opinion?
2. Why does a word clue like *believe* often tell you that the speaker is expressing an opinion?
3. How would the reference section of the library be able to help you to decide whether certain statements were facts or opinions?
4. When is it useful to be able to tell a fact from an opinion?

Pennsylvania Turnpike Commission

The Pennsylvania Turnpike was built between 1938 and 1940 (left). Gifford Pinchot (right) served two terms as governor of Pennsylvania.

LESSON 3

1900 1925 1946 1983 2000

A BETTER LIFE

Focus Activity

READ TO LEARN

What changes took place in Pennsylvania after World War II?

VOCABULARY

suburb
metropolitan area
commute
highway
discrimination
segregation
civil rights

PEOPLE

Martin Luther King, Jr.
Bayard Rustin
Robert Nix
W. Wilson Goode
Jeannette Reibman
Sophie Masloff

PLACES

Levittown
Monroeville
Easton
Three Mile Island

READ ALOUD

In 1951 Pennsylvanians rushed to Levittown to buy new homes. William Levitt described this new community that he built outside of Philadelphia: "We planned every foot of it—every store, filling station, school, house, apartment, church, color, tree, and shrub."

THE BIG PICTURE

Life was good for many Americans after World War II. After 1946 returning soldiers began to buy new homes and start families. Pennsylvanians joined other Americans in moving from cities to the new **suburbs**. A suburb is a community just outside of a city. A city and its suburbs together are called a **metropolitan area**.

After World War II, African Americans continued their struggle for equal rights. Women also wanted more rights as they sought work beyond the roles of housewives. Other people saw the damaged environment and struggled to end pollution.

As our country returned to peace, Americans turned their attention to making the country a better place to live for all people.

FROM CITY TO SUBURBS

The 1950s were a time of wealth and growth for many Americans. Many people had the money to buy new homes and cars. With special loans from the government, millions of soldiers and their families moved out of the cities. They built new homes in the suburbs.

Pennsylvania Suburbs

Pennsylvanians moved to the suburbs by the thousands. Suburbs offered yards for children to play in and quiet neighborhoods. Shopping centers, schools, and houses of worship were built nearby.

Homes in the suburbs could be built cheaply and quickly. During the 1950s, 250,000 new homes were built in the suburbs around Philadelphia. The suburb of Levittown sprang up overnight. Levittown was named after its builder, William Levitt.

Levittown began in 1951 with just a few small houses among spinach and broccoli farms. The suburb grew to 17,000 houses and more than 50,000 people by the late 1950s.

Outside of Pittsburgh, Monroeville also grew quickly during the 1950s. Businesses such as Westinghouse and U.S. Steel built new office buildings in the once rural area. Soon hundreds of new homes were built in the area. By 1960, Monroeville had more than 20,000 people.

Suburbs meant that people no longer needed to live close to where they worked. Instead they could commute, or travel back and forth, to work each day. With so many cars traveling to and from suburbs to cities, highways were built. A highway is a main road, and a major route of travel. The Schuylkill Expressway was built during the 1950s. This highway allowed people in the suburbs to commute to work in Philadelphia.

During the 1950s, many families moved to the suburbs. Many homes there had larger yards than homes in the city.

THE STRUGGLE FOR EQUAL RIGHTS

Many people in our country still did not have equal rights. African Americans could not live in Levittown or eat in the same restaurants as whites. This is called **discrimination**. Discrimination is the unfair difference in the treatment of people.

Martin Luther King, Jr., a Georgia minister, led marches for **civil rights** throughout our country. Civil rights are the rights of all people to be treated equally under the law. The largest civil rights march took place in Washington, D.C., in 1963. **Bayard Rustin** of West Chester helped organize this march. He also got young people involved in working for civil rights.

Finally the United States government passed The **Civil Rights Act** in 1964. It was now against the law for businesses to treat people differently because of their race, sex, or religion. In 1965 the United States government passed the Voting Rights Act. This law made illegal the practices that were used to keep African Americans from voting.

As a result, African Americans began to be chosen for government offices. In 1958 **Robert Nix** of Philadelphia became the first African American to be a United States Representative from our state. In 1983, **W. Wilson Goode** became the first African American to lead the city of Philadelphia.

Changes for Women

As you have read, women gained the right to vote in 1920. However, it was not until the 1960s that large numbers of women began to work outside the home. Many demanded to be paid the same as men for the same kinds of work.

Some Pennsylvania women have top jobs in state, local, and national government. **Jeannette Reibman** of **Easton** was the first woman to be chosen as a state senator in 1966. **Sophie Masloff** was the first woman to lead the city of Pittsburgh in 1988.

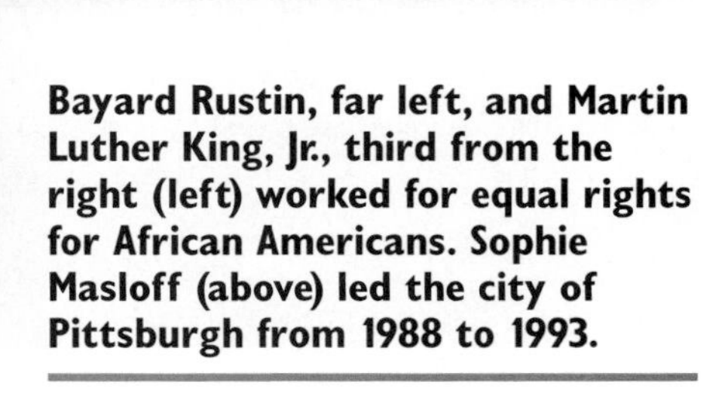

Bayard Rustin, far left, and Martin Luther King, Jr., third from the right (left) worked for equal rights for African Americans. Sophie Masloff (above) led the city of Pittsburgh from 1988 to 1993.

Protecting the Environment

A serious accident to the environment happened in our state on March 28, 1979. The **Three Mile Island** nuclear power plant south of Harrisburg began to leak. Dangerous steam filled the air. Thousands of people near the plant had to leave their homes. Some people moved away to other cities. One building at the plant was closed for good. Since the accident, many scientists have tried to find ways to use nuclear power more safely. In the Viewpoints on the next page, you will read more about what people think of nuclear power.

A protester urges Vice President "Fritz" Mondale to close the Three Mile Island Nuclear Plant in 1979.

WHY IT MATTERS

In the 1950s many people in Pennsylvania moved to the suburbs and commuted to cities to work. During the 1960s Pennsylvanians joined other Americans in an effort to win equal rights for all. The fight to gain equal rights for all people continues. So does the fight to protect our environment. In the next chapter, you will read about the economy of our state.

Reviewing Facts and Ideas

SUM IT UP

- Following World War II, thousands of Pennsylvanians moved from cities to the suburbs.
- The United States government passed the Civil Rights Act in 1964.
- Pennsylvanians, like many other Americans, continue to work for equal rights for all.

THINK ABOUT IT

1. What was the effect of the Civil Rights Act of 1964?
2. Describe what happened at Three Mile Island.
3. **FOCUS** What are some ways that life in Pennsylvania changed after World War II?
4. **THINKING SKILL** Identify one *fact* and one *opinion* on page 190 about why many Pennsylvanians moved to the suburbs.
5. **WRITE** Suppose you have just moved to Levittown from a big city. Write a postcard to a friend from your old neighborhood describing your new home and neighborhood in Levittown.

CITIZENSHIP VIEWPOINTS

The nuclear plant on Three Mile Island is still in operation, though part of it has been shut down.

WHAT DO PENNSYLVANIANS THINK ABOUT USING NUCLEAR POWER?

You read in Chapter 1 that someday nonrenewable fuels will be gone. You also read that scientists are looking for new sources of energy. Solar, wind, and nuclear power are some possibilities. Nuclear power is already used as a source for electricity. There are five nuclear power plants in Pennsylvania that supply more than one-third of our electricity. Some scientists believe nuclear power produces invisible rays that can be harmful to people's health. Accidents like the one at Three Mile Island nuclear plant can be dangerous. Also, the waste products from making nuclear power remain dangerous for thousands of years. They cannot be destroyed and must be buried.

You will read the viewpoint of Elaine Panella who supports nuclear power. You will also read the words of Dr. Rickie Sanders, who worries about getting rid of nuclear waste.

Some people, such as Terry Ganey, believe that as scientists find ways to make nuclear power plants safer, other sources of power should be explored. Read and consider three viewpoints on this issue. Then answer the questions that follow.

Three DIFFERENT Viewpoints

"... the price of electricity would go up."

1 TERRY GANEY
Middle School Teacher, Allentown
Excerpt from Interview, 1996

Our way of life depends on cheap electricity. Without nuclear power, the price of electricity would go up. There are dangers to nuclear power, but for now we have to live with the dangers while scientists look for safer sources of power.

Susquehanna Energy Information Center/ Pennsylvania Power & Light Company

"... saves our own nonrenewable resources."

2 ELAINE PANELLA
Pennsylvania Power and Light Employee, Berwick
Excerpt from Interview, 1996

Nuclear power is important to protect our environment. It helps us use less foreign oil and saves our own nonrenewable resources. Nuclear plants are designed to prevent nuclear material from poisoning our environment. They also do not pollute the air with gases.

"... we should rethink our energy policy."

3 DR. RICKIE SANDERS
College Professor, Philadelphia
Excerpt from Interview, 1997

We should not build any new nuclear power plants. The Three Mile Island accident shows that we should rethink our energy policy. The problem is not in making nuclear power, but in finding a safe way to get rid of the nuclear waste. Money for research should go into finding safer, cleaner energy sources.

BUILDING CITIZENSHIP

1. What is the viewpoint of each person? How do they support their views?
2. In what ways do the viewpoints agree? How do they disagree?
3. What other viewpoints might people have on this issue? How could you find out more about this issue in your community?

SHARING VIEWPOINTS

Discuss what you agree with or disagree with about these and other viewpoints. As a class, write three statements with which everyone agrees about the use of nuclear power.

CHAPTER 8 REVIEW

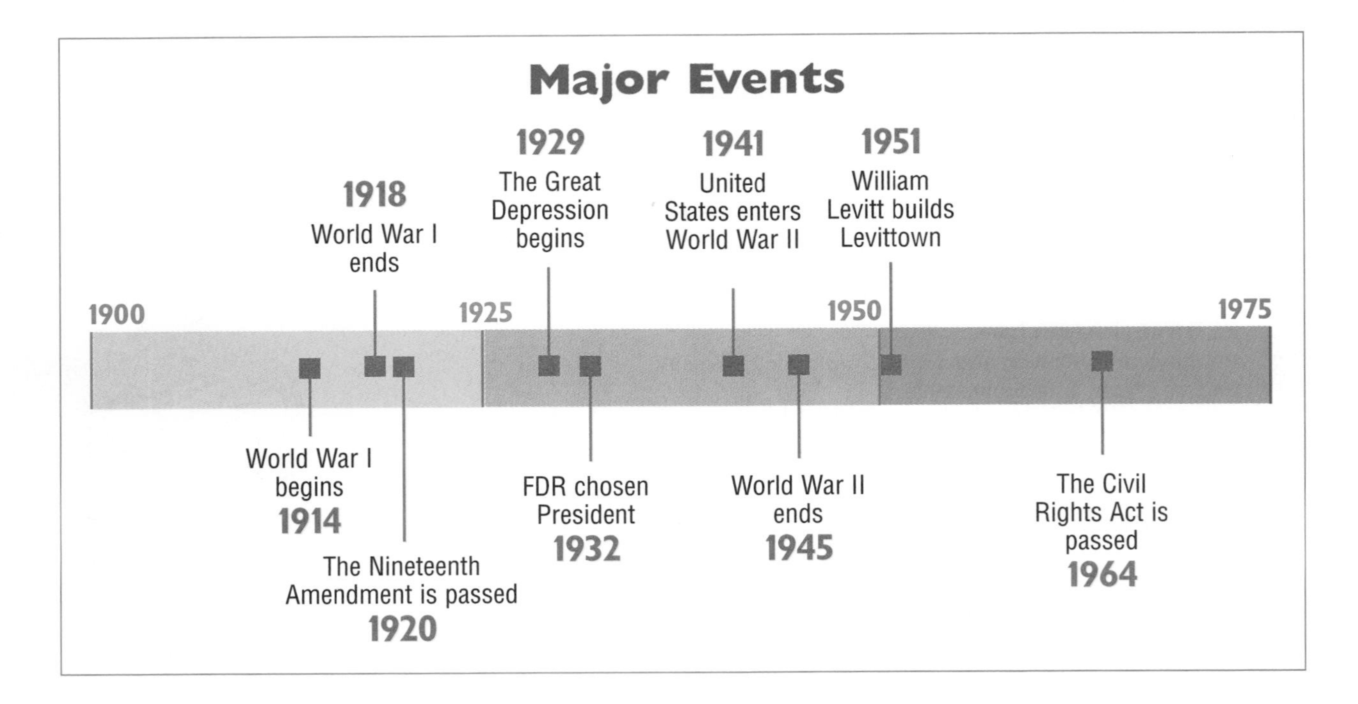

THINKING ABOUT VOCABULARY

Number a sheet of paper from 1 to 10. Next to each number write the word from the list that best completes each sentence.

amendment
commute
discrimination
Little New Deal
war bond

1. To _____ is to travel back and forth each day from one's home to one's workplace.
2. An addition to the United States Constitution is called an _____.
3. _____ is the unfair difference in the treatment of people.
4. To help the people of our state find jobs in the 1930s, Pennsylvania governors began programs known as the _____.
5. A _____ is a written promise by the government to pay back money it has borrowed to help pay for a war.

THINKING ABOUT FACTS

1. How did women in Pennsylvania help the war effort during World War I?
2. What did President Franklin D. Roosevelt do to help Americans get back on their feet during the Great Depression?
3. How were Pennsylvania's industries important in World War II?
4. Why did people want to move to the suburbs in the 1950s?
5. Looking at the time line above, tell how many years passed between the end of World War I and when the United States entered World War II.

THINK AND WRITE

WRITING A DESCRIPTION

Write a paragraph describing some of the new inventions of the 1920s and how they changed everyday life in our state.

WRITING A POSTER

Suppose you are living in Pennsylvania in 1941. Write and design a poster asking people to grow victory gardens or buy war bonds to help the war effort.

WRITING AN ADVERTISEMENT

You have read about many Pennsylvanians moving to the suburbs in the 1950s. Write an advertisement for Levittown that explains why this suburb is such a great place to live.

APPLYING THINKING SKILLS

IDENTIFYING FACT AND OPINION

1. What is the difference between a fact and an opinion?
2. What are some word clues that help you recognize opinions?
3. Identify the fact and the opinion in the following statement: *William Levitt began building Levittown in 1951. Many Pennsylvanians believed that life in the suburbs would be better than in large cities.*
4. Write a statement of your own including a fact *and* an opinion.
5. Why is it important to learn how to tell a fact from an opinion?

Summing Up the Chapter

Use the following word maps to organize information from the chapter. Copy the word maps on a sheet of paper. Then write at least one piece of information in each blank circle. When you have filled in the maps, use them to write a paragraph that answers the question "What were some of the important changes that took place in Pennsylvania during the 20th Century?"

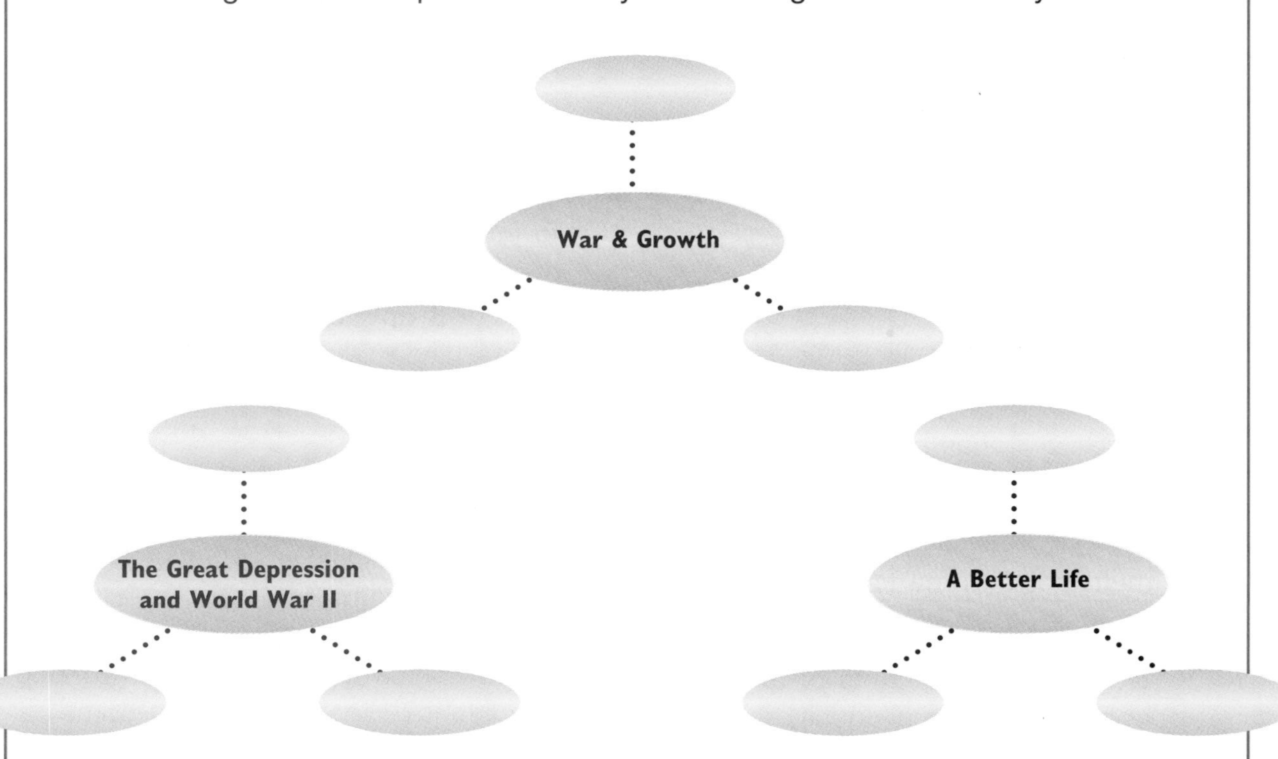

UNIT 4 REVIEW

THINKING ABOUT VOCABULARY

Number a sheet of paper from 1 to 10. Beside each number write **C** if the underlined word is used correctly. If it is not, write the word that would correctly complete the sentence.

1. Abolition was a system of secret routes through the Northern states that those escaping slavery followed to freedom.
2. All of the states that make up the United States are called the Confederacy.
3. A union is an organization formed by workers.
4. A dam is the stopping of work by workers in order to receive higher pay or to improve their working conditions.
5. A war bond is a written promise by the government to pay back money that has been loaned to help pay for the war.
6. Suffrage is the ending of slavery.
7. Stocks are shares, or parts, of ownership in a company.
8. World War II was started by the Allies, led by Germany, Italy, and Japan.
9. A metropolitan area is a community just outside of a city.
10. Civil rights are the rights of all people to be treated equally under the law.

THINK AND WRITE

WRITING A SHORT STORY

Suppose you are a conductor on the Underground Railroad. Write a short story about one of your experiences helping enslaved people escape to freedom.

WRITING A NEWSPAPER ARTICLE

Suppose you are a newspaper reporter who has arrived in Johnstown the day after the big flood. Write an article describing what happened and tell about the experiences of the people in Johnstown.

WRITING A LETTER

It is the early 1960s and you admire Dr. Martin Luther King, Jr., and his fight for civil rights. Write a letter to your local newspaper explaining why you believe in Dr. King's struggle.

BUILDING SKILLS

1. **Fact and opinion** Find one fact and one opinion in Unit 4. Explain how you made your choices.
2. **Fact and opinion** Andrew Carnegie believed that education was the way to improve communities. Is this a fact or an opinion? How do you know?
3. **Fact and opinion** The Civil War began when Confederate soldiers fired at Fort Sumter in April 1861. Is this a fact or an opinion? How do you know?
4. **Making conclusions** Give several examples of times when you might find it useful to make conclusions.
5. **Making conclusions** Did the use of unions and strikes during the late 1800s help workers get better working conditions? What helped you come to your conclusion?

YESTERDAY, TODAY & TOMORROW

The growth of technology and new inventions in the late 1800s brought about many changes in the lives of Pennsylvanians. During the 1900s, the invention of the automobile caused even greater changes. What kind of new technology do you think will cause great changes in the future of our state and country?

READING ON YOUR OWN

These are some of the books you could find at the library to help you learn more.

THE HOME FRONT
by R. Conrad Stein
This book describes what life was like on the "home front" during World War II.

THE BATTLE OF GETTYSBURG
by Alden R. Carter
This book tells the story of the Confederate Army's defeat at the Battle of Gettysburg and its effect on the Civil War.

THE DAY FORT SUMTER WAS FIRED ON: A PHOTO HISTORY OF THE CIVIL WAR
by Jim Haskins
This book illustrates the course of the Civil War in photographs.

UNIT PROJECT

Make a Pennsylvania History Mural

1. Think about the murals that artists for the WPA and other government agencies painted during the Great Depression.
2. Pick an event or time period in Pennsylvania history between the Civil War and the present to illustrate.
3. To begin your mural, sketch in pencil at least four scenes from the time period you chose.
4. Use crayons, markers, or paints to color the scenes. Paste your pictures on poster board.
5. Give your mural a title. Then share the mural and the history of the events it illustrates with your classmates.

STATE CAPITOL PLAZA (LEFT) CULTURAL FESTIVAL (RIGHT) PHILADELPHIA SYMPHONY ORCHESTRA (BELOW)

PITTSBURGH PENGUINS (LEFT) PENNSYLVANIA QUILTER (RIGHT)

UNIT FIVE

Pennsylvania Today

". . . rapidly-growing [center] of business . . ."

from a statement on the King of Prussia, Pennsylvania, Internet website
See page 208.

WHY DOES IT MATTER?

What do you think Pennsylvania will be like in the next century? Do you think Pennsylvanians will continue to work and play in the same ways they do now? What kinds of problems and opportunities do you think Pennsylvanians will have in the future?

As Pennsylvania faces the future, it has much to celebrate. We are lucky to live in a state where a blending of cultures gives us the opportunity to better understand the world we live in. In Unit 5 you will learn more about Pennsylvania's economy and government and what makes our state special.

HIGH-TECH INDUSTRY

CHAPTER 9

Economic Growth

THINKING ABOUT GEOGRAPHY AND ECONOMICS

Pennsylvania provides many important goods and services to the economy of the United States. We are lucky to have rich farmlands, booming cities, and the world's largest chocolate factory! Read on to find out about the many kinds of economic growth in Pennsylvania.

HERSHEY

Pennsylvanians are very proud of the Hershey Company, which is the world's largest producer of chocolate. This woman is taking a sample from a 10,000 pound tub of chocolate.

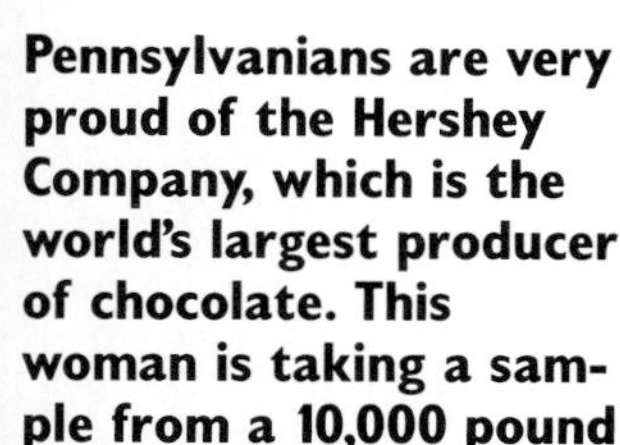

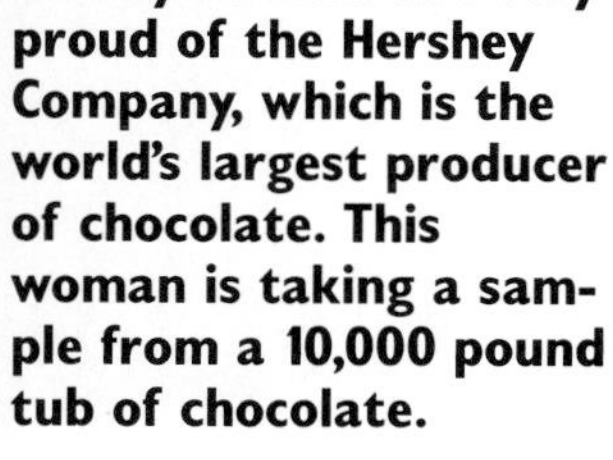

PHILADELPHIA

In this chapter you will read how many medicines and pills are made in our state. This vitamin factory in Philadelphia is just one of the many businesses that help make Pennsylvania a leader in the medical industry.

AVONDALE

Avondale mushroom growers help make Pennsylvania the mushroom capital of the world. But do you know how this affects our economy? Chapter 9 will explain.

NORTH EAST

Today farmers in North East, Pennsylvania use machinery to harvest grapes. In this chapter you will read more about farming in our state today.

LESSON 1

A FREE-ENTERPRISE ECONOMY

Focus Activity

READ TO LEARN

How does the free-enterprise economy work in Pennsylvania?

VOCABULARY

free-enterprise system
entrepreneur
profit
investor
consumer

PLACES

Zelienople

READ ALOUD

Mr. John Huesken [HUHS ken] is an adviser for a student-run business. He says that the free-enterprise system is "the best way known to give people economic power."

THE BIG PICTURE

One of the most important parts of life in Pennsylvania is its economy. As you have read in Chapter 1, the economy is the way a place uses its resources to meet people's needs and wants. Every time you spend or earn money, you are taking part in our economy.

One of the strengths of the economy in the United States is the free-enterprise system. Under this system people are free to own and run their own businesses. People in business decide what to make or buy. Shoppers can choose between many different products. The free-enterprise system allows Americans to make their own economic decisions.

A BUSINESS BLOOMS

People start thousands of businesses every year in our country. Here is how one business in Zelienople [zee lee NOHP uhl], Pennsylvania, got its start.

Getting Started

In 1995 a group of 13 students at Seneca Valley High School decided they wanted to learn about business by starting one themselves. They made ten products they thought the people in their community would buy. One product was a cookie sheet. Other products were boxes of candy and nuts, Christmas doorbells, and candles.

People who organize and run a business, such as these high school students, are called entrepreneurs (ahn truh pruh NURZ). Entrepreneurs take risks by creating products they think people will want to buy. When a business is successful, an entrepreneur makes a profit. Profit is the money a business earns after it pays for supplies, tools, salaries, and other costs. The profit is a return for hard work—and for taking a risk.

The First Steps

The group at Seneca Valley chose one student, Serenity Vincent, as president. Serenity Vincent chose four other students as vice presidents. Each vice president was put in charge of a different part of the business. The students decided to call their company "American Students Successfully Educating Themselves," or ASSET for short. The students also decided that if they got good advice, they would have a better chance of running a successful business. John Huesken, an employee of a local company, agreed to help them out.

The students (right) all helped to make products such as these cookie sheets (above) for ASSET.

A CLOSER LOOK

Starting and running a business means a lot of work. Let's take a closer look at how the Seneca Valley students made ASSET a success.

Investors and Consumers

Starting a business costs money. Most businesses need to borrow money to get started. Often businesses borrow money from **investors**. An investor is someone who puts money into a business. The investor usually expects to get some of the profit in return. The investors in ASSET were the 13 student entrepreneurs themselves. Each student bought from one to five shares for a total of 55 shares. The shares cost $5 each, so the business started with $275.

ASSET now had money to buy materials and tools. The students all helped to make the products. For example, to make the cookie sheets, the students bought pieces of stainless steel cut to the right size. Then they bent and shaped each piece into a cookie sheet. When the products were finished, the students needed to let **consumers** know about their products. Consumers are the people who buy a product or use a service.

The Service Side

"We thought the best way to tell people about our products was to talk to them in person," said Rachel Deere, a member of ASSET. Some of the products were sold door-to-door. The students also sold their products during the Zelienople Christmas parade and at a special sale in Pittsburgh.

A Successful Business

ASSET was a big success. The investors made a profit of 31 cents for each dollar they put in. The students sold $3,289 worth of goods. Their profit was over $85.

ASSET helped prepare 13 young people for a future in business. They gained first-hand business experience. The experience helped them learn how to get along with people—local businesspeople, consumers, and other students. The students can now feel sure that when they go for a job, they will be good employees.

Students (far left) gained real business skills in ASSET. In ASSET, small groups (center) each worked different jobs within their company. Student entrepreneurs (above) learned how to handle money for a business.

WHY IT MATTERS

In a free enterprise system, people make their own economic decisions. ASSET made some good decisions to become a successful business. Our economy depends on businesses that are willing to take risks.

Different parts of our state have different resources and make different products. In the next lesson, you will learn about other kinds of business in our state.

Reviewing Facts and Ideas

SUM IT UP

- In a free enterprise system, people can start their own businesses.
- Whenever you spend or earn money, you are taking part in the economy.
- Services, such as selling things to people, are an important part of our economy.

THINK ABOUT IT

1. What is free about the free-enterprise system?
2. What are two ways in which you take part in your community's economy?
3. **FOCUS** How does ASSET show the free-enterprise system working in Pennsylvania?
4. **THINKING SKILL** *Sequence* the steps that the students took to make their business a success.
5. **WRITE** Suppose you worked for ASSET. Write an advertisement explaining why people should buy your products.

LESSON 2

MANUFACTURING AND SERVICES

Focus Activity

READ TO LEARN

How have manufacturing and services changed in Pennsylvania?

VOCABULARY

high-tech industry
assembly line
service industry
tourist

PLACES

King of Prussia
Bowmansville

READ ALOUD

King of Prussia is a city near Philadelphia. If you have a computer at school that is connected to the Internet, you can learn things about King of Prussia. With your teacher, type www.Kingof-Prussia.com, and you will read, "King of Prussia is located in one of the country's most rapidly-growing centers of business and industry."

THE BIG PICTURE

Why is King of Prussia growing so fast? It is because thousands of new businesses have opened there. Some businesses are stores, hotels, and manufacturing companies. The headquarters of many large businesses have also moved to King of Prussia. This is very different from in the past. Through World War II, "heavy" industries such as coal mining and steel making were some of Pennsylvania's biggest businesses. These businesses still provide jobs for thousands of Pennsylvanians, but other businesses have grown to be more important.

The banking, printing, and chemical industries, for example, have continued to grow in recent years. Technology has also become more important. Technology allows fewer workers to create more goods. This helps to bring down prices. Thanks to our state's natural resources and our hard-working people, Pennsylvania is an important part of the free-enterprise economy of the United States.

MANUFACTURING

Today, one out of every five workers in Pennsylvania has a job in manufacturing. As you have read, manufacturing means making things in large quantities, usually by machine. Most of the items manufactured in Pennsylvania are produced in factories. These items include everything from ice cream to wheels for railroad cars.

Food Processing

Pennsylvania is among the leading states in food processing. As you have read, food processing is any of hundreds of ways of turning raw food into different kinds of products. For example, vegetables grown in Erie are made into soup in Pittsburgh. Animals eat processed food, too, and our state is number one in the production of dog and cat food.

Chemicals

Another major industry in Pennsylvania is the production of chemicals. Chemicals are used to make paint, soap, and medicine. Philadelphia is among our country's leading cities in the production of pills and other medicines.

High-Tech Industry

Did you know that the first modern computer was created in Philadelphia? Today, several companies in Pittsburgh make robots that work in factories. A robot is a machine that can do some of the things that a human being can do. These companies are part of the **high-tech industry**. This industry produces goods that require a great knowledge of science and math. Technology is the "tech" in *high tech*.

Making baby food (top) is one of the many food processing businesses in Pennsylvania. Our state's steel industry (above) still plays a strong role in our economy.

AN ASSEMBLY LINE

In many Pennsylvania factories, people work along an assembly line. On an assembly line, the work of making a product is divided into many different steps. Each worker specializes in performing a single task.

In Bowmansville, for example, about 30 people work on an assembly line to make pretzels. As the chart below shows, it takes many steps to make something even as simple as a pretzel. Working together, the men and women in the factory can make and package 64,000 large pretzels in a single day.

Work at this small pretzel company affects more than just the people in Bowmansville. Stores in states as far away as California sell the company's pretzels. By advertising on the Internet, the company receives orders from nearly every state in the United States and places in Canada.

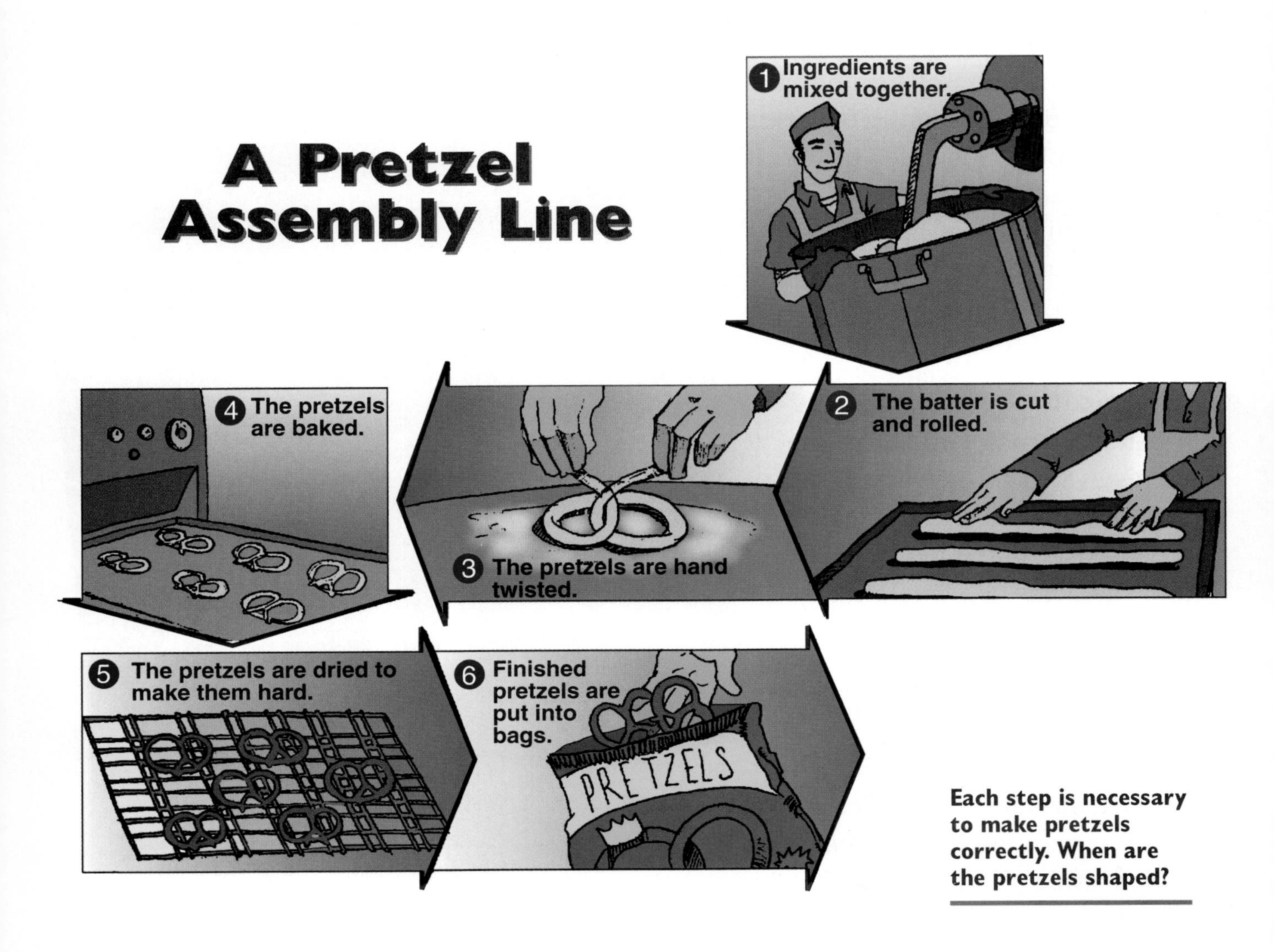

Each step is necessary to make pretzels correctly. When are the pretzels shaped?

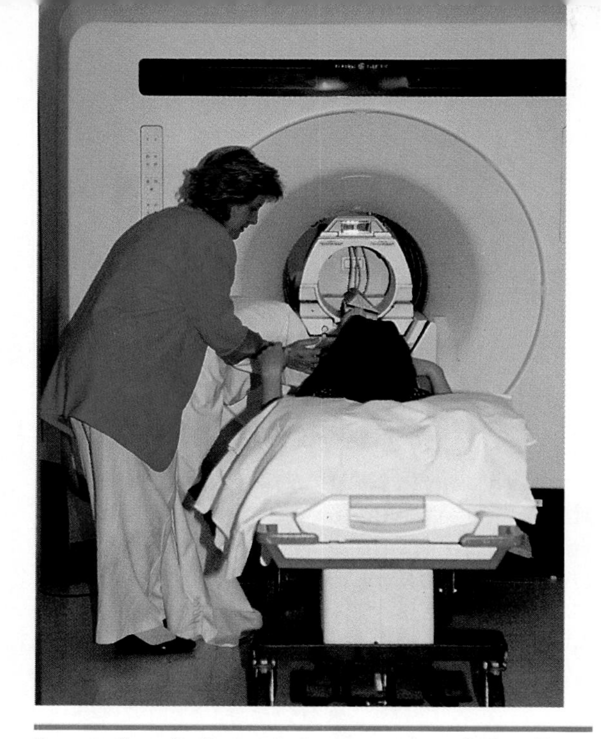

Pennsylvania is one of our country's leading centers for medical research and technology.

BIG CITIES, BIG ECONOMIES

As you know, Philadelphia and Pittsburgh are the largest cities in our state. Many people who live in these metropolitan areas work in the service industry. The service industry is made up of all the people whose jobs are to help other people. The service industry makes up the largest part of our economy.

The Service Industry

Doctors, nurses, salespeople, and teachers work in the service industry. So do government workers such as police officers, postal workers, and firefighters.

In Chapter 8 you read that Monroeville began as a small suburb. Today, this suburb is still growing. Both King of Prussia and Monroeville are important business centers in Pennsylvania.

Large malls in King of Prussia and Monroeville attract thousands of shoppers. The salespeople, restaurant workers, and visitor information workers who take care of them are part of the service industry.

The Tourist Industry

Large numbers of tourists visit Pennsylvania every year. Tourists are people who travel for pleasure or to learn about other places. They come to hike and fish, visit museums, see historical sites, or go to any of the hundreds of other attractions in our state.

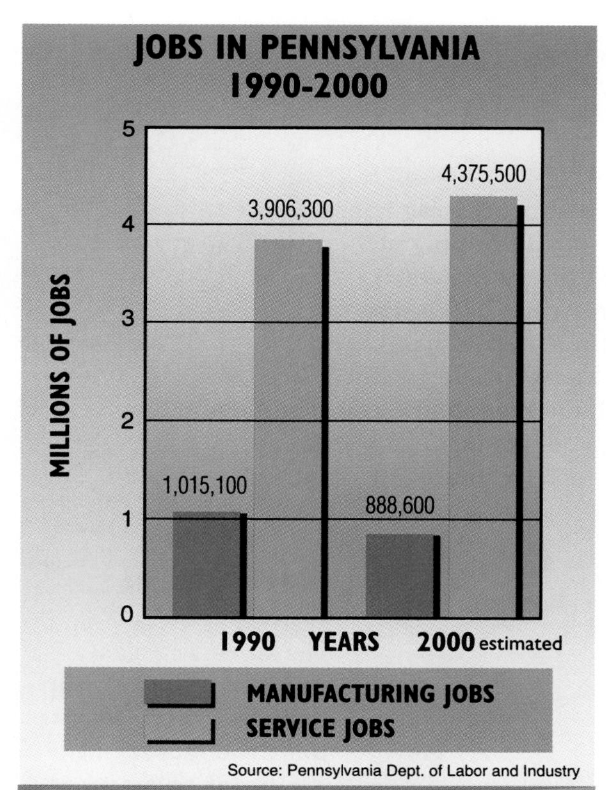

CHART WORK

This chart predicts jobs in the future.

1. Were there more manufacturing jobs or service jobs in 1990?
2. Why do you think the service industry is expected to grow?

Infographic

The Economy of Pennsylvania

Food processing and chemicals are two of Pennsylvania's largest industries. What other goods and services are important to our state's economy?

Dress for Success

Pennsylvania is the fourth-leading state in the manufacturing of clothing. Factories turn out suits and coats for men and boys, children's clothing, and women's dresses.

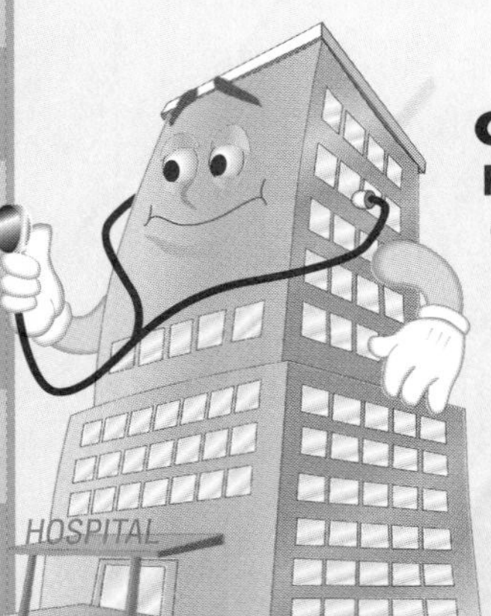

Get Well Soon

Pittsburgh is one of our country's top medical centers. More than 50 hospitals are located there. Many perform life-saving heart and liver operations.

In the Soup

Food processing has been an important industry in Pennsylvania since 1800, when flour mills dotted the landscape. Today there are over 1,200 companies producing many hundreds of products including bread, preserved vegetables, and many different kinds of soup.

Heavy, Man

One of every 10 tons of our country's steel is produced in Pennsylvania. Most of it is made in or around Pittsburgh.

How Sweet It Is!

The world's largest chocolate factory is in Hershey. Milton Hershey built the factory in 1905 in order to be near the cows that would supply the fresh milk for the chocolate. Millions and millions of pounds of chocolate candy are produced here each year.

Hi, Tech

Pennsylvania produces many high-tech products, such as electronic parts for robots and computers. New companies are starting all the time.

Can You Dig It?
Coal is still our state's most important mineral. Over 70 million tons are mined each year. In addition to being burned for heat or to make electricity, coal is also used to make some medicines and plastics.

Which Came First?
Pennsylvania is second in our country in egg production. Every year, Pennsylvania chickens lay 5 billion eggs. That's enough for each American to have a 20-egg omelet!

I'll Be Seeing You
Each year, millions of tourists bring billions of dollars to Pennsylvania's economy. On a busy summer day, 20,000 tourists may visit Independence National Park in Philadelphia. What tourist site is nearest your school?

WHY IT MATTERS

People in Pennsylvania have jobs in many fields—from high-tech industries to service industries. As our free-enterprise economy grows and changes, new jobs and businesses are created. As you grow older, you will play a more important role in our state's growing economy.

Reviewing Facts and Ideas

SUM IT UP

- Major industries in our state include service, tourist, food processing, and high-tech.
- In many Pennsylvania factories, people work along an assembly line.
- Pennsylvania cities, such as King of Prussia and Monroeville, have grown because of new businesses and industries.

THINK ABOUT IT

1. Name five different kinds of products manufactured in Pennsylvania.
2. Why do tourists from all over the country come to Pennsylvania?
3. **FOCUS** How have the manufacturing and service industries in Pennsylvania changed in recent years?
4. **THINKING SKILL** *Predict* whether or not our state's cities will continue to grow. Explain the reason for your prediction.
5. **GEOGRAPHY** Look again at the Infographic. How do you think the geography and resources of Pennsylvania influence our economy?

GEOGRAPHYSKILLS

Reading Time Zone Maps

VOCABULARY

time zone

WHY THE SKILL MATTERS

Many people today are able to do business over long distances with the help of computers, telephones, fax machines, and plane travel. Suppose a businessperson in Harrisburg wants to talk to someone in Phoenix, Arizona. She would need to know what time it is in Phoenix before making her calls. If it is 9:00 A.M. in Harrisburg, it's only 7:00 A.M. in Phoenix.

USING THE SKILL

Until the late 1800s towns across the country set their own time by the location of the sun in the sky. For example, it would be noon in Harrisburg when the sun was directly overhead. However, a person traveling across the country by train would have no way of knowing what time it was in each town along the way. It was also hard for people who set train schedules to know when trains from different cities would arrive.

Time zones were set up to solve this problem in 1884. Earth is divided into 24 time zones—one for each hour of the day. The difference in time between most neighboring time zones is exactly one hour.

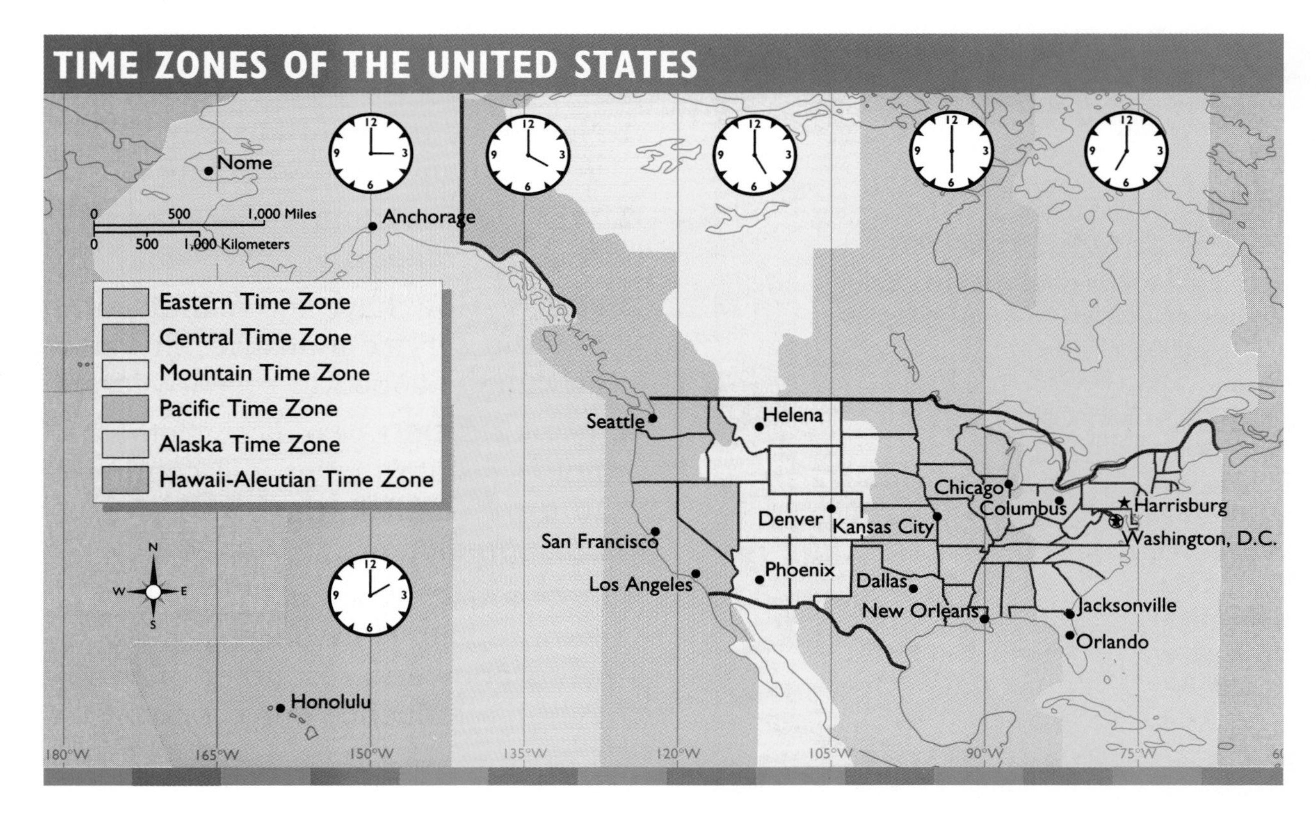

HELPING Yourself

- **A time zone is one of 24 parts of Earth used to measure standard time.**
- **Find your starting point on the map.**
- **Add an hour for each time zone east of you. Subtract an hour for each time zone west of you.**

Look at the Time Zone map. As you can see, most states in the United States are located within one time zone. However, some states are located within more than one time zone.

Because Earth rotates from west to east, in time zones east of yours it is always later than it is in your time zone. In time zones west of yours it is always earlier than it is in your time zone. For example, suppose it is 7:00 P.M. where you live. In the time zone just west of yours it is 6:00 P.M.

What time is it in Seattle, Washington, if it is 4:00 P.M. in Pittsburgh? To figure this out, count the number of time zones to the west of Pittsburgh until you reach Seattle. How many time zones are there? Now subtract one hour for each time zone going west. Pittsburgh and Seattle are three time zones apart. When it is 4:00 P.M. in Pittsburgh, it is 1:00 P.M. in Seattle.

TRYING THE SKILL

Answer the following questions about time zones using the Time Zone map. Use the Helping Yourself box for hints.

What is the name of the time zone to the west of Phoenix? What time zone is to the east?

If the President of the United States plans to make a speech on television from Washington, D.C. at 5:00 P.M., what time will people hear the broadcast in Los Angeles, California? What time would people hear it in Dallas, Texas? How did you figure out the broadcast times?

Suppose your family is on vacation in Honolulu, Hawaii, and wants to call friends in Erie, Pennsylvania. It is 9:00 P.M. in Honolulu. What time is it in Erie? Is it too late to make the call?

Suppose you live in Allentown. Your family is planning a trip to Washington, D.C. After school, you want to call the visitor center to find out about fun things to do. The visitor center is open until 5:00 P.M. every day. You get home from school at 3:30 P.M. Will you be able to call the office before it closes? Why or why not?

REVIEWING THE SKILL

1. What is a time zone?
2. What time zone do you live in?
3. When people in San Francisco, California, are waking up at 7:00 A.M., what time is it in your town? In Anchorage, Alaska? How do you know?
4. If you leave at 4:00 P.M. to take an hour-long plane trip from Columbus, Ohio, to Chicago, Illinois, what time will it be when you arrive in Chicago?
5. Why is it important to be able to use a time zone map?

MODERN AGRICULTURE

Focus Activity

READ TO LEARN

How has modern technology changed farming in Pennsylvania?

VOCABULARY

agribusiness
agriculture
organic farming

PLACES

Penns Creek
West Chester
Avondale

READ ALOUD

David Johnson is a farmer in the Susquehanna River Valley. He says, "The Susquehanna River Valley here is all about dairy farming. . . . The valley is a natural transportation [route]. My milk goes straight to New York City by truck every other night. Besides, the climate is good. River fog can hold back the frost, and that gives us a longer growing season. . . ."

THE BIG PICTURE

Today, only about one out of every 100 Pennsylvanians is a farmer like David Johnson. Yet their farms cover almost one-fourth of all Pennsylvania's land. In the early 1800s, 80 out every 100 Pennsylvanians worked on farms across our state. That number has been getting smaller year after year. Modern machines have made it possible for large farms to be run by a few people.

Another change that came to rural Pennsylvania was the growth of agribusiness. Agribusiness is a farm combined with other businesses, such as food processing. These farms often grow several different crops and ship them across the country. Together they produce an amazing variety of food products that end up on kitchen tables across the United States. How do these farmers do it?

MODERN FARMING

Today farming in Pennsylvania is big business. Modern equipment has made **agriculture**, or the business of growing crops and raising animals, a high-tech industry.

Agribusiness

Paul Keene and his family own a farm with more than 500 acres near the town of **Penns Creek**. The Keenes practice **organic farming**. Organic farming means using natural products, such as manure, instead of manufactured chemicals to enrich the soil. Paul Keene says that this allows "the soil to feed the plants." Keene also uses ladybugs instead of chemicals to help control insects that might eat the plants.

The Keenes run an agribusiness. Every year their farm produces 700 tons of food such as potatoes, apples, and corn. The Keenes package more than 350 different products for sale all over the country. There is a factory right on the farm. It can produce 60 cans of soup every minute. Other products include cereal, jelly, and pancake mix. Look at the map on this page. What farm products can be found near where you live?

In an agribusiness, some of the foods grown on a farm may be canned there also.

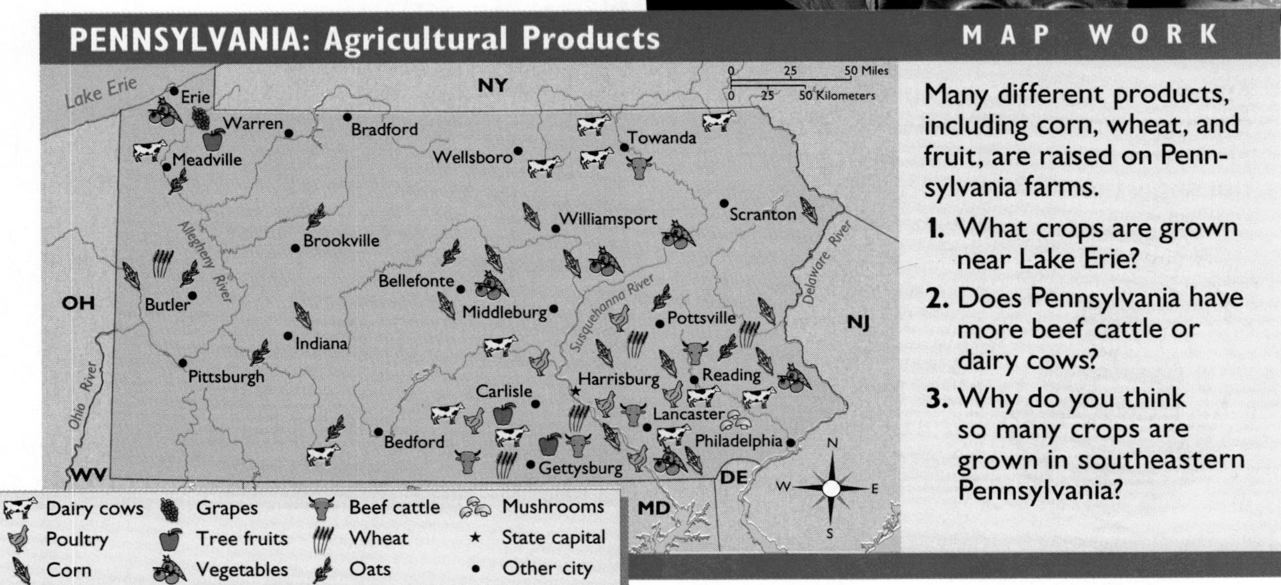

MAP WORK

Many different products, including corn, wheat, and fruit, are raised on Pennsylvania farms.

1. What crops are grown near Lake Erie?
2. Does Pennsylvania have more beef cattle or dairy cows?
3. Why do you think so many crops are grown in southeastern Pennsylvania?

FARMING AS A BUSINESS

Pennsylvania farms produce many kinds of products. However, milk is our state's number one product. Only three other states produce more milk than Pennsylvania.

Dairy Farming

High technology has changed dairy farming in our state. With modern milking machines, one farmer can milk as many as 20 cows at the same time.

On some dairy farms, computers are used to keep track of how much milk each cow produces. Farmers also use computers to figure out the healthiest mixture of grains to feed each cow for the least amount of money. Computers measure out the amount of grain that each cow will need every day.

Links to **ART**

Our Farming Heritage

How does Pennsylvania's seal show the importance of agriculture to our state?

Among the symbols on Pennsylvania's state seal are three bundles of wheat, a plow, and a cornstalk. This is to honor the importance of agriculture in our state's history. Draw the symbols you would use if you were making a seal for your school.

With modern technology, cows today can produce twice as much milk as cows did 40 years ago. Our state has more than 600,000 dairy cows. They produce over ten billion pounds of milk every year. That's about 40 pounds—or over 7 gallons—per cow per day.

The Pick of the Crop

One of the most important crops in our state is mushrooms. Farmers around West Chester and nearby Avondale make Pennsylvania the mushroom capital of the country.

Our state is also among the top five states that grow apples, grapes, and peaches.

The Amish Farmer

There are only 25,000 Amish living in Pennsylvania—about as many people as live in a small city such as Easton or Lebanon. Yet they are some of our state's best-known farmers. As you have read, the Amish live today much as they lived in the past. On Amish farms horses still pull the plows. The Amish feel strongly about taking care of the land on which they live and work. They think they should leave it in better condition than when they first began to work it.

Although the Amish continue to farm the way their ancestors did, the changes around them are causing them to change too. Much of the farmland around Lancaster, the center of Amish country, is being used to build new homes, stores, and tourist sites. About half of the Amish men in this area have jobs other than farming. In recent years, many Amish families have moved to other states so they might have more land for farming.

In a modern dairy barn (left), milk is collected by machinery into large glass jars. On Amish farms (below), horses still pull the machinery.

WHY IT MATTERS

Agriculture is an important part of our state's economy. Modern technology has helped farmers to produce more food than in the past. it has also helped our state become one of the leading agricultural states in our country.

Reviewing Facts and Ideas

SUM IT UP

- Major Pennsylvania farm products include mushrooms, apples, grapes, peaches, and milk.
- By using new technology, farmers are finding better ways of raising crops and dairy cows.

THINK ABOUT IT

1. Name some major Pennsylvania crops.
2. What is organic farming?
3. **FOCUS** How has technology changed farming in Pennsylvania?
4. **THINKING SKILL** *Compare* and *contrast* a modern Pennsylvania farmer with one from the 1800s.
5. **GEOGRAPHY** Why do you think so many farms in Pennsylvania are found in valleys and on flat areas near Lake Erie?

CHAPTER 9 REVIEW

THINKING ABOUT VOCABULARY

Number from 1 to 10 on a sheet of paper. Next to each number write the word or term from the list below that best completes the statement.

assembly line	**investor**
consumer	**organic farming**
entrepreneur	**profit**
free-enterprise system	**service industry**
high-tech industry	**tourist**

1. All the companies that use science and mathematics to produce their goods are part of the _____.
2. Farming without factory-made chemicals is called _____.
3. An _____ is person who organizes and runs a business.
4. A _____ is a person who visits an area just to enjoy himself or herself.
5. When people work on an _____, each worker specializes in performing a single task.
6. Someone who puts money into a business is called an _____.
7. People are free to own and run their own businesses under the _____.
8. People whose jobs are to help other people make up the _____.
9. A _____ is a person who buys a product or uses a service.
10. The money a business earns after it pays for supplies, tools, salaries, and other costs, is called a _____.

THINKING ABOUT FACTS

1. Describe how the free-enterprise system works.
2. What are some of the first steps in starting a business?
3. Name three industries that have continued to grow in recent years.
4. Name three products that are made with chemicals.
5. What are some examples of service jobs? Think of one kind of service job that is not listed in the chapter.
6. How much of Pennsylvania's land is covered by farms?
7. How have modern machines affected the number of people needed to run farms in our state?
8. Name four farm products that can be found in Pennsylvania.
9. How has technology changed dairy farming in our state?
10. How is Amish farm life changing as the farmland around Lancaster is being used for homes and stores?

THINK AND WRITE

WRITING A BUSINESS PLAN

Think of a product or service that people might buy. Write a business plan for your idea, and name your company. Include the things you would need to get started, such as time, money, and supplies.

WRITING A LETTER

Imagine you and your classmates are planning to start a business. Write a letter to a person in your community asking for advice in beginning that business. Be sure to tell the person why you chose to contact him or her.

WRITING A JOB DESCRIPTION

Choose an industry in our state that you might like to work in someday. Write a description of a job in that industry that you might enjoy doing.

APPLYING GEOGRAPHY SKILLS

READING TIME ZONE MAPS

Refer to the map on page 214 to answer the following questions.

1. Why were time zones created?
2. Into how many time zones is Earth divided?
3. In time zones west of yours, is it always earlier or later than in your time zone? Why?
4. The Dodgers are playing a baseball game in Los Angeles, California. The game is going to start at 2:00 P.M. What time does it start in your town?
5. You get home from school at 4:00 P.M. You want to call a friend in New York City. Will he or she be home from school yet? Why?

Summing Up the Chapter

Use the following chart to organize the information from the chapter. Copy the chart on a sheet of paper. Then write at least two pieces of information under each topic. When you have filled in the chart, use it to write a paragraph that answers the question, "How do people in Pennsylvania make a living?"

HIGH-TECH INDUSTRY	SERVICE INDUSTRY	AGRICULTURE

CHAPTER 10

Pennsylvania Government and You

THINKING ABOUT GEOGRAPHY AND CITIZENSHIP

Have you ever wondered how you could help make changes in your community? Have you ever thought about ways you would like to help our state? Do you know what your responsibilities are as an American? This chapter is all about government. Read on to learn how our local, state, and national governments work.

HARRISBURG

Pennsylvanians across the state are proud of our State Capitol in Harrisburg. The governor and other state leaders depend on citizens like you to help keep our government running smoothly.

City of Erie, Office of the Mayor

OUR LOCAL GOVERNMENT

Focus Activity

What role do citizens play in our local governments?

VOCABULARY
citizen
elect
borough
township
municipal
commission
council
mayor
manager
home rule
county
county commissioner

PEOPLE
Joyce A. Savocchio

PLACES
Erie

READ ALOUD

Mayor Joyce A. Savocchio of Erie is proud of her city and wants people of all ages to share in her pride. In 1996 she said:

"Cities are important. Our cities hold all the things that make up our identity. I want to encourage our young people to stay and rebuild our cities and help to improve the quality of life that we all share."

THE BIG PICTURE

You already know that Pennsylvania is a part of the United States. Pennsylvanians are citizens of the United States. Citizens are people who are born in a country or who have earned the right to become members of this country. United States citizens have special rights and freedoms and also have special responsibilities.

In our country, citizens elect leaders for their government. To elect means to choose by voting. Leaders carry out the wishes of the people who elected them. Citizens have the duty of paying taxes. Governments use tax money to pay for services such as fixing roads and building new schools.

Later in this chapter, you will learn about the government and the leaders of our state and our country. In this lesson, you will read about the ways in which our local governments affect our lives.

GOVERNMENT IN YOUR COMMUNITY

Think about the community where you live. What is it called? Besides its name, your community is probably known as a city, a **borough**, or a **township**. A borough is a community that usually has fewer people than a city. A township is a community for citizens who live in areas outside of cities or boroughs. All communities have local governments elected by the people who live there.

What Local Governments Do

Why is it important to have a government in your local community? Local government is needed to make decisions. Of course you—and your family—make decisions all the time. Some decisions affect only you. Other decisions affect your whole community. What if you thought that your street needed a new stop sign? You could not make this decision alone. It would probably be made by your local government.

In Pennsylvania, local governments have many responsibilities. They run police and fire departments. They make sure that the community has water and that the garbage gets picked up. Local governments take care of parks, roads, and traffic lights. Some even run libraries and hospitals.

How do our governments pay for all of these important services? They use tax money from citizens to pay for community programs.

Local government workers help us in many ways. Police officers (top) help carry out a city's laws. Firefighters (above) are always prepared to battle a blaze.

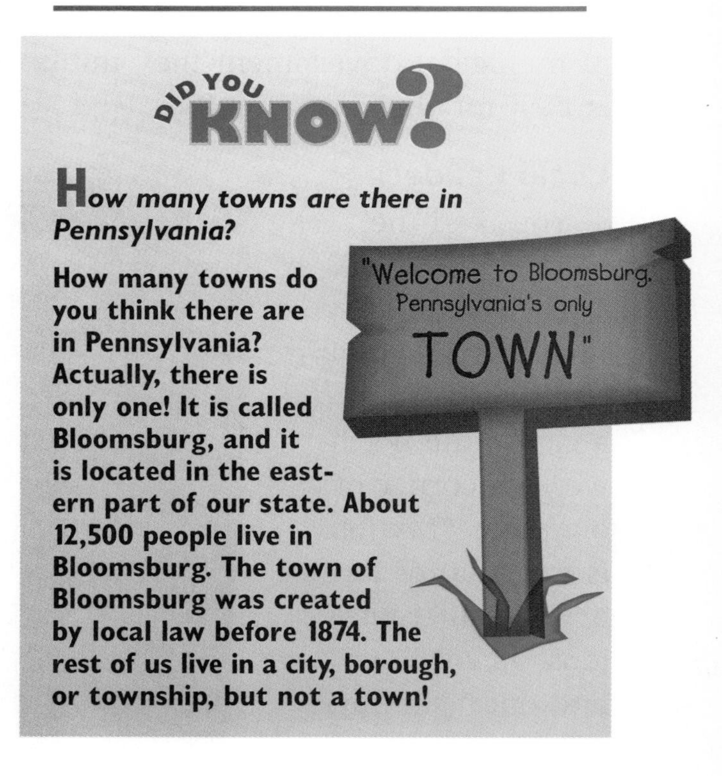

How many towns are there in Pennsylvania?

How many towns do you think there are in Pennsylvania? Actually, there is only one! It is called Bloomsburg, and it is located in the eastern part of our state. About 12,500 people live in Bloomsburg. The town of Bloomsburg was created by local law before 1874. The rest of us live in a city, borough, or township, but not a town!

MUNICIPAL GOVERNMENT

Another name for local government is municipal government. Municipal governments are made up of a group of elected leaders. In townships this group is usually called a commission. In boroughs the elected group is usually called a council. Cities may have either a commission or a council.

Most cities and boroughs also have a mayor. A mayor oversees a municipal government and carries out its laws. Some local governments have a manager in addition to, or instead of, a mayor. A manager is appointed by the council to take care of the community's daily business.

Home Rule

Why are there different kinds of municipal government? The state of Pennsylvania allows home rule. This means people can vote for the kind of municipal government they think is best for their community.

Local Leaders

You read the words of Joyce A. Savocchio in the Read Aloud. She is the mayor of Erie, a city in the northwestern corner of our state. "My job is made up of three or four different jobs, all rolled up into one," she says.

Mayor Savocchio helps other city officials decide how to spend the city's taxes. She oversees the services that the city provides, such as the police and fire departments. Mayor Savocchio also represents the people of Erie to our country and state governments, and to people who are visiting from other countries. She also works to create more jobs for Erie.

Mayor Savocchio helps to set goals for the city. She has a Neighborhood Outreach Program in which she travels around the city of Erie. In this program she talks to people of all ages to find out what is important to them. One project Mayor Savocchio is very excited about is a new high school in Erie. "It really is a school for the 21st century," she says. "It is very important that we use technology and information to prepare our students."

A mayor and the municipal government decide where new homes and businesses should be built.

COUNTY GOVERNMENT

Each municipal government is part of a larger community called a county. A county is one of the sections into which a state is divided. There are 67 counties in Pennsylvania. Look at the county map on page R13. Can you find the county in which you live?

What County Governments Do

Most counties are run by a group of three elected people called the county commissioners. County commissioners are usually elected every four years. Other counties choose to organize their government differently under home rule.

The county commissioners, along with other elected county leaders, are responsible for many things. For example, county governments must make sure that elections run smoothly. This means having citizens sign up to vote, deciding where the voting will take place, counting the votes, and sending the election results to Harrisburg.

County governments have other duties. For example, our county governments must decide how best to use county taxes. County governments in Pennsylvania repair county roads and buildings. Many also run hospitals, airports, libraries, and community colleges. In addition, county governments support different programs for people in the community who need help.

Voting is an important role citizens play in our government (below, left). By running libraries, many county governments play a role in education.

School boards make many student sports activities possible.

SCHOOL DISTRICTS

School districts are a special kind of local government. They are separate from our municipal and county governments. Voters in a school district elect a group of leaders called the school board. School boards in Pennsylvania have nine members. In most districts, school board members are elected for six-year terms. School boards hire teachers, decide on school programs, and make sure that you have the supplies a student needs. Have you ever been to a meeting of the school board in your school district? Most are open to the public. Going to these meetings is a good way to learn about your local government.

WHY IT MATTERS

Government leaders make decisions that affect our health, safety, and education. It is important for citizens to be involved with our local governments. Mayor Savocchio says, "What you think is very important. Write to your mayor, your city council, and your school board. Local officials are very interested in what young people have to say."

Reviewing Facts and Ideas

SUM IT UP

- Every community has some kind of local government.
- Municipal government runs a township, borough, or city. Home rule allows citizens to vote for the kind of municipal government they want.
- County governments are usually run by three county commissioners.
- School districts are special kinds of government that make decisions about education.

THINK ABOUT IT

1. What is a citizen?
2. What is a county?
3. **FOCUS** How can citizens play a role in our local governments?
4. **THINKING SKILL** *Classify* the following as the duties of either municipal or county government: organizing elections, making sure the community has water, and running the local fire department.
5. **WRITE** Write to the leader of your municipal government to find out more about what he or she does.

CITIZENSHIP

MAKING A DIFFERENCE

Speaking Out for Safety

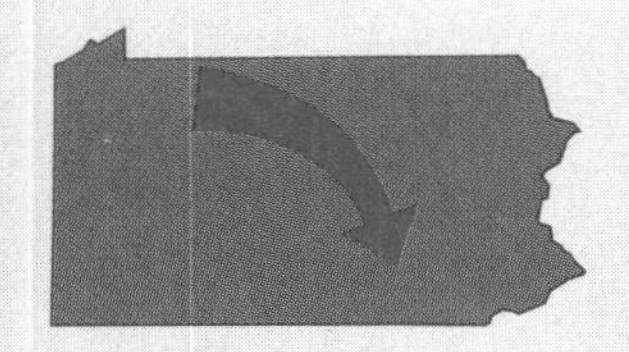

HERSHEY, PA—In 1993 Lena Malcolm and Joshua Etterman were students at Hershey Intermediate School. One day an emergency room nurse there talked to them about bicycle injuries. "I was shocked when I heard what happened to kids who didn't wear helmets," said Lena.

Lena, Joshua, and over 200 other students were taking part in a program called Kids Around Town. These students had to pick a community problem and decide how to solve it. Lena, Joshua, and other students decided to learn more about bicycle accidents. Some students wrote to the National Safety Council for information. Others asked all the fifth graders about bicycle safety and helmet use.

After they examined all the information they had collected, Lena, Joshua, and the other students wanted all children under age 12 to wear helmets while riding their bicycles. They asked if they could speak at a meeting of the Hershey Board of Supervisors. The supervisors are local government officials who make the laws for the Hershey community.

Joshua Etterman was one of the students who went to the board meeting. He said, "At first I thought we shouldn't force people to wear helmets, but when I saw that people died from not wearing helmets, I changed my mind." After sharing their information with the supervisors, the students asked the Board to pass a helmet safety law.

That same year, lawmakers in Pennsylvania's state government passed a helmet law for all Pennsylvanians, not just the people living in Hershey.

The Hershey students felt their work had helped the state lawmakers pass the new law. "Our work," said Lena, "showed that young people should speak out. If people hear us, good things can happen."

". . . good things can happen."

Lena N. Malcolm

Joshua M. Etterman

OUR STATE'S GOVERNMENT

Focus Activity

READ TO LEARN

What are the jobs of the three branches of state government?

VOCABULARY
checks and balances
executive branch
governor
budget
legislative branch
General Assembly
bill
veto
judicial branch

PEOPLE
Tom Ridge

PLACES
Harrisburg

READ ALOUD

In January 1995, Tom Ridge became the Governor of our state. He spoke about working together: "As a community, we agree there is much to be done. As neighbors, we sense the immediate need. As individuals, we must realize that the responsibility of change lies . . . within ourselves."

THE BIG PICTURE

The Pennsylvania Constitution is the guide for running our state's government. It explains that the government is divided into three branches, or sections. The Constitution describes the responsibilities of each branch. The Constitution also describes the responsibilities and the rights of our state's citizens.

The government is divided into three branches so that no person or group of people will have too much power. Each branch of government keeps watch over the other two branches. This is called the principle of checks and balances.

THE EXECUTIVE BRANCH

Have you ever visited Harrisburg, our state capital? Many important decisions are made there every day. These decisions affect the lives of every Pennsylvanian—including you!

It is the job of the executive (eg ZEK yoo tihv) branch to carry out the laws of our state. The head of the executive branch is called the governor. The governor's office is in Harrisburg, along with many other state government offices.

The Governor

You read the words of Governor Tom Ridge in the Read Aloud. The governor is elected by the people of our state to serve for a term of four years. Each Pennsylvania governor may be elected for two terms in a row.

The governor helps set goals for our state. He or she also chooses people to run some executive departments such as the Department of Health and the Department of Environmental Resources. These departments work to provide people such services as public health programs and the protection of state land and water. State workers also take care of our state highways and buildings.

Pennsylvanians pay state taxes to provide for these services. The governor is responsible for making a plan to use the taxes. This plan is called a budget. The budget shows how much the state will spend on each service. The circle graph on this page shows how Pennsylvania spends taxes and other money.

Pennsylvania state park rangers protect state land, water, and wildlife. This ranger at Canoe Creek State Park helps educate visitors about bears.

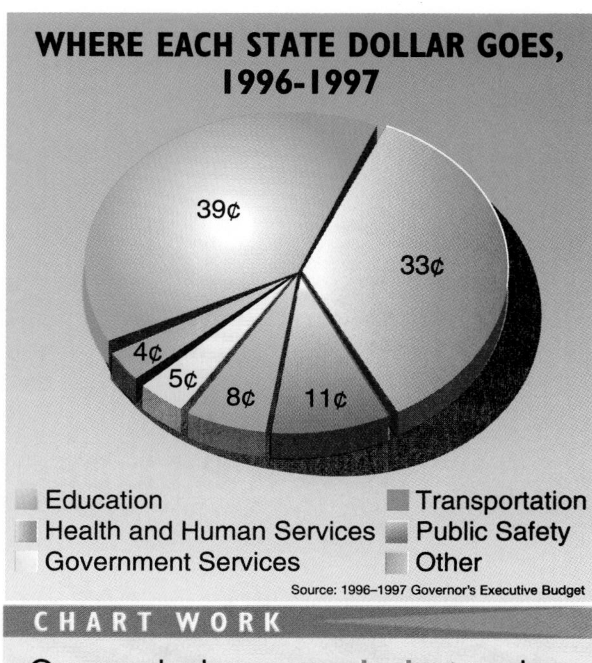

CHART WORK

Our state leaders create a budget to plan how to spend state money.

1. On which kind of service does our state spend the most money?
2. How much is spent on transportation?
3. In which area would you like to see our state spend more? Why?

THE LEGISLATIVE BRANCH

The **legislative** (LEJ is lay tihv) **branch** of our state government is responsible for making the laws. Our legislative branch meets in the State Capitol Building in Harrisburg.

The General Assembly

In Pennsylvania, the legislative branch is called the **General Assembly**. The General Assembly has two parts—the Senate and the House of Representatives. The 50 senators and 203 representatives are elected by Pennsylvania voters. State senators serve four-year terms and state representatives serve two-year terms. Senators and representatives in the General Assembly vote on **bills**. Bills are proposals for laws.

How does a bill become a law? Let's follow the history of one bill. Our state song is "Pennsylvania" by Eddie Khoury and Ronnie Bonner. You can read the words to this song in Chapter 11. But how did this song become our state song?

In 1988 several members of the Pennsylvania legislative branch proposed a bill making "Pennsylvania" our state song. The House of Representatives and the Senate voted to pass the bill. Then it went to the governor, who at that time was Robert P. Casey. If he had disagreed with the bill, he could have decided to **veto**, or reject it. Instead, in 1990, he signed it and "Pennsylvania" became our state song.

Follow the steps showing how a bill becomes a law.

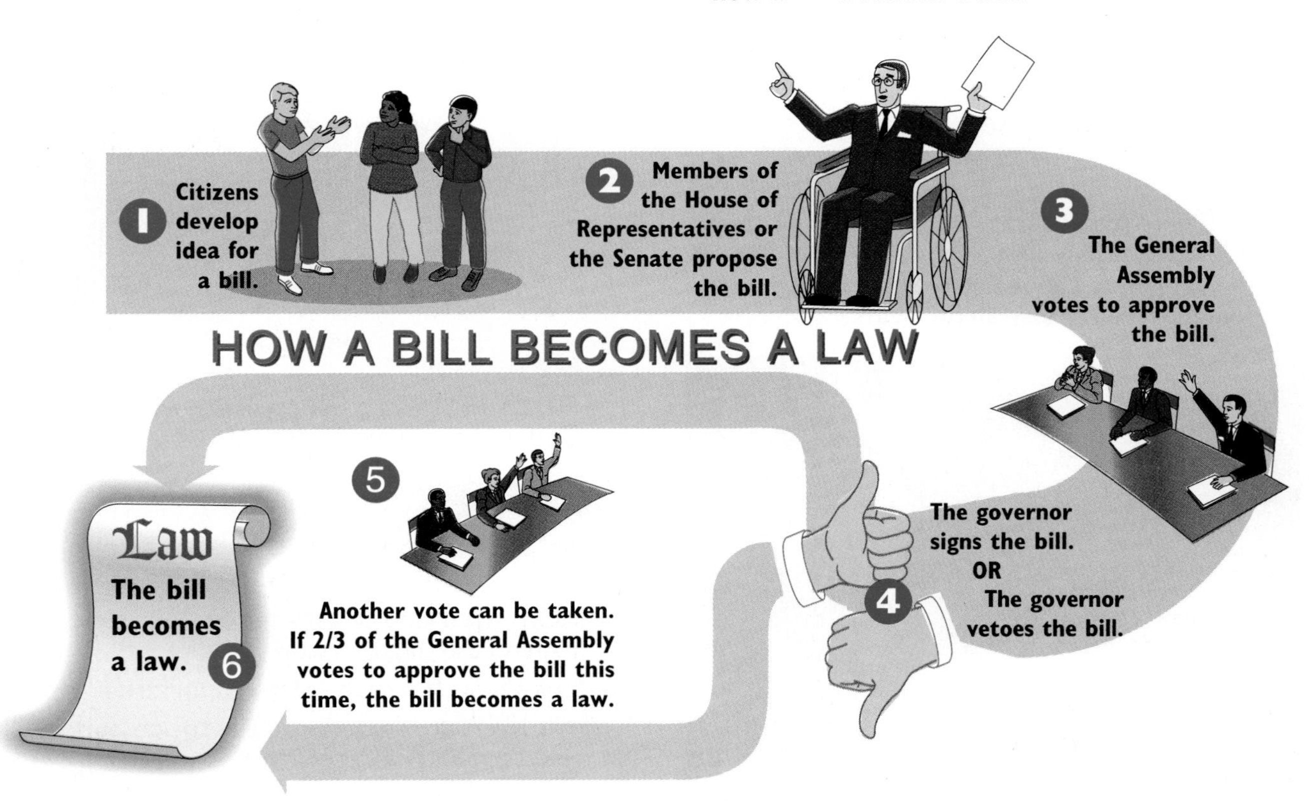

In Pennsylvania, the Supreme Court (left) explains our state's laws. In the State Capitol Building (below, left) where the General Assembly meets, any member may propose a new bill.

THE JUDICIAL BRANCH

The judicial (joo DISH uhl) branch of state government interprets, or explains, our state's laws. This branch is made up of judges, people who hear cases in courts. The highest court in Pennsylvania is the Supreme Court, which has seven judges.

The Supreme Court hears cases from lower courts. It may also decide to hear any case that it considers to be very important. If the Supreme Court judges decide that a law goes against the Pennsylvania Constitution, they can reject that law.

WHY IT MATTERS

A government works well when its citizens take an interest in what is happening. There are many ways to take part in government. What issues interest you? Write letters to your representatives. Elected officials need to hear from citizens in order to represent their view.

Reviewing Facts and Ideas

SUM IT UP

- The checks and balances system makes sure that no one branch of government has too much power.
- Our state government provides services to Pennsylvanians.
- The state government is made up of the executive, legislative, and judicial branches.

THINK ABOUT IT

1. What is the principle of checks and balances?
2. How does a bill become a law?
3. **FOCUS** What is the job of each branch of our state government?
4. **THINKING SKILL** *Make a conclusion* about why it is important to communicate with state leaders.
5. **GEOGRAPHY** Look in your local telephone book. Name any state offices in or near your community.

STUDYSKILLS

Reading Newspapers

VOCABULARY

news article
feature article
editorial
headline
byline
dateline

WHY THE SKILL MATTERS

You have just read that Pennsylvania's state government is run by the governor and the state legislature. What if you wanted to learn more about the decisions officials make? A good way to find out is to read a newspaper.

Reading a newspaper is often the best way to get information about what is happening today. Many newspapers cover events from all over our country and around the world. Some focus on events from a state, city, or town.

USING A NEWSPAPER

When you read a newspaper, it helps to know the different parts. Use the Helping Yourself box on page 235 to guide you in reading newspapers. The front section of a paper includes mostly **news articles**. These articles contain facts about recent events.

Another kind of article is a **feature article**. A feature article takes a detailed look at a specific person, subject, or event.

Newspapers also include sports articles, letters to the editor, and **editorials**. In an editorial, the editors—the people who run the paper—share their ideas about an issue. Unlike a news article, an editorial gives opinions rather than facts.

USING A NEWS ARTICLE

A news article usually begins with a **headline**—a title printed at the top of the story. The headline tells the main idea of the story in just a few words.

Look at the news article on the facing page. It is based on an article that appeared in the *Lancaster Sunday News*. Find the headline "State Senator Adds Amendment for New Motorcycle Riders."

News articles often have a **byline**. The byline names the writer of the article. The writer of this story is Jon Rutter.

Finally, many news articles include a **dateline**. This tells when and where the article was written. The dateline here tells you that this article was written on March 17, 1996, in Lancaster.

A well-written news article should answer five questions: (1) *Who* was involved in the event? (2) *What* took place? (3) *When* did the event happen? (4) *Where* did the event happen? (5) *Why* did the event happen?

Read this article. Does the article answer the five questions? The first answer, for example, would be "State Senator Gibson Armstrong." Can you explain *what* happened in your own words? Can you say *why* it happened?

HELPING *Yourself*

- **Identify whether you are reading a news article, a feature article, or an editorial.**
- **Study the headline, byline, and dateline.**
- **Ask yourself the "five questions" about the story.**

TRYING THE SKILL

You just read a news article about an amendment written by State Senator Gibson Armstrong to make new motorcycle riders take part in a safety program. Why do you think that reading a newspaper is a good way to learn about such an event? Can you think of any other sources for this kind of information?

Now suppose that your class is curious about a different topic: the construction of a new state highway. An article in the newspaper is called "Highway Opening Delayed." What kind of article do you think this is? Another is called "New Highway is a Step in the Right Direction." What kind of article do you think this is? How do you know?

REVIEWING THE SKILL

1. Name three different kinds of articles that appear in newspapers.
2. How can you tell that the article printed below is a news article and not an editorial?
3. Why is it important for some news articles to have a dateline?
4. How would a newspaper help you learn more about Pennsylvania?

State Senator Adds Amendment for New Motorcycle Riders

By Jon Rutter

LANCASTER, Pennsylvania, March 17—State Senator Gibson Armstrong on Tuesday introduced an amendment to a transportation bill to improve motorcycle safety. The amendment would make all new motorcycle riders take part in the state's Motorcycle Safety Program. The program teaches riders the importance of wearing a helmet, giving turn signals, and staying within the speed limit.

The cost would be expensive—perhaps $25 for each person taking the course. But Armstrong thinks that would be a small price to pay to save lives.

"We have a lot of people who think it's cool to be on a motorcycle," he said, "but some do not know the first thing about riding. That, plus the fact that some young riders like to go fast, makes the motorcycle a dangerous machine."

The legislature is expected to pass the bill by the end of summer.

OUR NATION'S GOVERNMENT

Focus Activity

READ TO LEARN

What are the rights and responsibilities we have as Americans?

VOCABULARY

democratic republic
candidate
political party
United States Congress
United States Supreme Court
jury

PLACES

Washington, D.C.

READ ALOUD

"I pledge allegiance to the flag of the United States of America, and to the Republic for which it stands, one Nation under God, indivisible, with liberty and justice for all."

THE BIG PICTURE

When you say the Pledge of Allegiance, you make a promise. You are promising to be loyal to the United States and support our country's government.

Running a government is not easy. After declaring the United States an independent country in 1776, our country's first leaders found out just how tough the job is. As you have read they wrote the United States Constitution, the plan for running our government, in Philadelphia in 1787.

The United States Constitution explains how the government is to be set up. The Constitution made our country a democratic republic. In our democratic republic, people pick representatives to run the government. Democracy means that the power to rule comes from the people.

THE UNITED STATES GOVERNMENT

In 1863 President Abraham Lincoln said that we have a "government of the people, by the people, for the people." His words remind us that democracy cannot work without its citizens. People in a democratic republic must care about choices that affect each other.

But the United States is a big country. Not every citizen can take part directly in every decision. They take part by voting. Voters elect people to make decisions for them.

In an election, the people running for office are called **candidates**. Usually candidates are members of a **political party**. A political party is a group of citizens who share many of the same ideas about government. The Democratic and Republican parties are the largest political parties in the United States.

Like our local and state governments, the United States government provides services. One of these is defense. The United States government runs the Army and the rest of our armed forces. Our government pays for the building of ships, airplanes, and weapons to defend our country—as well as other countries.

Another service our government provides is disaster relief. The Federal Emergency Management Agency helps people recover from hurricanes, earthquakes, and other natural disasters. In Chapter 1 you read about the Flood of '96 that caused much damage in Wilkes-Barre and other parts of Pennsylvania. This agency provided temporary shelter, replaced people's damaged belongings, and helped rebuild roads and homes.

Laws are passed by our government in the United States Capitol Building.

Pennsylvanians pay taxes on the money they earn to the national government. This kind of tax is called an income tax. Pennsylvanians also pay an income tax to the state government. In addition, we pay sales taxes to our state and local governments on things we buy. Local governments in Pennsylvania also collect taxes on houses, businesses, and other property. Without taxes, the different levels of government could not provide the services we need.

THE THREE BRANCHES

Our national government is located in Washington, D.C. Like our state government, our country's government has three branches. Each branch has different duties. Find these branches on the chart below.

Congress

The legislative branch of our national government is called the United States Congress. Congress makes laws for the whole country. Congress has two parts, the Senate and the House of Representatives.

The voters of every state elect two senators to the United States Senate. The number of representatives voters elect depends on how many people live in their state. Pennsylvania, which has a large population, elects 21 people to the United States House of Representatives. The state of Vermont, on the other hand, elects only one representative. Senators serve for six years and representatives serve for two years.

The President

The President is elected every four years. This person is head of the executive branch of government. The President makes sure that laws passed by Congress are carried out. The President also meets with leaders of other countries and is the Commander-in-Chief of our military forces. The President chooses people to head national departments in charge of areas such as transportation and defense.

NATIONAL GOVERNMENT: Three Branches

EXECUTIVE **President**	LEGISLATIVE **Congress (100 Senators, 435 Representatives)**	JUDICIAL **Supreme Court (9 Judges)**
• Carries out laws • Meets with leaders of other countries • Leads military	• Makes laws for our country • Decides how much money to spend	• Makes sure our laws follow the Constitution

CHART WORK

Our national government, located in Washington, D.C., has three branches.

1. How many senators does Congress have? How many representatives?
2. Which branch does the President head?
3. What are the President's duties?
4. Who are the highest officials of the judicial branch of our government?

The Supreme Court's Chief Justice is William H. Rehnquist (center).

THE COURTS

The President also selects the United States Supreme Court judges. The Supreme Court is the highest court in our country. The courts make up the third branch of our national government. It is called the judicial branch.

Nine justices, or judges, serve on the United States Supreme Court. Once chosen and approved by the Senate, they serve for life. These judges hear cases that come from the lower courts. They also decide whether laws that are passed by Congress agree with the United States Constitution.

The lower courts decide whether laws have been obeyed. If a person is accused of breaking the law, the courts may hold a trial by jury. A jury is a group of citizens that decides whether the accused person is guilty under the law. United States citizens who are 18 or older may be called to serve on a jury.

Rights and Responsibilities

The Congress, the President, and the Supreme Court all work to protect the rights of American citizens. With rights come responsibilities. Citizens must pay taxes and obey our country's laws. At election time, it's important that we vote.

WHY IT MATTERS

The United States is a democratic republic. Citizens elect leaders to serve in government. When you turn 18, you will be able to vote for national, state, and local leaders. Voting will be your right and your responsibility.

Reviewing Facts and Ideas

SUM IT UP

- The United States is a democratic republic.
- The United States government uses taxes to pay for services such as defense and disaster relief.
- The three branches of our national government are headed by Congress, the President, and the Supreme Court.

THINK ABOUT IT

1. What is a democratic republic?
2. What is a political party?
3. **FOCUS** What are the rights and responsibilities that we have as American citizens?
4. **THINKING SKILL** How can voters *make a decision* about which candidate to elect?
5. **WRITE** What qualities do you think are important in a citizen? Write a paragraph to explain.

CHAPTER 10 REVIEW

THINKING ABOUT VOCABULARY

A. Write a sentence for each pair of words below. Include details that give clues to the meaning of the first term in each pair.

1. citizen, elect
2. municipal, mayor
3. county, county commissioners
4. bill, veto
5. candidate, United States Congress

B. Number a sheet from 1 to 10. Next to each number write the word or term from those in Part A that best completes the sentence.

1. A _____ is one of the sections into which a state is divided.
2. A _____ is a proposal for a law.
3. A person who runs for office is called a _____.
4. A _____ is a person born in a country or who has earned the right to become a member of that country.
5. The town or city where you live has a _____ government.
6. Three elected officials who run the county are called the _____.
7. The head of the municipal government is the _____.
8. In our country, citizens _____ government leaders.
9. The _____ is the legislative branch of our national government.
10. To _____ a bill is to reject it.

THINKING ABOUT FACTS

1. How do the citizens of the United States take part in our government?
2. Who is the head of the municipal government? What does home rule mean?
3. What is the purpose of the Pennsylvania Constitution?
4. What are the three branches of our national and state governments? How does the system of checks and balances apply to them?
5. In which city is the office of our state's governor located? How is the governor chosen and how long does he or she serve?
6. What is the state song of Pennsylvania? How was it chosen?
7. What services are provided by the United States government?
8. How many senators are elected by each state to the United States Senate? How many representatives to the United States House of Representatives are elected by Pennsylvania?
9. Who is the head of the executive branch of the United States government? Name two responsibilities that belong to this person.
10. What are the responsibilities of all Americans? What will be your right and your responsibility when you turn 18?

THINK AND WRITE

WRITING A BILL
Suppose you are a senator from Pennsylvania. Write a bill proposing something that would make our state a better place to live.

WRITING A POSTER
Write a poster showing the three branches of our state government. Label the responsibilities of each branch.

WRITING AN ARTICLE
Suppose you are an editor of a newspaper. Write an editorial encouraging people to vote in the next election. Explain why it is an important responsibility for each citizen to vote.

APPLYING STUDY SKILLS

READING NEWSPAPERS

1. What five questions should a well-written news article answer?
2. Look at the news article about the amendment for motorcycle riders on page 235. Identify the headline, the byline, and the dateline.
3. What is an editorial? How does it differ from a news article?
4. Look again at the news article on page 235. How would you change the article to an editorial?
5. What can you learn from reading newspapers?

Summing Up the Chapter

Use the following table to organize information from the chapter. Copy the table on a sheet of paper. Then list the people and groups that run each level of government. When you have filled in the table, use it to write a paragraph that answers the question "What do the local, state, and national governments have in common? How are they different?"

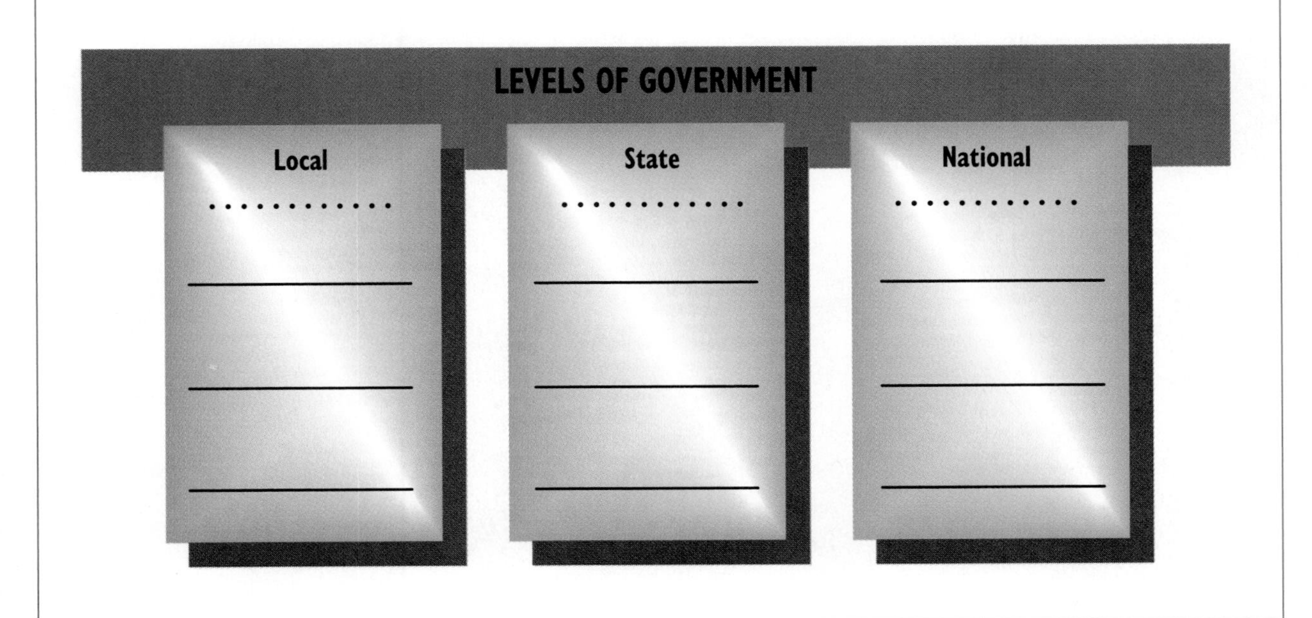

CHAPTER 11

Our Special State

THINKING ABOUT GEOGRAPHY AND CITIZENSHIP

What is your favorite way to enjoy your free time? Maybe you like to play football, paint pictures, or go for long walks outdoors. We Pennsylvanians have many ways to enjoy and celebrate our special state and our many cultures. Read Chapter 11 to find out more about the rich cultures of Pennsylvania.

OHIOPYLE STATE PARK

Many people enjoy the natural beauty of Pennsylvania's many scenic rivers. A favorite activity of visitors to our state parks is whitewater rafting. These adventurers are braving the wild waters on the Youghiogheny River.

A BLEND OF CULTURES

Focus Activity

READ TO LEARN

How have different cultures made Pennsylvania a special state?

VOCABULARY

census

PLACES

Kittanning
Punxsutawney
Manheim
State College
Allentown
Reading
Strasburg
Edinboro
Everett
Enon Valley

READ ALOUD

In an interview, a Philadelphia woman named Helen remembered one of the city's special celebrations she enjoyed as a child: "The Mummer's Parade strutted past the corner of Marshall and Girard every year. . . . A piece of America, right down our street. And it happened only in Philadelphia. The rest of the world didn't have what we had on New Year's Day."

THE BIG PICTURE

How people have fun is an important part of their culture. So too, are the languages they speak and their beliefs about the world. Ways of having fun, languages, and beliefs vary from Pennsylvanian to Pennsylvanian. As you will read in this lesson, Pennsylvania is a blend of many cultures. We are lucky to live in a state where these differences in heritage come together. They create a special Pennsylvania way of life.

In its early days, people from Sweden, England, Germany, Scotland, Ireland, France, and Africa called Pennsylvania home. Later, immigrants from Poland, Italy, and other European countries arrived. Today, Asians and people from Spanish-speaking countries also live in Pennsylvania.

WHO WE ARE

Every ten years the national government sends a census (SEN sus) to every home in Pennsylvania. A census is a count of the people who live in a place. The 1990 census showed that almost 12 million people live in our state. This makes Pennsylvania the fifth-largest state in the United States.

Where We Came From

Most Pennsylvanians have ancestors who came here as immigrants. One way to learn about the different people who are our ancestors is to study the names of Pennsylvania's towns and cities. Kittanning and Punxsutawney are Native American words, and remind us of the first settlers in our state. Other cities, such as Quakertown, are reminders of the Quakers who came here in the 1600s. Some people brought names from their old homes, like the Germans who settled Manheim.

Some of the recent immigrants to our state have come from different parts of the world—from India, China, and Vietnam [vee et NAHM]. If you've visited cities such as Philadelphia, Pittsburgh, State College, Allentown, and Reading, you've probably seen Indian and other Asian restaurants there.

Other recent immigrants to our state have come from places where most people speak the Spanish language. Two of these countries are Puerto Rico [PWAIR tuh REE koh], which is controlled by the United States, and Mexico. Look at the circle graph below to see the five largest immigrant groups to recently come to our state.

Religion in Pennsylvania

Today, Roman Catholics are the largest religious group in Pennsylvania. Our state is also known as a center of the Quaker religion. Other Christian groups include Methodists, Amish, Mennonites, Lutherans, and Presbyterians.

Jews began arriving from Europe in the 1600s and settled mostly in Philadelphia. Today, about 330,000 Jews live in Pennsylvania. Among Asian immigrants, the main religions are Hinduism [HIHN doo ih zum] and Buddhism [BOO dih zum].

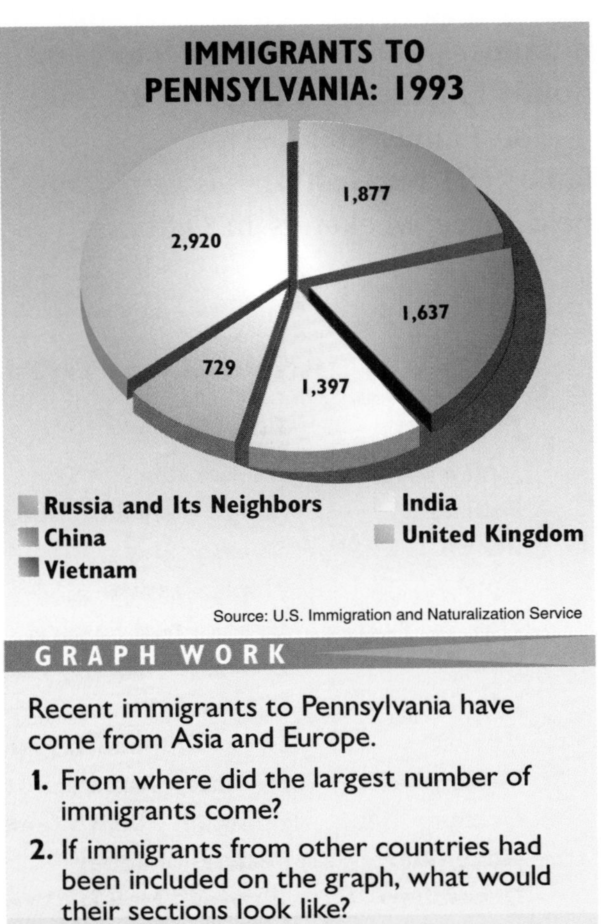

GRAPH WORK

Recent immigrants to Pennsylvania have come from Asia and Europe.

1. From where did the largest number of immigrants come?
2. If immigrants from other countries had been included on the graph, what would their sections look like?

A CELEBRATION OF CULTURES

Pennsylvanians are proud of the many different cultures that make up our state. Throughout the year, there are festivals and special events to celebrate our different traditions. Perhaps you have taken part in or gone to one of them.

Let's Celebrate!

As you have read in the Read Aloud, only in Philadelphia will you find the fun-filled Mummer's Parade. This eye-popping New Year's Day parade has hundreds of banjo players and marchers in bright, feathered costumes. *Mumming* means to go masked or in disguise. Groups of mummers paraded the streets of South Philadelphia as early as 1800.

The Family Oktoberfest [ahk TOH bur fest] in Strasburg is held three weekends in October. There are German bands, with lots of dancing and singing. You can sample German foods like bratwurst, a kind of hot dog, and sauerkraut.

Every August, African Americans in Philadelphia remember their heritage with a lively African American celebration. During this festival, the streets are filled with the sounds of African drums and the sweet smell

At many cultural events such as the Slovenfest, people often wear traditional dress and perform dances to celebrate their heritage.

ANNUAL FESTIVALS IN PENNSYLVANIA

MONTH	FESTIVAL	CITY
January	Ice Carving Festival	White Haven
February	Sleigh Rally and Ride	Forksville
March	Charter Day	Statewide
April	Maple Festival	Meyersdale
May	Greek Food Festival	Pittsburgh
June	Lancaster County Food, Farm, and Fun Fest	Ephrata
July	Oil Fields Picnic	Titusville
August	Great Stoneboro Fair	Stoneboro
September	Northern Appalachian Storytelling Festival	Mansfield
October	Pumpkin Patch Weekend	Lancaster
November	Festival of Trees	New Castle
December	Victorian Holiday Weekend	Lewisburg

of barbecued pork. People from all over Pennsylvania enjoy eating, dancing, and listening to music at this popular celebration.

At the Spring Highlands Festival in **Edinboro**, Scottish traditions are celebrated. Boys and girls of Scottish descent dress in colorful plaid kilts and dance the "Highland Fling." Bagpipe bands fill the air with their music. Many people enjoy the contests of skill such as tossing the caber, or large pole, and wrestling.

Native Americans celebrate their heritage at different events. At the Down River Pow-Wow in **Everett**, Native Americans wear the traditional dress of their ancestors. They take part in special dances and songs. Many Native American crafts such as weaving and making jewelry can be enjoyed as well.

People dance the polka almost nonstop at the Slovenfest [SLOH ven fest], in **Enon Valley**. They also enjoy traditional eastern European foods such as potato-filled dumplings called pirogi [pir OH gee], and kielbasa [keel BAH suh], a Polish sausage. Look at the chart to see some other festivals that take place in our state.

Special foods are prepared as part of many festivals.

WHY IT MATTERS

Pennsylvanians have ancestors who came from countries all around the world. As a result, we have different beliefs and celebrate different traditions. Yet, as Pennsylvanians, we also have a great deal in common. We share the responsibility of taking care of our state, because its future is our future.

Reviewing Facts and Ideas

SUM IT UP

- Pennsylvanians have ancestors from many different cultures.
- Many festivals in our state celebrate our different cultures.

THINK ABOUT IT

1. Name three countries from which recent immigrants to our state have come.
2. Name three religious groups in our state.
3. **FOCUS** How have different cultures made Pennsylvania a special state?
4. **THINKING SKILL** *Make a generalization* about what makes a Pennsylvanian a Pennsylvanian.
5. **WRITE** Write a story describing a festival you've seen.

STUDYSKILLS

Writing Notes and Outlines

VOCABULARY
outline

WHY THE SKILL MATTERS

You have just read about Pennsylvania's many festivals and celebrations. Suppose you were asked to write a report about one of them. How would you collect and organize your information?

A plan for organizing written information about a subject is called an **outline**. First take notes in your own words as you read. Write down the main ideas of what you are reading. You should also jot down important facts that support the main ideas.

For your outline, place a roman numeral beside each main idea. Under each of your main ideas, group the facts that support it. Write a capital letter beside each fact.

USING THE SKILL

The following article describes a historical celebration in Pennsylvania. Try taking notes. Then study the outline below it to see how it organizes the information.

According to the outline, what is the first main idea of this article? What facts support this idea?

There are many exciting historical celebrations in Pennsylvania. Some honor places and events like the Pennsbury Manor Fair or the Reenactment of Washington Crossing the Delaware. Others celebrate the heritage of ethnic groups that have settled in our state, such as the Kutztown Pennsylvania German Festival.

One of the newest historical events celebrates both. The Johan Printz Challenge is a canoe race held every July. This race was started in 1993 on the 350th Anniversary of Printz's arrival in New Sweden. The Challenge honors the settlers of New Sweden and their most popular governor, Johan Printz. Viewers enjoy learning about life in the Swedish Colony and watching sailboats pass by on the Delaware River.

I. Historical celebrations in Pennsylvania
   A. celebrate places and events
   B. celebrate heritage
II. Johan Printz Challenge
   A. canoe race started in 1993
   B. honors Johan Printz and settlers of New Sweden
   C. viewers learn about life in New Sweden

HELPING Yourself

- **An outline is a way of organizing what you learn.**
- **Take notes in your own words.**
- **Label each main idea with a roman numeral. Then under each main idea write two or more supporting facts.**

TRYING THE SKILL

Now read the article about another Pennsylvania celebration, the Bark Peelers Convention. Take notes as you read, then write an outline. Use the Helping Yourself box on this page for hints. What are the main ideas? Be sure to use facts from the article to support them. Do main ideas or supporting facts get roman numerals in your outline?

REVIEWING THE SKILL

1. How does writing outlines help you to organize information?
2. How did you decide which statements were main ideas and which were supporting facts?
3. In your outline on the Bark Peelers Convention, what are the supporting facts? How can you tell?
4. How can taking notes and writing an outline help you learn about history?

One of Pennsylvania's entertaining and educational festivals is the Bark Peelers Convention. This celebration honors the traditions of Pennsylvania lumber workers. It is held for two days each July at the Pennsylvania Lumber Museum between Galeton and Coudersport.

The beginnings of the Bark Peelers Convention go back to the late 1800s when the lumbering industry in Pennsylvania was booming. Every year on the fourth of July, the lumber camp workers would gather to celebrate the country's birthday and another year's hard work. They would dance, sing, and hold contests to test their skills.

There are many things to do at the Bark Peelers Convention today. You can watch lumber workers hewing, or cutting wood, making ax handles, peeling bark, and sawing. A circular steam-powered sawmill runs both days. The lumberjacks hold contests that include greased pole climbing, frog jumping, and fiddling. The celebration also has lots of music to enjoy and hand-crafted products to buy. On the final day, a traditional log cake is cut and served to everyone.

Legacy

LINKING PAST AND PRESENT

Pennsylvania Quilting

One form of folk art in our state is quilting. A quilt is a kind of cloth sandwich, usually used as a bed cover. The top is often made by sewing together different pieces of cloth to make designs. The middle is filled with stuffing, such as cotton fluff. The bottom is usually a plain cloth. Sewing the three layers together is called quilting.

There are many different quilt designs. The Amish continue to use the same designs as their ancestors did. They often use solid color fabrics and simple shapes to make patterns such as Center Diamond.

Quilts made of log-shaped strips were created by African Americans. Strip designs are still used today in Africa.

Today, many Pennsylvanians belong to quilting groups called guilds that get together to share their knowledge. In this way they hope to keep alive the legacy of quilt making.

HERITAGE QUILT

Quilting has long been a part of our state's heritage. The designs shown here are just some of the many made by Pennsylvania's quilters.

ARTS, SPORTS, AND RECREATION

Focus Activity

READ TO LEARN
How do arts, sports, and recreation make our state a fun place to live?

VOCABULARY
recreation
folk art
mobile
Pulitzer Prize
professional team

PEOPLE
August Wilson
Mary Cassatt
John Sloan
Andrew Wyeth
Alexander Calder
Annie Dillard
Jerry Spinelli
Martha Graham
Stephen Foster
Keith Jarrett
Marian Anderson
Joe Montana

PLACES
Allegheny National Forest
Williamsport

READ ALOUD

"I like Pittsburgh's rivers and hills, which allow for different people to live on different sides, each with their own neighborhood and story."

August Wilson, a poet and writer of plays, grew up in Pittsburgh. His hometown is important to the stories he tells in his plays. In fact, several of his plays take place in Pittsburgh. Wilson likes to write about the everyday lives of ordinary African Americans throughout the 1900s.

THE BIG PICTURE

August Wilson is part of the tradition of art in Pennsylvania. Art is made up of things like the pictures people paint, the songs they sing, and the stories they write. Writing, painting, dancing, and creating music are all forms of art. Art is one important part of our state's culture. So, too, are sports and recreation. Recreation is what people do for relaxation or enjoyment. Our state provides opportunities for people to enjoy art, sports, and recreation, no matter what their interests might be.

PENNSYLVANIA ARTISTS

The tradition of art in Pennsylvania dates back to the earliest Native Americans living in our state. They made rock paintings and stone carvings of animals and humans.

Later immigrants to Pennsylvania brought their own art forms, adding to our old and rich tradition. Some of this art was folk art. Folk art is the traditional art of the common people of a country or region.

In the 1800s and 1900s, many Pennsylvania painters became famous. One of them, Mary Cassatt, grew up in Pittsburgh and studied painting in Paris. In the early 1900s, John Sloan of Lock Haven painted scenes of everyday life in New York City. Andrew Wyeth lived his entire life in the small village of Chadds Ford. Many of his paintings of the land, people, and animals around him have a lonely feeling.

Born in Philadelphia, Alexander Calder, was one of the inventors of an entirely new kind of art called the mobile [moh BEEL]. A mobile is a sculpture made out of metal, plastic, cardboard, or other material. The parts of a mobile are often hung from wires and set in motion by the movement of air. In Calder's mobiles, shapes of painted metal and wood hang from wires linked together. The shapes seem to float in space.

You can see works by these and other Pennsylvania artists at some of our state's museums, such as the Philadelphia Museum of Art and the Carnegie Museum in Pittsburgh.

This famous painting (above) by Mary Cassatt is called *The Boating Party.* Alexander Calder made this mobile (right), which hangs in the National Gallery of Art in Washington, D.C.

Links to **ART**

Swinging Art

The most important thing about a mobile is the way it moves. The connected shapes are balanced so they can swing in the wind. Mobiles can be any size and shape. You can make a mobile from many different kinds of materials. Study the picture of Calder's mobile. Then try making your own mobile using sticks or coathanger wire and shapes cut from cardboard.

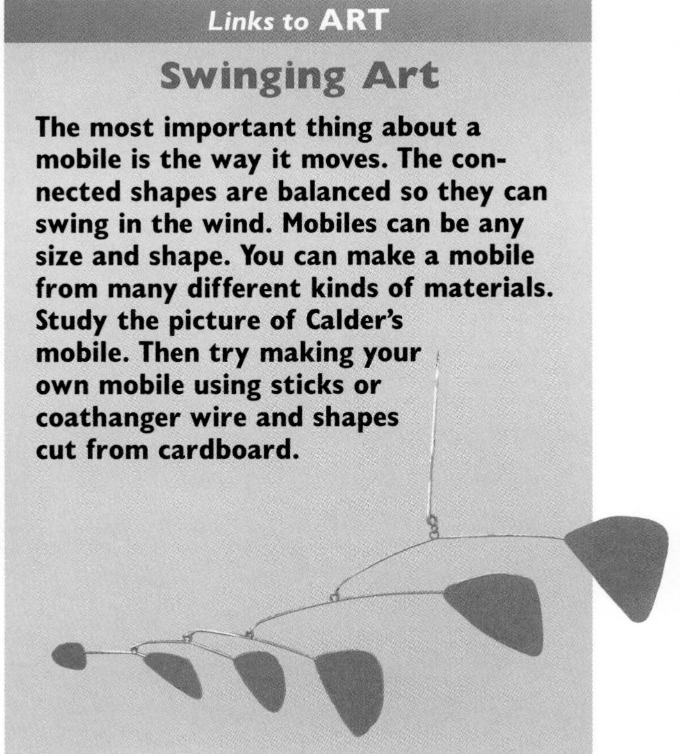

BOOKS, MUSIC, AND DANCE

Many Pennsylvanians have stressed the beauty and hardships of everyday life in their work. Their books, music, and dance are only a part of the rich heritage of our state.

Pennsylvania Writers

Annie Dillard has written books about her life and the thoughts she has had in the places she has lived. In 1974 she won the Pulitzer [PUHL iht zur] Prize for *Pilgrim at Tinker Creek,* a book about nature. Pulitzer Prizes are awarded every year for the best work in literature, music, and newspaper writing.

Jerry Spinelli [spih NEL lee], from Norristown, is also well-known for writing funny stories about the ups and downs of teenage life. Perhaps you have read one of his books, *Fourth Grade Rats.*

Pennsylvania Musicians and Dancers

Pennsylvania also has a rich musical and dance heritage. Dancer Martha Graham was born in Allegheny in 1894. Graham helped to invent "modern dance."

Stephen Foster was born in 1826 in Lawrenceville. He was one of the best-known writers of popular songs. Many of his songs, such as "Oh! Susanna," are still sung today.

Pianist Keith Jarrett, of Allentown, combines jazz and classical music to create a different music style. He plays to packed concert halls around the world.

Singer Marian Anderson was born in Philadelphia in 1902. With a beautiful and powerful voice, Anderson became the first African American to sing with the Metropolitan Opera in New York.

What songs do you enjoy singing? You can find the words and music to our state song, "Pennsylvania," on the next page. What is the "bell of independence" mentioned in the song?

Opera singer Marian Anderson (far left) was known all over the world. Author Annie Dillard (left) discusses her work in an interview.

Pennsylvania

Music and Words by
Eddie Khoury and Ronnie Bonner

Many Pennsylvanians enjoy fishing (left) or taking a drive to see our state's beautiful covered bridges (above).

ENJOYING OUR STATE

Pennsylvania offers many kinds of recreation, from rafting rivers and skiing to watching football and baseball games. No matter where you live, there is always something fun to do around our state.

The Great Outdoors

Some of the best places for recreation are our state and national parks. The Allegheny National Forest is the largest recreational area in our state. It is in the Allegheny Plateau region. This forest has over a million acres of trees. You can hike up tree-covered mountains and along quiet creeks. You can see deer, turkeys, elk, and black bears. In the winter months there is plenty of snow for cross-country skiing.

Hiking and skiing are popular in the Laurel Highlands in southern Pennsylvania and the Pocono Mountains in the northeastern part of our state. Families also camp and picnic at our state parks.

If you'd rather be near water, there are lots of places you can go. Pennsylvania has almost 50 miles of shoreline on Lake Erie. It's a great place to swim, fish, and sail. Our state also has many rivers. The swiftly moving Delaware and Youghiogheny [YAHK uh gay nee] rivers are perfect for rafting.

Autumn is a great time to be outdoors in Pennsylvania. You can take a drive or ride a bicycle to enjoy the fall colors. If you do, you might see one of Pennsylvania's many covered bridges.

Sports in Pennsylvania

As you have read, Pennsylvania is a great place for sports. For those who enjoy watching sports, both

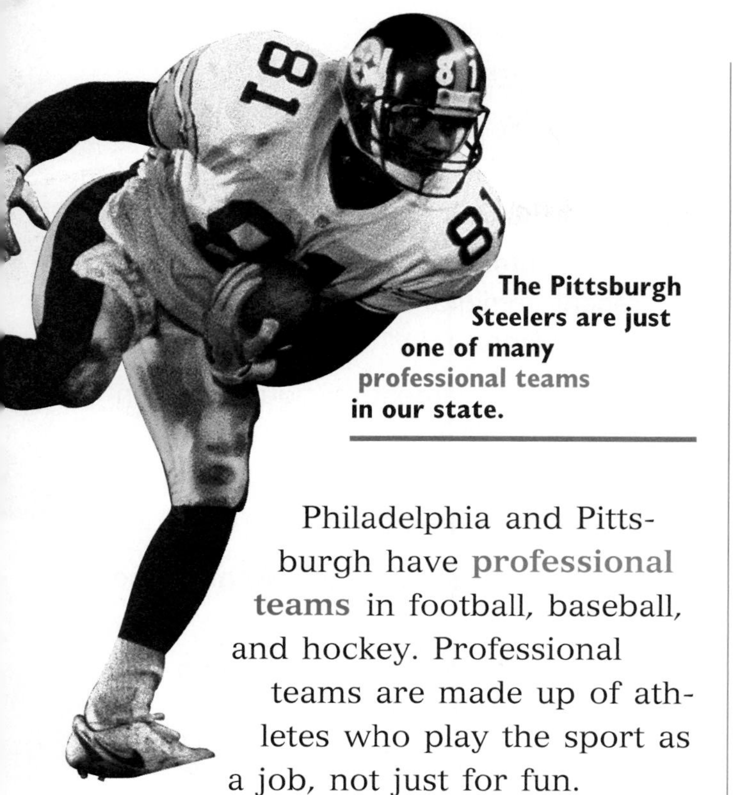

The Pittsburgh Steelers are just one of many **professional teams** in our state.

Philadelphia and Pittsburgh have **professional teams** in football, baseball, and hockey. Professional teams are made up of athletes who play the sport as a job, not just for fun. Philadelphia also has a professional basketball team, the 76ers. **Joe Montana**, one of the best professional football players of all time, was born in Monongahela.

Pennsylvania also has many college teams. Thousands of people attend college football games. Many people also enjoy track and field. The Villanova women's cross-country team won national championships for six straight years.

Pennsylvanians also enjoy baseball, from Little League to the pros. Little League started in **Williamsport** in 1939, and the Little League World Series is held there every year. Teams from all over the world take part in this exciting event. Handicapped children also take part in sporting events. The Special Olympics is held every year in Pennsylvania.

WHY IT MATTERS

You don't have to be a star to create art. You can write stories, songs, or paint at home or in school. Whenever you choose to make art yourself, you are adding to the rich heritage of our state.

From football to baseball, hiking, and canoeing, our state provides a variety of recreation. Thanks to our plentiful resources, we always have something fun to do in our state.

Reviewing Facts and Ideas

SUM IT UP

- Painting, writing, dancing, and making music are some of the art forms that make up our state's rich heritage.
- Pennsylvania's state and national parks and forests offer outdoor recreation such as hiking, skiing, and fishing.
- Football, baseball, and basketball are popular sports in Pennsylvania.

THINK ABOUT IT

1. Name two writers who have lived in Pennsylvania and one work written by each of them.
2. List three places in our state where you can hike or ski.
3. **FOCUS** How do the arts, sports, and recreation make Pennsylvania a fun place to live?
4. **THINKING SKILL** *Predict* what life might be like if people did not take the time for recreation.
5. **WRITE** Choose an event from your life. Write a poem or story that tells about it.

CHAPTER 11 REVIEW

THINKING ABOUT VOCABULARY

Number from 1 to 5 on a sheet of paper. Next to each number write the word or term from the list below that best completes the sentence.

census
folk art
mobile
Pulitzer Prize
recreation

1. The _____ is awarded each year for the best work in literature, music, and newspaper writing.
2. The traditional art of the common people of a country or region is called _____.
3. A _____ is a count of the people who live in a place.
4. _____ is what people do for relaxation or enjoyment.
5. A sculpture made out of metal, cardboard, or other material that is hung from wires and set in motion by the movement of the air is a _____.

THINKING ABOUT FACTS

1. Name three countries from which recent immigrants to Pennsylvania have come.
2. What is the largest religious group in Pennsylvania today?
3. Name three festivals that are celebrated in Pennsylvania.
4. Who was Mary Cassatt? What is she known for?
5. Name a Pennsylvania writer who has won the Pulitzer Prize.
6. Who is Stephen Foster? What is he known for?
7. List three kinds of recreation popular in Pennsylvania today.
8. What is the largest recreational area in our state?
9. Where was Little League baseball started?
10. What is the name of one sporting event where handicapped children in Pennsylvania can take part?

THINK AND WRITE

WRITING A RESEARCH REPORT
Choose an artist or a writer you read about in Lesson 1. Learn more about the person, write a report, and share it with the class.

WRITING A DESCRIPTION
Write a description of a recreation area in Pennsylvania. Include details about what you might do or see there.

WRITING AN ARTICLE
Suppose you are a sports reporter for the local newspaper. Write an article about one of the sports events mentioned in Lesson 2. Include a headline, byline, and dateline.

APPLYING STUDY SKILLS

WRITING NOTES AND OUTLINES
1. What is an outline? How can writing outlines help you organize information?
2. What are the steps in writing an outline?
3. Read the section in Lesson 1 titled "Where We Came From" on page 245. Take notes as you read, then write an outline of the section.
4. Read the section in Lesson 2 titled "The Great Outdoors" on page 256. Then write an outline of the section.
5. How can taking notes and writing an outline help you to write a research report about recreation in Pennsylvania?

Summing up the Chapter

Use the following main-idea chart to organize information from the chapter. Copy the chart on a sheet of paper. Then fill in the blank spaces on the chart. When you have filled in the chart, use it to write a paragraph answering the question, "How have art, recreation, and culture contributed to making Pennsylvania a special state?"

CULTURE	SPORTS AND RECREATION		THE ARTS
language	rafting	hiking	writing

UNIT 5 REVIEW

THINKING ABOUT VOCABULARY

Number a sheet of paper from 1 to 10. Beside each number, write the word from the list below that best matches the description.

agribusiness	General Assembly
budget	governor
checks and balances	jury
council	political party
executive branch	professional team

1. A farm combined with other businesses
2. A municipal government made up of a group of elected leaders
3. A government system where each branch keeps watch over the other branches
4. The branch of government that carries out the laws of our state
5. A plan that shows how much a state will spend on each service
6. The legislative branch of Pennsylvania's government
7. A group of citizens who share many of the same ideas about government
8. A group of citizens who decide if a person accused of a crime is guilty or innocent
9. A team that plays a sport as a job
10. The head of the executive branch of Pennsylvania's government

THINK AND WRITE

WRITING AN EXPLANATION

Choose a manufactured product made on an assembly line. Research and illustrate the different steps on that product's assembly line.

WRITING A REPORT

Choose a cultural group from Chapter 11, Lesson 1 that you know little about. Do some research about that cultural group. Then write a report and share it with the class.

WRITING A SPEECH

Suppose that you are a candidate for the council or commission in your community. Write a speech explaining how you will try to make your town or city a better place to live.

BUILDING SKILLS

1. **Reading time zone maps** Into how many time zones is Earth divided?
2. **Reading time zone maps** Is the time in zones west of where you live earlier or later than your time?
3. **Reading newspapers** Why is it important to read newspapers?
4. **Reading newspapers** If you wanted to learn the editor's opinion about an issue, what kind of news article would you read?
5. **Notes and outlines** How can writing outlines help you organize information?

YESTERDAY, TODAY & TOMORROW

Through the years, new machinery has been invented to help farmers with their work. Today, fewer people and less land are needed to produce enough food. What new machines do you think will improve farming in the future?

READING ON YOUR OWN

Here are some books you might find at the library to help you learn more.

LETTER TO THE WORLD: THE LIFE AND DANCES OF MARTHA GRAHAM
by Trudy Garfunkel
This book details the creative life led by this Pennsylvania native.

THE VOICE OF THE PEOPLE
by Betsy Maestro
Here is a guide to voting and elections in the United States.

REVOLUTION AND TECHNOLOGY
by Ann Kramer
This book looks at the changes that happened during the Industrial Revolution to show how they affect us today.

UNIT PROJECT

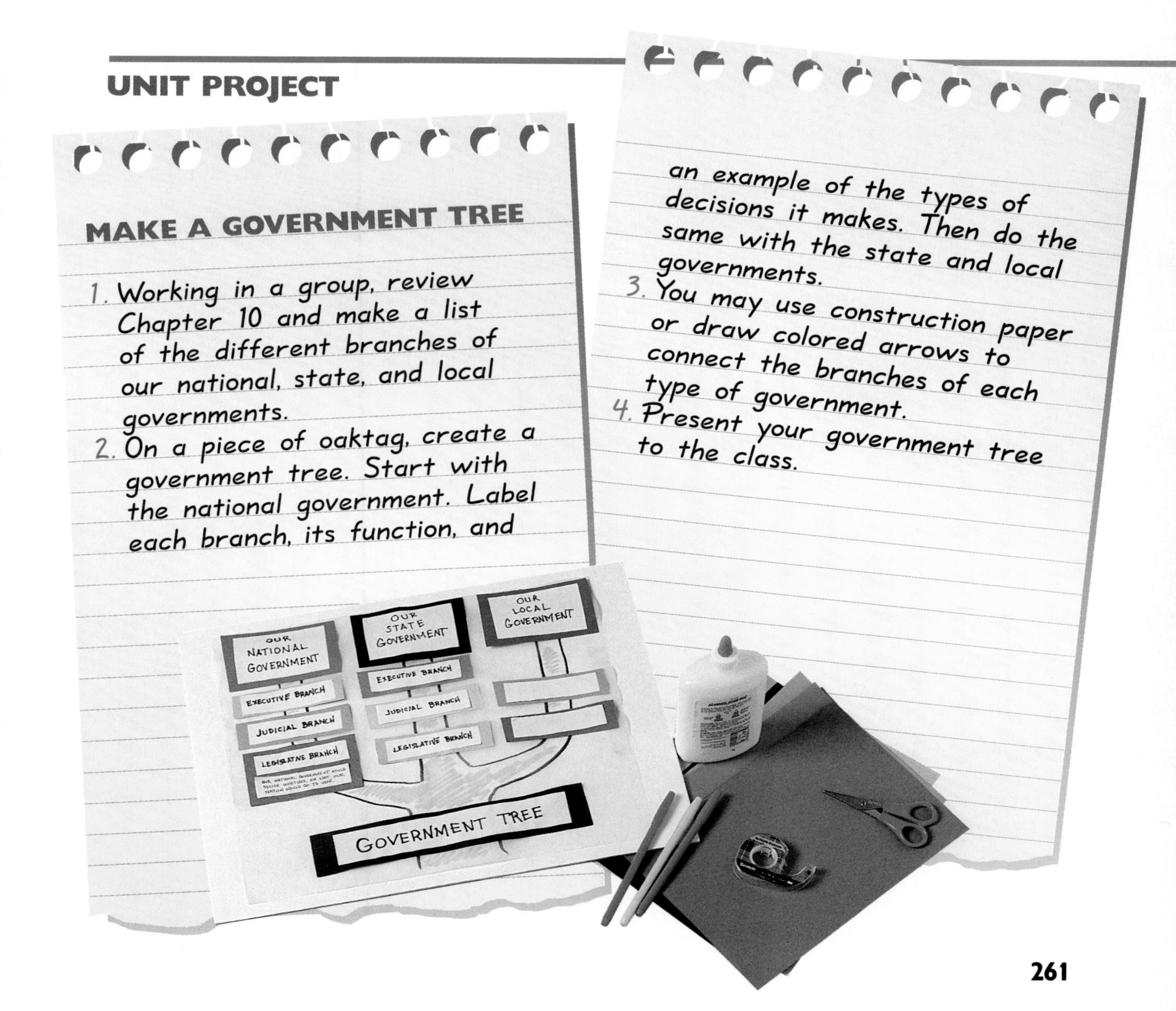

MAKE A GOVERNMENT TREE

1. Working in a group, review Chapter 10 and make a list of the different branches of our national, state, and local governments.
2. On a piece of oaktag, create a government tree. Start with the national government. Label each branch, its function, and an example of the types of decisions it makes. Then do the same with the state and local governments.
3. You may use construction paper or draw colored arrows to connect the branches of each type of government.
4. Present your government tree to the class.

REFERENCE SECTION

The Reference Section has many parts, each with a different type of information. Use this section to look up people, places, and events as you study.

R4 Atlas

Maps of our state, country, and the world

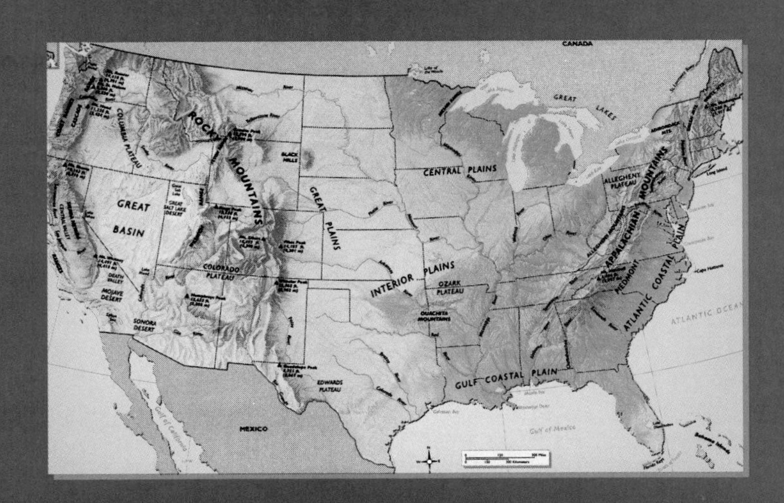

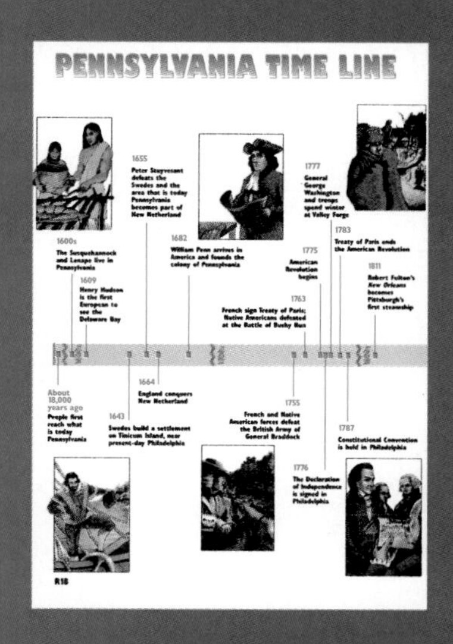
PENNSYLVANIA TIME LINE

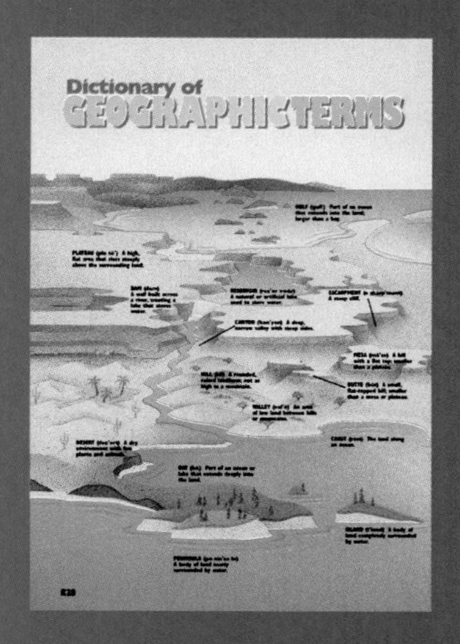
Dictionary of
GEOGRAPHIC TERMS

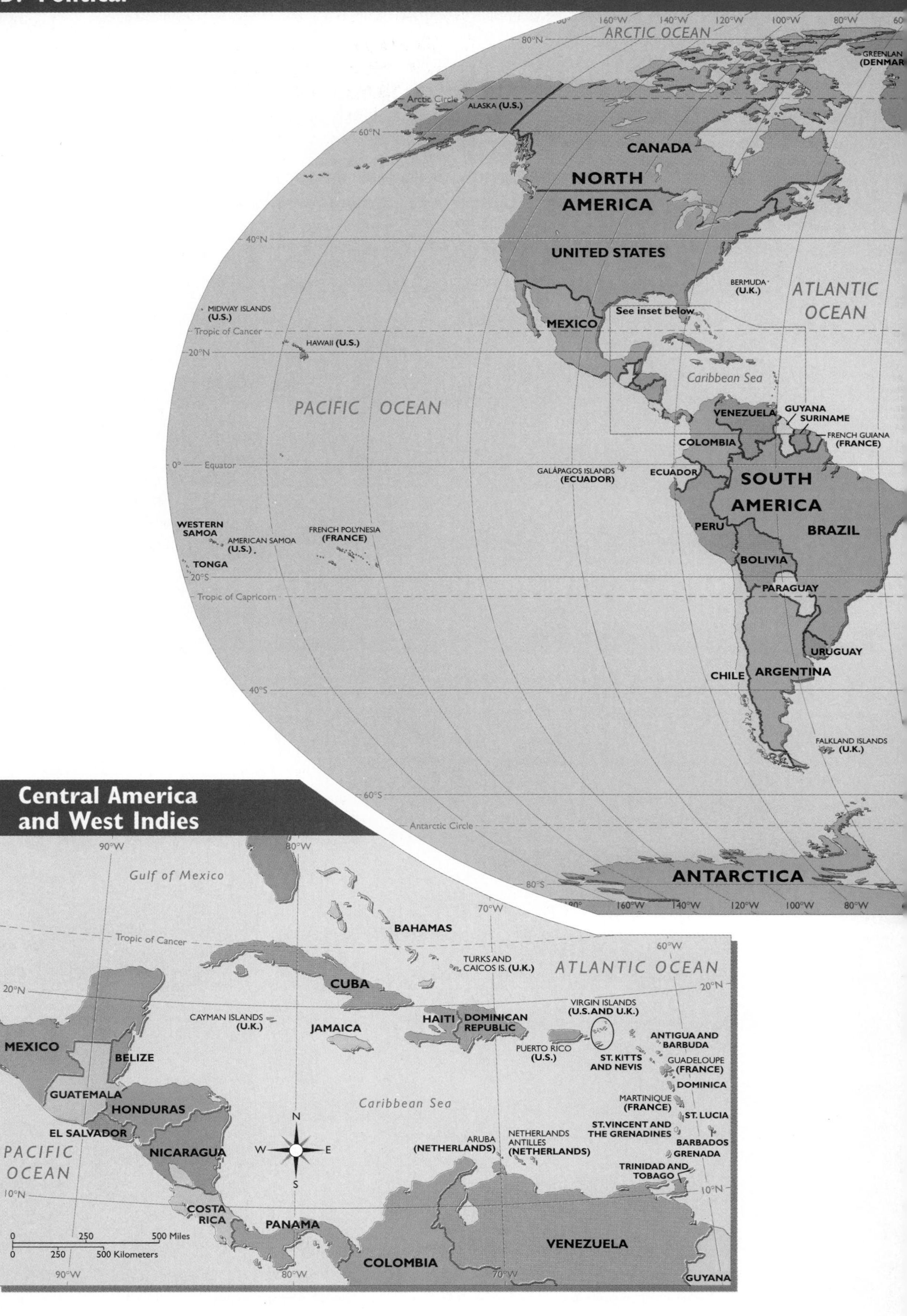
ARCTIC OCEAN
GREENLAND (DENMARK)
Arctic Circle
ALASKA (U.S.)
CANADA
NORTH AMERICA
UNITED STATES
BERMUDA (U.K.)
ATLANTIC OCEAN
MIDWAY ISLANDS (U.S.)
Tropic of Cancer
HAWAII (U.S.)
MEXICO
See inset below
Caribbean Sea
PACIFIC OCEAN
VENEZUELA
GUYANA
SURINAME
FRENCH GUIANA (FRANCE)
COLOMBIA
Equator
GALÁPAGOS ISLANDS (ECUADOR)
ECUADOR
SOUTH AMERICA
WESTERN SAMOA
AMERICAN SAMOA (U.S.)
FRENCH POLYNESIA (FRANCE)
PERU
BRAZIL
TONGA
BOLIVIA
Tropic of Capricorn
PARAGUAY
URUGUAY
CHILE
ARGENTINA
FALKLAND ISLANDS (U.K.)
Antarctic Circle
ANTARCTICA
Central America and West Indies
Gulf of Mexico
BAHAMAS
Tropic of Cancer
TURKS AND CAICOS IS. (U.K.)
ATLANTIC OCEAN
CUBA
VIRGIN ISLANDS (U.S. AND U.K.)
CAYMAN ISLANDS (U.K.)
JAMAICA
HAITI
DOMINICAN REPUBLIC
ANTIGUA AND BARBUDA
MEXICO
PUERTO RICO (U.S.)
ST. KITTS AND NEVIS
GUADELOUPE (FRANCE)
BELIZE
DOMINICA
GUATEMALA
HONDURAS
Caribbean Sea
MARTINIQUE (FRANCE)
ST. LUCIA
EL SALVADOR
ST. VINCENT AND THE GRENADINES
PACIFIC OCEAN
NICARAGUA
ARUBA (NETHERLANDS)
NETHERLANDS ANTILLES (NETHERLANDS)
BARBADOS
GRENADA
TRINIDAD AND TOBAGO
COSTA RICA
PANAMA
VENEZUELA
COLOMBIA
GUYANA
0 250 500 Miles
0 250 500 Kilometers

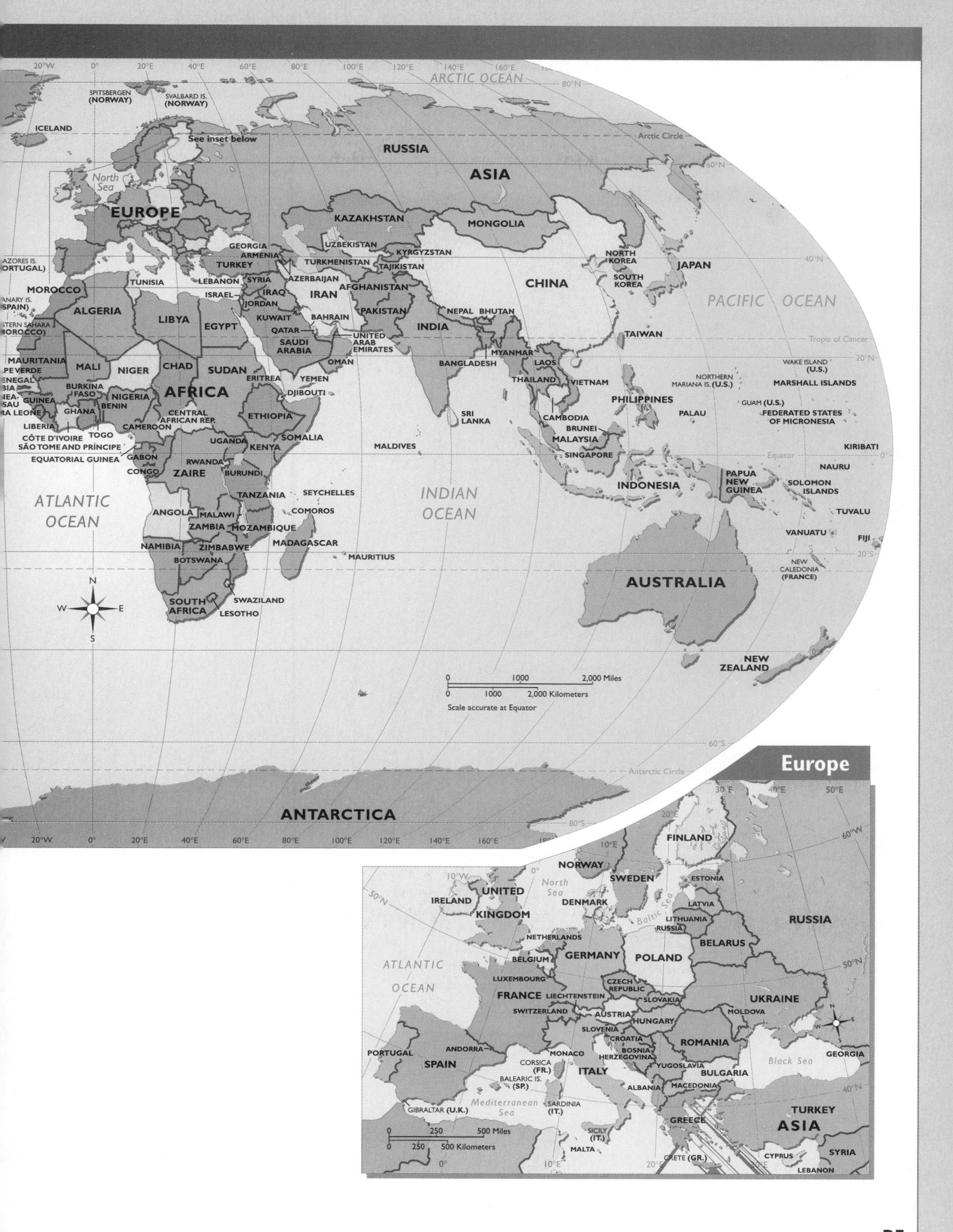
ARCTIC OCEAN
SPITSBERGEN (NORWAY)
SVALBARD IS. (NORWAY)
ICELAND
See inset below
North Sea
EUROPE
RUSSIA
ASIA
KAZAKHSTAN
MONGOLIA
GEORGIA
ARMENIA
TURKEY
UZBEKISTAN
KYRGYZSTAN
TURKMENISTAN
TAJIKISTAN
AZERBAIJAN
NORTH KOREA
SOUTH KOREA
JAPAN
CHINA
PACIFIC OCEAN
MOROCCO
TUNISIA
LEBANON
SYRIA
IRAQ
ISRAEL
JORDAN
IRAN
AFGHANISTAN
PAKISTAN
KUWAIT
BAHRAIN
QATAR
SAUDI ARABIA
UNITED ARAB EMIRATES
OMAN
ALGERIA
LIBYA
EGYPT
NEPAL
BHUTAN
INDIA
TAIWAN
MAURITANIA
MALI
NIGER
CHAD
SUDAN
ERITREA
YEMEN
MYANMAR
BANGLADESH
LAOS
THAILAND
VIETNAM
NORTHERN MARIANA IS. (U.S.)
WAKE ISLAND (U.S.)
MARSHALL ISLANDS
BURKINA FASO
NIGERIA
BENIN
AFRICA
DJIBOUTI
GUINEA
GHANA
CENTRAL AFRICAN REP.
ETHIOPIA
SRI LANKA
PHILIPPINES
PALAU
GUAM (U.S.)
FEDERATED STATES OF MICRONESIA
LIBERIA
CÔTE D'IVOIRE
TOGO
CAMEROON
SÃO TOME AND PRÍNCIPE
EQUATORIAL GUINEA
GABON
CONGO
UGANDA
KENYA
SOMALIA
RWANDA
ZAIRE
BURUNDI
MALDIVES
CAMBODIA
BRUNEI
MALAYSIA
SINGAPORE
KIRIBATI
NAURU
INDONESIA
PAPUA NEW GUINEA
SOLOMON ISLANDS
ATLANTIC OCEAN
TANZANIA
SEYCHELLES
INDIAN OCEAN
COMOROS
ANGOLA
MALAWI
ZAMBIA
MOZAMBIQUE
TUVALU
VANUATU
FIJI
NAMIBIA
ZIMBABWE
MADAGASCAR
MAURITIUS
BOTSWANA
NEW CALEDONIA (FRANCE)
AUSTRALIA
SOUTH AFRICA
SWAZILAND
LESOTHO
NEW ZEALAND
Arctic Circle
Tropic of Cancer
Equator
Antarctic Circle
0 1000 2,000 Miles
0 1000 2,000 Kilometers
Scale accurate at Equator
ANTARCTICA
Europe
FINLAND
NORWAY
SWEDEN
ESTONIA
UNITED KINGDOM
IRELAND
DENMARK
LATVIA
Baltic Sea
LITHUANIA
RUSSIA
NETHERLANDS
BELARUS
BELGIUM
GERMANY
POLAND
LUXEMBOURG
CZECH REPUBLIC
UKRAINE
FRANCE
LIECHTENSTEIN
SLOVAKIA
SWITZERLAND
AUSTRIA
MOLDOVA
HUNGARY
SLOVENIA
CROATIA
ROMANIA
PORTUGAL
ANDORRA
MONACO
BOSNIA-HERZEGOVINA
GEORGIA
SPAIN
CORSICA (FR.)
ITALY
YUGOSLAVIA
Black Sea
BULGARIA
BALEARIC IS. (SP.)
ALBANIA
MACEDONIA
Mediterranean Sea
SARDINIA (IT.)
GIBRALTAR (U.K.)
TURKEY
GREECE
ASIA
0 250 500 Miles
0 250 500 Kilometers
SICILY (IT.)
MALTA
CRETE (GR.)
CYPRUS
SYRIA
LEBANON

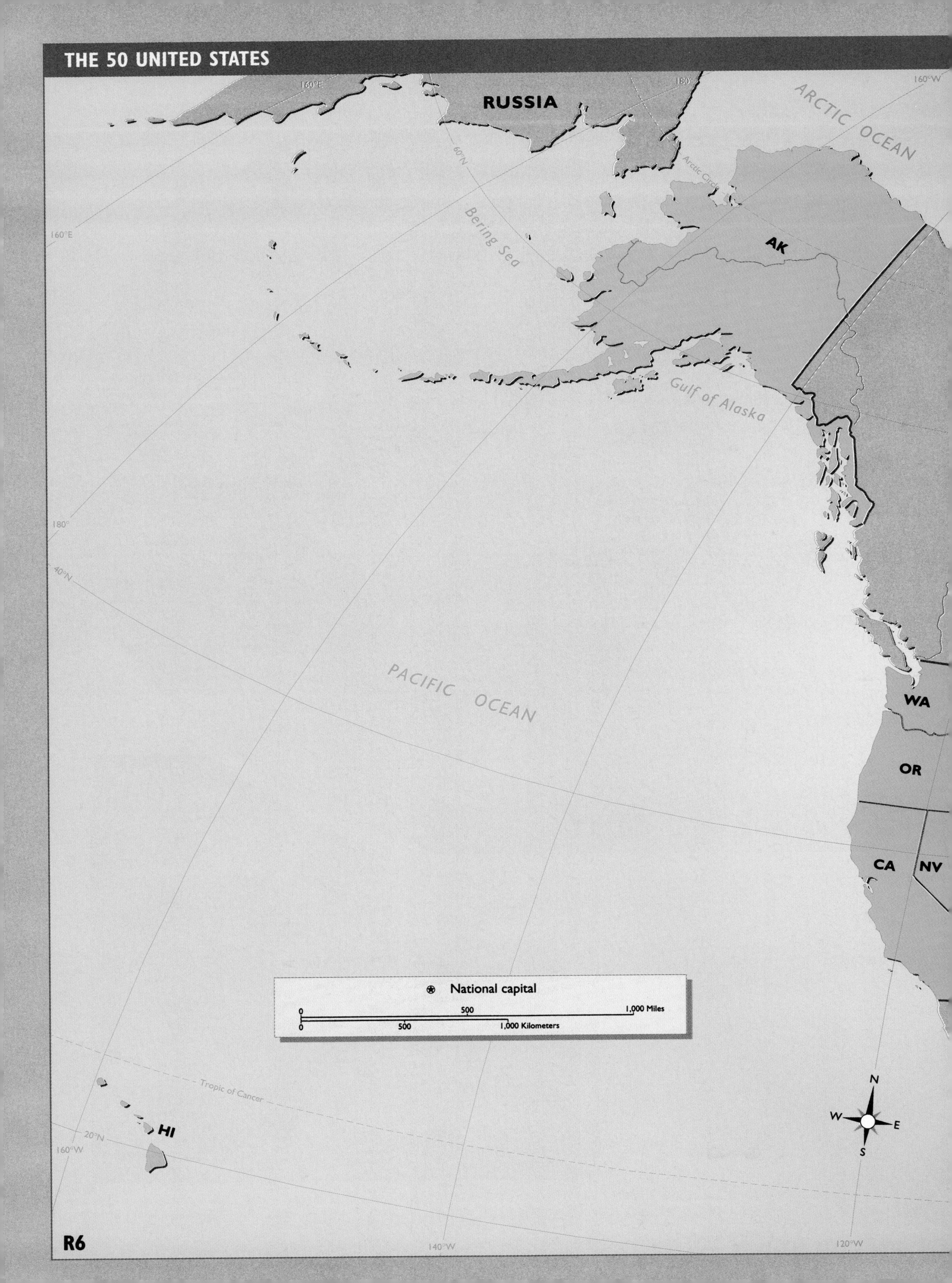
RUSSIA
ARCTIC OCEAN
Arctic Circle
Bering Sea
AK
Gulf of Alaska
PACIFIC OCEAN
WA
OR
CA
NV
HI
Tropic of Cancer
160°E
180°
160°W
140°W
120°W
60°N
40°N
20°N
National capital
0
500
1,000 Miles
0
500
1,000 Kilometers
N
S
E
W

Greenland
(DENMARK)
Hudson Bay
CANADA
Great Lakes
MT
ND
MN
MI
ME
VT
NH
ID
WY
SD
WI
MI
NY
MA
CT
RI
NE
IA
PA
NJ
UT
CO
KS
IL
IN
OH
Washington, D.C.
MD
DE
WV
VA
ATLANTIC OCEAN
MO
KY
AZ
NM
OK
AR
TN
NC
SC
MS
AL
GA
LA
TX
FL
Gulf of Mexico
MEXICO
CUBA

RUSSIA
ARCTIC OCEAN
ALASKA
Arctic Circle
Nome
Yukon River
Fairbanks
CANADA
Anchorage
Juneau
PACIFIC OCEAN
0 250 500 Miles
0 250 500 Kilometers
70°N
60°N
180°
170°W
160°W
150°W
140°W
CANADA
WASHINGTON
Seattle
Olympia
Spokane
Columbia River
Portland
Salem
Eugene
OREGON
IDAHO
Boise
Snake River
Pocatello
MONTANA
Great Falls
Missouri River
Helena
Billings
WYOMING
Casper
Cheyenne
NEVADA
Reno
Carson City
Great Salt Lake
Ogden
Salt Lake City
Provo
UTAH
COLORADO
Denver
Colorado Springs
Pueblo
San Francisco
Oakland
San Jose
Sacramento
CALIFORNIA
Las Vegas
Colorado River
Los Angeles
Long Beach
San Diego
ARIZONA
Phoenix
Tucson
NEW MEXICO
Santa Fe
Albuquerque
El Paso
Rio Grande
MEXICO
PACIFIC OCEAN
40°N
30°N
20°N
130°W
120°W
110°W
PACIFIC OCEAN
Kauai
Niihau
Oahu
Honolulu
Molokai
Lanai
Maui
Kahoolawe
HAWAII
Hawaii
Hilo
160°W
155°W
20°N
0 100 200 Miles
0 100 200 Kilometers

CANADA
Lake Superior
Lake Michigan
Lake Huron
Lake Ontario
Lake Erie
NORTH DAKOTA
Grand Forks
Bismarck
Fargo
SOUTH DAKOTA
Pierre
Sioux Falls
MINNESOTA
Duluth
Minneapolis
St. Paul
WISCONSIN
Green Bay
Madison
Milwaukee
MICHIGAN
Grand Rapids
Lansing
Detroit
IOWA
Cedar Rapids
Davenport
Des Moines
NEBRASKA
Omaha
Lincoln
Platte River
Missouri River
ILLINOIS
Rockford
Chicago
Peoria
Springfield
INDIANA
Gary
Fort Wayne
Indianapolis
Evansville
OHIO
Toledo
Cleveland
Columbus
Cincinnati
Ohio River
NEW YORK
Buffalo
Albany
New York
PENNSYLVANIA
Pittsburgh
Harrisburg
Philadelphia
Newark
Trenton
NEW JERSEY
Dover
DELAWARE
Baltimore
Annapolis
MARYLAND
Washington, D.C.
WEST VIRGINIA
Wheeling
Charleston
VIRGINIA
Richmond
Norfolk
MAINE
Augusta
Portland
VERMONT
Burlington
Montpelier
NEW HAMPSHIRE
Concord
MASSACHUSETTS
Boston
Providence
RHODE ISLAND
Hartford
CONNECTICUT
KANSAS
Topeka
Wichita
Arkansas River
MISSOURI
Kansas City
Kansas City
Jefferson City
St. Louis
Mississippi River
KENTUCKY
Frankfort
Louisville
TENNESSEE
Nashville
Knoxville
Memphis
Tennessee River
NORTH CAROLINA
Raleigh
Charlotte
SOUTH CAROLINA
Columbia
Charleston
ATLANTIC OCEAN
OKLAHOMA
Tulsa
Oklahoma City
Red River
ARKANSAS
Fort Smith
Little Rock
MISSISSIPPI
Jackson
Biloxi
ALABAMA
Birmingham
Montgomery
Mobile
GEORGIA
Atlanta
Columbus
Savannah
FLORIDA
Tallahassee
Jacksonville
Tampa
Miami
TEXAS
Fort Worth
Dallas
Austin
Houston
San Antonio
Laredo
Corpus Christi
LOUISIANA
Shreveport
Baton Rouge
New Orleans
Gulf of Mexico
THE BAHAMAS
CUBA
National capital
State capital
Other city
0 150 300 Miles
0 150 300 Kilometers
50°N
40°N
30°N
70°W
100°W
90°W
80°W

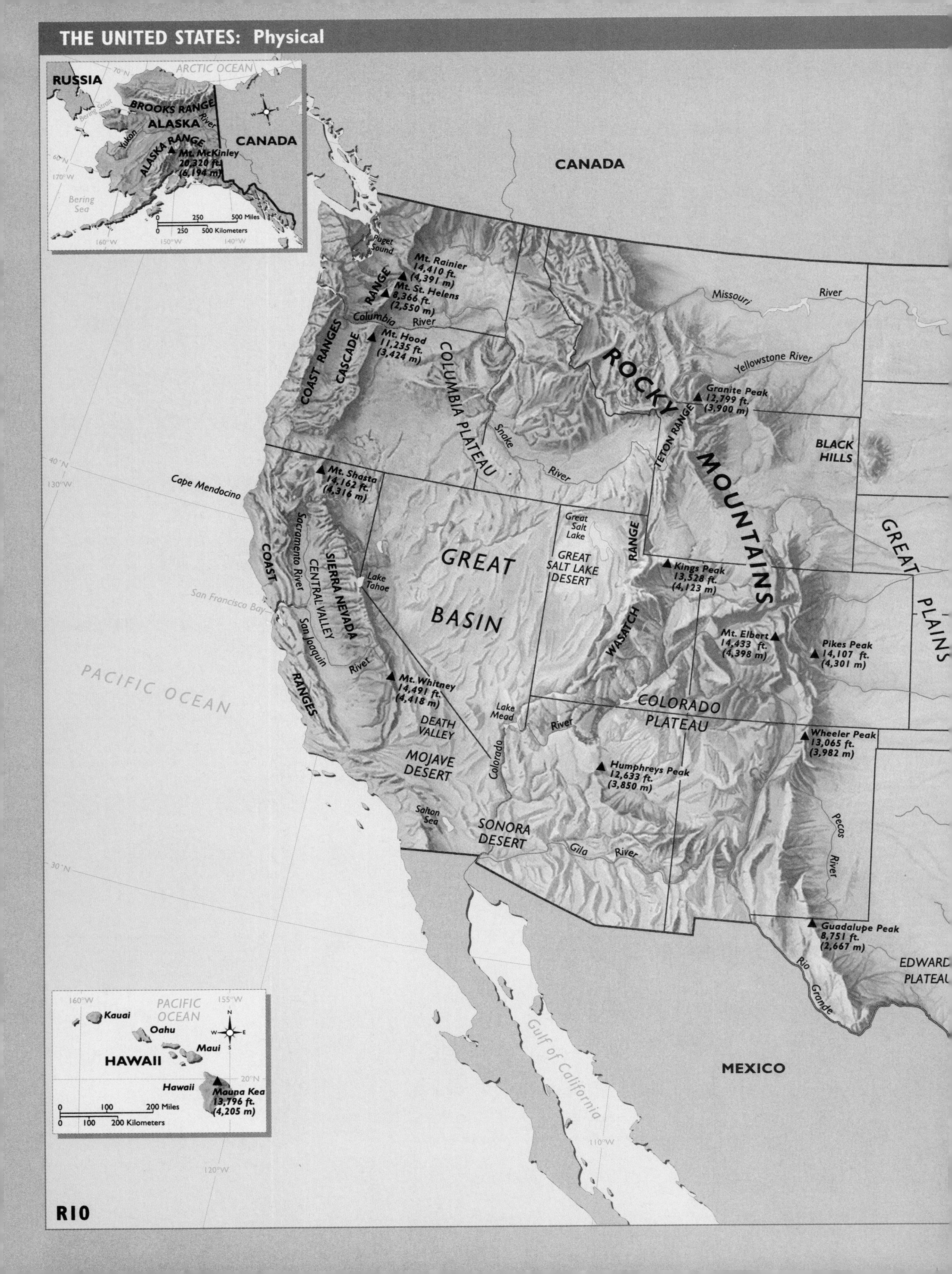
RUSSIA
ARCTIC OCEAN
BROOKS RANGE
ALASKA
CANADA
Yukon
River
ALASKA RANGE
Mt. McKinley 20,320 ft. (6,194 m)
Bering Sea
0 250 500 Miles
0 250 500 Kilometers
CANADA
Puget Sound
Mt. Rainier 14,410 ft. (4,391 m)
Mt. St. Helens 8,366 ft. (2,550 m)
Columbia River
Mt. Hood 11,235 ft. (3,424 m)
COAST RANGES
CASCADE RANGE
COLUMBIA PLATEAU
ROCKY MOUNTAINS
Missouri River
Yellowstone River
Granite Peak 12,799 ft. (3,900 m)
TETON RANGE
BLACK HILLS
Snake River
Cape Mendocino
Mt. Shasta 14,162 ft. (4,316 m)
Great Salt Lake
GREAT SALT LAKE DESERT
GREAT BASIN
GREAT PLAINS
Kings Peak 13,528 ft. (4,123 m)
Lake Tahoe
Sacramento River
COAST RANGES
SIERRA NEVADA
CENTRAL VALLEY
San Francisco Bay
San Joaquin River
WASATCH RANGE
Mt. Elbert 14,433 ft. (4,398 m)
Pikes Peak 14,107 ft. (4,301 m)
PACIFIC OCEAN
Mt. Whitney 14,491 ft. (4,418 m)
COLORADO PLATEAU
Lake Mead
DEATH VALLEY
River
Colorado
Wheeler Peak 13,065 ft. (3,982 m)
MOJAVE DESERT
Humphreys Peak 12,633 ft. (3,850 m)
Pecos River
Salton Sea
SONORA DESERT
Gila River
Guadalupe Peak 8,751 ft. (2,667 m)
EDWARDS PLATEAU
Rio Grande
PACIFIC OCEAN
Kauai
Oahu
Maui
HAWAII
Hawaii
Mauna Kea 13,796 ft. (4,205 m)
0 100 200 Miles
0 100 200 Kilometers
Gulf of California
MEXICO

CANADA
Lake of the Woods
Lake Superior
GREAT LAKES
MESABI RANGE
Lake Michigan
Lake Huron
Lake Ontario
Lake Erie
St Lawrence River
WHITE MTS.
Mt. Washington 6,288 ft. (1,917 m)
GREEN MTS.
ADIRONDACK MTS.
Hudson River
Cape Cod
Long Island
Mississippi River
CENTRAL PLAINS
ALLEGHENY PLATEAU
APPALACHIAN MOUNTAINS
Susquehanna River
Potomac River
Delaware Bay
Chesapeake Bay
ALLEGHENY MOUNTAINS
Platte River
Missouri River
Wabash River
Ohio River
Mt. Mitchell 6,684 ft. (2,037 m)
Cape Hatteras
PIEDMONT
ATLANTIC COASTAL PLAIN
Arkansas River
INTERIOR PLAINS
OZARK PLATEAU
OUACHITA MOUNTAINS
Tennessee River
Savannah River
ATLANTIC OCEAN
Red River
Alabama River
Chattahoochee River
Brazos River
Colorado River
GULF COASTAL PLAIN
Mobile Bay
Mississippi Delta
Galveston Bay
Gulf of Mexico
Lake Okeechobee
Bahama Islands
Florida Keys
Straits of Florida
CUBA
50°N
40°N
30°N
70°W
80°W
90°W
N S E W
0 150 300 Miles
0 150 300 Kilometers

PENNSYLVANIA: Physical

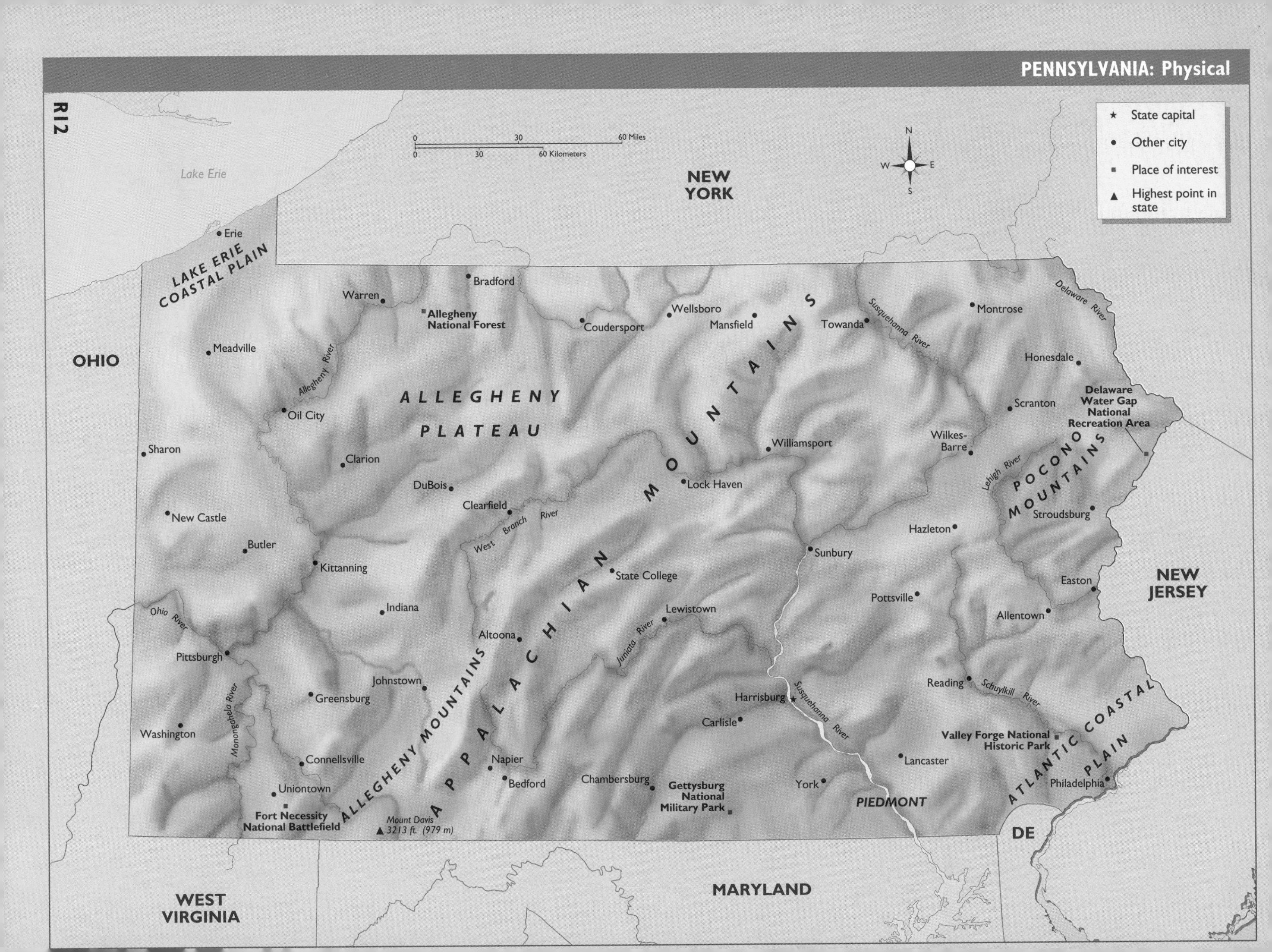

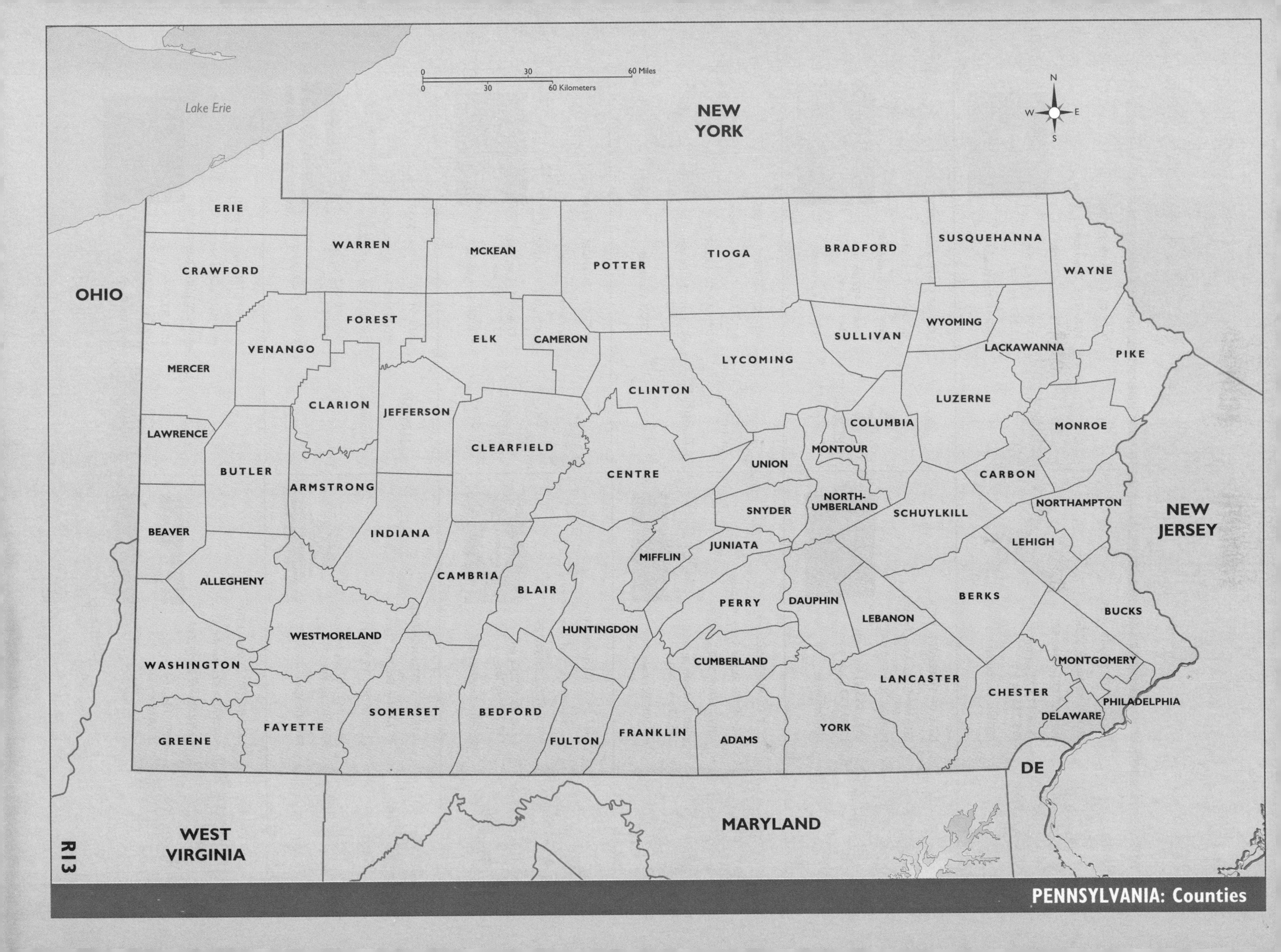
PENNSYLVANIA: Counties
Lake Erie
0
30
60 Miles
0
30
60 Kilometers
N
S
E
W
NEW YORK
OHIO
NEW JERSEY
DE
MARYLAND
WEST VIRGINIA
ERIE
WARREN
MCKEAN
POTTER
TIOGA
BRADFORD
SUSQUEHANNA
WAYNE
CRAWFORD
FOREST
ELK
CAMERON
LYCOMING
SULLIVAN
WYOMING
LACKAWANNA
PIKE
MERCER
VENANGO
CLINTON
LUZERNE
CLARION
JEFFERSON
COLUMBIA
MONROE
LAWRENCE
CLEARFIELD
MONTOUR
BUTLER
CENTRE
UNION
CARBON
ARMSTRONG
NORTH-UMBERLAND
NORTHAMPTON
SNYDER
SCHUYLKILL
BEAVER
INDIANA
JUNIATA
LEHIGH
MIFFLIN
ALLEGHENY
CAMBRIA
BLAIR
BERKS
PERRY
DAUPHIN
BUCKS
LEBANON
HUNTINGDON
WESTMORELAND
MONTGOMERY
CUMBERLAND
WASHINGTON
LANCASTER
CHESTER
PHILADELPHIA
DELAWARE
SOMERSET
BEDFORD
FAYETTE
FRANKLIN
YORK
GREENE
FULTON
ADAMS

OUR FIFTY STATES

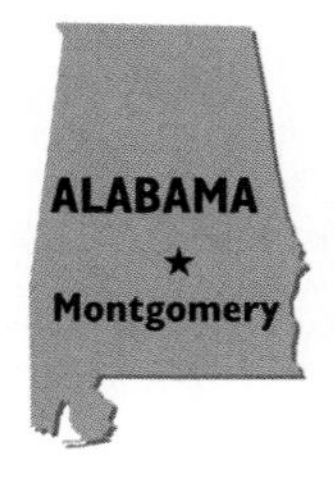

DATE OF STATEHOOD **1819**

NICKNAME **Heart of Dixie**

POPULATION **4,040,587**

AREA **52,423 sq mi; 135,776 sq km**

REGION **Southeast**

DATE OF STATEHOOD **1959**

NICKNAME **The Last Frontier**

POPULATION **550,043**

AREA **656,424 sq mi; 1,700,138 sq km**

REGION **West**

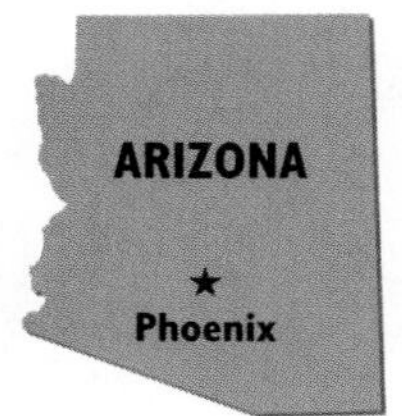

DATE OF STATEHOOD **1912**

NICKNAME **Grand Canyon State**

POPULATION **3,665,228**

AREA **114,006 sq mi; 295,276 sq km**

REGION **Southwest**

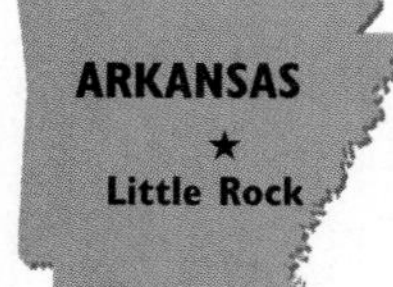

DATE OF STATEHOOD **1836**

NICKNAME **Land of Opportunity**

POPULATION **2,350,725**

AREA **53,182 sq mi; 137,741 sq km**

REGION **Southeast**

DATE OF STATEHOOD **1850**

NICKNAME **Golden State**

POPULATION **29,760,021**

AREA **163,707 sq mi; 424,001 sq km**

REGION **West**

Denver ★

COLORADO

DATE OF STATEHOOD **1876**

NICKNAME **Centennial State**

POPULATION **3,294,394**

AREA **104,100 sq mi; 269,619 sq km**

REGION **West**

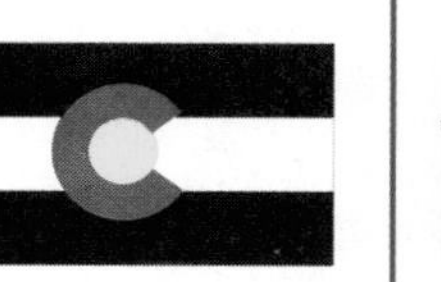

★ Hartford

CONNECTICUT

DATE OF STATEHOOD **1788**

NICKNAME **Constitution State**

POPULATION **3,287,116**

AREA **5,544 sq mi; 14,359 sq km**

REGION **Northeast**

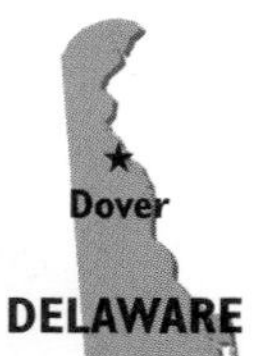

DATE OF STATEHOOD **1787**

NICKNAME **First State**

POPULATION **666,168**

AREA **2,489 sq mi; 6,447 sq km**

REGION **Northeast**

DATE OF STATEHOOD **1845**

NICKNAME **Sunshine State**

POPULATION **12,937,926**

AREA **65,758 sq mi; 170,313 sq km**

REGION **Southeast**

DATE OF STATEHOOD **1788**

NICKNAME **Peach State**

POPULATION **6,478,216**

AREA **59,441 sq mi; 153,952 sq km**

REGION **Southeast**

HAWAII

★ Honolulu

DATE OF STATEHOOD **1959**

NICKNAME **The Aloha State**

POPULATION **1,108,229**

AREA **10,932 sq mi; 28,314 sq km**

REGION **West**

★ Boise

IDAHO

DATE OF STATEHOOD **1890**

NICKNAME **Gem State**

POPULATION **1,006,749**

AREA **83,574 sq mi; 216,457 sq km**

REGION **West**

ILLINOIS

DATE OF STATEHOOD **1818**

NICKNAME **The Prairie State**

POPULATION **11,430,602**

AREA **57,918 sq mi; 150,008 sq km**

REGION **Middle West**

INDIANA

DATE OF STATEHOOD **1816**

NICKNAME **Hoosier State**

POPULATION **5,544,159**

AREA **36,420 sq mi; 94,328 sq km**

REGION **Middle West**

IOWA

DATE OF STATEHOOD **1846**

NICKNAME **Hawkeye State**

POPULATION **2,776,755**

AREA **56,276 sq mi; 145,755 sq km**

REGION **Middle West**

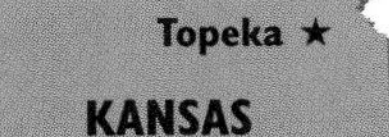

KANSAS

DATE OF STATEHOOD **1861**

NICKNAME **Sunflower State**

POPULATION **2,477,574**

AREA **82,282 sq mi; 213,110 sq km**

REGION **Middle West**

KENTUCKY

DATE OF STATEHOOD **1792**

NICKNAME **Bluegrass State**

POPULATION **3,685,296**

AREA **40,411 sq mi; 104,664 sq km**

REGION **Southeast**

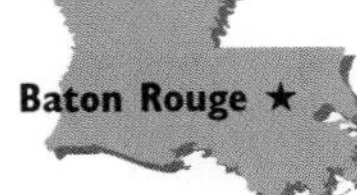

LOUISIANA

DATE OF STATEHOOD **1812**

NICKNAME **Pelican State**

POPULATION **4,219,973**

AREA **51,843 sq mi; 134,273 sq km**

REGION **Southeast**

MAINE

Augusta

DATE OF STATEHOOD **1820**

NICKNAME **Pine Tree State**

POPULATION **1,227,928**

AREA **35,387 sq mi; 91,652 sq km**

REGION **Northeast**

MARYLAND

DATE OF STATEHOOD **1788**

NICKNAME **Free State**

POPULATION **4,781,468**

AREA **12,407 sq mi; 32,134 sq km**

REGION **Northeast**

MASSACHUSETTS

DATE OF STATEHOOD **1788**

NICKNAME **Bay State**

POPULATION **6,016,425**

AREA **10,555 sq mi; 27,337 sq km**

REGION **Northeast**

MICHIGAN

DATE OF STATEHOOD **1837**

NICKNAME **Wolverine State**

POPULATION **9,295,297**

AREA **96,810 sq mi; 250,738 sq km**

REGION **Middle West**

MINNESOTA

DATE OF STATEHOOD **1858**

NICKNAME **North Star State**

POPULATION **4,375,099**

AREA **86,943 sq mi; 225,182 sq km**

REGION **Middle West**

MISSISSIPPI

DATE OF STATEHOOD **1817**

NICKNAME **Magnolia State**

POPULATION **2,573,216**

AREA **48,434 sq mi; 125,444 sq km**

REGION **Southeast**

OUR FIFTY STATES

DATE OF STATEHOOD **1821**
NICKNAME **Show Me State**
POPULATION **5,117,073**
AREA **69,709 sq mi; 180,546 sq km**
REGION **Middle West**

MONTANA
★ Helena

DATE OF STATEHOOD **1889**
NICKNAME **Treasure State**
POPULATION **799,065**
AREA **147,046 sq mi; 380,849 sq km**
REGION **West**

NEBRASKA
Lincoln ★

DATE OF STATEHOOD **1867**
NICKNAME **Cornhusker State**
POPULATION **1,578,385**
AREA **77,358 sq mi; 200,357 sq km**
REGION **Middle West**

NEVADA
★ Carson City

DATE OF STATEHOOD **1864**
NICKNAME **Silver State**
POPULATION **1,201,833**
AREA **110,567 sq mi; 286,369 sq km**
REGION **West**

NEW HAMPSHIRE

DATE OF STATEHOOD **1788**
NICKNAME **Granite State**
POPULATION **1,109,252**
AREA **9,351 sq mi; 24,219 sq km**
REGION **Northeast**

NEW JERSEY
★ Trenton

DATE OF STATEHOOD **1787**
NICKNAME **Garden State**
POPULATION **7,730,188**
AREA **8,722 sq mi; 22,590 sq km**
REGION **Northeast**

DATE OF STATEHOOD **1912**
NICKNAME **Land of Enchantment**
POPULATION **1,515,069**
AREA **121,598 sq mi; 314,939 sq km**
REGION **Southwest**

NEW YORK
Albany ★

DATE OF STATEHOOD **1788**
NICKNAME **Empire State**
POPULATION **17,990,455**
AREA **54,475 sq mi; 141,090 sq km**
REGION **Northeast**

NORTH CAROLINA

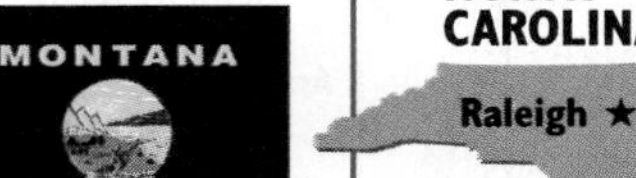

DATE OF STATEHOOD **1789**
NICKNAME **Tar Heel State**
POPULATION **6,628,637**
AREA **53,821 sq mi; 139,396 sq km**
REGION **Southeast**

NORTH DAKOTA
Bismarck ★

DATE OF STATEHOOD **1889**
NICKNAME **Peace Garden State**
POPULATION **638,800**
AREA **70,704 sq mi; 183,123 sq km**
REGION **Middle West**

OHIO
★ Columbus

DATE OF STATEHOOD **1803**
NICKNAME **Buckeye State**
POPULATION **10,847,115**
AREA **44,828 sq mi; 116,105 sq km**
REGION **Middle West**

OKLAHOMA
★ Oklahoma City

DATE OF STATEHOOD **1907**
NICKNAME **Sooner State**
POPULATION **3,145,585**
AREA **69,903 sq mi; 181,049 sq km**
REGION **Southwest**

OREGON
★ Salem

DATE OF STATEHOOD **1859**
NICKNAME **Beaver State**
POPULATION **2,842,321**
AREA **98,386 sq mi; 254,820 sq km**
REGION **West**

PENNSYLVANIA
Harrisburg ★

DATE OF STATEHOOD **1787**
NICKNAME **Keystone State**
POPULATION **11,881,643**
AREA **46,058 sq mi; 119,290 sq km**
REGION **Northeast**

RHODE ISLAND
Providence ★

DATE OF STATEHOOD **1790**
NICKNAME **Ocean State**
POPULATION **1,003,464**
AREA **1,545 sq mi; 4,002 sq km**
REGION **Northeast**

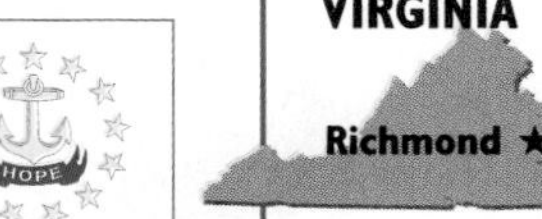

SOUTH CAROLINA
★ Columbia

DATE OF STATEHOOD **1788**
NICKNAME **Palmetto State**
POPULATION **3,486,703**
AREA **32,007 sq mi; 82,898 sq km**
REGION **Southeast**

SOUTH DAKOTA
Pierre ★

DATE OF STATEHOOD **1889**
NICKNAME **Mount Rushmore State**
POPULATION **696,004**
AREA **77,121 sq mi; 199,743 sq km**
REGION **Middle West**

TENNESSEE
★Nashville

DATE OF STATEHOOD **1796**
NICKNAME **Volunteer State**
POPULATION **4,877,185**
AREA **42,146 sq mi; 109,158 sq km**
REGION **Southeast**

TEXAS
Austin ★

DATE OF STATEHOOD **1845**
NICKNAME **Lone Star State**
POPULATION **16,986,510**
AREA **268,601 sq mi; 695,677 sq km**
REGION **Southwest**

UTAH
★ Salt Lake City

DATE OF STATEHOOD **1896**
NICKNAME **Beehive State**
POPULATION **1,722,850**
AREA **84,904 sq mi; 219,901 sq km**
REGION **West**

VERMONT
★ Montpelier

DATE OF STATEHOOD **1791**
NICKNAME **Green Mountain State**
POPULATION **562,758**
AREA **9,615 sq mi; 24,903 sq km**
REGION **Northeast**

VIRGINIA
Richmond ★

DATE OF STATEHOOD **1788**
NICKNAME **Old Dominion**
POPULATION **6,187,358**
AREA **42,769 sq mi; 110,772 sq km**
REGION **Southeast**

WASHINGTON
★ Olympia

DATE OF STATEHOOD **1889**
NICKNAME **Evergreen State**
POPULATION **4,866,692**
AREA **71,303 sq mi; 184,675 sq km**
REGION **West**

WEST VIRGINIA
★ Charleston

DATE OF STATEHOOD **1863**
NICKNAME **Mountain State**
POPULATION **1,793,477**
AREA **24,231 sq mi; 62,758 sq km**
REGION **Southeast**

WISCONSIN
Madison ★

DATE OF STATEHOOD **1848**
NICKNAME **Badger State**
POPULATION **4,891,769**
AREA **65,503 sq mi; 169,653 sq km**
REGION **Middle West**

WYOMING
Cheyenne ★

DATE OF STATEHOOD **1890**
NICKNAME **Equality State**
POPULATION **453,588**
AREA **97,818 sq mi; 253,349 sq km**
REGION **West**

Sources: population—U.S. Bureau of Census, 1990; area—U.S. Bureau of Census, 1991; capital—World Almanac, 1995.

PENNSYLVANIA TIME LINE

About 18,000 years ago
People first reach what is today Pennsylvania

1600s
The Susquehannock and Lenape live in Pennsylvania

1609
Henry Hudson is the first European to see the Delaware Bay

1643
Swedes build a settlement on Tinicum Island, near present-day Philadelphia

1655
Peter Stuyvesant defeats the Swedes and the area that is today Pennsylvania becomes part of New Netherland

1664
England conquers New Netherland

1682
William Penn arrives in America and founds the colony of Pennsylvania

1755
French and Native American forces defeat the British Army of General Braddock

1763
French sign Treaty of Paris; Native Americans defeated at the Battle of Bushy Run

1775
American Revolution begins

1776
The Declaration of Independence is signed in Philadelphia

1777
General George Washington and troops spend winter at Valley Forge

1783
Treaty of Paris ends the American Revolution

1787
Constitutional Convention is held in Philadelphia

1811
Robert Fulton's *New Orleans* becomes Pittsburgh's first steamship

1600s 1700s 1800s

1829

The United States' first steam locomotive, the *Stourbridge Lion,* runs between Carbondale and Honesdale

1840s

Underground Railroad workers help enslaved African Americans escape to freedom

1850

Women's Medical College of Pennsylvania opens in Philadelphia

1854

Ashmun Institute opens in Oxford

1859

Oil is discovered in Titusville

1861-1865

The Civil War

1863

At the Battle of Gettysburg, Union soldiers defeat Confederate forces

1875

Andrew Carnegie opens the J. Edgar Thomson Works steel mill in Braddock

1889

The Johnstown Flood kills over 2,000 people

1900s

1914-1918

World War I

1920

Women given the right to vote; Pittsburgh station makes first commercial radio broadcast in the United States

1929

Stock Market crashes and the Great Depression begins

1939-1945

World War II

1966

Jeanette Reibman becomes first woman state senator in Pennsylvania

1979

Accident at Three Mile Island nuclear power plant causes environmental concern

1990

Nearly four out of five Pennsylvania workers have jobs in the service industry

GOVERNORS *of* PENNSYLVANIA

GOVERNORS OF THE STATE OF PENNSYLVANIA	TERM
Thomas Wharton, Jr.	1777–1778
George Bryan	1778
Joseph Reed	1778–1781
William Moore	1781–1782
John Dickinson	1782–1785
Benjamin Franklin	1785–1788
Thomas Mifflin	1788–1799
Thomas McKean	1799–1808
Simon Snyder	1808–1817
William Findlay	1817–1820
Joseph Hiester	1820–1823
John Andrew Schulze	1823–1829
George Wolf	1829–1835
Joseph Ritner	1835–1839
David Rittenhouse Porter	1839–1845
Francis Rawn Shunk	1845–1848
William Freame Johnston	1848–1852
William Bigler	1852–1855
James Pollock	1855–1858
William Fisher Packer	1858–1861
Andrew Gregg Curtin	1861–1867
John White Geary	1867–1873
John Frederick Hartranft	1873–1879
Henry Martyn Hoyt	1879–1883
Robert Emory Pattison	1883–1887
James Addams Beaver	1887–1891
Robert Emory Pattison	1891–1895
Daniel Hartman Hastings	1895–1899
William Alexis Stone	1899–1903
Samuel W. Pennypacker	1903–1907
Edwin Sydney Stuart	1907–1911
John Kinley Tener	1911–1915
Martin Grove Brumbaugh	1915–1919
William Cameron Sproul	1919–1923
Gifford Pinchot	1923–1927
John Stuchell Fisher	1927–1931
Gifford Pinchot	1931–1935
George Howard Earle	1935–1939
Arthur Horace James	1939–1943
Edward Martin	1943–1947
John C. Bell, Jr.	1947
James H. Duff	1947–1951
John S. Fine	1951–1955
George Michael Leader	1955–1959
David Leo Lawrence	1959–1963
William W. Scranton	1963–1967
Raymond P. Shafer	1967–1971
Milton J. Shapp	1971–1979
Richard L. Thornburgh	1979–1987
Robert Casey	1987–1995
Tom Ridge	1995–present

Tom Ridge is our state's fifty-first governor.

PENNSYLVANIA CITIES

City Name	City Population	County	Population Rank
Abington	56,322	Montgomery	12
Allentown	105,090	Lehigh	4
Altoona	51,881	Blair	16
Ben Salem	56,788	Bucks	11
Bethlehem	71,428	Lehigh	8
Bristol	57,129	Bucks	10
Chester	41,856	Delaware	23
Erie	108,718	Erie	3
Harrisburg	52,376	Dauphin	15
Haverford	49,848	Delaware	18
Lancaster	55,551	Lancaster	13
Levittown	55,362	Bucks	14
Lower Merion	58,003	Montgomery	9
Lower Paxton	39,162	Dauphin	24
Middletown	43,063	Bucks	21
Millcreek	46,820	Erie	20
Northampton	35,406	Bucks	26
Pennhills	51,479	Allegheny	17
Philadelphia	1,585,577	Philadelphia	1
Pittsburgh	369,879	Allegheny	2
Reading	78,380	Berks	7
Scranton	81,805	Lackawanna	5
State College	38,923	Centre	25
Upper Darby	81,177	Delaware	6
Wilkes-Barre	47,523	Luzerne	19
York	42,192	York	22

All cities with a population greater than 35,000 in the 1990 census have been listed.

Famous Pennsylvanians

Ed Bradley
Born in Philadelphia in 1941; broadcast journalist; co-anchor on "60 Minutes"; started as a reporter for WDAS in Philadelphia

Marilyn Horne
Born in Bradford in 1934; opera singer known for a broad vocal range; sang with the Metropolitan Opera in New York City

Lola Falana
Born in Philadelphia in 1946; actor, dancer; known as "First Lady of Las Vegas"

Gelsey Kirkland
Born in Bethlehem in 1953; world-famous ballerina for the American Ballet Theater until 1981; now teaches young dancers

Michael Keaton
Born in Pittsburgh in 1951; actor; known for his roles in movies such as *Beetlejuice*, *Mr. Mom*, and *Batman*

Patricia Prattis Jennings
Born in Pittsburgh in 1941; songwriter and keyboardist; played with Pittsburgh Symphony and founded *Symphonium*, an African American musicians' magazine

Patti Labelle
Born in Philadelphia in 1944; singer; won a Grammy award for "Burnin'" album and a Special Citation from President Reagan

Fred Rogers
Born in Latrobe in 1928; actor; known as host of television's long-running children's program, "Mister Rogers' Neighborhood"

Guion S. Bluford, Jr.
Born in Philadelphia in 1942; astronaut; first African American to travel in space on the *Challenger* in 1983

Jimmy Stewart
Born in Indiana in 1908; famous actor who has appeared in more than 70 movies, including *Harvey* and *It's a Wonderful Life*; won an Academy Award for *The Philadelphia Story*

John Updike
Born in Shillington in 1932; famous writer of novels, short stories, essays, and poetry; won a Pulitzer Prize for *Rabbit is Rich* in 1982

Warren Christopher
Born in Scranton in 1925; Secretary of State under President Clinton; awarded the U. S. Medal of Freedom

Sharon Stone
Born in Meadville in 1958; actor; appeared in such movies as *Total Recall* and *Last Dance*, and television's "War and Remembrance"

Jonathan Taylor Thomas
Born in Bethlehem in 1981; actor; known for his role in television's "Home Improvement"; starred in movies *Tom and Huck* and *Adventures of Pinocchio*

Bill Cosby
Born in Philadelphia in 1937; comedian, actor, producer, writer; known for his role on "The Cosby Show," once the most watched television show in the United States; now stars in "Cosby"

Sally Jesse Raphael
Born in Easton in 1943; talk show host; known for television's "Sally Jesse Raphael Show"; won Emmy Awards in 1989 and 1990

Reggie Jackson
Born in Wyncote in 1946; baseball player; led American League in home runs four times; Most Valuable Player in 1973

Gloria Skurzynski
Born in Duquesne in 1930; writer; known for children's books *The Magic Pumpkin* and *What Happened in Hamelin*

August Wilson
Born in Pittsburgh in 1945; poet and play writer; won Pulitzer Prizes for *Fences* and *The Piano Lesson*

Sarah Yong-chu Chang
Born in Philadelphia in 1980; child violinist; played with New York Philharmonic, Montreal Symphony, and Philadelphia Symphony

Annie Dillard
Born in Pittsburgh in 1945; poet, writer; wrote *An American Childhood* about growing up in Pittsburgh; won a Pulitzer Prize for *Pilgrim at Tinker Creek*

Places to Visit

Our state is filled with places that people find interesting and fun to visit. You can see why many Pennsylvanians spend their vacations right in our own state. How many of these places have you visited?

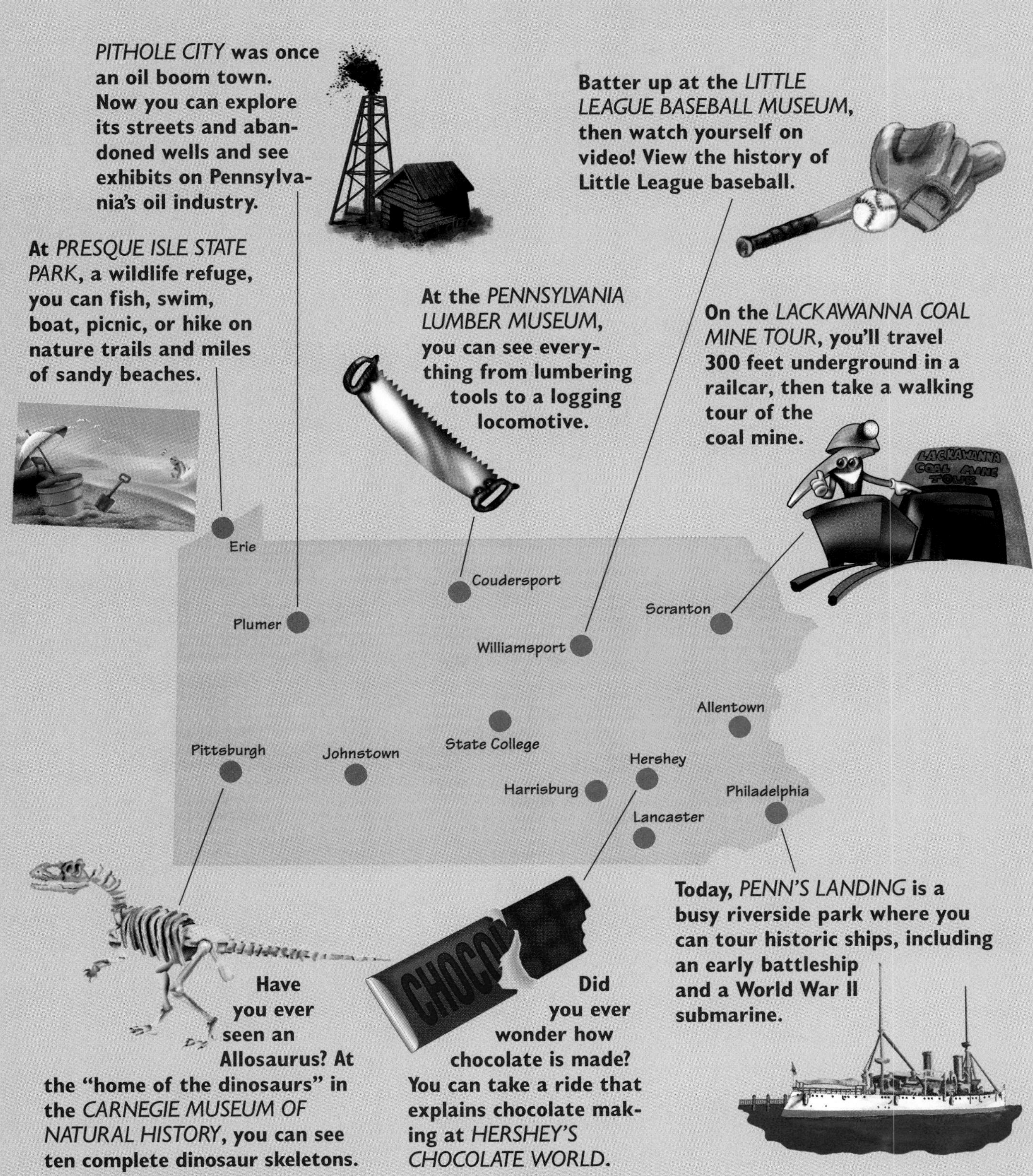

PITHOLE CITY **was once an oil boom town. Now you can explore its streets and abandoned wells and see exhibits on Pennsylvania's oil industry.**

Batter up at the ***LITTLE LEAGUE BASEBALL MUSEUM*****, then watch yourself on video! View the history of Little League baseball.**

At ***PRESQUE ISLE STATE PARK*****, a wildlife refuge, you can fish, swim, boat, picnic, or hike on nature trails and miles of sandy beaches.**

At the ***PENNSYLVANIA LUMBER MUSEUM*****, you can see everything from lumbering tools to a logging locomotive.**

On the ***LACKAWANNA COAL MINE TOUR*****, you'll travel 300 feet underground in a railcar, then take a walking tour of the coal mine.**

Today, ***PENN'S LANDING*** **is a busy riverside park where you can tour historic ships, including an early battleship and a World War II submarine.**

Have you ever seen an Allosaurus? At the "home of the dinosaurs" in the ***CARNEGIE MUSEUM OF NATURAL HISTORY*****, you can see ten complete dinosaur skeletons.**

Did you ever wonder how chocolate is made? You can take a ride that explains chocolate making at ***HERSHEY'S CHOCOLATE WORLD*****.**

ANIMALS AND PLANTS OF PENNSYLVANIA
18
19
16
14
17
15
12
13
11
10
9
8
7
3
6
5
2
1
4

1. Fowler's toad
2. Raccoon
3. Muskrat
4. Carp
5. Brown trout
6. White bass
7. One-flowered wintergreen
8. Red fox
9. Gray partridge
10. Ring-necked pheasant
11. Ruffed grouse
12. Milkweed
13. White-tailed deer
14. Eastern white pine
15. Virginia opossum
16. Barn swallow
17. Cardinal
18. Bald eagle (T)
19. Eastern hemlock
20. White ash
21. American beech
22. American sycamore
23. Shagbark hickory
24. Northern flying squirrel
25. Bobcat (R)
26. House sparrow
27. Red maple
28. Eastern gray squirrel
29. Striped skunk
30. Beaver
31. Bigtooth aspen
32. Mountain laurel
33. Black bear
34. Eastern cottontail rabbit
35. Bouncing Bet
36. Eastern mole
37. Timber rattlesnake
38. Five-lined skink
39. American robin
40. Blue jay
(T) Threatened
(R) At Risk
20
21
22
23
24
25
26
27
28
29
30
31
32
33
34
35
36
37
38
39
40

Dictionary of GEOGRAPHIC TERMS

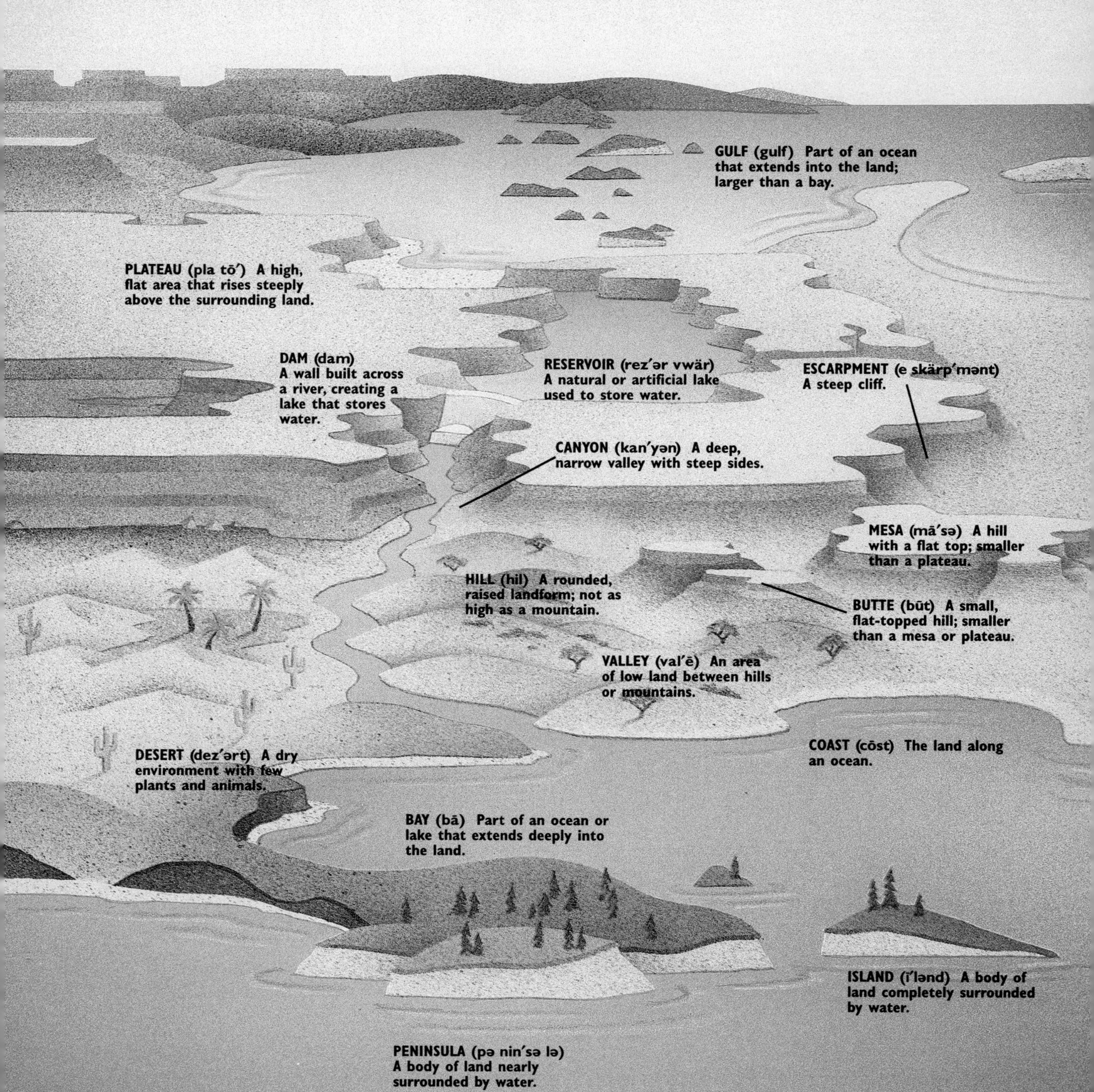

VOLCANO (vol kā′nō) An opening in Earth's surface through which hot rock and ash are forced out.

MOUNTAIN (moun′tən) A high landform with steep sides; higher than a hill.

PEAK (pēk) The top of a mountain.

HARBOR (här′bər) A sheltered place along a coast where boats dock safely.

GLACIER (glā′shər) A huge sheet of ice that moves slowly across the land.

CANAL (kə nal′) A channel built to carry water for irrigation or transportation.

LAKE (lāk) A body of water completely surrounded by land.

TRIBUTARY (trib′yə ter ē) A smaller river that flows into a larger river.

PORT (pôrt) A place where ships load and unload their goods.

SOURCE (sôrs) The starting point of a river.

TIMBERLINE (tim′bər līn) A line beyond which trees do not grow.

RIVER BASIN (riv′ər bā′sin) All the land that is drained by a river and its tributaries.

WATERFALL (wô′tər fôl) A flow of water falling vertically.

MOUNTAIN RANGE (moun′tən rānj) A row or chain of mountains.

RIVER (riv′ər) A stream of water that flows across the land and empties into another body of water.

PLAIN (plān) A large area of nearly flat land.

BASIN (bā′sin) A bowl-shaped landform surrounded by higher land.

DELTA (del′tə) Land made of soil left behind as a river drains into a larger body of water.

MOUTH (mouth) The place where a river empties into a larger body of water.

BARRIER ISLAND (bar′ē ər ī′lənd) A narrow island between the mainland and the ocean.

OCEAN (ō′shən) A large body of salt water; oceans cover much of Earth's surface.

Gazetteer

This Gazetteer is a geographical dictionary that will help you to pronounce and locate the places discussed in this book. Latitude and longitude are given for cities and some other places. The page numbers tell you where each place first appears on a map or in the text.

A

Allegheny Mountains (al′ə gā nē maun′tənz) Highest part of the Appalachian Mountains in Pennsylvania. (m. 7, t. 9)

Allegheny National Forest (al′ə gā nē na′shə nəl for′əst) The largest national forest in Pennsylvania, located in the northwest region of the state. (t. 256)

Allegheny Plateau (al′ə gā nē pla tō′) High, hilly area of land to the west of the Allegheny Mountains. (m. 7, t. 9)

Allegheny River (al′ə gā nē riv′ər) A river that joins with the Monongahela River to form the Ohio River. (m.7, t.11)

Allentown (al′en toun) City in eastern Pennsylvania; 40°N, 75°W.° (m. 7, t. 245)

Appalachian Mountains (ap ə lā chən maun′tənz) Range of mountains stretching from Maine to Alabama. (m. 7, t. 8)

Appomattox, Virginia (ap ə mat′əks) Town in Virginia where a treaty ending the Civil War was signed; 37°N, 78°W. (t. 165)

Atlantic Coastal Plain (ət lan′tik kōs′təl plān) Sandy, flat lowland that lies along the Delaware River. (m. 7, t. 8)

Austria-Hungary (ôs′trē yə hung′ə rē) Large empire that once combined several countries in central Europe. (t. 180)

B

Bedford (bed′ fərd) Borough in southern Pennsylvania; 40°N, 78°W. (m. 95, t. 95)

Bering Strait (bə′ring strāt) Body of water that separates North America from Asia. (m. R10, t. 58)

Beringia (bə rin′jē ə) A land bridge believed to have connected Asia with North America for about 2,000 years during the Ice Age. (m. 59, t. 58)

Bethlehem (beth′li hem) City in eastern Pennsylvania; 40°N, 75°W. (m. 93, t. 88)

Bowmansville (bō′mənz vil) Borough in southeastern Pennsylvania; 40°N, 76°W. (t. 210)

Bradford (brad′ford) City in northern Pennsylvania; 42°N, 78°W. (m. 15, t. 16)

Brandywine Creek (bran′dē wīn krēk) Site of American Revolution battle in southeastern Pennsylvania. (m. 119, t. 119)

Bushy Run (bu′shē rən) Site of 1763 battle that ended Native American resistance in Pennsylvania, approximately 25 miles east of Fort Pitt. (m. 107, t. 109)

C

Camp Reynolds (kamp ren′ əldz) World War II prisoner of war camp in northwestern Pennsylvania; 40°N, 80°W. (t. 187)

Camp William Penn (kamp wil′yəm pen) Camp outside Philadelphia where African American soldiers were trained during the Civil War. (t. 162)

Carbondale (kär′bən dāl) City in northeastern Pennsylvania. The railroad train, the *Stourbridge Lion*, ran between Carbondale and Honesdale; 41°N, 75°W. (t. 137)

pronunciation key

a	**at**	ī	**ice**	u	**up**	th	**thin**
ā	**ape**	îr	**pierce**	ū	**use**	<u>th</u>	**this**
ä	**far**	o	**hot**	ü	**rule**	zh	**measure**
âr	**care**	ō	**old**	ů	**pull**	ə	**about, taken, pencil, lemon, circus**
e	**end**	ô	**fork**	ûr	**turn**		
ē	**me**	oi	**oil**	hw	**white**		
i	**it**	ou	**out**	ng	**song**		

Carlisle (kär′ līl) Borough in southern Pennsylvania, established in 1751 by pioneers; 40°N, 77°W. (m. 95, t. 95)

Carpenters' Hall (kär′pən tərz hôl′) Meeting place of the First Continental Congress in Philadelphia. (t. 113)

Central Plains (sen′trəl plānz) Eastern part of the Interior Plains, an area of gently rolling hills where much corn is grown. (m. R11, t. 37)

Chambersburg (chām′bərz bərg) Borough in southern Pennsylvania which was burned by the Confederate Army during the Civil War; 40°N, 78°W. (t. 163)

Chester (ches′tər) City in southeastern Pennsylvania; 39°N, 75°W. (t. 181)

Columbia (kə ləm′ bē a) Borough on the Susquehanna River in southeastern Pennsylvania, important in early 1800s agricultural trade; 40°N, 76°W. (t. 145)

Cumberland Valley (kəm′bər lənd val′lē) Valley in central Pennsylvania, west of the Susquehanna River. (t. 95)

D

Delaware Bay (de′lə wâr bā) Body of water that connects the Delaware River with the Atlantic Ocean. (m. 77, t. 10)

Delaware River (de′lə wâr ri′vər) River that forms the eastern border of Pennsylvania. (m. 7, t. 8)

E

Edinboro (ed′ən bər ə) Borough in northwestern Pennsylvania; 42°N, 80°W. (t. 247)

Enon Valley (ēn′ən val′ē) Borough in western Pennsylvania; 41°N, 80°W. (t. 246)

Ephrata (ef′rət ə) Borough in southeastern Pennsylvania, settled by German Seventh-Day Baptists; 40°N, 76°W. (t. 88)

Erie (ir′ē) City in northwestern Pennsylvania; 42°N, 80°W. (m. 7, t. 226)

Everett (ev′ ə rət) Borough in southern Pennsylvania; 40°N, 78°W. (t. 247)

Exeter (ek′ sə tər) Borough in northeastern Pennsylvania, hometown of Daniel Boone; 40°N, 76°W. (t. 95)

F

Fort Christina (fôrt′ kris tē′nə) Swedish settlement in 17th century Pennsylvania. (m. 77, t. 77)

Fort Duquesne (fôrt dü kān′) French fort during the French and Indian War, built where the Allegheny and Monongahela rivers meet. (m. 107, t. 107)

Fort Necessity (fôrt ni se′sə tē) British fort during the French and Indian War, built near present-day Pittsburgh. (m. 107, t. 107)

Fort Pitt (fôrt pit) British fort in the French and Indian War, built on the site of Fort Duquesne. (m. 107, t. 108)

Fort Sumter (fôrt sum′ tûr) Union fort in South Carolina where the first Civil War battle took place; 33°N, 80°W. (m. 161, t. 161)

G

Germantown (jər′mən taun) A section of Philadelphia settled by Mennonites; 40°N, 75°W. (t. 87)

Gettysburg (get′ēz bərg) City in southern Pennsylvania, site of a decisive battle of the Civil War; 40°N, 77°W. (t. 162)

Grand Canyon (grand kan′yən) Canyon on the Colorado River in northwestern Arizona. (t. 38)

Great Lakes (grāt lāks) A chain of five lakes (Superior, Michigan, Huron, Erie, and Ontario) in central North America that drain through the St. Lawrence Seaway into the Atlantic Ocean. (m. G11, t. 10)

Great Meadows (grāt me′dōz) Site of Fort Necessity, a British fort in the French and Indian War, near present-day Pittsburgh. (t. 107)

Great Plains (grāt plānz) Western part of the Interior Plains, an area of dry grassland where much wheat is grown. (m. R10, t. 37)

H

Harrisburg (har′əs bərg) Capital of Pennsylvania, located in the southeastern region of the state; 40°N, 77°W. (m. 13, t. 8)

Homestead (hōm′sted) Borough near Pittsburgh, site of a violent steelworkers' strike in 1892; 40°N, 80°W. (t. 169)

Honesdale (hōnz′dāl) Borough in northeastern Pennsylvania. The railroad train, the *Stourbridge Lion*, ran between Carbondale and Honesdale; 41°N, 75°W. (t. 137)

I

Indiantown Gap (in′dē ən taůn gap) Area near Harrisburg where soldiers trained during World War II; 40°N, 77°W. (t. 186)

Interior Plains (in tîr′ē ər plānz) The large plain in the central part of the United States that includes the Central Plains and the Great Plains. (m. R10, t. 37)

Ireland (īr′lənd) Island off Great Britain. Many poor Irish immigrated to Pennsylvania. (m. R5, t. 95)

J

Johnstown (jän′staůn) City in southwestern Pennsylvania, site of a flood in 1889; 40°N, 79°W. (t. 171)

Juniata River (ju nē ät′ə riv′ər) A tributary of the Susquehanna River. (t. 11)

K

King of Prussia (king əv prəsh′ə) Borough outside Philadelphia; 40°N, 75°W. (t. 208)

L

Lake Conemaugh (lāk kän′ə mo) Former lake In Southwestern Pennsylvania, near Johnstown. (t. 171)

Lake Erie (lāk ir′ē) Great Lake forming part of Pennsylvania's northern border. (m. 7, t. 6)

Lancaster (lan′kəs tər) City in southeastern Pennsylvania, settled by Amish and Mennonites; 40°N, 76°W. (m. 7, t. 87)

Lehigh River (lē′hī riv′ər) A major tributary of the Delaware River. (m. 7, t. 10)

Levittown (le′vit toun) City in eastern Pennsylvania; 40°N, 75°W. (t. 191)

M

Mississippi River (mis ə sip′ē riv′ər) One of the longest rivers in North America. It flows south from northern Minnesota into the Gulf of Mexico. (m. R11, t. 36)

Monongahela River (mə non gə hē′lə riv′ər) A river that joins with the Allegheny River to form the Ohio River. (m. 7, t. 11)

Monroeville (mun rō′vil) Borough in southwestern Pennsylvania, outside Pittsburgh; 40°N, 80°W. (t. 191)

N

New Brighton (nü brīt′ən) Borough in western Pennsylvania, a stop on the Underground Railroad; 40°N, 80°W. (t. 159)

New Gothenburg (nü gäth′ən bərg) Seventeenth-century Swedish settlement on Tinicum Island. (m. 77, t. 78)

New Hope (nü′ hōp) Borough on the Delaware River in eastern Pennsylvania; 40°N, 70°W. (t. 118)

New Netherland (nü ne′thər lənd) Seventeenth-century Dutch colony in North America. (t. 78)

New Sweden (nü swē′dən) Swedish colony in the Delaware Bay area, founded in 1636. (m. 77, t. 77)

O

Ohio River (ō hī′ō ri′vər) A river in western Pennsylvania formed by the joining of the Allegheny and Monangahela rivers. (m. 13, t. 11)

P

Penns Creek (penz krēk) Borough in central Pennsylvania; 41°N, 77°W (t. 217)

Philadelphia (fil ə del′fē ə) City on the Delaware River. The largest city in Pennsylvania; 40°N, 75°W. (m. 7, t. 7)

Phoenixville (fē′niks vil) Borough in southeastern Pennsylvania; 40°N, 75°W. (m. 15, t. 15)

Piedmont (pēd′mont) A plateau of gentle hills that lies east of the Appalachian Mountains. (m. 7, t. 8)

Pittsburgh (pits′bərg) City in southwestern Pennsylvania; 40°N, 80°W. (m. 7, t. 7)

Pottstown (pots′toun) Borough in southeastern Pennsylvania; 40°N, 76°W. (t. 88)

Presque Isle (presk īl) A narrow strip of land that reaches out from the Pennsylvania shoreline into Lake Erie. (t. 45)

R

Reading (red′ing) City in southeastern Pennsylvania; 40°N, 76°W. (m. 7, t. 181)

Rocky Mountains (rok′ē moun′tənz) A high mountain range that stretches from Canada through the western United States into Mexico. (m. R10, t. 38)

S

Schuylkill River (skül′kil riv′ər) A major tributary of the Delaware River. (m. 7, t. 10)

Scotland (skät′lənd) Part of the island of Great Britain. (t. 95)

Scranton (scran′ tən) City in eastern Pennsylvania; 41°N, 75°W. (m. 7, t. 44)

St. Lawrence Seaway (sānt lô′rents sē′wā) A body of water in southeastern Canada through which the Great Lakes drain into the Atlantic Ocean. (m. G11, t. 10)

State College (stāt kol′ij) Borough in central Pennsylvania, site of Pennsylvania State University; 40°N, 78°W. (t. 245)

Susquehanna River (səs kwə ha′nə riv′ər) River in central Pennsylvania. (m. 7, t. 11)

T

Tamaqua (tə mäk′wə) Borough in eastern Pennsylvania; 40°N, 78°W. (m. 15, t. 15)

Three Mile Island Site of a nuclear energy plant near Harrisburg that had a serious accident in 1979; 40°N, 77°W. (t. 193)

Tinicum Island (tin′i kəm ī′lənd) Seventeenth-century Swedish settlement on the Delaware River, near present-day Philadelphia. (m. 77, t. 78)

Titusville (tī′təs vil) City in northwestern Pennsylvania, site of the first oil well in 1859; 40°N, 75°W. (p. 140)

Trenton, New Jersey (tren′ tən nü jər′sē) City along the Delaware River in western New Jersey; site of an American victory in the Revolutionary War; 40°N, 76°W. (m. 119, t. 118)

V

Valley Forge (va′lē fôrj) Winter camp of the Continental Army during the Revolutionary War, about 21 miles northwest of Philadelphia. (m. 119, t. 119)

W

Washington, D.C. (wô′shing tən dē sē) Capital of the United States; 39°N, 77°W. (m. R9, t. 131)

West Chester (west ches′ tər) Borough in southeastern Pennsylvania famous for mushroom industry; 40°N, 75°W. (t. 218)

Wilkes-Barre (wilks′ bar ə) City in eastern Pennsylvania, on the Susquehanna River; 41°N, 75°W. (m. 15, t. 17)

Williamsport (wil′yəmz port) City in central Pennsylvania, birthplace of the Little League; 41°N, 77°W. (t. 257)

Wrightsville (rīts′vil) Borough on the Susquehanna River, easternmost point of the Old Pennsylvania Road; 40°N, 77°W. (t. 136)

Z

Zelienople (zē lē nō′pəl) Borough north of Pittsburgh; 41°N, 80°W. (t. 205)

pronunciation key

a **at**; ā **ape**; ä **far**; âr **care**; e **end**; ē **me**; i **it**; ī **ice**; îr **pierce**; o **hot**; ō **old**; ô **fork**; oi **oil**; ou **out**; u **up**; ū **use**; ü **rule**, ů **pull**; ûr **turn**; hw **white**; ng **song**; th **thin**; th **this**; zh **measure**; ə **about**, **taken**, **pencil**, **lemon**, **circus**

Biographical Dictionary

Biographical Dictionary

The Biographical Dictionary tells you about the people you have learned about in this book. The Pronunciation Key tells you how to say their names. The page numbers tell you where each person first appears in the text.

A

Anderson, Marian (an′dər sən), 1897–1993 African American opera singer from Philadelphia. (p. 254)

B

Barton, Clara (bär′tən), 1821–1912 Nurse who founded the American Red Cross. (p. 171)

Blankenburg, Lucretia (blang′kən bûrg, lü krē′shə), 1845–1937 President of the Pennsylvania Women's Suffrage Association that fought for women's rights. (p. 183)

Boone, Daniel (bün), 1734–1820 Trapper and skilled trail guide who helped to build trails and lead many pioneers westward. (p. 95)

Booth, John Wilkes (büth), 1838–1865 Confederate supporter who shot and killed President Abraham Lincoln after the Civil War. (p. 165)

Bouquet, Henry (bō kā′), 1719–1765 British colonel in the French and Indian War who defeated the Native Americans at the Battle of Bushy Run. (p. 108)

Braddock, Edward (brad′ ək), 1695–1755 British general in the French and Indian War who was defeated and killed in battle near Fort Duquesne. (p. 108)

Buchanan, James (bū kan′ən), 1791–1868 Fifteenth President of the United States from Pennsylvania who supported the rights of slave owners. (p. 160)

C

Calder, Alexander (käl′dər), 1898–1976 Pennsylvania artist famous for creating mobiles. (p. 253)

Carnegie, Andrew (kär′nə gē), 1835–1919 Scottish immigrant who became rich making steel. Gave money to build more than 3,000 public libraries and founded a university. (p. 167)

Cassatt, Mary (kə sat′), 1844–1926 Pittsburgh painter who became famous for her paintings of mothers with their children. (p. 253)

Charles II (Chärlz), 1630–1685 King of England who gave William Penn the land where he started the colony of Pennsylvania. (p. 80)

Coble, Frances (kō′bəl), 1911–1968 Pennsylvanian who was chief nurse of an army hospital in North Africa and was honored for outstanding service to our country. (p. 186)

D

Davis, Jefferson (dā′ vis) 1808–1889 President of the Confederacy during the Civil War.

Dickinson, John (dik′in sən), 1732–1808 Member of the Second Continental Congress who hoped the colonies would make peace with Great Britain instead of breaking away. (p. 114)

Dillard, Annie (dil′ərd), 1945– Writer and poet from Pittsburgh who won a Pulitzer Prize for her book, *Pilgrim at Tinker Creek*. (p. 254)

Drake, Edwin L. (drāk), 1819–1880 New Yorker who discovered oil near Titusville. (p. 140)

Duryea, Charles and J. Frank (dûr ē′ə), 1861–1938, 1869–1967 Brothers from Reading who built some of the first automobiles in the United States. (p. 182)

E

Earle, George (ûrl), 1890–1974 Pennsylvania governor during the Great Depression who began state programs to help people find jobs. (p. 185)

pronunciation key

a	**at**	ī	**ice**	u	**up**	th	**thin**
ā	**ape**	îr	**pierce**	ū	**use**	<u>th</u>	**this**
ä	**far**	o	**hot**	ü	**rule**	zh	**measure**
âr	**care**	ō	**old**	u̇	**pull**	ə	**about, taken, pencil, lemon, circus**
e	**end**	ô	**fork**	ûr	**turn**		
ē	**me**	oi	**oil**	hw	**white**		
i	**it**	ou	**out**	ng	**song**		

F

Fitch, John (fich), 1743–1798 Started Pennsylvania's first steamboat service on the Delaware River in 1787. (p. 135)

Forbes, John (fôrbz), 1710–1759 British general in the French and Indian War who led an army to capture Fort Duquesne. (p. 108)

Forten, James (fôr′tən), 1766–1842 A free African American patriot who worked on an American warship during the Revolution. Later became a successful businessman who helped organize abolitionists. (p. 123)

Foster, Stephen (fos′tər), 1826–1864 Writer of popular songs like "Oh! Susanna." (p. 254)

Franklin, Benjamin (frang′klən), 1706–1790 Printer, writer, inventor, scientist, and American statesman. A delegate to the Continental Congress, signer of the Declaration of Independence, and delegate to the Constitutional Convention. (p. 88)

Franklin, Deborah (frang′klən), 1707–1774 Benjamin Franklin's wife who ran his printing business. (p. 89)

Frick, Henry Clay (frik), 1849–1919 Pennsylvanian who owned one of the largest coke companies in the world. (p. 167)

Fulton, Robert (fu̇l′tən), 1765–1815 Built the first steamboat in Pittsburgh, the *New Orleans*. (p. 135)

G

Garrison, William Lloyd (gâr′əs ən), 1805–1879 Abolitionist who helped form the American Anti-Slavery Society. (p. 158)

George III (jôrj), 1738–1820 King of Great Britain during the American Revolution. (p. 114)

Goode, W. Wilson (gu̇d), 1938– First African American elected mayor of Philadelphia. (p. 192)

Graham, Martha (grā′əm), 1894–1991 Dancer from Allegheny who helped develop modern dance. (p. 254)

Grant, Ulysses S. (gränt), 1822–1885 Led the Union Army during the Civil War and later became the 18th president of the United States. (p. 165)

H

Half King (haf king) 1700?–1754 A Seneca chief who was a guide for the British. (p. 107)

Hays, Mary (hāz), 1752–1832 Known as Molly Pitcher, she carried water to the American soldiers in the Battle of Monmouth during the Revolutionary War. (p. 122)

Heinz, Henry Jo (hīnz), 1844–1919 Business leader who helped develop the food processing industry. (p. 168)

Hendrickson, Cornelis (hen′drik sun, kôr′nə lis), 1500s–1600s Dutchman who came to the Delaware Bay area to trade with Native Americans. (p. 77)

Hoskens, Jane (häs′kənz), 1694–? Indentured servant from England whose autobiography described life in colonial Pennsylvania. (p. 87)

Howe, William (hou), 1729–1814 Commander of British troops who captured Philadelphia during the American Revolution. (p. 119)

Hudson, Henry (hud′sən) 1565–1611 English explorer who came upon Delaware Bay while looking for a Northwest Passage to Asia. (p. 76)

J

Jarrett, Keith (jâr′ət, kēth), 1945– Pianist from Allentown. (p. 254)

Jefferson, Thomas (jef′ər sən), 1743–1826 Principal writer of the Declaration of Independence and third President of the United States. (p. 115)

K

Kelly, Alexander (ke′ lē) 1800s Awarded Medal of Honor for gallantry during the Civil War.

Kier, Samuel (kîr), 1813–1874 Discovered a way to use oil in lamps. (p. 140)

King, Martin Luther, Jr. (king), 1929–1968 African American minister and civil rights leader during the 1950s and 1960s. (p. 192)

L

Lampkin, Daisy (lamp′kən), 1884–1965 African American from Reading who raised over two million dollars for war bonds during World War I. (p. 181)

Lappawinzoe (lap′pa win zō), 1600s–1700s Lenni Lenape chief who watched the Walking Purchase. (p. 83)

Lee, Robert E. (lē), 1807–1870 Commander of the Confederate Army during the Civil War. (p 162)

Lincoln, Abraham (ling′kən), 1809–1865 Sixteenth President of the United States who led the country during the Civil War. (p. 160)

M

Madison, James (mad′ə sən), 1751–1836 Fourth President of the United States and Virginia delegate to the Constitutional Convention. (p. 129)

Marshall, George C. (mär′shəl), 1880–1959 General who commanded the U.S. forces during World War II. (p. 186)

Masloff, Sophie (maz′lof, sō′fē), 1917– First woman mayor of Pittsburgh. (p. 192)

Masters, Sybilla (mas′terz) 1600s–1720 Philadelphia businesswoman who invented a machine for cleaning corn. (p. 89)

McCormick, Cyrus (mə kôr′mik, sī′rəs) 1809–1884 Inventor of mechanical horse-drawn reaper. (p. 147)

McKim, J. Miller (mə kim′), 1800s Quaker abolitionist who helped many enslaved African Americans escape to freedom. (p. 159)

Meade, George (mēd), 1815–1872 General who led the Union soldiers at the Battle of Gettysburg. (p. 162)

Minuit, Peter (min′yə wət) 1580–1638 Dutch leader who set up the colony of New Sweden. (p. 77)

Montana, Joe (mon tan′ə), 1956– Professional football player from Monongahela. (p. 257)

Morris, Gouverneur (môr′əs, gəv ər nûr′), 1752–1816. Delegate from Pennsylvania to the Constitutional Convention. (p. 130)

Morris, Robert (môr′əs), 1734–1806. Delegate from Pennsylvania to the Constitutional Convention. (p. 129)

Mott, Lucretia (mot, lü krē′shə), 1793–1880 Abolitionist and women's rights leader. (p. 156)

N

Nix, Robert, Sr. (nix), 1928–1987 First African American U.S. Representative from Pennsylvania. (p. 192)

O

Owens, Mary (ō′wəns), 1800s Disguised herself as a man and fought in battle during the Civil War. (p. 162)

P

Paine, Thomas (pān), 1737–1809 American patriot who wrote *Common Sense* explaining why the colonies should break away from England. (p. 114)

Penn, Hannah (pen), 1671–1726 William Penn's wife who ruled the Pennsylvania colony after he died in 1718. (p. 82)

Penn, Thomas (pen), 1702–1775 One of William and Hannah Penn's sons who led the colony. (p. 83)

Penn, William (pen), 1644–1718 Englishman who started the colony of Pennsylvania based on Quaker beliefs. (p. 80)

Pinchot, Gifford (pin′shō), 1865–1946 Pennsylvania governor who began state programs to help people find jobs during the Great Depression. (p. 185)

Pitt, William (pit), 1708–1778 Government leader in Great Britain who sent a large army to the colonies during the French and Indian War. (p. 108)

Powel, Eliza (paủ′əl), 1742?–1830 Wife of a Philadelphia leader during the time of the Constitutional Convention. (p. 130)

Preston, Ann (pres′tən), 1813–1872 Medical doctor and professor who attended the first medical college for women in the United States. (p. 157)

Printz, Johan (prins, yō′hän), 1592–1663 Swedish soldier who became the leader of New Sweden. (p. 78)

Purvis, Robert (pûr′vis), 1810–1898 Successful African American businessman who helped organize the first national African American anti-slavery meeting. (p. 158)

R

Reibman, Jeannette (rēb′man, jə net′) 1915– First woman elected to Pennsylvania's state senate. (p. 192)

Ridge, Tom (rij), 1945– Elected governor of Pennsylvania in 1994. (p. 231)

Rising, Johan (rī′zing, yō′hän) 1617–1672 Replacement for Johan Printz as leader of New Sweden. (p. 79)

Rittenhausen, Wilhelm (rit′ən haus, vil′helm), 1732–1796 Built the colonies' first paper mill in Germantown. (p. 88)

Roosevelt, Franklin D. (rō′zə velt), 1882–1945 Thirty-second President of the United States who created the New Deal programs during the Great Depression and led the country during World War II. (p. 185)

Ross, Betsy (rôs) 1752–1836 Believed to have helped design and sew the first American flag. (p. 123)

Rustin, Bayard (rus′tən), 1910–1987 Civil rights organizer from West Chester. (p. 192)

Rutter, Thomas (rut′tər), 1600s–1700s Manufactured iron on Manatawny Creek near Pottstown in 1716. (p. 88)

S

Salomon, Haym (sal′ə mən), 1740–1785 Banker who loaned his fortune to the Continental Congress to help the American Revolution. (p. 122)

Savocchio, Joyce A. (sə vok′kē ō), 1942– Mayor of Erie. (p. 226)

Shikellamy, John (shi kel′ə mē), ?–1748 Chief of the Native American groups in Pennsylvania who worked for peace between the pioneers and Native Americans. (p. 97)

Sims, William S. (simz), 1838–1906 Pennsylvanian who led American naval forces in Europe during World War I. (p. 181)

Skinner, George (skin′ər), 1800s African American hero who saved a young girl's life during the Johnstown Flood. (p. 171)

Sloan, John (slōn), 1871–1951 Painter known for his paintings of life in New York City. (p. 253)

Smith, Robert and Joseph (smith), 1700s–1800s Invented an iron plow in 1800. (p. 147)

Smith, Stephen (smith), 1797–1873 Wealthy African American businessman who bought and sold lumber and coal. (p. 141)

Spinelli, Jerry (spi nel′ē), 1941– Norristown writer who has written many children's books. (p. 254)

Steuben, Baron Friedrich von (stü′bən, frēd′rik von), 1730–1794 Skilled Prussian soldier who helped train Americans at Valley Forge. (p. 120)

Stevens, Thaddeus (stē vəns, thad′ē us), 1792–1868 Gettysburg lawmaker who supported public education. (p. 157)

Still, William (stil), 1821–1902 African American abolitionist who helped people escape from slavery. (p. 159)

Stuyvesant, Peter (stī′və sənt), 1610–1672 Leader of the Dutch colony of New Netherland. (p. 78)

T

Tamenend (tam′ə nənd), 1625?–1701? Lenape chief with whom historians think William Penn signed a Great Treaty of friendship. (p. 82)

Thorpe, Jim (thôrp), 1886–1953 Native American football hero from Carlisle. (p. 182)

Tubman, Harriet (tub′mən), 1820?–1913 Abolitionist and Underground Railroad conductor who helped hundreds of enslaved African Americans escape to freedom. (p. 158)

W

Wanamaker, John (wän′ə māk ər), 1838–1922 Opened the country's first department store in Philadelphia. (p. 168)

Washington, George (wô′shing tən), 1732–1799 First President of the United States and general of the Continental Army during the American Revolution. (p. 107)

Washington, Martha (wô′shing tən), 1731–1802 Wife of George Washington and the First Lady of the United States. (p. 120)

Wayne, Anthony (wān), 1745–1796 American general known as "Mad Anthony" for his bravery in battle. (p. 122)

Weiser, Conrad (vī′zər), 1696–1760 German immigrant who worked with Native Americans to keep the peace. (p. 97)

Westinghouse, George (wes′ting hous), 1846–1914 Inventor and businessman who invented the railroad brake. (p. 168)

Wilson, August (wil′sən), 1945– African American poet and playwright from Pittsburgh. (p. 252)

Woolworth, Frank W. (wůl′wûrth), 1852–1919 Businessman who started a chain of "Five and Dime" stores. (p. 168)

Wyeth, Andrew (wī′əth), 1917– Painter from Chadds Ford who painted lonely scenes of the land and people around him. (p. 253)

pronunciation key

a **at**; ā **ape**; ä **far**; âr **care**; e **end**; ē **me**; i **it**; ī **ice**; îr **pierce**; o **hot**; ō **old**; ô **fork**; oi **oil**; ou **out**; u **up**; ū **use**; ü **rule**, ů **pull**; ûr **turn**; hw **white**; ng **song**; th **thin**; <u>th</u> **this**; zh **measure**; ə **about**, **taken**, **pencil**, **lemon**, **circus**

Glossary

This Glossary will help you to pronounce and understand the meanings of the vocabulary in this book. The page number at the end of the definition tells where the word first appears.

A

abolition (ab ə lish′ən) End or do away with completely; often used in reference to slavery. (p. 156)

agribusiness (ag′rə biz nes) A farm that is combined with other businesses. (p. 216)

agriculture (ag′ri kul chər) The business of growing crops and raising animals. (p. 217)

Allied Powers (al′īd pow′ərs) Countries that fought in World War I on the side led by England, France, Russia, and the United States. *See* **Central Powers**. (p. 180)

Allies (al′īz) Countries who fought in World War II on the side led by England, France, Russia, and the United States. *See* **Axis Powers**. (p. 186)

ally (al′ī) A person or country that joins with another for a common purpose. (p. 108)

amendment (ə mend′mənt) Addition to the United States Constitution. *See* **constitution**. (p. 183)

American Revolution (ə mer′ə kən rev ə lü′shən) The war fought by the American colonies to end British Rule, 1775–1783. (pp. 114, 118–123)

ancestor (an′ses tər) A person in your family, starting with your parents, who was born before you. (p. 42)

anthracite coal (an′thrə sīt kōl) A hard coal that burns very hot and produces very little smoke. (p. 139)

archaeology (är kē ol′ə jē) also archeology. The study of the way people lived in the past, including prehistoric times. (p. 59)

artifact (är′tə fakt) Object made by people who lived in the past, often found and studied by archaeologists. (p. 59)

assembly line (ə sem′blē līn) A line of workers and machines along which a product is moved to be put together. (p. 210)

Axis Powers (ak′sis pow′ərz) Countries who fought in World War II on the side led by Germany, Italy, and Japan. *See* **Allies**. (p. 186)

B

Battle of Brandywine (bat′əl uv bran′dē wīn) Revolutionary War battle during which the Continental Army unsuccessfully tried to stop the British from marching into Philadelphia, on September 11, 1777. (p. 119)

Battle of Germantown (bat′əl uv jər′mən toun) Revolutionary War battle during which the Continental Army unsuccessfully attempted to drive the British out of Pennsylvania, October 4, 1777. (p. 119)

Battle of Gettysburg (bat′əl uv get′ēz bərg) Civil War battle in which thousands of lives were lost. It was a turning point for the war. (pp. 162–163, 164)

Battle of Trenton (bat′əl uv trent′n) Revolutionary War battle at which the Continental Army successfully attacked British-hired soldiers at Trenton, New Jersey on Christmas Day, 1776. *See* **Continental Army**. (p. 118)

bay (bā) A part of an ocean or lake that cuts deeply into the land. (p. 10)

bill (bil) An idea for a law. (p. 232)

bituminous coal (bī tü′mə nəs kōl) A soft coal that burns easily and produces much smoke. (p. 139)

boom town (büm town) A community that has grown at a rapid rate. (p. 140)

border (bôr′dər) A line that people agree on to separate two places. (p. 6)

borough (bu′rō) A community in Pennsylvania that usually has fewer people than a city. (p. 225)

boycott (boi′kot) To join with others in refusing to buy a product. (p. 113)

pronunciation key

a	**at**	ī	**ice**	u	**up**	th	**th**in
ā	**ape**	îr	**pierce**	ū	**use**	<u>th</u>	**th**is
ä	**far**	o	**hot**	ü	**rule**	zh	mea**s**ure
âr	**care**	ō	**old**	u̇	**pull**	ə	**a**bout, tak**e**n, penc**i**l, lem**o**n, circ**u**s
e	**end**	ô	**fork**	ûr	**turn**		
ē	**me**	oi	**oil**	hw	**white**		
i	**it**	ou	**out**	ng	**song**		

budget (buj′it) Plan for using an amount of money for a specific purpose. (p. 231)

byline (bī′līn) A line at the beginning of a newspaper article that names the writer. (p. 234)

C

canal (kə nal′) A waterway dug across land for transportation or irrigation. *See* **transportation**. (p. 135)

candidate (kan′də dāt) A person running for office in an election. (p. 237)

cardinal directions (kär′də nəl dī rek′shənz) The main directions of the globe: north, south, east, and west. (p. G8)

cash crop (kash krop) A crop that is grown to be sold for money rather than to be used on the farm where it is grown. *See* **profit**. (p. 144)

cause (kôz) An event or person that makes something else happen. *See* **effect**. (p. 62)

CD-ROM (sē dē rom′) A reference source on a compact disc that you "read" with a computer; it may include writing, pictures, sounds, or short movies. *See* **reference source**. (p. 111)

census (sen′səs) A count of the population. (p. 245)

Central Powers (sen′tral pow′ərs) Countries that fought in World War I on the side which included Germany, Austria-Hungary, and Italy. *See* **Allied Powers**. (p. 180)

checks and balances (cheks and bal′əns əs) The idea that each branch of government keeps watch over the others. (p. 230)

circle graph (sûr′kəl graf) A graph in the shape of a circle that shows the sizes of different parts of a whole; also called a pie graph. *See* **graph**. (p. 142)

citizen (sit′ə zən) A person who is born in a country or who has earned the right to become a member of that country by law. (p. 224)

civil rights (siv′əl rīts) The rights of people to be treated equally under the law. (p. 192)

Civil War (siv′əl wôr) The war in the United States between the Union States of the North and the Confederate States of the South, 1861–1865. *See* **Union** *and* **Confederacy**. (p. 161)

clan (klan) A group of families who share the same ancestor. (p. 65)

climate (klī′mit) The pattern of weather of a certain place over many years. (p. 14)

coke (kōk) A gray-black solid fuel made by heating bituminous coal; coke is used to make iron. (p. 139)

colony (kol′ə nē) A place that is ruled by another country. (p. 77)

commission (kō mish′ən) A group of elected leaders in townships and cities. (p. 226)

commute (kəm myūt′) To travel back and forth to work. (p. 191)

compass rose (kum′pəs rōz) A small drawing on a map that shows directions. (p. G8)

conclusion (kən klü′zhen) A statement that pulls together several pieces of information and gives them a meaning. (p. 172)

Conestoga wagon (kon ə stō′gə wag′ən) Large canvas-covered wagons used by pioneers to cross America. (p. 96)

Confederacy (kən fed′ər ə sē) The government formed by 11 Southern states that seceded from the United States, 1860–1865. *See* **Civil War** *and* **secede**. (p. 161)

conquer (kong′kər) To defeat, to win. (p. 108)

conservation (kon sər vā′shən) The careful use of a natural resource. (p. 28)

constitution (kon sti tü′shən) A document that has the basic rules to govern a state, country, or other organized group. (p. 128)

Constitutional Convention (kon sti tü′shə nəl kən ven′shən) The historic meeting at which our country's plan of government, or constitution, was written, 1787. (p. 128)

consumer (kon sü′mər) Person who buys a product or uses a service. (p. 206)

continent (kon′tə nənt) One of Earth's seven great bodies of land—Africa, Antarctica, Asia, Australia, Europe, North America, and South America. (p. G6)

Continental Army (kon tə nen′təl är′mē) The army of the American colonies, led by George Washington. *See* **Second Continental Congress**. (p. 114)

council (koun′səl) A group of people who meet to discuss problems, give advice, or make decisions. (p. 67)

A group of elected leaders in boroughs and cities. (p. 226)

county (koun′tē) One of the sections into which a state is divided. (p. 227)

county commissioner (koun′tē kō mish′ən ər) Elected official who runs county government. (p. 227)

crop rotation (krop rō tā shən) Method of planting a different crop each year on the same soil to help keep the soil healthy. (p. 147)

culture (kul′chər) The way of life shared by a group of people, including language, beliefs, music, arts, and foods. (p. 64)

custom (kus′təm) The special way a group of people does something. (p. 42)

D

dam (dam) A wall built across a river to control the flow of water. (p. 171)

dateline (dāt′līn) The lead-in to a newspaper article, telling when and where the story was written. (p. 234)

decision (di sizh′ən) A choice that helps you reach a goal. (p. 46)

Declaration of Independence (dek lə rā′shən uv in di pen′dəns) The document declaring independence from Great Britain for the thirteen American colonies, adopted on July 4, 1776 by the Second Continental Congress. (p. 115)

degree (di grē′) A unit for measuring distance on Earth's surface; also a unit for measuring temperature. Represented by the symbol °. (p. 18)

delegate (del′i gət) A person chosen to represent others. (p. 129)

democratic republic (dem ə krat′ik ri pub′lik) A government in which citizens elect representatives to run the government. (p. 236)

descendants (di sen′dənts) The people who come after a particular ancestor or group of ancestors. *See* **ancestor**. (p. 70)

desert (dez′ərt) A dry area that gets less than 10 inches of precipitation each year. (p. 38)

dictionary (dik′shə ner ē) A book that explains the meaning of words and shows how to pronounce and spell them. (p. 110)

discrimination (di skrim ə nā′shən) Unfair difference in the treatment of people. (p. 192)

E

economy (i kon′ə mē) The way a country or other place produces and uses natural resources, goods, and services. (p. 25)

editorial (ed ə tôr′ē al) A newspaper article that gives opinions rather than facts. (p. 234)

effect (i fekt′) An event that happens as a result of another event. *See* **cause**. (p. 62)

elect (i lekt′) Choose by voting. (p. 224)

elevation (el ə vā′shən) The height of land above sea level. (p. 12)

Emancipation Proclamation (i man sə pā′shən präk lə mā′shən) Announcement by President Lincoln in 1863 that all enslaved people living in Confederate states were free. (p. 165)

encyclopedia (en sī klə pē′dē ə) A book or set of books that gives facts about people, places, things, and events. (p. 111)

entrepreneur (än trə prə nûr′) A person who has the skill and leadership to start a new business and to produce new products. (p. 205)

environment (en vī′rən mənt) The surroundings in which people, plants, or animals live. (p. 22)

equator (i kwā′tər) An imaginary line that lies halfway between the North Pole and the South Pole, at 0° latitude. (p. G7)

ethnic group (eth′nik grüp) A group of people whose ancestors are from the same country or area. (p. 42)

executive branch (eg zek′yə tiv branch) The branch of government that carries out the laws. (p. 231)

explore (ek splôr′) To travel in unfamiliar places in order to learn about them. (p. 76)

F

feature article (fē chər är′ti kəl) A newspaper story that takes a detailed look at a person, subject, or event. (p. 234)

First Continental Congress (fûrst kon tə nen′təl kong′gris) A meeting of the leaders of the American colonies at which they talked about their problems with Great Britain, held in Philadelphia on September 5, 1774. *See* **Second Continental Congress**. (p. 113)

folk art (fōk ärt) The traditional art of the common people of a country or region. (p. 253)

food processing (füd pros′es ing) Any of hundreds of ways of turning crops and livestock into different food products. (p. 168)

free-enterprise system (frē en′tər prīz sis′təm) The economic system that allows people to own and run their own businesses. (p. 204)

French and Indian War (french and in′dē ən wôr) A North American war in which Great Britain fought France and its Native American allies, 1754–1763. (p. 108)

frontier (frun tîr′) The edge of a settled area. (p. 94)

fuel (fū′əl) A substance burned as a source of heat and power, such as coal, wood, or oil. (p. 24)

G

General Assembly (jen′ər əl ə sem′blē) The legislature of the state of Pennsylvania. (p. 232)

geography (jē og′rə fē) The study of Earth and the way people, plants, and animals live on and use it. (p. 6)

Gettysburg Address (get′ēz bərg ə dres′) A speech given by President Lincoln at the site of the Battle of Gettysburg. (pp. 163, 164)

glacier (glā shər) A huge sheet of ice that moves slowly over the land. (p. 58)

global grid (glō′bəl grid) The crisscrossing lines of latitude and longitude found on a map or globe. (p. 20)

governor (guv′ərn ôr) Elected official who heads the executive branch of state government. (p. 231)

graph (graf) A diagram that show information in a picture. *See* **circle graph** *and* **line graph**. (p. 142)

Great Depression (grāt di presh′ən) Period of widespread economic hardship in the 1930s. (p. 184)

Great Law (grāt lô) A set of laws to rule the colony of Pennsylvania, written by William Penn. (p. 82)

Great Migration (grāt mī grā′shən) The movement of African Americans in the early and middle 1900s from the rural areas of the Southeast to urban areas of the Northwest and Middle West. (p. 181)

Great Runaway (grāt run′ə wā) The flight south of scared settlers when Native Americans and Loyalists from the New York colony attacked the Wyoming Valley. (p. 121)

Great Treaty (grāt trē′tē) A treaty of friendship believed to be made between William Penn and the Lenape chief, Tamenend. (p. 82)

growing season (grō′ing sē′zən) The time of the year when the weather is suitable for crops to grow in a certain place. (p. 45)

guide words (gīd wûrdz) Words appearing at the top of each page of a dictionary that tell you the first and last words that are defined on that page. (p. 110)

H

headline (hed′līn) A title printed in large letters at the beginning of a newspaper article. (p. 234)

hemisphere (hem′əs fîr) Half a sphere; one of the four hemispheres of Earth—Northern, Southern, Eastern, and Western Hemispheres. *See* **equator** *and* **prime meridian**. (p. G7)

heritage (her′ə tij) The history and traditions that a group of people share. (p. 42)

high-tech industry (hī tek in′dus trē) The use of advanced scientific ideas and special skills and tools to meet people's needs. (p. 209)

highway (hī′wā) A main road and a major route of travel. (p. 191)

history (his′tə rē) The story of what happened in the past, usually as preserved in written records. (p. 41)

home rule (hōm rül) A system where people can vote for the kind of municipal government they think is best for their city. (p. 226)

hunter-gatherers (hun′tər gath′ər ərz) People who get their food by hunting game and gathering plants, fruits, and nuts. (p. 60)

hurricane (hûr′i kān) A storm with very strong winds and heavy rains. (p. 17)

I

Ice Age (īs āj) A period of time when glaciers covered much of Earth's surface. (p. 58)

immigrant (im′i grənt) A person who comes to a new country to live. (p. 86)

indentured servant (in den′chərd sûr′vənt) A person who agrees to work for another person for a fixed amount of time to pay for a debt, usually travel expenses. (p. 87)

industry (in′də strē) All the businesses that make one kind of product or provide one kind of service. (p. 138)

intermediate direction (in tər mē′dē it di rek shəns) Any direction between two cardinal directions: northeast, southeast, southwest, northwest. (p. G8)

invention (in ven′shən) A newly created product. (p. 168)

investor (in ves′tər) Someone who puts money into a business and expects a share of the profit. *See* **profit**. (p. 206)

J

judicial branch (jü dish′əl branch) The branch of government that interprets, or explains, laws. (p. 233)

jury (jür′ē) A group of citizens in a court of law who decide if someone is innocent or guilty. (p. 239)

L

labor union (lā′bər ūn′yən) A group of workers organized to get better working conditions (p. 169)

lake effect (lāk i fekt′) A weather condition where cold air blowing across a lake is warmed and picks up water; the water eventually falls from the sky as snow. (p. 45)

landform (land′fôrm) Any of the shapes that make up Earth's surface. (p. 7)

latitude (lat′i tüd) A measure of how far north or south a place on Earth is from the equator. *See* **parallel**. (p. 18)

legislative branch (leg′is lā tiv branch) The branch of government that makes laws. (p. 232)

pronunciation key

a **at**; ā **ape**; ä **far**; âr **care**; e **end**; ē **me**; i **it**; ī **ice**; îr **pierce**; o **hot**; ō **old**; ô **fork**; oi **oil**; ou **out**; u **up**; ū **use**; ü **rule**, ů **pull**; ûr **turn**; hw **white**; ng **song**; th **thin**; <u>th</u> **this**; zh **measure**; ə **about**, **taken**, **pencil**, **lemon**, **circus**

line graph (līn graf) A graph that shows how a piece of information changes over time. *See* **graph**. (p. 142)

Little New Deal (lit′əl nü dēl) State government programs introduced by Pennsylvania Governors Gifford Pinchot and George Earle to help people find jobs during the Great Depression. (p. 185)

locator (lō kā tər) A small map or globe set onto another map that shows where the main map is set. (p. G10)

longhouse (long hous) A long, covered building in a Native American village that houses many families together. (p. 65)

longitude (län′ji tüd) A measure of distance on Earth east or west of the prime meridian. *See* **prime meridian**. (p. 19)

M

manager (man′i jər) Person hired by a city government to run its daily business. (p. 226)

manufacture (man yə fak′chər) To make goods by machine. (p. 88)

map key (map kē) An explanation of what the symbols on a map represent. *See* **symbol**. (p. G9)

mayor (mā′ər) Elected head of the government of a city. (p. 226)

meridian (mə rid′ē ən) A line of longitude. *See* **longitude** *and* **prime meridian**. (p. 19)

metropolitan area (met rō pol′it ən âr′ē ə) A city and its suburbs. (p. 190)

mineral (min′ər əl) A nonrenewable natural resource that is found in the ground. (p. 24)

minuteman (min′it man) A colonist who was armed and ready to fight at a minute's notice. (p. 113)

mobile (mō′bēl) A movable sculpture made of metal, plastic, cardboard, or other material. (p. 253)

mouth (mouth) The place where a river empties into an ocean or another large body of water. (p. 36)

municipal (myū nis′ə pəl) Having to do with the running of a city. (p. 226)

N

nation (nā′shən) A group of Native Americans who share the same culture. (p. 65)

natural resource (nach′ər əl rē′sôrs) Something found in the environment that people can use. (p. 22)

New Deal (nü dēl) Government programs introduced during the Depression by President Franklin D. Roosevelt. (p. 185)

news article (nüz är′ti kəl) A newspaper story that contains facts about recent events. (p. 234)

nonrenewable resource (non ri nü′ə bəl rē′sôrs) A resource available in a limited supply. When used it is gone forever. (p. 24)

Northwest Passage (nôrth west′ pas′ij) A water route through North America to Asia. (p. 76)

O

ocean (ō′shən) One of Earth's four largest bodies of water—the Atlantic, Arctic, Indian, and Pacific Oceans. (p. G6)

organic farming (ôr gan′ik färm ing) Using natural products, such as manure, instead of manufactured chemicals to enrich the soil. (p. 217)

outline (out′līn) A plan for organizing written information about a subject. (p. 248)

P

parallel (par′ə lel) A line of latitude. *See* **latitude**. (p. 18)

pioneer (pī ə nîr′) A person who leads the way. (p. 94)

plain (plān) A large area of flat or nearly flat land. (p. 7)

plateau (pla tō′) A high, flat area of land that rises steeply above the surrounding land. (p. 9)

political party (pə lit′i kəl pär′tē) Group of people who share similar ideas about government. (p. 237)

pollution (pə lü′shən) Result of carelessly using resources, such as chemicals, that make air, water, or soil dirty. (p. 28)

population (pop yə lā′shən) The number of people who live in a place or area. (p. 140)

port (pôrt) A place where ships load and unload their goods. (p. 88)

precipitation (pri sip ə tā′shən) The moisture that falls to the ground as rain, snow, sleet, or hail. (p. 15)

prehistory (prē his′ tə rē) The time before written records. (p. 59)

prime meridian (prīm mə rid′ē ən) The line of longitude, marked 0°, from which other meridians are measured. *See* **longitude**. (p. 19)

professional (prō fe′shən əl) Athlete who plays a sport as a job. (p. 257)

profit (prof′it) The money a business earns after it pays for tools, salaries, and other costs. (p. 205)

Pulitzer Prize (pu̇l′it zər) Awarded every year for the best work in American literature, music, and newspaper writing. (p. 254)

R

rain shadow (rān shad′ō) The side of a mountain that is usually dry because precipitation falls on the other side. (p. 39)

reaper (rē′pər) A person or machine that cuts and gathers grain. (p. 147)

recreation (rek rē ā′ shən) What people do for relaxation or enjoyment. (p. 252)

recycle (rē sī′kəl) To use something again instead of discarding it. (p. 28)

reference source (ref′ər əns sôrs) A book or any form of information that contains facts about many different subjects. (p. 110)

region (re′jən) An area with common features that set it apart from other areas. (p. 34)

renewable resource (ri nü′ə bəl rē′sôrs) A natural resource that can be replaced for later use, such as a forest. (p. 23)

ridge (rij) Narrow chain of mountains. (p. 8)

river system (riv′ər sis′təm) All the streams and rivers that flow into a larger river. (p. 10)

Roaring Twenties (rôr′ing twen′tēz) A period of success, excitement, and good times for many Americans during the 1920s. (p. 182)

rural (rur′əl) Of the countryside. (p. 40)

S

scale (skāl) The relationship between the distance on a map and the real distance on Earth. (pp. 92, G10)

secede (sə sēd′) To withdraw or formally leave an organization such as a government. (p. 161)

Second Continental Congress (sek′ənd kon tə nen′təl kong′gris) The second meeting of the leaders of the American colonies held in Philadelphia starting in May 1775 at which they formed the Continental Army and approved the Declaration of Independence. *See* **Continental Army** *and* **Declaration of Independence**. (p. 114)

service industry (sûr′vis in′də strē) Businesses or jobs in which people help others. (p. 211)

slavery (slā və rē) The practice of making one person the property of another. (p. 87)

source (sôrs) The place where a river begins. (p. 36)

Stamp Act (stamp akt) A British tax on everything made of paper that was sold in the American colonies. (p. 113)

states' rights (stāts rīts) Belief that the people of each state have the right to decide laws for themselves. (p. 160)

steamboat (stēm′bōt) Large boat powered by steam used to carry heavy loads. (p. 135)

stock (stok) A share of ownership in a company. (p. 184)

Stourbridge Lion (stər′brij lī′ən) The first steam locomotive to run on rails in the United States. It traveled between the towns of Carbondale and Honesdale, Pennsylvania. (p. 137)

strike (strīk) Refusal by a group to work until demands are met. (p. 169)

subsistence farming (səb sis′təns fär′ming) Growing only enough food to live, not any extra to sell. (p. 96)

suburb (sub′ûrb) A community just outside a big city. (p. 190)

suffrage (suf′rij) The right to vote. (p. 183)

symbol (sim′bəl) Anything that stands for something else. (p. G9)

T

tax (taks) Money people pay to a government. (p. 113)

technology (tek nol′ə jē) The use of skills, ideas, and tools to meet people's needs. (p. 168)

temperature (tem′pər ə chər) A measurement of how hot or cold something is. (p. 15)

textile (tex′tīl) A word to describe articles made from thread or yarn. (p. 140)

time line (tīm līn) A diagram that shows when events took place. (p. 84)

time zone (tīm zōn) A region in which all the clocks are set to the same time. (p. 214)

tornado (tôr nā′dō) A swirling funnel of wind that moves over the ground at high speeds. (p. 17)

tourist (tür′ist) Person who travels for pleasure or to learn about other places. (p. 211)

township (toun′ship) A community for citizens who live in areas outside of cities or boroughs. (p. 225)

trading post (trād′ing pōst) A store in a sparsely settled area where local people can barter, usually trading products for other goods. (p. 77)

transportation (trans pər tā′shən) A way to move goods and people from one place to another. (p. 134)

treaty (trē′tē) A formal agreement between countries or peoples. (p. 82)

Treaty of Paris (trē′tē uv par′is) Treaty ending the French and Indian War in which France agreed to give up all its land in North America, signed in 1763. (p. 108)

pronunciation key

a **at**; ā **ape**; ä **far**; âr **care**; e **end**; ē **me**; i **it**; ī **ice**; îr **pierce**; o **hot**; ō **old**; ô **fork**; oi **oil**; ou **out**; u **up**; ū **use**; ü **rule**, ů **pull**; ûr **turn**; hw **white**; ng **song**; th **thin**; th **this**; zh **measure**; ə **about**, **taken**, **pencil**, **lemon**, **circus**

tributary (trib′yə ter ē) A smaller river or stream that flows into a larger river. (p. 11)

turnpike (tərn′pīk) A highway that travelers pay to use. (p. 136)

U

underground railroad (ən′dər ground rāl′rōd) A system of secret routes through which people helped enslaved people escape to the free states or Canada before and during the Civil War. (p. 158)

Union (ūn′yən) The states that make up the United States. Used during the Civil War to refer to the government of the Northern States. *See* **Civil War**. (p. 161)

United States Congress (ū nī′təd stāts kong′ris) The legislative branch of the United States government. (p. 238)

United States Supreme Court (ū nī′təd stāts sə prēm kôrt) The highest court of the United States. (p. 239)

urban (ûr bən) Of a city. (p. 40)

V

valley (val′ē) Low patches of land between hills. (p. 8)

veto (vē′tō) The power of the executive branch to reject a bill passed by the legislative branch. (p. 232)

W

Walking Purchase (wô′king pûr′chəs) A treaty supposedly signed by William Penn and Lenape chiefs that gave Penn the land west of the Delaware River as far "as a man can go in one day and a half." (p. 83)

war bond (wôr bond) A written promise by the government to pay back money that has been loaned to pay for the war. (p. 181)

weather (weth′ər) The condition of the air at a certain time in a certain place, including temperature, precipitation, and wind. (p. 14)

wigwam (wig′wom) A one-room Native American hut, usually rounded, made of poles covered with bark, skins, or woven grass. (p. 66)

World War I (wûrld wôr wən) The first war between countries from around the world, fought mostly in Europe from 1914 to 1918. The Allied Powers fought the Central Powers. *See* **Allied Powers** *and* **Central Powers**. (p. 181)

World War II (wûrld wôr tü) War fought mostly in Europe, North Africa, and the Pacific from 1939 to 1945. The Allies fought against the Axis Powers. *See* **Allies** *and* **Axis Powers**. (p. 186)

pronunciation key

a **a**t; ā **a**pe; ä f**a**r; âr c**ar**e; e **e**nd; ē m**e**; i **i**t; ī **i**ce; îr p**ier**ce; o h**o**t; ō **o**ld; ô f**o**rk; oi **oi**l; ou **ou**t; u **u**p; ū **u**se; ü r**u**le, ů p**u**ll; ûr t**ur**n; hw **wh**ite; ng so**ng**; th **th**in; th **th**is; zh mea**s**ure; ə **a**bout, tak**e**n, penc**i**l, lem**o**n, circ**u**s

index

This index lists many topics that appear in the book, along with the pages on which they are found. Page numbers after an *m* refer you to a map. Page numbers after a *p* indicate photographs, artwork, or charts.

CREDITS

COVER PHOTOGRAPHY: Macmillan/McGraw-Hill School Division

Maps: Geosystems

Chapter Opener Globes: Greg Wakabayashi

PHOTOGRAPHY CREDITS: All photographs are by the Macmillan/McGraw-Hill School Division (MMSD) except as noted below.

Table of Contents: iii: l.: Gregory K. Scott, Photo Researchers, Inc.; r.: D. Young-Wolff, Photo Edit. iv: t.l.: The Historical Society of Pennsylvania; b.l.: Stock Montage, Inc.; b.r.: Landis Valley Museum, Pennsylvania Historical and Museum Commission. v: t.: The Granger Collection; b.: The Granger Collection. vi: t.: Stock Montage, Inc.; b.l.: Corbis-Bettmann; b.r.: Corbis-Bettmann. vii: l.: AP/Wide World Photos, Inc.; r.: Blair Seitz. viii: Carla Messinger. ix: Museum of American Folk Art. **Front Matter:** G2: bkgd: Larry Ulrich, Tony Stone Images; l.: Scott Goldsmith, Tony Stone Images. G3: t.l.: Bill Luster; t.r.: Ed Wheeler, The Stock Market; b.l.: Cary Wolinsky, Stock Boston; b.r.: Robert Llewellyn, Uniphoto. G4: bkgd: Elizabeth Wolf; t: Sylvain Grandadam, Tony Stone Images; b: J. Irwin, H. Armstrong Roberts. G5: t: Bill Ballenberg; b.l.: Larry Ulrich, Tony Stone Images; b.r.: Sam Abell. **Chapter 1:** 2: t.l.: Lori Adamski Peek, Tony Stone Images; t.r.: H. Mark Weidman; c: H. Mark Weidman; b.l.: H. Mark Weidman; b.r.: Blair Seitz. 3: t.: H. Mark Weidman; b.: H. Mark Weidman. 5: t., b.m., & b.: H. Mark Weidman; t.m.: Blair Seitz. 6: Blair Seitz. 8: l.: Blair Seitz; r.: H. Mark Weidman. 9: l. & r.: H. Mark Weidman. 10: H. Mark Weidman. 14: Gregory K. Scott, Photo Researchers, Inc. 15: Blair Seitz. 16: l.: H. Mark Weidman; r.: Sally Weigand. 17: Gene J. Puskar, AP/Wide World Photos, Inc. 21: SuperStock, Inc. 22: John R. Patton. 23: l.: H. Mark Weidman; r.: Bob Daemmrich, Stock Boston. 24: John R. Patton. 25: H. Mark Weidman. 26: Michael Newman, Photo Edit. 27: t.l.: Cline Oil/Bradford, Pennsylvania; t.r.: John R. Patton; c.: H. Mark Weidman; b.r.: Denver Bryon, Images on the Wild Side; b.l.: Blair Seitz. 28: D. Young-Wolff, Photo Edit. 29: Elisabeth Lynch. **Chapter 2:** 33: t.: Sally Weigand; t.m.:Blair Seitz; b.m.: H. Armstrong Roberts; b.: Charles J. Benson, Lechner & Benson Advertising Design. 34: Jim Simmern, Tony Stone Images, Inc. 36: t.: Bettman; b.: John Elk, Tony Stone Images, Inc. 37: l.: Felicia Martinez, Photo Edit; r.: Chuck Pefley, Tony Stone Images, Inc. 38: t.: Tom Bean, Tony Stone Images, Inc.; b.: Tom Till, Tony Stone Images, Inc. 40: Courtesy of Carnegie Museums of Pittsburgh. 41: Blair Seitz. 42: t. & b.: Raymond Bial. 43: t.: Blair Seitz; c.: Raymond Bial; b.: ETV Productions. 44: l.: H. Mark Weidman; r.: Eric R. Berndt. 45: H. Mark Weidman. 46: t. & b.: H. Mark Weidman. 48: H. Mark Weidman. 49: b.: H. Mark Weidman; c.: John R. Patton; b.: Sally Weigand. 53: Greg Miller. **Chapter 3:** 54: t.: The Granger Collection; t.l.: North Wind Pictures; t.r.: Blair Seitz; c.: John T. Kraft, Waterloo Village; b.l.: Blair Seitz; b.r.: Landis Valley Museum, Pennsylvania Historical and Museum Commission. 55: Sally Weigand. 58: Roy Anderson, National Geographic Society. 59: The State Museum of Pennsylvania, Section of Archaeology. 60: SuperStock, Inc. 61: Blair Seitz. 62: From: *Smithsonian Exploring the Ancient World, Search for The First Americans* by David J. Meitzer, St. Remy Press and Smithsonian Books. © St. Remy Press and Smithsonian Institution. Illustration © Greg Harlini/Wood, Ronsaville, Harlin. Used with permission. 63: Tony Freeman, Photo Edit. 64: The Granger Collection. 66: l.: John T. Kraft, Waterloo Village; r.: Herbert C. Kraft, Seton Hall University. 68: t.l. & c.l.: Buffalo Museum of Science; t.r. & c.: Thaw Collection, Fenimore House Museum, Cooperstown, NY, Photo by John Bigelow Taylor, NYC; b.l.: National Museum of the American Indian, Smithsonian Institution; b.r.: The Ohio Historical Society. 69: t.l. & t.r.: The State Museum of Pennsylvania, Section of Archaeology; b.l. & b.r.: National Museum of the American Indian, Smithsonian Institution. 70: Donald Secondine. 71: Carla Messinger. **Chapter 4:** 76: The Historical Society of Pennsylvania. 78: American Swedish Historical Museum. 79: Courtesy of the Friends of the Swedish Cabin. 80: Stock Montage, Inc. 81: t.: The Historical Society of Pennsylvania; b.: Corbis-Bettman. 82: The Historical Society of Pennsylvania. 86: North Wind Pictures. 87: The Granger Collection. 88: The New York Public Library/Prints Division. 89: t.: W. Metzen, H. Armstrong Roberts; c.: The Granger Collection. 90: C.W. Peale, FPG International. 91: t.l.: North Wind Pictures; t.r.: Bettman; c.: The Granger Collection; b.l.: Corbis-Bettman; b.r.: The Metropolitan Museum of Art, Rogers Fund, 1922. 94: Pennsylvania Historical and Museum Commission. 95: Stock Montage, Inc. 96: l.: North Wind Pictures; r.: Corbis-Bettman. 101: Greg Miller. **Chapter 5:** 102: t.l.: The Historical Society of Pennsylvania; t.r.: Colonial Williamsburg Foundation; c. & b.r.: The Granger Collection; b.l.: Pennsylvania State Archives. 103: t.: The Granger Collection; b.: Blair Seitz. 106: The Granger Collection. 107: BRT Photographic Illustrations. 108: The Granger Collection. 109: c.: Thaw Collection, Fenimore House Museum, Cooperstown, NY, Photo by John Bigelow Taylor, NYC; r.: Historical Artist, Robert Griffing. 111: David Chambers, Tony Stone Images, Inc. 112: National Society Daughters of the American Revolution. 113: The Granger Collection. 114: l. & r.: North Wind Pictures; c.: The Granger Collection. 116: The Granger Collection. 117: t.: The Historical Society of Pennsylvania; c.: John Singleton Copley/The Historical Society of Pennsylvania. 118: North Wind Pictures. 119: North Wind Pictures. 120: c.: The Granger Collection; b.: Hunt Commercial Photo/Pennsylvania Capitol Preservation Committee. 121: North Wind Pictures. 122: t.l.: Bettman; t.r. & c.: The Granger Collection; b.: Stock Montage, Inc. 123: The Historical Society of Pennsylvania, Leon Gardiner Collection. **Chapter 6:** 128: The Granger Collection. 129: The Granger Collection. 130: The Granger Collection. 131: The Granger Collection. 132: Blair Seitz. 133: all: Blair Seitz. 134: Smithsonian Institution. 135: Pennsylvania State Archives. 136: John R. Patton. 138: The Granger Collection. 139: Richard Richardson, Memoir of Josiah White (Philadelphia, 1873). 140: Photograph from the Collection of the Drake Well Museum. 141: The Historical Society of Pennsylvania. 144: The Granger Collection. 145: The Carnegie Museum of Art. 146: Cunningham/Feinknopf Photography/Scott Cunningham. 147: The Granger Collection. 151: Greg Miller Photography. **Chapter 7:** 152: t.l.: Corbis-Bettman; t.r. & b.r.: Bettman; l.c. & c.: The Granger Collection; b.l.: John R. Patton. 153: t.: The Ohio Historical Society; b.: The Granger Collection. 156: Friends Historical Library, Swarthmore College. 157: all: Courtesy of the Archives and Special Collections on Women in Medicine, Allegheny University of the Health Sciences. 158: all: The Granger Collection. 160: The Granger Collection. 162: Historical Society of Pennsylvania. 163: all: The Granger Collection. 164: t.r.: The State Museum of Pennsylvania, Pennsylvania Historical and Museum Commission; b.l.: The Granger Collection; b.r.: Sally Weigand. 166: The Bettman Archive. 167: t.: Commonwealth of Pennsylvania, Division of Archives and Manuscripts; c.: The Granger Collection; b.: Commonwealth of Pennsylvania, Division of Archives and Manuscripts. 168: all: Corbis-Bettmann. 170: Special Collections Office, The Research Libraries, New York Public Library. 171: Clara Barton National Historic Site. 172: The Historical Society of Schuylkill County. 173: Corbis-Bettmann. 174: Corbis-Bettmann. 175: t.: Carnegie Mellon University; c.: Carnegie Museums and Library of Pittsburgh; b.: Blair Seitz. **Chapter 8:** 180: The Ohio Historical Society. 181: l.: Fisk University Library; r.: The Granger Collection. 182: The Granger Collection. 183: Bettmann. 184: AP/Wide World Photos, Inc. 185: t.: National Archives; b.: AP/Wide World Photos, Inc. 186: l.: Bettmann; r.: AP/Wide World Photos, Inc. 187: Meehan Military Posters/Nurick: Shools at War. 188: Pennsylvania Turnpike Commission. 189: Stock Montage, Inc. 190: Blair Seitz. 191: FPG International. 192: l.: UPI/Corbis-Bettmann; r.: Nathan Benn, National Geographic Image Collection. 193: UPI/Corbis-Bettmann. 194: SuperStock, Inc. 195: t.: Terry Ganey; c.: Pennsylvania Power & Light Company; b.: Rickie Sanders. **Chapter 9:** 200: t.l.: Blair Seitz; t.r.: AP/Wide World Photos, Inc.; c.: AP/Wide World Photos, Inc.; b.l.: Blair Seitz; b.r.: B. Taylor, H. Armstrong Roberts. 201: H. Mark Weidman. 203: all: H. Mark Weidman. 204: Richard F. Krosel. 205: all Richard F. Krosel. 206: all: Richard F. Krosel. 207: Richard F. Krosel. 208: Sally Weigand. 209: t.: H. Mark Weidman; b.: Zefa, H. Armstrong Roberts. 211: Sally Weigand. 216: SuperStock, Inc. 217: Walnut Acres Organic Farms. 218: Blair Seitz. 219: John R. Patton. **Chapter 10:** 222: Blair Seitz. 224: City of Erie, Office of the Mayor. 225: t.: Sally Weigand; c.: H. Mark Weidman. 226: AP/Wide World Photos, Inc. 227: r.: Sally Weigand. 228: Sally Weigand. 229: Laura A. Walker. 230: John Zeedick, Commonwealth Media Services. 231: John R. Patton. 233: t.: John Zeedick, Commonwealth Media Services; c.: Blair Seitz. 236: t.l.: Charles Gupton, Stock Boston; b.: FPG International. 237: FPG International. 239: AP/Wide World Photos, Inc. **Chapter 11:** 243: Blair Seitz. 244: Blair Seitz. 246: Dolder Huber, H. Armstrong Roberts. 247: J. Miles Wolf. 249: Leader Publishing Co., Inc. 250: t.: Museum of American Folk Art; b.: B. Taylor, H. Armstrong Roberts. 251: t.l.: Gerry Benton; t.r., c.r., & b.l.: Museum of American Folk Art. 252: AP/Wide World Photos, Inc. 253: l.: The Granger Collection; r.: Photri Inc. 254: all: AP/Wide World Photos, Inc. 256: l.: Blair Seitz; r.: H. Mark Weidman. 257: AP/Wide World Photos, Inc. **Reference Section:** R20: John Zeedick, Commonwealth Media Services. R22: t.l.: Frank Capri/Saga, Archive Photos; t.r., c.l., & c.: AP/Wide World Photos, Inc., c.r.: Archive Photos; b.l.: Lauren Studies, Inc.; b.r.: AP/Wide World Photos, Inc. R23: t.l. & t.r.: AP/Wide World Photos, Inc.; c.l.: Reuters/Csilla Cseke/Archive Photos; c.: Nancy R. Schiff/Saga, Archive Photos; c.r.: AP/Wide World Photos, Inc.; b.l. & b.r.: Bob Grant, Archive Photos. R24: t.l.: AP/Wide World Photos, Inc.; t.r.: Frank Capri/Saga, Archive Photos; c.t.l.: AP/Wide World Photos, Inc.; c.r.: Gloria Skurzynski; c.b.l.: AP/Wide World Photos, Inc.; b.l.: AP/Wide World Photos, Inc.; b.r.: Brigitte LaCombe, EMI Classics.

The Princeton Review Handbook of Test-Taking Strategies

STANDARDIZED TEST SUPPORT

READ QUESTIONS CAREFULLY

The most common mistake students make when they take a test is to answer the questions too quickly. Rushing through a test causes careless mistakes. Don't rush. Read each question carefully. Make sure you understand the question BEFORE you try to answer it.

Use the map to answer questions 1 through 3.

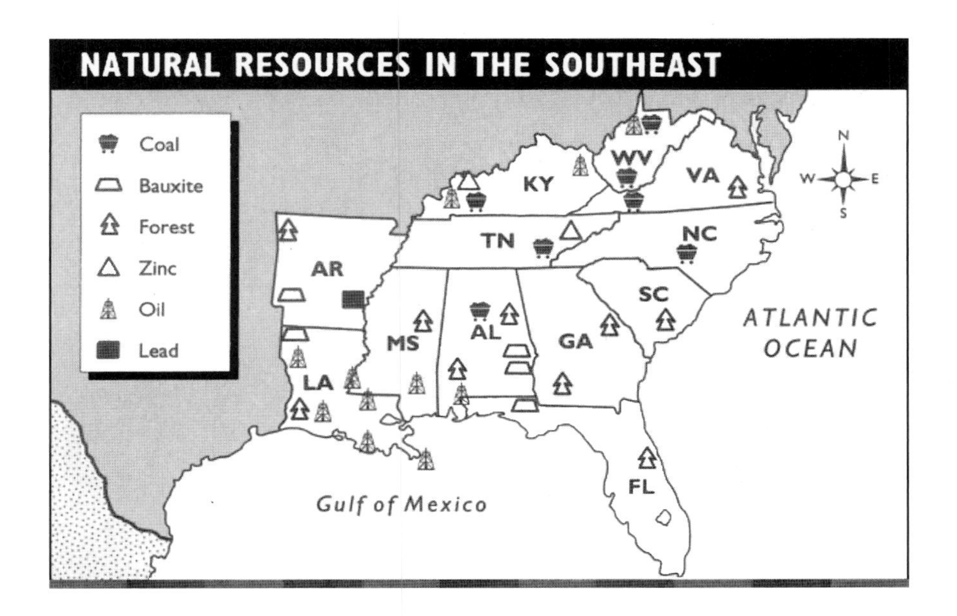

1 In which state is oil an important natural resource?

A Georgia
B North Carolina
C Louisiana
D Tennessee

2 South Carolina's natural resources include

F bauxite
G zinc
H coal
J forest

3 In which state would a lead miner be most likely to find a job?

A Arkansas
B West Virginia
C Florida
D Alabama

Remember: Do not write in your textbook.

TIME LINES

Historical information is sometimes presented in the form of a time line. A time line shows events in the order in which they happened. Time lines are usually read from left to right, like a sentence. If the time line is drawn vertically, it is usually read from top to bottom.

If you read carefully, you should do very well on time line questions.

Look at the time line below. Then answer questions 1 and 2.

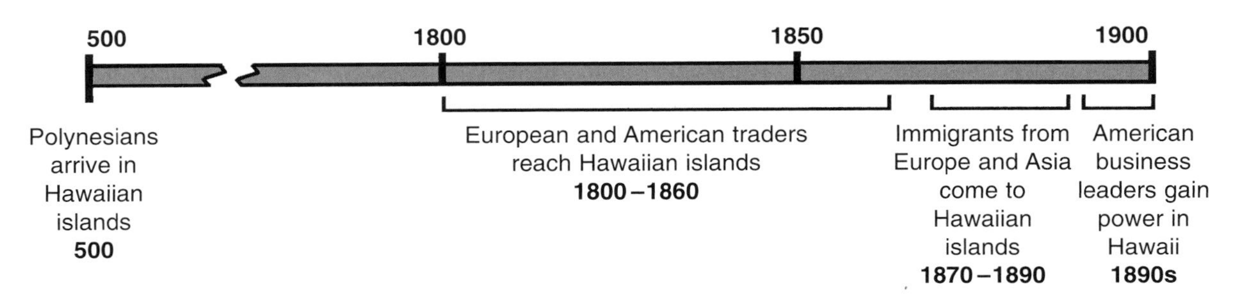

1 Which group was the first to reach the Hawaiian islands?

A Europeans
B Americans
C Asians
D Polynesians

2 Which of the following most likely occurred in 1845?

F Traders from Europe and America came to the Hawaiian islands.
G The first Polynesians arrived in the Hawaiian islands.
H American business leaders gained power in Hawaii.
J Asian immigrants came to the Hawaiian islands.

Remember: Do not write in your textbook.

LOOK AT THE DETAILS BEFORE YOU START

Some test questions contain lots of details. These questions may use:

- charts
- graphs
- flow charts
- time lines
- word webs
- maps

Before you try to answer questions like these, take a few moments to study the information that the charts, graphs, maps, or other visuals contain. The questions will be much easier to answer, because you will know exactly where to look for information!

Study the bar graph. Then do questions 1 and 2.

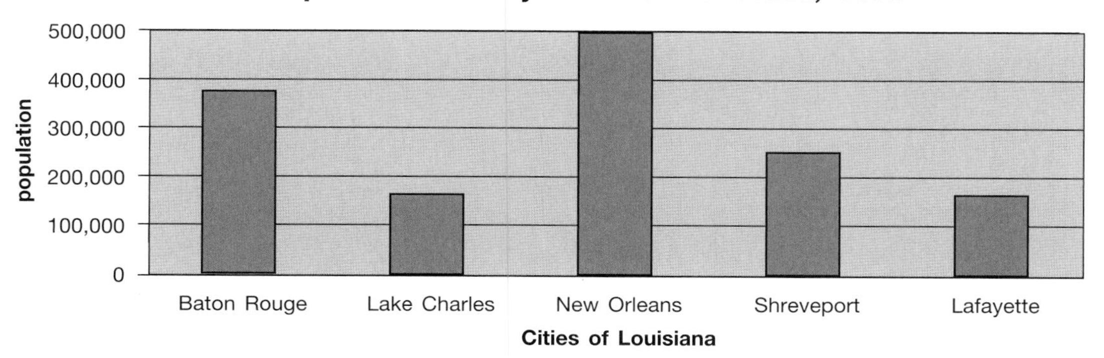

1 In 1990, which Louisiana city had a population of about 380,000?

A Lake Charles
B New Orleans
C Shreveport
D Baton Rouge

2 In 1990, which two Louisiana cities had approximately the same population?

F Baton Rouge and New Orleans
G Lake Charles and Lafayette
H Shreveport and Baton Rouge
J New Orleans and Lake Charles

DIFFERENT TYPES OF GRAPHS

Different types of graphs are used to present numerical information. A **line graph** shows how something changes over time. A line graph might be used to show how the population of the United States has grown over the years. A **bar graph** compares amounts. A bar graph might show the population of different United States cities. A **circle graph** shows how a whole is divided into smaller parts. For example, a circle graph might show how the government divides its budget to pay for roads, education, and other services.

Sometimes you will see a set of questions accompanied by more than one graph. Each question will contain clues to tell you which graph you should read to find the answer. Take the extra time to make sure you are looking at the correct graph. This will help you avoid careless mistakes.

Use the graphs below to answer questions 1 and 2.

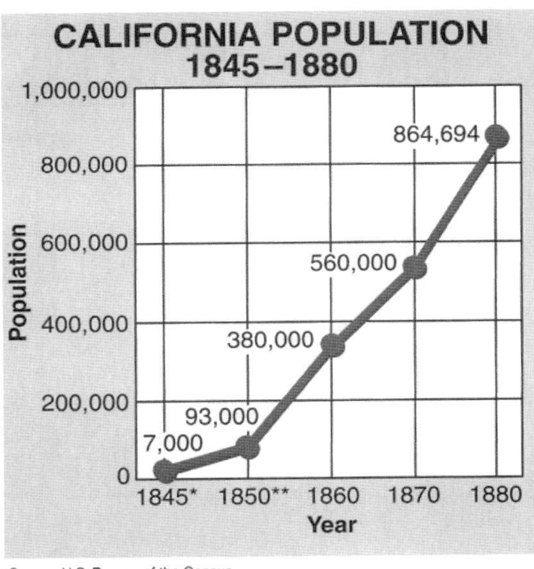

Source: U.S. Bureau of the Census

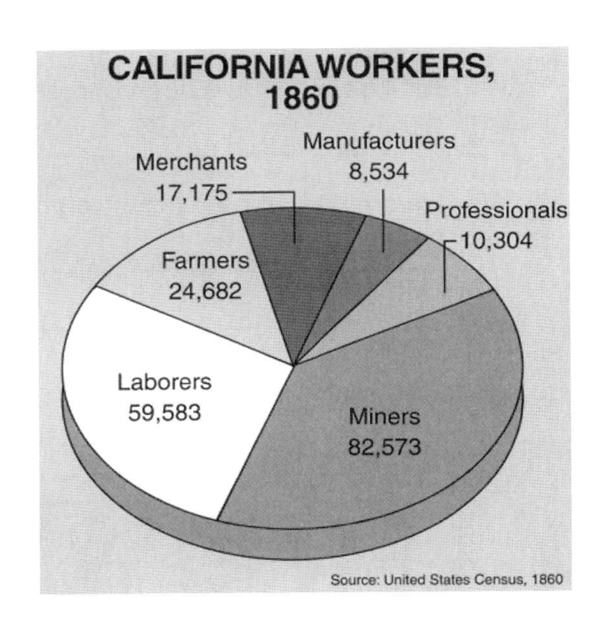

1 In what year did the population of California reach 380,000?

A 1840
B 1850
C 1860
D 1870

2 How many people were working as professionals in California in 1860?

F 10,304
G 17,175
H 59,583
J 82,573

Remember: Do not write in your textbook.

PROCESS OF ELIMINATION

Sometimes when you read a test question, you will not know the answer right away. If you don't know the answer, don't give up. You may be able to find the correct answer another way.

On a multiple-choice test, you can look at the answer choices. One of the answers will be the best answer. The others will be wrong, or not as good. Look at the choices and see if there are any that you know are definitely wrong. If there are, you can ELIMINATE, or ignore, those answers.

Sometimes you will be able to eliminate all of the answers except one. When that happens, it means that you have found the best answer by the PROCESS OF ELIMINATION.

Try using the process of elimination to answer this question:

1 The largest city in South Dakota is

A Los Angeles
B Dallas
C Sioux Falls
D Mexico City

Were you able to eliminate any *wrong* answers? How many?

Now try using the process of elimination to answer this question:

2 The section of the United States Constitution that protects the freedom of Americans is called the

F Declaration of Independence
G Bill of Rights
H Civil War
J Star Spangled Banner

OUTSIDE KNOWLEDGE

Many questions on multiple-choice tests ask you to look at a map, a chart, a graph, or a drawing. Then you are asked to choose the correct answer based on what you see. On these questions, the information you need to answer the question will be in the map, chart, graph, or drawing.

Sometimes, however, multiple-choice tests will ask you to remember a fact that you learned in social studies class. You won't be able to find the correct answer on a map, chart, graph, or drawing; the correct answer will be in your memory. We call these OUTSIDE KNOWLEDGE questions.

If you are sure you know the answer to an OUTSIDE KNOWLEDGE question, choose the correct answer. It's that simple! When you're NOT sure what the correct answer is, use the PROCESS OF ELIMINATION to answer the question.

1 Which of these books would probably provide the most information about the life of Martin Luther King, Jr.?

A an atlas
B an encyclopedia
C a novel about the South during the Civil War
D a collection of poetry

2 Which of the following statements about the southern portion of the United States is true?

F The South does not have many farms.
G The South is home to the largest cities in the United States.
H The South is the most mountainous region in the United States.
J The South has a warmer climate than the northern United States.

Remember: Do not write in your textbook.

FLOW CHARTS

A flow chart shows the sequence of steps used to complete an activity. It shows the steps in the order they happen. A flow chart usually uses arrows to show which step happens next.

The first thing to do when you look at a flow chart is to see if it has a title. The title will tell you what the flow chart is about. The next thing you should do is find the arrows. The arrows tell you the order in which to read the chart.

Read flow charts carefully. Don't just look at the illustrations. Make sure to read any text beneath the illustrations.

Study the flow chart. Then do questions 1 and 2.

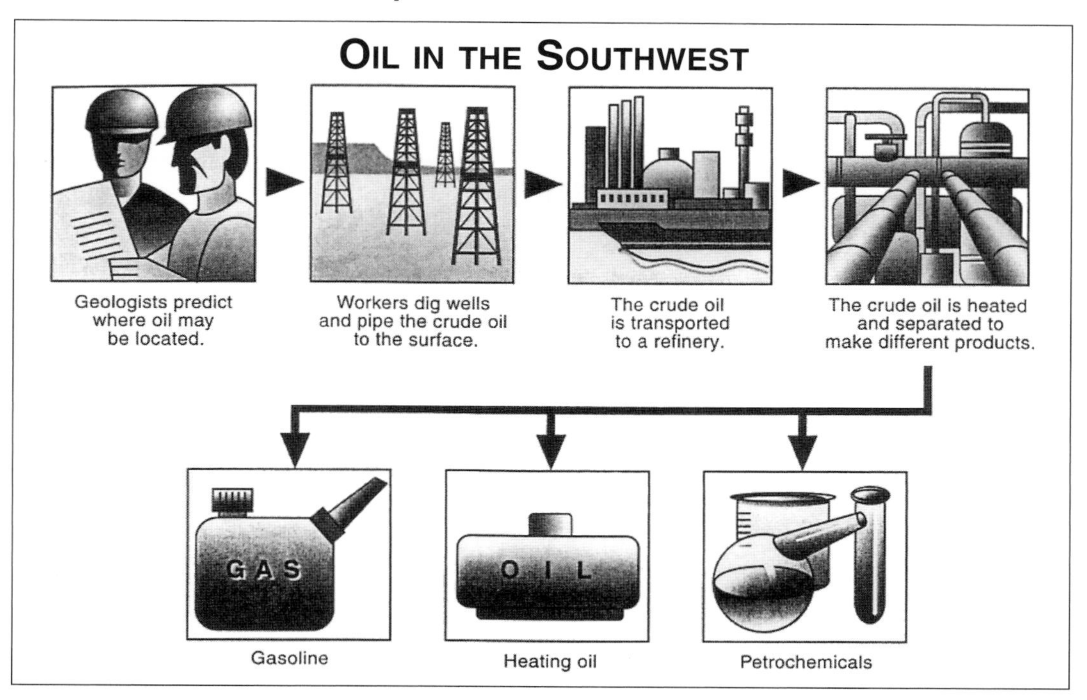

1 Which of these questions is answered by the flow chart?

A What are some of the products that can be made from crude oil?

B How much does it cost to produce heating oil?

C Where in the United States is the most crude oil found?

D How many automobiles are there in the United States?

2 The crude oil is probably transported to the oil refinery in

F automobiles

G large ships

H helicopters

J tractors

Remember: Do not write in your textbook.

MAPS

The ability to read and understand maps is an important skill in social studies. Many of the multiple-choice tests you take will require you to read a map.

Look carefully at all the parts of a map. Maps contain a lot of information. Whenever you see a map, you should ask yourself questions like these:

- What does the title of the map tell you?
- Where is the map key?
- What symbols are on the map key? What do they stand for?
- Where is the compass rose?
- What does the compass rose tell you?
- Is there a map scale?

Use the map of Pennsylvania to answer questions 1 and 2.

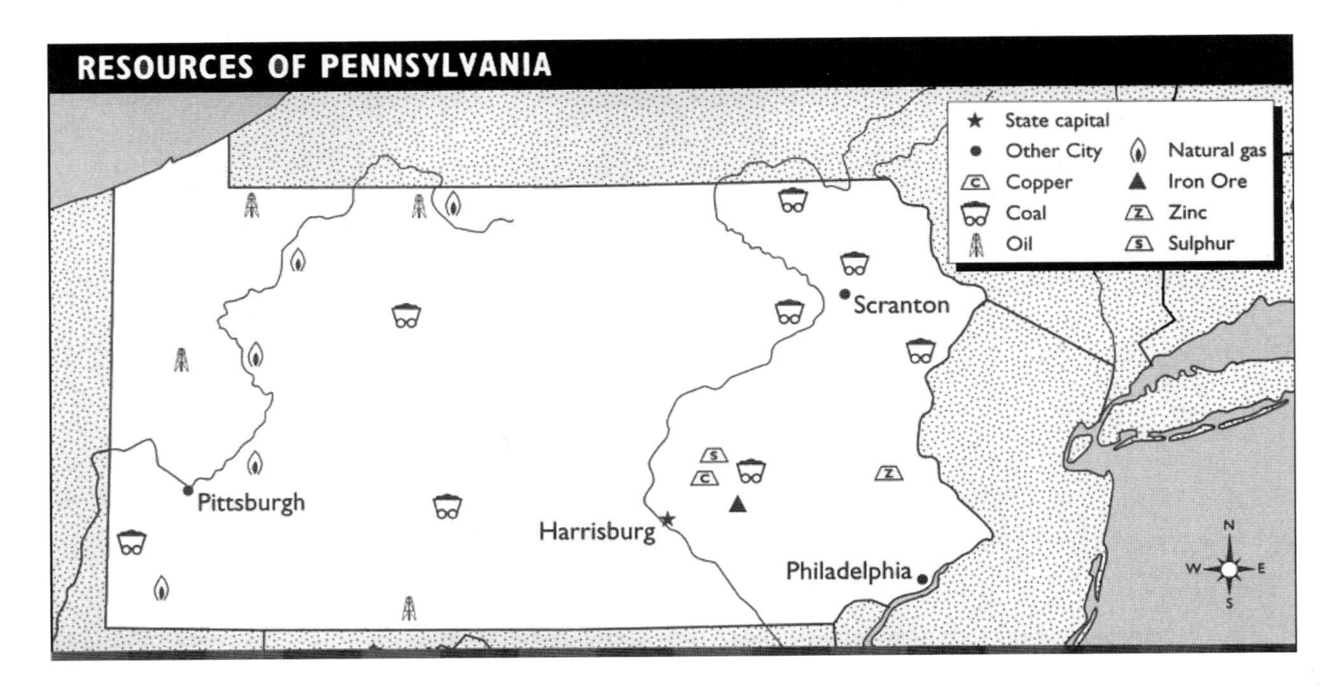

1 Which natural resource is found only in the western part of Pennsylvania?

A zinc

B natural gas

C coal

D iron ore

2 Which of these people would be most likely to find a job near Scranton?

F a driller of oil wells

G a coal miner

H a miner of iron ore

J a zinc miner

Remember: Do not write in your textbook.

CIRCVLVS ARCTICVS.
ANIAN regnum.
AMERICA SIVE IN DIA NOVA. Ao 1492. a Christophoro Colombo nomine regis Castellæ primum detecta.
Tolm
Totonteac
Noua Francia.
Chilaga
Estotilant
Canagadi
Calicuas
Tagil.
Florida
La Bermuda
La Emperadada
Marata
Las dos hermanas
Los Bolcanes
TROPICVS CANCRI
Trinidad
Archipelago di
S. Thomas
Anubiada
Rocca partida
Abrego
Hispania noua
MAR DEL NORT
S. Lazaro
CIRCVLVS AEQVINOCTIALIS
Caribana.
Labarbada
Los Bolcanes
Ins di los Tiburones
MAR DEL ZVR
Insulæ incognitæ
ins di S. Pedro
Peru
Amazones
Tisnada
Brasil
TROPICVS CAPRICORNI.
EL MAR PACIFICO
Chica
Chile
Rio de la Pla
Hanc continentem Australem, nonnulli Magellanicam regionem ab eius inuentore nuncupant.
Archipelago
CIRCVLVS ANTARCTICVS.
Terra del Fuego.
190 200 210 220 230 240 250 260 270 280 290 300 310 320 330
TERRA AVSTR